CW01457449

MILITARY AIR POWER IN EUROPE PREPARING FOR WAR

A STUDY OF EUROPEAN NATIONS' AIR FORCES
LEADING UP TO 1939

MILITARY AIR POWER IN EUROPE PREPARING FOR WAR

A Study of European Nations' Air Forces Leading up to 1939

NORMAN RIDLEY

AIR WORLD

AIR WORLD

MILITARY AIR POWER IN EUROPE PREPARING FOR WAR
A Study of European Nations' Air Forces Leading up to 1939

First published in Great Britain in 2022 by
Air World
An imprint of
Pen & Sword Books Ltd
Yorkshire – Philadelphia

Copyright © Norman Ridley, 2022

ISBN 978 1 39906 685 3

The right of Norman Ridley to be identified as Author of this work has been asserted by him in accordance with the Copyright, Designs and Patents Act 1988.

A CIP catalogue record for this book is available from the British Library.

All rights reserved. No part of this book may be reproduced or transmitted in any form or by any means, electronic or mechanical including photocopying, recording or by any information storage and retrieval system, without permission from the Publisher in writing.

Typeset by SJmagic DESIGN SERVICES, India.

Printed and bound in the UK by CPI Group (UK) Ltd.

Pen & Sword Books Limited incorporates the imprints of Atlas, Archaeology, Aviation, Discovery, Family History, Fiction, History, Maritime, Military, Military Classics, Politics, Select, Transport, True Crime, Air World, Frontline Publishing, Leo Cooper, Remember When, Seaforth Publishing, The Praetorian Press, Wharncliffe Local History, Wharncliffe Transport, Wharncliffe True Crime and White Owl.

For a complete list of Pen & Sword titles please contact

PEN & SWORD BOOKS LIMITED
47 Church Street, Barnsley, South Yorkshire, S70 2AS, England
E-mail: enquiries@pen-and-sword.co.uk
Website: www.pen-and-sword.co.uk

Or
PEN AND SWORD BOOKS
1950 Lawrence Rd, Havertown, PA 19083, USA
E-mail: Uspen-and-sword@casematepublishers.com
Website: www.penandswordbooks.com

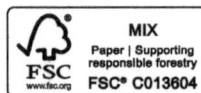

MIX
Paper | Supporting
responsible forestry
FSC
www.fsc.org
FSC® C013604

Contents

Abstract

During the years following the Wright Brothers' first heavier-than-air flight at Kitty Hawk in 1903, air power began to force its way towards the centre of military doctrine, driven by revolutionary scientific and technological advances, and fired the imagination of military theorists with its almost limitless potential. At the core of air power is air doctrine. This is not something that emerges ready-formed at the moment an air force is created, but has to be defined according to what are perceived to be the broad tenets of a service. The concepts by which air forces organise and train, target their enemies and conduct large-scale operations are encapsulated in written regulations and documents and it is this collection that comprises the doctrine of an air force. Air forces the world over grew out of established army and navy organisations which had their own special doctrines built up over many years out of their values beliefs, practices and aspirations. There are three basic military doctrines: fundamental doctrine, organisational doctrine and tactical doctrine. This book examines the way in which these competed with each other for prominence within the military structures of six major European nations, with different resources, ambitions and philosophies, in the years from the beginning of aviation right up to the start of the Second World War.

The First World War had seen the mechanisation of warfare. Battle fronts had become immobilised in the grip of machine guns and heavy artillery leading to slaughter on an unprecedented scale. The end of the war saw exhausted governments extricating themselves from the carnage, but given the level of upheavals seen since 1914 with the disintegration of the Hapsburg Empire, the rise of communism in Russia, the emasculation of Germany through the Treaty of Versailles and the many smaller conflicts that continued to rage across Eastern Europe and the wider world, few leaders

ABSTRACT

doubted that, sooner or later, another major war would follow. As France's Marshal Foch put it, the Treaty of Versailles was only a 'twenty-year truce'. The overriding concern was to find ways in future of avoiding the kind of static battle fronts that had consumed so many in such futile efforts.

Military aviation was seen as the one great innovation that had the potential to do this by revolutionising warfare. It would not only augment the effectiveness of ground forces in a tactical role, but also had the means of reaching out strategically beyond the battlefronts to strike at the enemy's trade, supplies, communications and industrial production. All through the First World War, military aviation had been firmly under the control of army commanders but there was soon a fierce debate over the way it should be developed. The evolution of an air doctrine within each of the major European powers was fraught with difficulty as the nascent air-arms struggled, with varying degrees of success, to free themselves from army control and find a new, independent identity.

While traditional military leaders refused to concede legitimacy to the idea of an air force having equal status to either the army or navy, theorists were quick to recognise the way in which the boundaries of warfare would be hugely expanded into the third dimension by this revolutionary concept. Long before there was the slightest capability of realising it in practice, the 'terror bombing' theory of such as Guilio Douhet with its apocalyptic scenarios, envisaging whole cities razed to rubble, invaded the collective imagination and had politicians almost rigid with fear. Here was introduced, for the first time, the idea that war would henceforth be waged by whole countries, including civilians, and not just trained and armed military forces. Nothing and nobody would be outside the combat zone with civilian casualties rivalling or exceeding those of the military. It was even hoped by some optimists that the very threat of such a conflagration would act as a deterrent to war itself, but history would prove that the proponents of air power were both willing and able to scale the heights of destruction and ultimately threaten the very existence of humanity.

Chapter 1

Air Doctrine

During World War I, airplanes proved their worth in a variety of realms. Indeed, nearly every modern mission of aircraft received at least a rudimentary trial between 1914 and 1918.[1]

The tenets of air doctrine evolve over time through the analysis of experience and the teachings of prominent theorists. To a greater or lesser extent, air doctrine was only one part of the overall military doctrine of each country considered in this study and each nascent air force was obliged to follow its own trajectory as they struggled to create their own individual identity and purpose. The air forces of Europe up to 1939 adopted different air doctrines according to their military, geographical and political situations. For instance, an island state such as Britain had looked out at its near neighbours and potential enemies across the sea comforted by its possession of the world's largest navy, while Germany lived uneasily with danger lurking just across several of its land borders. France had emerged from the First World War proud in victory with the world's biggest army, but with an unstable political structure rent by deep internal divisions. Two other nations had undergone fundamental change at a time when they were also dealing with the fallout from Versailles. Poland was to find itself reborn as a country, albeit insecure and impoverished, with its overriding ambition to simply survive and avoid being devoured once again by mortal enemy nations to the east and the west. Russia was consumed by revolution and war as it struggled to establish secure borders and, internally, convert an agricultural feudal state into a modern industrial giant. Further south and pursuing its destiny within a Mediterranean context, Italy had decided to reinvent itself as the head of a new Roman Empire, but inevitably found

1

that it could not do so while ignoring events taking place on the other side of the Alps.

The concepts by which air forces organise and train, target their enemies and conduct large-scale operations are encapsulated in written regulations and documents and it is this collection that comprises the doctrine of an air force. Basic air doctrine describes the fundamental philosophy behind the uses of air power and incorporates the basic principles by which the military forces support national objectives. Doctrine is usually based on theory, historical experience and current technological capabilities and, given that all three sources will be different for each country, the individual nature of their doctrine will be unique to them. Technology may well dictate the types of weapons a particular country might possess and thus influence the doctrine it chooses, while its concept of war might determine whether it adopts a strategic or tactical approach to air power.

Air forces the world over grew out of established army and navy organisations which had special doctrines built up over many years from their own values, beliefs, practices and ambitions, which meant that any attempt to create a new one within existing structures would be bound to meet resistance. The US air strategist Brigadier General William Lendrum Mitchell wrote, 'The armed forces of a nation are the most conservative elements in its whole make-up.'

There are three basic military doctrines: fundamental doctrine, organisational doctrine and tactical doctrine.[2] Fundamental doctrine defines the basic institutional values of a service and may be illustrated, in one instance, by its attitude towards the Douheist concept of strategic bombing or, in another, by the philosophy instilled into its recruits, best illustrated by the early Royal Air Force with its elitist ex-public school and university intake of pilots. Organisational doctrine is administrative and describes the internal structure of an organisation and the way it interacts with other services to achieve common goals, while tactical doctrine describes how the resources of a service are to be deployed as a means of realising an end.

There are also essentially only three main missions that all air forces have set for themselves: to win and hold air superiority, to strike at the enemy's centre of gravity, and to support ground forces in close air support. Air superiority requires that the effectiveness of enemy air forces is reduced sufficiently to allow one's own aircraft to carry out missions within a given area with minimal prohibitive interference. Striking at the 'centre of gravity' enables aircraft, operating in a strategic role, to influence the outcome of a war by air power alone. These two, by definition, are operations that are carried out by air forces independently of other services, but close air support is significantly more complex in that it demands close cooperation with ground forces. Close air support may be defined as air action against hostile targets which are in close proximity to friendly forces and is encapsulated in Blitzkrieg tactics or ground support which, in turn, is defined as air operations conducted to destroy, neutralise or delay the enemy's military potential within the battle area. The degree of importance afforded each of these missions is rarely governed by military doctrine alone since political and economic considerations usually require a certain level of compromise.

Doctrine in the context of ground support was often subsumed by the seductive narratives of close air-support heroics on the one hand, and Douhetist theories of mass 'terror-bombing' on the other which, between them, tended to drown out arguments for a middle way. The difficulties over defining ground-support objectives and the 'command and control' systems required for implementation, which usually boiled down to the 'who' rather than the 'what', were not easily resolved and continued to bedevil discussions for years. Nor can ground support be separated from the requirement for air superiority, since without the latter there is little chance of being able to concentrate exclusively on the mission at hand.

Between the two world wars, European air forces debated two basic air power theories. The first was that the primary role of air forces was to act as an independent force in pursuit of strategic objectives (long-distance bombing) to undermine the enemy war effort by attacking its war industry, transport systems and civilian morale, and the second, that it should be a support arm for land and naval forces. For the most part Italy, the Soviet Union and Germany allowed considerable free debate on theory and doctrine, but France discouraged it. Germany, the Soviet Union and Italy were able to test their respective air power theories and doctrines as the primary air combatants in Spain from 1936 to 1939 and all three concluded that the theory of support aviation held sway over strategic doctrine.

Military theorists were not slow to debate the merits of each doctrine. In 1917, Major General Hugh Trenchard, commander-in-chief of the Royal Flying Corps had fervently maintained that the primary purpose of an air force was to be offensive, preferably with heavy bombers, and that any money spent on producing fighters and anti-aircraft guns was 'a virtual waste of resources', but he diverged from Douhetist strategic doctrine by arguing that the target of such bomber fleets should be the enemy's military, and not civilian, centres. The civilian theorist Basil Liddell Hart argued against 'terror-bombing' of civilian populations as an effective means of destroying 'the general will to resist', which would not, as Douhet claimed, 'decide the fate of a nation within days or weeks'. Squadron Leader John Cotesworth Slessor, who became Director of Plans at the Air Ministry in 1939, wrote an influential book in 1936 *Air Power and Armies* in which he advocated the use of air power in a tactical role in support of ground forces. The overriding air doctrine of France, who in the early 1920s had the most powerful air force in the world and was a leader in aviation technology, was the tactical use of air power to support ground forces, but they too were subjected to strident calls for an independent air force having strategic capabilities.[3]

Air power first became a factor in warfare almost from the moment that the first balloon ascended in 1783. The French had been swift to see the military potential and had included corps of balloonists in their ranks during the years of revolution at the end of the eighteenth century. The Austrians took the next step by touching on tactical applications when they dropped 'balloon torpedoes' on Venice in 1849. Ten years later, Frenchmen Godard and Nadir brought reconnaissance firmly into the fold when they took photographs of enemy positions from a balloon at the Battle of Solferino. The French were in the vanguard again after the Franco-Prussian War of 1871, when they set up a permanent department to study military aeronautics. By 1884, there were balloon units in the armies of Russia, Germany, Italy and Spain, where they were used as observation platforms – but apparently were seen as having no further use, as H.W.L. Mödebek wrote in 1885, 'the value of the balloon as a weapon is still very much in doubt'.[4] However, when the First Hague Conference on the Laws of War convened in May 1899, the Russian delegation, anticipating a surge of interest in their military uses and already fearful of the range and potential consequences of those uses 'the prohibition of the discharge of any kind of projectile or explosive from balloons or by similar means'.[5] Others chose to keep the debate open while possibilities and potential advantage were weighed. The US delegate, William Crozier, was one such, and argued that prohibition should only be temporary on the basis that such 'means' had the potential to revolutionise warfare and a much longer deliberation period was required before making binding commitments. He won the day, and the ban was imposed, not permanently as was first called for, but for only five years, after which it was to be reviewed but, of course, it lapsed and was never revisited.

While kite balloons had become commonplace as aerial reconnaissance platforms with balloon units attached to all the great European armies, a new generation of aircraft, gas-filled dirigibles, emerged as a natural development and extended the range of possibilities in as much as they offered more scope for control and navigation than did the tethered balloon. For a few years, France continued to make the greatest progress along with Italy, who had introduced the first civilian airship in 1905. A new age was born, and when the fears of military exploitation expressed by the delegates at The Hague in 1899 re-emerged, all talk of renewing the five-year ban was forgotten. In the interim, Crozier's vision of a new dawn of military aviation had become a reality. In just a few short years military forces across the world were introducing dirigibles as weapons to supplement balloons as warfare took off into the third dimension. The Germans, particularly, accelerated their development programme and introduced three types of dirigible into their armed services built by Zeppelin and Schütte-Lanz.

Into this rapidly evolving landscape there now emerged the greatest revolutionary development of all in the form of the heavier-than-air flying machine as demonstrated by Wilbur and Orville Wright who brought their 'Flyer' aircraft for a public display in France in August 1908 and established a flying school at Pau. Other establishments followed in Germany and Italy. A.V. Roe made the first flight in Britain, while in France, Henri Farman set endurance records and Louis Blériot, who would later manufacture SPAD fighters for the French air force, crossed the Channel in his Type XI monoplane powered by a 50-hp Anzani engine. While the French were excelling with powered aircraft, the Germans, whose aviation budget was eight times that of France, had become the world leaders in airships which they described as 'implements of war far superior to anything of the kind our opponents have', from which they were stepping up experiments in aerial bombardment.[6] Much to the chagrin of their neighbours, they had sited airship facilities along their border with France at Escaty and with Russia at Königsberg, Allenstein, Thorn and Posen. This prompted an immediate response. In immediate reaction to this threat, by 1913 the French had begun developing counter-measures and had invented a benzene-filled dart which they called an 'incendiary arrow', for the specific use of bringing down dirigibles. There was great interest in airships within the wider community also and major fundraising campaigns were launched to finance aerial armament such as the one in Britain where a 'National Airship Fund' was set up; in France, where the publication *Auto* led a campaign to raise funds to buy aircraft for the military; and also in Italy, where the king and his citizens raised 3 million lira for the purpose. As early as 1911, prophesies about the destructive powers of aircraft in warfare were rife. There was much public disquiet over the idea of airships flying over cities and bombarding a defenceless population and this gave rise to political nervousness. Given that the industrialised European nations of Britain, Germany and France were essentially on a par technologically, war between them was seen as progressively less likely because no country would want to risk the certainty of the destruction of its cities overnight. With aircraft seen as having the power to 'strike everywhere without being hindered by political or physical borders', war could bring no gain if both sides had their populations decimated. Mutual deterrence or unilateral disarmament were seen as the only two ways to avoid warfare – and even put an end to large-scale war, heralding an age of cooperation within a 'United States of Europe', a concept first mooted at the Paris Peace Congress of September 1849. The writer Rudyard Kipling optimistically spoke of peace under a world government founded on air power.[7] Well, so much for ambition!

Competitions and demonstrations of air transport abounded and achievements in civil aviation became inextricably tied up with national prestige, but the real engine of technological development, as ever, would be war. Even civil events had military overtones. Non-stop flights from one city to another across Europe, beyond national boundaries, were excellent opportunities for crews to gather strategic and tactical intelligence about the land traversed. The rapid development of aircraft design generated by civilian competition fuelled, in turn, by the massive public interest was carefully nurtured by governments and industrialists, both of whom stood to benefit. Technical innovations abounded such as those developed by Eugene Ruchonnet and Louis Béchereau who had experimented with 'monocoque' smooth fuselage construction in an aircraft of their design which, in 1912, was the first aircraft to fly at more than 100mph. Meanwhile, in Germany, Anthony Fokker and Reinhold Platz were experimenting with steel-tube structures to form the body of the aircraft and scientists were beginning to explore air flows around aircraft in flight using classical theories of fluid dynamics and wind tunnels. Some governments, anxious to exploit their military potential, had already made provision to commandeer civil aircraft in time of war.

In an operational context, aircraft were being used by the Italians in Libya and the French in Morocco to test their usefulness as adjuncts to infantry. As an indication of how prevalent air power was becoming, in the Balkan War of 1912–13 all sides, Bulgaria, Greece, Serbia and Turkey, deployed aircraft operationally, albeit on a very limited scale. All flew French aircraft with French-trained pilots. By 1914, the air component of the military was seen to have a discernible structure and function in warfare with more than 1,000 military aircraft in use, many of which had been designed and built with particular military specifications in mind although the wider potential, beyond observation and reconnaissance, was not yet fully appreciated.

The expanded roles and missions of modern military aircraft that would become commonplace over the following decades were first explored during the First World War and 'what differences existed between the nature of military air power in 1914 and 1939 were more in the nature of technological change than in the nature of doctrine and strategy.'[8] Despite government incentives, the air fleets of all belligerents in 1914 were still mostly made up of sporting types which were slowly adapted to perform a range of services, but the most striking contribution of aviation on the early battle fronts was still the huge number of tethered kite balloons. Hundreds of Caquots on the French side and Drachens on the German side would be seen rising up to as much as 4,000ft above the battlefield, acting as the artillery's 'eye in the sky', giving a field of view up to five miles behind enemy lines. The most important element at play on the battle front was the artillery and, to gain the approbation of the army, all else had to prove its worth in support of that. Here the aeroplane was yet to make its impact but balloons, for all their utility as artillery spotters, were also acutely liable to present themselves as static targets for enemy ground fire and for enemy aircraft which attacked them armed with crude rockets or hand-held guns.

At the outbreak of the war, little was expected of what aircraft might contribute beyond a general consensus that they might serve a useful purpose as elaborate observation platforms offering more mobility and greater scope than tethered balloons. Initially aircraft from opposite sides avoided each other in flight, but as more were deployed their roles inevitably would bring them into direct confrontation and in that moment the concept of the fighter aircraft was born. In search of what other roles aircraft could play, governments, who had little concept of air power, had expressed vague aspirations; as in the case of the French, where fear of German airship attacks had spawned research into incendiary projectiles to destroy them, or in Italy where air-launched torpedoes, delivered from aircraft, were given priority as means of attacking enemy ground positions.[9] It was still reconnaissance, however, that was the aircraft's main contribution, as was dramatically demonstrated on 2 September 1914, when French pilot Louis Charles Breguet reported that he had observed surprising new German troop movements which threatened to isolate Paris. French Army commanders initially dismissed his report but French commander-in-chief General Joffre intervened and acted upon the intelligence, halting the German advance on the Marne in a manoeuvre that shaped the future trajectory of the whole war. German reconnaissance aircraft were equally useful on the Russian front at the Battle of Tannenberg, where Leutnant Mertens in a Gotha Taube monoplane, which had become the standard German military aircraft in 1914, observed the Russian Army advancing with exposed flanks and reported back immediately to headquarters, which allowed the Germans to surprise, encircle and destroy them. In this way, reconnaissance aircraft had achieved 'an undreamed-of importance', and armies 'scrambled [to support] the infrastructure and the productive base of their air services'.[10]

When the war turned into a stalemate of trench warfare the aircraft began to exhibit its potential as a weapon in its own right. Aerial reconnaissance had become invaluable for artillery spotting, although still very much the domain of balloons, which prompted ground forces on both sides to try and restrict aircraft movements through ground fire and then by arming aircraft to attack each other. As a result, aircrews started shooting at each other to try to prevent reconnaissance, which elevated 'control of the air' to become a very desirable objective and aerial combat was born. The French fighter 'ace' René Paul Fonck, 'an aviator without equal',[11] wrote of his experiences in the trenches: 'a thousand faces turned hypnotised toward the sky. Two planes, one French and the other German, were clashing in a ferocious aerial duel … turn to turn, plunge to plunge.'[12] This led to creation of the dedicated fighter aircraft with enhanced aerobatic capabilities and flown by pilots with specialised skills heralding what, in popular imagination, was a time of 'chivalrous engagements' between 'heroic figures' who embodied the spirit of a nation and deflected attention away from the slaughter in the trenches. The image, however, disguises the fact that most aerial 'victories' were won by stealth, surprise and ambush rather than by aerial jousting. As a caveat, Fonck later described how, 'hidden from the target', he had from the ground shot down a German reconnaissance aircraft which, 'without having the time to know what was happening … fell into a tailspin and was lost among the reeds of a marsh'. The age of the lone fighter pilot as 'gladiator' was short because soon, aircraft were combined into large formations of fighters used to apply concentrated force in a bid to establish control of the air above combat zones, and thus 'air supremacy' became one of the first practised doctrinal concepts of air warfare. In this regard, the invention of the synchronised machine gun designed to fire forward through the propeller under the direct control of the pilot allowing him to 'really hunt down the enemy' was a significant technological advance.[13]

Early moves towards militarisation of aircraft had consisted of making low-altitude reconnaissance flights of short duration over enemy territory and reporting back the intelligence gained in person. The single-occupancy aircraft was soon joined by larger twin-engine types, with pilot and an extra crewman for observation and as a gunner. They were initially adjuncts of army operations with three basic functions: observation, interdiction and bombing. Observation aircraft would assist the army as required; combat and pursuit aircraft would attack enemy aircraft attacking friendly ground forces, and bombers would attack and harass enemy troops in the field, destroying their communications, weapons stores and ammunition dumps. Later, a fourth function was introduced: ground attack or the harassment of enemy troops on the ground with machine-gun fire. The idea of strategic bombing took hold in the later stages of the war, at which time a new dimension in warfare emerged which encouraged the air forces to seek recognition as independent arms of the military. It was rapidly becoming a 'given' that mastery of the skies would be the deciding factor in future wars. This tempted military theorists to believe that the 'correct' application of air power would assure swift victory, but it also appalled politicians to see that losing meant the nightmare prospect of destruction on a scale hitherto unimagined. Air doctrine across Europe during the first decade of the twentieth century grew out of a perceived threat of the offensive potential of air power. The psychological nightmare of death raining out of the skies upon helpless civilians had spawned conferences on international law and disarmament that considered proposals as extreme as completely banning aerial bombing altogether, even before its effects

9

had been observed. Annexes to the Second Hague convention of 1907 had explicitly prohibited air attacks on towns, villages, houses, churches, hospitals and the like, even though the capability to do so scarcely existed at the time.

Following on from the concept of air supremacy came the belief, not universally shared at first, that air power should primarily be used, in the manner espoused by Douhet, as an unrelentingly offensive strike force rather than defensively.[14] Despite the poor record of aerial bombing before 1914, the concept was revived as part of a wide-ranging review of the overall potential of military aircraft. The idea of dropping bombs from the sky was latched onto early in the era of manned flight, but the first aircraft had no mechanical facilities for carrying and delivering heavy bombs, so only small devices could be deployed and the crew had to drop them by hand. At first, crews simply dropped artillery shells, the only explosives to hand, but soon innovated with bigger and more destructive items, especially in the case of the Zeppelins which were capable of carrying a greater weight. In the first dedicated bombing missions of late 1914, Zeppelin Z VI struck at Liege and German Taube aircraft made tentative raids on French railway stations around Belfort and Lunéville and even Paris was on the receiving end of small attacks on more than a dozen occasions.[15] The British had become unnerved by the attacks on France and feared similar attacks against themselves from the newly formed Brieftauben Abteilungen Ostende German bomber force in Belgium. On 21 November they chose to launch a pre-emptive strike and sent four Avro 504 bombers from Belfort in Alsace to attack the main Zeppelin factory at Friedrichshafen on Lake Constance in southern Germany. In retaliation one German aircraft dropped a few small bombs on Dover on 22 December establishing a pattern of strike and counter-strike. While targets abounded, many of them undefended, hitting them with any sort of accuracy proved difficult. Between March and June 1915, the Western Allies tried 141 times to bomb German railway stations and succeeded in hitting the target a mere three times.[16] When the forces along the Western Front became entrenched and it became clear that the war would not be over quickly, a great deal of thought went into technological developments that might break the deadlock, one of which was air power. As well as bombing and reconnaissance, in another development, aircraft had on occasion harassed enemy ground forces and this was recognised as an effective tactic gaining official endorsement as 'close support' of ground forces. In this role, aircraft operated either in simultaneous attacks with ground forces directly against enemy troops, or by attacking supply dumps and communications facilities just behind enemy lines. After its early reputation as an interesting novelty, but of limited military value, the aircraft was quickly coming into its own as 'a legitimate weapon of war.'[17]

On the Western Front both sides expanded their bombing operations, but the British and French were bolder in extending the war behind enemy lines. On 26 April 1915 the British bombed Courtrai rail yards and on 27 May, sixteen French aircraft from the 1re Groupe de Bombardement made the three-hour flight from Nancy to Ludwighafen to bomb the Badische Aniline explosives plant. The Germans picked up the French idea of strategic bombing to open a new 'front' to the war, but, as their preferred option, they chose dirigibles over aircraft, given their greater carrying capacity. Their first significant raids were by naval Zeppelins on 19 January 1915 against Yarmouth. At first their Zeppelin airships, which were ideally equipped to carry a heavy load of bombs, took the war onto the streets of London after the Kaiser reversed an earlier ban. Powerful airships up to 600ft long prowled the skies over London throughout the summer of 1915, killing 277 civilians. They eventually proved to be particularly vulnerable to both ground fire and aircraft interdiction and were withdrawn in favour of German heavy bombers, the 'Gotha' G-plane or 'Grossflugzeug' and the 'Giant' R-plane or 'Riesen flugzeug' of the Kagohl-3 bombing unit, which further increased the paranoia created by the lumbering giant Zeppelins by delivering a more concentrated bombardment. The British government reacted to attacks on the capital with panic, fearing an immediate breakdown of civil order. In particular, two raids on London on 13 June and 7 July 1917 were important landmarks, leaving 227 people dead and 677 wounded. Both raids showed existing defensive measures to be totally inadequate. In the British political mindset the bombings of London created an urgent requirement for an effective defensive strategy. There were not enough anti-aircraft guns and fighters, and the early warning system was virtually non-existent. When the British government called for aircraft to be withdrawn from France for home defence, the army commander Sir Douglas Haig and his air advisor Major General Hugh Trenchard, commander-in-chief of the Royal Flying Corps, resisted the call. Trenchard viewed this as a misuse of aircraft, offence being their only proper role; in the end, however, he had no choice but to comply.

On the Western Front, tactical bombing by day of enemy front-line positions practically ceased in the autumn of 1916 owing to the high levels of casualties. The Germans, who had always prioritised fighter defence over bomber attack on the battlefield, began to exact a heavy toll of French bombers. This prompted a refocusing of attention on strategic targets well behind enemy lines, but again, casualties were high and night-bombing became the only option with any degree of sustainable losses. The difficulties of navigation, especially at night, and the inaccuracy of bomb-aiming techniques argued against strategic bombing as an effective means of forcing a resolution to the war, but rather than dismiss strategic bombing as a viable doctrine, all countries felt that despite its obvious limitations, strategic air power, in the imagination, had limitless potential if air fleets were afforded the kind of resources currently consumed by army or naval budgets.[18] Given the proximity of Paris to the German border, France refused to consider the idea of an arms race with strategic bombing of populated areas as its focus. Playing 'who blinks first' in such a potentially catastrophic scenario was not to its taste. Neither were they enamoured of a military doctrine that abolished the separation between citizen and soldier.[19]

The problem for strategic air war theorists lay in the limited capability of aircraft to inflict sufficient damage to actually influence the course of the war. All the major powers had invested resources in creating a strategic bomber capability, none more so than the Italians in their war with Austria-Hungary, in the hope that they might be able to break the stalemate on the ground. In the West, the Germans were better situated to attack French cities, but their Zeppelin still had to travel considerable distances to attack British targets from bases at Tondern, Fuhlsbuttel, Nordholt and Hoge on the North Sea. When Zeppelin bases were moved up to operate from the front lines in France, however, they became dangerously close to London and Paris, but the prime German targets were still a considerable distance from Allied air bases. Although the Zeppelin raids caused little physical damage, they had a considerable psychological effect on the terrified citizens cowering under their massive forms prowling overhead. However ominous and frightening the Zeppelins were, they did prove to be vulnerable to the increased defensive ground fire and were prone to accidents in less than perfect weather conditions. When excessive losses prompted their replacement by Gotha bombers, random attacks such as the one on a shopping arcade in Folkestone, killing 95 and wounding 260, caused a furious reaction in the

British press which demanded increased protection for civilians. A week later London was hit with a death toll of 162. Raids continued but were now met with an increasing level of interdiction, eventually leading to an unsustainable 20 per cent casualty rate which persuaded the Germans to give up their strategic bombing initiative altogether. The consequences of the bombings, over Britain especially, proved to be far-reaching in two particular respects. While it dampened German enthusiasm for strategic bombing, it also started a chain of events that resulted in the formation of an independent Royal Air Force and that would set the scene for, and have a great influence on, another great air battle more than twenty years later.

There emerged, nevertheless, a general consensus that bomber aircraft would dominate future wars, both in a tactical and strategic role, and air power was likely to become the single most important deciding factor. While this was tacitly accepted by ground forces, they insisted that air power should remain firmly under their control. This, however, did not prevent Britain, in response to the attacks on London, implementing the recommendations of the 'Smuts Report' of 1917. Within three months they alone of all European powers had decided to let air power 'off the lead' and had established the 'Independent Force' based in France, to carry out an ambitious programme of strategic bombing raids against Cologne and, a year later, created the Royal Air Force with freedom to operate completely separate from the army or navy.

In the matter of tactical air power it was generally conceded that air attack against ground forces could have a decisive impact if correctly integrated with ground offensives, but the risk of significant casualties was ever present if low-level attacks were made against well-trained and well-equipped troops. The RAF manual warned that fighter aircraft should not be deployed against well-defended positions, neither should they be given licence to roam lest they encounter such positions by accident. It was emphasised that they should only conduct missions against targets that had been thoroughly investigated by reconnaissance aircraft and such attacks should be made without delay so that target intelligence did not become redundant. The British, especially, developed complex methods of communication involving radio and visual signals.

Control of the air first began to play an important part in the great land battles of the First World War at Verdun and later on the Somme, where intelligence brought back by closely protected reconnaissance flights gave significant advantages. With the acknowledgement of the important role of aircraft in reconnaissance, urgent research began on developing high-resolution cameras to bring back detailed images of enemy positions, but this also had its problems. Photographic plates had to be inserted and changed after every shot. As a measure of the level of interest shown in flying and all the technical issues surrounding it, Giulio Douhet had developed an automatic camera with his colleague and aviation pioneer Giovanni Caproni even before the war started in 1914. To make observation easier for air crews, one of the areas new aircraft designers were exploring when developing the second generation of wartime aircraft was the field of vision available to them. In this respect German aircraft were less well designed, but that was less of a problem for them since their main operational roles were in defence behind their own lines and they did not venture far from home.

The war had given a tremendous impetus to technological and doctrinal innovation. Stephen Budiansky believed that the effect of the First World War on military aviation was greater than the effect of military aviation on the war. Between 1914 and 1918, as many as five generations of aircraft superseded each other and quickly made the preceding one redundant. In 1914 no country had more than about fifty generally underpowered and lightly armed military aircraft, but by the end of the war, France alone had 260 squadrons on the Western Front.[20] As a result of their experiences, different countries had developed air power doctrine in their own different ways. Britain and Italy came out with a firm strategic ambition, with Britain the only country having an independent air arm. Germany had been eager to explore strategic air war with their Zeppelins and heavy Gotha bombers but the losses sustained only convinced them that the future lay in tactical air support of ground forces. Since aircraft were such a modern phenomenon, the training of airmen proved especially problematical. There was a distinct shortage of experienced airmen to guide new recruits given the high attrition rate of flyers during the war and so, with no particular example to follow, flyers were left pretty much to their own devices to come up with ways of achieving a broad range of objectives in their training.[21]

The most important and challenging element in the development of aviation was engine technology; essentially, extracting more power from a given weight of engine. In terms of innovation, engines generally lagged behind airframes due to the much greater technological challenges in designing, testing and mass-producing them. Early types such as the Motorenfabrik Oberursel rotary engine of the Fokker E.I, the Le Rhône 9C of the Bristol Scout and the Morane-Saulnier L generated a meagre 80-hp but by the end of the war, while five generations of airframes had been rolled out, the engines for even the Siemens-Schuckert D.IV, a fifth generation aircraft, still only had a Siemens-Halske 160-hp engine.

For the fighter pilot, as well as speed and manoeuvrability, a critical factor in terms of survival was offensive armament. At first the only weapon a pilot could carry was the hand gun or rifle, but the obvious problem of flying the aircraft and aiming a weapon at the same time exposed the limitations of that and soon led to innovation. The fixed machine gun was installed on single-seater fighters but, out of necessity, positioned so that its line of fire did not cause catastrophic damage to the propeller. This meant that the pilot had to stand up to operate the gun fixed to the top of the upper wing, which still left him flying without hands on the controls. Apart from that, the guns required frequent reloading, often jammed and had to be cleared by hitting them with a wooden mallet.[22] A second crewman was added to man the weapon, but even with a two-man crew the pilot and gunner had difficulty working together to manoeuvre the aircraft and keep the enemy in the gunsights. Two-seater aircraft were seen as an early solution. Pusher aircraft such as the Vickers 'Gunbus' had the engine facing backwards behind the pilot, allowing a second crewman to occupy a position right at the front of the aircraft and operate a fixed machine gun there, but the extra weight slowed the aircraft and still left the single-seater fighter with a problem, especially since tractor aircraft (i.e. having the propeller right at the front of the aircraft), such as the French Nieuport 17 were now significantly out-performing pushers. A Frenchman, Eugene Adrien Roland Georges Garros, had experimented with a synchronising mechanism that prevented the gun from discharging when the propeller was in its line of fire. While the synchronising device was reliable, the irregular firing mechanism of the guns and the lack of consistency in ammunition threatened to shred the propeller, so he had armoured propellers fitted to his Morane-Saulnier L allowing bullets to ricochet off if the synchronisation failed. This soon proved unsound, however, as the armour-plating was unable to protect the propeller when more powerful ammunition was developed. A German Fokker engineering team that captured Garros's aircraft made the next breakthrough with more efficient ammunition and a modified cam-operated synchroniser mechanism that allowed pilots such as Oswald Boelcke and Max Immelmann, 'the Eagle of Lille', to begin what became known as the 'Fokker scourge', when German fighters gained temporary ascendancy in the air war in 1917.[23]

Right from the start of the war, Britain and France had adopted fundamentally different bombing doctrines.[24] The idea of 'total war' intrinsic to the strategic bombing doctrine which saw the mobilisation of the whole of society onto a war footing and the erosion of distinction between military personnel and civilian populations was, at the outset, unpopular with the French, who chose to exercise a considerable degree of restraint by mostly restricting its actions to munitions factories and railways, despite significant pressure to extend the war to target German civilians. On the few occasions where attacks were carried out against German cities in 1915, French bomber units suffered unsustainable high losses for limited gains. Crossing many miles of enemy air space with the risk of fighter interdiction and only rudimentary navigation techniques to locate targets, the meagre bomb loads did little damage to vital areas. Bombing a city like Frankfurt was considerably more difficult for the French than the bombing of Paris was for the Germans, and the bombing of territory such as Alsace-Lorraine, which the French were hoping to have restored to them after the war, would be counter-productive. The proximity of French cities to German airfields meant that, according to the commander of French aviation General Maurice Duval, France needed a bomber force 10–20 times that of Germany to redress the imbalance caused by geography. Where strategic bombing was carried out, Britain, Germany and France all suffered heavy losses. When Germany bombed French towns, reprisal raids were condoned, but initially only by government decree and each raid was considered separately to avoid escalation which could only be to France's detriment. This involved delays in carrying out the reprisal raids leading to a pre-approved list of targets in a 'quid pro quo' policy, but still Deputy Pierre-Étienne Flandin agitated for the bombing of enemy factories and cities to make the German people feel the weight of the war and lobbied for massive bombing fleets under American control.[25]

The bombing of British cities in 1917 prompted a different approach from its government and led to a rapid escalation of British reprisal raids. They were encouraged by the fact that German munitions industries in Düsseldorf and Essen were much more concentrated than those of the Allies but the French objected, fearing that it would be they who felt the weight of German reaction. The British set up the Independent Force based in France to attack German military and industrial targets including those found in cities.[26] Trenchard had at first objected strongly to the notion of strategic bombing, but very quickly came round to being a powerful advocate and argued that the word 'reprisal' should be expunged from official documents. Supported by the RFC Chief of Staff, Brigadier General Frederick Hugh Sykes, he rejected any restraint on bombing policy. If its major assets were attacked, Germany, he argued, would be forced to withdraw much of its fighter force from the front to defend the cities and improve Allied prospects of victory on the ground.

As a measure of how far technology had advanced during the First World War, the aviator Roland Garros emerged from three years in a German prison in 1918 to find that he was unable to fly the current generation of aircraft without extensive retraining. Viewed from the perspective of 1918, the aircraft of four years previously were 'ancient and extinct'.[27] Part of the reason for innovation was attrition, which stripped units of their aircraft at an impressive rate forcing production of replacements incorporating all the latest technology, and all made possible by the vast national resources allocated to the aircraft manufacturing industries. With so many countries at war and so much material being consumed, the shortage of raw materials had the effect of encouraging innovative solutions to the challenges of both airframe design and engine power. The impetus of war ensured that there were four, or possibly five, generations of aircraft developed during the four years of conflict. Aircraft speeds had doubled and engine power had quadrupled. The concept of lift and wing-loading, rate-of-climb and ceiling became better understood as was the relationship between them, where positive changes to one might be to the detriment of another. The relationship matured between the military, whose battlefield experiences informed requirements, and the government, who issued specifications for new aircraft and industry who submitted designs based upon them.

Engine design was probably the most challenging for industry. There was a constant demand for ever greater performance, but the internal combustion engine designed for motor vehicles was not particularly suitable for aircraft, in which it would be required to operate at full throttle for extended periods. There were two basic types: the rotary engine, which revolved around a stationary crankshaft, and the stationary engine that drove a revolving crankshaft. The stationary type had three variants which could be air-cooled or water-cooled, while the rotary was air-cooled. Rotary engines such as the Gnome-Rhône, which were reliable and excellent in many respects, reached a ceiling of efficiency in power output early in the war and were replaced by stationary engines which could be scaled up more effectively. Some engines were notoriously unreliable and had 'a reputation for insincerity'. All engines required frequent servicing, rotaries especially, which could only run for about thirty hours before being dismantled and refitted. Although numbers of aircraft, especially later in the war, were impressive on paper, a significant percentage at any one time would be unserviceable due to engine wear.

The intensity and duration of the First World War at a time of accelerating technological progress saw huge advances in all spheres of military innovation and doctrine, not least of which was in the application of air power. From almost a standing start, air forces had battled to define their own purpose and ambitions; their own strengths and weaknesses and their place within the military structure. So many challenges in such a short time, against a background of struggle for an independent identity called for 'leadership, wisdom and commitment'.[28] While the French air force remained no more than semi-independent from the army and restricted themselves essentially to an air-support role and the British RAF had broken free to explore strategic air doctrine, the German air force had, in theory at least, ceased to exist. Whatever role the air forces found themselves playing, evidence from the battlefield had shown that technical superiority, aircraft manufacturing capacity and superior crew training, all of which fluctuated according to circumstances, were the essential ingredients for success in the air war.

Most air operations during the First World War had been tactical in nature and carried out in support of ground forces over and around the battlefront but there had been notable exceptions, such as the German bombing of London. It was in response to this experience that Britain, in 1918, marked the beginning of its strategic air doctrine by creating an independent air force: the RAF. For some, military inertia had proved to be as difficult to disturb as ever with its traditional inclination to base its doctrine on fighting the previous war all over again by lauding its victories and failing to learn the lessons of its defeats. For others, like Germany, having little option after being stripped of its military air arm at Versailles, it was a chance to start all over again. Wherever they emerged, the challenge for air forces was to prise funding and control away from the army and navy, which often involved political intervention and realignment of military budgets. The new inter-service relationships varied from country to country and where, as in the case of the RAF, an independent force emerged, albeit uneasily, internal rivalries developed between the strategic bomber arm and the tactical fighter arm. Germany, in contrast, had managed to retain and develop an air doctrine throughout its years of purgatory thanks to subterfuge and secret training and development facilities in the Soviet Union. They nurtured and encouraged a close bond between air and ground forces even after the Luftwaffe was created as an independent force in 1935, and that was the basis of their spectacularly successful Blitzkrieg doctrine.[29]

There were five important factors that came together to shape air power between the wars: defence expenditure, perceived threats, national strategies, technology and personalities. Two lesser influences were: experiences and consequences of the First World War and the resulting diplomatic rivalries. The level of funding determined the extent to which new technologies and doctrines were adopted, while geographic factors had a huge influence on defence thinking. Britain had an Empire to govern and, surrounded by sea, was comforted by having the most powerful navy in the world, which left the air force to find its own place. France boasted the most powerful army, which maintained an iron grip on its air force. Germany and the newly created Poland were politically volatile and both faced potential threats along their east and west land borders. The Soviet Union, meanwhile, was in the throes of post-revolutionary transformation.

The collapse of the old European order during and after the First World War brought instability with numerous small conflicts and wars as governments squabbled over boundaries and resources, and subjugated nations agitated for independence. These conflicts were played out in an era of rapid technological developments but in ways that did not advance military doctrine to any great extent. New weapons were seen as enhancement of old ones and used in similar ways. Only slowly did ideas of how to implement new weapons systems break out of conservative straitjacketed thought and take on a separate, unique character. All of these conflicts involved scenarios in which the air components played some part and encouraged military theorists to explore its role in isolation from ground forces, but it had to overcome ingrained military dogma and a huge burden of 'slavish adherence to a particular military design philosophy'.[30] Of all the ideas that wore the mantle of dogma, strategic air power was the most intransigent. Hippler, in reference to strategic air doctrine asks 'how, despite all common sense, a strategy came to prevail that was, according to all available indicators, militarily ineffective'.[31] Few denied that experience of the war had exposed the 'uselessness of strategic bombing', but this was conveniently attributed to poor implementation rather than incorrect doctrine and therefore the question of its effectiveness was allowed to remain moot. The explanation for its failure, its adherents blindly argued, was that the aeroplane had simply not had sufficient opportunity to prove itself and the rationale was that once technology had raised it to a certain level of proficiency and performance, all doubt would be erased.

Military aviation had developed at a tremendous rate during the First World War, but after 1919 countries adopted different air doctrines according to their evaluation of their war experience and the fundamental constraints imposed by each of their financial and geographical situations. It is possible to argue that Germany, initially frustrated by the ban on military aviation imposed upon it by the Treaty of Versailles, may have benefited from its freedom to explore new aircraft design, technology and doctrine from a theoretical viewpoint, while taking note of the best aircraft and technologies that each of the other countries were turning out. Of major concern to all nations was the discussion about the extent to which an air force should be independent of other armed services. The idea of an independent air force was inexorably tied to the concept of strategic air warfare. Could an air force carrying out operations unrelated to the ground battlefront situation and not under the control of ground commanders have a significant positive, or even decisive, effect on the progress of a war? Theory had it that there were two ways in which this might happen. Either by degrading an enemy's capacity to wage war by destruction of critical assets such as ammunition dumps, armament factories and communications networks, or by direct attacks on cities to exert psychological pressure on the civilian population, and by extension on their government, to capitulate. In a memo to the Cabinet in October 1917, Winston Churchill expressed his doubt that attacking civilians would weaken their will to make war. Britain and France had tried the first military option with attacks on Zeppelin sheds, but the French later extended operations to the bombing of cities at Karlsruhe and Munich in June 1915. The Germans had gone straight for the jugular with

Zeppelin raids on British towns and cities, but it might be argued that it was as much the sight of these monstrous ships hovering above and not the small amount of damage their bombs caused that so stirred the imagination and caused such panic. The Italians, for their part, had launched strategic bombing attacks on military targets at Lubjiana and Pola.

Because the aircraft, by the end of the First World War, had displayed 'a degree of mobility, and psychological impact … that surpassed the most sanguine expectations of its pre-war supporters', it had the power to generate a level of expectation that was quite unrealistic.[32] Theories of strategic air power were creating an ambivalent mood of trepidation and ambition which threatened to take over as more conservative doctrine struggled to retain control. Experience from the war was overwhelmingly of tactical operations with aircraft engaged along the battle front very much as part of cooperative operations with the army. Where strategic missions had been flown, they had proved costly and largely ineffective. This bolstered the conservative view, but the sheer freedom of action displayed by machines operating in three dimensions was a powerful stimulus to explore the broader horizons of air doctrine. The many small wars, of disparate natures, that continued to erupt across the world after 1919 involved aviation to a greater or lesser extent which allowed proponents of both views to collect evidence in support of their position, but the limited nature of such wars would not significantly inform the debate.

A number of influential theorists such as Guilio Douhet, Billy Mitchell, Alexander de Seversky and Sir Hugh Trenchard laid the foundations of air doctrine in the immediate post-war years, but none 'attempted a balanced history of air power'.[33] Douhet, especially, concentrated on only one aspect and is often accredited with the advent of strategic bombing doctrine, but his works were only translated from the Italian and widely distributed in the early 1930s. The extent of his influence before this time is debatable, but that does not detract from the wide interest shown in strategic bombing since the first Zeppelin raids in 1915. Whether promulgated by Douhet or by others, the doctrine of the strategic deployment of aircraft was: 'To conquer command of the air means victory, to be beaten in the air means defeat and acceptance of whatever terms the enemy may be pleased to impose.' For them, war is the business of the whole population, since a modern country can only prosecute warfare if a significant proportion of its economy, and the people involved in that, are engaged in war-related activities such as munitions manufacture. Furthermore, the growing trend toward democratisation of the political process gave the people the power to influence political decisions, the gravest of which was to take a country to war, and so the population could be held responsible for the actions of its government and pressure applied to the people through bombing could influence the progress of the war. The people would be bombed 'in order to destroy their unity [of the body politic] with a view to releasing the forces of anarchy and revolt'.[34] Intrinsic to this view, which sees air offensive as the means of destroying the unity between the people and the state, is the converse which sees defence against air attack as a 'moral and political [unifier] of a people'. So powerful was the idea of bombers dominating a future war, and so universal was its acceptance, that the merest mention of its flaws seems to have been frowned upon at every level. Such weaknesses in the argument are clear in retrospect but, at the very least, the abysmally poor bomb-aiming technology should have given pause for thought when precision targeting was such a central tenet of the doctrine.

The concept of the 'precision bombing of node points', to bring about economic collapse of the enemy promulgated by the US theorist Billy Mitchell, was enthusiastically pursued, but the only country that could really apply it was the US with its advanced Norden bombsight. For Britain, who knew it simply could not bomb anywhere near accurately enough for a 'military' bombing strategy, the idea of breaking enemy civilian morale became the 'go-to' argument. This would have greater impact than the destruction of property, they claimed, and a strategic air war would be one of attrition until the weaker side capitulated. The idea that an adequate defence could be put up against strategic bombing was obviously counter to this philosophy and examination of its virtues was not encouraged. The whole atmosphere of the early 1930s was dominated by the 'terror-bombing' theory that held the world's governments in its grip. A concept of 'mutually assured destruction' in a short, sharp war with minimal involvement of ground forces, it was hoped, might dissuade any country from starting another major European war and, coincidentally, allowed governments to proceed without any commitment to detailed planning for a long war and let them winnow down their defence budgets.[35]

Strategic air doctrine after the war would evolve in different ways in different countries and it is worth, at this stage, looking briefly at how that happened. Britain, under Trenchard's influence, had adopted an offensive doctrine based on strategic bombing 'to defeat the enemy nation' well before the publication of Douhet's *Command of the Air*. Aircraft procurement was heavily biased towards bombers, with fighters seen as a sop to public opinion but of no real value. Discussion of civilian casualties resulting from strategic bombing was not encouraged except to say that 'the dislocation of civilian morale was the true object of war'.[36] Liddell Hart went further by saying that after laying enemy cities in ruins, 'the general will to resist [will] vanish'. A number of leading airmen such as Slessor would dispute this doctrine, but Trenchard's dominance of the RAF establishment was such that his influence was extremely slow to wane and persisted right up to the latter part of the 1930s. The French Air Force was much slower than the RAF to break free of army control, essentially because of the immense political power of the army establishment. There was really no compelling case to be argued for separating the air force command from the army if it was to continue to play an army support role so airmen, who yearned for independence, tried to redefine the air force in Douhetist terms. This was an uphill struggle at a time when the French Army was busy making extensive plans to bury itself deep inside the gargantuan defensive Maginot Line, but slowly, with the creation of an air ministry in 1928, the dream of air independence was starting to become a reality. The problem was that, although separation of the two services was completed in 1933, the dispute over fundamental air doctrine was never resolved and since there was never a clear doctrine, aircraft procurement vacillated between offensive and defensive types, resulting in a mixture of aircraft that suited neither purpose. In Italy, which was the home of Douhetist strategic bombing doctrine, the concept initially suited the mood of the times and was taken up by the fascist movement as typifying its modern revolutionary and brutally disciplined philosophy. Ironically, however, it was the Italian Air Force that began to reject Douhet's ideas in favour of the more nuanced approach of Air Marshal Italo Balbo and General Amadeo Mecozzi, who disparaged Douhetist doctrine as 'war against the unarmed'.[37] In the immediate aftermath of the Bolshevik Revolution the Soviet Union had doctrine, but not much of an air force with which to practice it. Their penchant for strategic air power was purely theoretical but it changed when the Germans set up their research centre at Lipetsk, after which Soviet doctrine began to be very strongly influenced by their guests.

Experiences of, and lessons learned from, the Russo-Polish War which broke out in 1920 were quite different from those of the First World War. The vast Russian-Polish border areas over which the conflict raged rarely brought aircraft into direct confrontation, which allowed them almost unfettered freedom of action across much of the battle front. Most air actions were against cavalry and infantry ground forces and many of the aircraft were old, worn-out and badly maintained war-surplus machines resulting in significant numbers of casualties from accidents rather than combats. Under such circumstances there was little scope for either the Russians or the Poles to develop anything resembling an air doctrine. Flying the flimsy Austro-Hungarian-built Albatros D.III fighter, the high-speed, Italian-built Ansakldo A.1 Balilla, and the excellent French designed Breguet XIV light bomber, the Poles did manage to evolve attack stratagems to avoid enemy ground fire during their attacks but were generally unable to muster sufficient fire-power to have a decisive influence until they encountered a large Russian force advancing south of the Pripet Marshes. This force of Semyon Budenny's cavalry was spotted by the US-crewed Kosciuśko squadron and scattered by repeated strafing attacks until it was driven back in disarray. It was a significant defeat for the Russians and helped to turn the tide of war in Poland's favour. So much so that Budenny cabled Moscow and demanded that a bounty of 25,000 gold roubles be put on the head of each US pilot in the squadron.

Despite the rout of Buddeny's cavalry, it was ground forces that settled the issue and forced an armistice in October. Air power alone could not really be said to have 'won the war' for the Poles, but the requirement for a narrative to stir national pride as the newly created country struggled to find its feet in the shifting sands of East European border realignments gave the Polish Air Ministry a platform on which to boast of its achievements and build a service. Air power, however, fell victim to political machinations which dragged it back under army control with emphasis on reconnaissance and ground support and limited doctrinal development. This, in turn, fed into choices of aircraft types, either to buy or manufacture. For the Russians, the ground-attack role also dominated doctrine. Production of the Polikarpov R-5 Shturmovik in 1931 was the result of a decade-long preference for attack aircraft (Shturmovaya Aviatsia).

For Britain in the years immediately after the First World War, it was the security of its Imperial possessions that fuelled its interest in air power as a policing tool. Interventions by aircraft in a number of campaigns against insurgents in the Middle East had shown them to be a relatively inexpensive means of controlling rebellions. Even though many of the aircraft were often under-powered and obsolete, such as the B.E.2c, they had mobility and were able to cause panic among tribesmen who had never seen the like before. While aircraft in no way replaced ground forces they did add a new capability, especially in reconnaissance and occasionally bombing, which was appreciated by the army who were effulgent in their praise for the airmen and 'the courage and skill which they displayed in performing their duties in these antiquated machines'.[38]

In Somaliland, a year later, a flight of British DH.9 two-seater bombers undertook intensive and very successful independent bombing and strafing attacks against Dervisher positions, but the army command on the spot was not minded to allow the upstart service to take the credit for suppressing the revolt and reined them in by restricting all further action to ground support. Again, recounting of the events exaggerated the role of aircraft with Viscount Milner noting that aircraft in the campaign 'contributed greatly to its success', but leaders at home remained sceptical. Trenchard and Churchill, however, saw merit in promoting the new Royal Air Force as a success and secured political approval to station eight squadrons in the Middle East to help police the Empire. This initially proved to be an economic and effective substitute for large-scale infantry and cavalry operations, especially against Wahabi tribesmen, where air units were able to gain some initial advantage but soon the enemy learned to disperse in the face of air attack which then left the aircraft with no targets to aim at. On top of this, air units were often accused of being slow to respond to calls for air support from ground forces, but when, by design or accident, cooperation between aircraft and infantry was achieved, the results of combined action left 'camelmen riding madly towards every point of the compass'.[39]

The British theorist Wing Commander John Slessor, who was to become a Marshal of the Royal Air Force, was a champion of the single-seater fighter, but he believed that 'aircraft are not normally battlefield weapons', indicating a preference for strategic attack roles deep in the enemy's rear.[40] Despite this view, however, as commander of air forces later on the North-West Frontier he seems to have had a change of heart and called for close air and army cooperation, his concept of which was encapsulated in a manual *Close Support Tactics*. He was forced to review his thoughts once again, however, when a later action at Dakai Kalai in which he was involved resulted in heavy casualties showed just how difficult this type of operation was to implement in practice. The main problem, Slessor found, was the lack of efficient ground-air communications so that 'clear orders can be conveyed quickly to pilots in the air'.[41]

France had its own experiences in support of Spanish forces in the Moroccan 'Rif' Wars of the early 1920s. Here it worked with colonial Groupe Mobile forces of infantry, artillery and mechanised transport. These units were renowned for their flexibility, speed of manoeuvre and concentration of force. They had significant successes using aircraft in combined attack with armoured vehicles, but only where the enemy was 'powerless to oppose them'.

Between the wars, the threat posed by air power played a significant role in international affairs, and predisposed politicians to accept strategic bombing as a potentially war-winning force in itself and a way of avoiding any more slaughter in the trenches. However, the terror caused by bombing of civilians during the First World War had led to a commission convening under the auspices of the League of Nations in 1925 to urge severe limits on aerial warfare. British officials called for a total abolition of aerial bombardment, but it was rejected. This at a time when the whole British air doctrine was coagulating around strategic bombing. We are quite prepared to adopt terror-bombing as a policy, they seemed to say, but we don't like it and we will refrain from carrying it out if everyone else agrees to do likewise.

Germany, under the constraints of Versailles, had opted to develop skills and technologies associated with air power through ostensibly non-military entities such as glider clubs and civilian airlines, but had also secretly established three military aviation research stations far away from prying eyes in the forbidding landscape of Soviet Russia. The French remained fearful of German resurgence and held onto much of its air force after 1919 while working assiduously to build up the Polish Air Force so as to threaten a second front in the event of German belligerence. At the same time they kept a watch over their shoulder at the unpredictable, aloof and 'not quite trustworthy' British. Italian fascist leader Benito Mussolini was known to be a keen student of Douhetian doctrine, allowing him to strike beyond the Alpine ranges at little cost while Britain retreated into its shell, adopting a defensive posture and cutting back military expenditure, confident that it could not be embroiled in another continental war for at least ten years.

The experiences of strategic bombing in the several minor wars that took place during the 1920s and '30s might well have given cause to revise ideas about strategic air warfare, but some governments stubbornly refused to allow any doubt to creep in. When the Spanish bombarded Moroccan villages with gas and fragmentation bombs in 1924 the population, rather than cowering in defeat, responded with a fierce will to resist. Only the introduction of massive ground forces brought the insurrection to an end. In similar fashion, Kurdish nationalists endured seven months of bombing by the British before eventually being subdued by land forces. The Spanish citizens of Barcelona emerged from cellars and makeshift shelters to defy Italian bombers during the Spanish Civil War. The Japanese bombing of Nanking provoked similar resistance.[42] These experiences might well have been used as evidence to counter the still all-pervading idea, built on First World War experience, that people could be terrified by the very sight of aircraft, but the case never came to court and dogma prevailed.

In France, at the close of the First World War, the air force was one of the largest and most well respected in the world, but the paralysis that gripped the traumatised army pervaded the entire defence establishment. With the exception of Air Minister Pierre Cot and a handful of his disciples, the French were simply not interested in a defence policy that advocated offensive operations, especially strategic air operations that might bring retaliation down on French cities. It was a different story in the Soviet Union. When the Russian Empire collapsed in 1917, the country's air arm was weak and outmoded. For the next few years, this downward trend continued but began to change in the mid-1920s, when the revolutionaries started rebuilding their military forces. Marshal Mikhail Tukhachevski, army chief of staff, articulated the concept of 'deep battle' in *Field Regulations of 1929* and *Instructions on Deep Battle* in 1935, which became official doctrine in 1936 with the *Provisional Field Regulations*. This concept was to dominate Soviet military thinking for several decades, and air power played a major role in that through interdiction of enemy troops and supplies. The enthusiasm for tactical air power was partly a consequence of their close relationship between the wars with the German military, which also emphasised tactical over strategic air power. Although the Soviets did not neglect bombardment doctrine or the development of bomber aircraft, by the outbreak of the Second World War, the Soviet air force had a distinctly tactical focus.

On 3 October 1935, Italian forces invaded Ethiopia and started a war in which Italian air power was employed and proved to be 'tremendously effective'.[43] Aircraft were able to respond much more quickly than armoured vehicles in fluid engagements across rugged terrain. They did, however, suffer equally from the sort of drawbacks seen by other air forces operating against tribal opponents where often there was no mass of enemy on which to concentrate their fire. One tactic, which brought international condemnation (although many countries were developing their capacity to employ it), was to counter the ability of the enemy to disperse into caves and find cover by dropping mustard gas bombs. Cooperation between air and ground forces proved to be a problem resulting in debacle, as in the attack on Gorrahei, where air attack drove off Ethiopian forces before General Luigi Frusci's infantry could engage them. Once dispersed, a body of troops taking advantage of ground cover was nigh on impossible to root out either by air or ground forces. On the other hand, the campaign also flagged up the difficulties that air support had in trying to maintain contact with rapidly advancing infantry. Their ground facilities for refuelling and rearming could not keep up, leaving aircraft flying from airfields further and further from the front.

The Italian Air Force used two main types of air action. In a Douhetian strategy, they bombed towns, fortifications, caravans and troop assembly points from height with Ca.101 and SM.81 aircraft, but also employed low-level attack aircraft to strike at predetermined targets and then range far and wide to locate targets of opportunity. One important lesson they took from this was that strategic bombing did not have the effect that Douhet had predicted against civilian populations, who remained defiant, but was very effective against concentrations of troops on the march. The Italian commander, Marshal Pietro Badoglio, later said that Italian aircraft had, 'in the absence of enemy aviation ... dominated the sky', which was a fairly obvious expectation and did not necessarily warrant his conclusion that aviation, in coordination with the army, was 'the combat arm of the future'.[44] Other observers saw it a little differently and concluded that the Italian aircraft 'could not afford to [operate at low altitude] against a well-armed and well-trained opponent'.

Apart from the Russo-Polish War, it is clear that the lessons of these conflicts had only marginal significance in the wider picture given their colonial character, where relatively sophisticated weaponry was ranged against tribal forces lacking the means of proper defence. It is also noteworthy that, even without any sort of heavy weaponry or opposing air power, the tribesmen were able to inflict casualties and force modification of tactics. The lessons learned from these operations, however, were interpreted by air theorists and policy makers according to their own prejudices when developing air doctrine, which is unfortunate since the conditions under which air forces would have to operate during the next great conflagration would be quite different from colonial wars and require a very significant and rapid review of both tactics and strategy.

As war clouds gathered over Europe in the mid-1930s, thoughts of placing an international prohibition on air striking forces was abandoned in favour of a rush by governments to acquire a capability of delivering a 'knock-out' blow of their own. In Britain during the 1920s, Trenchard had dominated the air power debate and his voice continued to carry immense authority within the RAF. His doctrine, which persisted, was to give the RAF maximum offensive power by establishing as many bomber squadrons as possible. As commander of the British air arm in war and peace, he had been responsible not only for imparting a vision for the use and future of the air weapon, but also for carrying out the sobering task of organising, equipping, training, and leading a combat organisation on a day-to-day basis. Initially not a strong advocate of strategic air power, he soon became a passionate proponent. Specifically, he was convinced that air bombardment of a country's industrial infrastructure would have a devastating and decisive psychological effect on the morale of the civilian population. Attempting to reconstruct his air doctrine views is difficult. He was, for a time, thought also to be an advocate of 'terror bombing' of civilians, but nothing in the meagre collections of his writings supports this, and his widely reported poor lecturing skills and inability to clearly articulate his ideas may have led others to paraphrase and exaggerate.

The inescapable consequence of strategic bombing was mass civilian casualties. The immunity of civilian populations from war was bound up in the concept of war as a relation between states, but democracy had blurred the boundary between people and state, and war was now nation against nation. Chief of the German General Staff Erich Ludendorff had called the people the 'centre of gravity [of modern warfare]'.[45] Trenchard was a little more circumspect when he likened bombing to economic blockade and said its purpose was to 'induce the enemy government, by pressure from the population, to sue for peace'. Still there was no effort made to explain exactly how the one could translate into the other, and experience from Barcelona to London to Berlin would show that the gap between the two was vast and unbridgeable by simplistic notions. Hippler argued that strategic bombing showed 'class difference [to be] the cornerstone of air strategy'. Perceived as the least politically integrated and most intrinsically unstable element of the 'social order', the working class were targeted above all others, he claimed, because not only did they man industry, they also had the power, through strikes or revolt, to halt industrial production.[46]

The flaws in British bomber doctrine were clear for all to see and applied to a greater or lesser extent to all other air forces. Bombers did not have the ability to carry out the kind of precision bombing this policy demanded and would inevitably lead to indiscriminate destruction of civilian populations. Crews did not possess the navigation skills that would allow them to accurately home in on their targets by day and night, in unfavourable weather and over unfamiliar territory. Furthermore, from the British perspective, the great distance between British airfields and German targets meant that full fuel loads would limit the weight of bombs each aircraft could carry and, perhaps most important of all, fighter aircraft that would come up against the bombers were now significantly faster and more manoeuvrable than their prey. The British, in particular, clung to the strategic concept while continental powers such as Germany, the Soviet Union and France remained committed to the development of tactical air doctrine. The German doctrine of close ground support was developed out of the fact of Luftwaffe officers who had been, for the most part, ex-army personnel, while the British ideas may well have been strongly influenced by the long-standing of the RAF as an independent service with an ethos and philosophy developed during a time of some antagonism between them and the army.[47]

In 1936, the German armed forces had carried out three major exercises including army-Luftwaffe manoeuvres to test blitzkrieg tactics. In the following year, a six-day exercise, with Generalleutnant Albert Kesselring in charge of the Luftwaffe contingent, included most Luftwaffe operational units in ground-support roles in both night-time and poor weather conditions.

These proved to be invaluable sources of enlightenment. Naturally many things had not gone to plan, but the purpose of the exercises was to uncover such flaws and address strategies to overcome them. Probably the most important initiative to emerge from the 1937 manoeuvres was the setting up of a night-fighter force to defend German cities against bomber attack. There was no place in Kesselring's philosophy for a 'bomber will always get through' mindset. As a result, at this point the fighter started to take priority over the bomber in Luftwaffe doctrine.[48]

That is not to say, however, that the idea of strategic bombing had been abandoned. One of the most vocal advocates was Luftwaffe Major Hans-Detlef Herhundt von Rohden, whose theories stemmed from Germany's geographical situation making it vulnerable to attack from all sides. This, he argued, made the Luftwaffe its first line of defence and the Luftwaffe's primary asset was its strategic bomber force, which was the only means of striking back quickly. He published a book, *Vom Luftkriege*, in which he argued that, by its very nature, the air force was a strategic weapon and should be controlled from the highest level of operational command. He denied Douhet's assertion that air power could win wars on its own, but it was capable of decisive action if employed in concentration against vital points. The first objective would be destruction of the enemy air force in the air and on the ground, opening the way for attacks on industrial targets which, because of their nature and diverse locations, would be less well defended than military forces. This was a concept popular with Luftwaffe officers, but overall it required a great deal of work in order to make it a practical proposition. Most importantly, the doctrine had to be supported by detailed analysis of potential targets which would require significant intelligence work and aerial photography. The Luftwaffe intelligence chief, Josef Schmid, did try to supply this information in relation to Britain, in his *Studie Blau* of 1939, and intensive photo-reconnaissance was carried out prior to September 1939, but thereafter it proved difficult to update the information. By the summer of 1940, when the Luftwaffe attempted its first strategic bombing campaign in the Battle of Britain, its lack of up-to-date target information proved to be a critical factor contributing to its failure.

Trenchard had been able to mute, if not silence completely, opposition from within his own forces, and decided that the RAF's fighters should be short-range, so they would be employed only for home defence, and that long-range fighters would not be needed to protect bombers which would look after themselves. Intrinsic to the British attitude was the idea that bombers would decide the war, but that was a weak argument and would apply only if one side had significantly stronger forces. If both sides were evenly matched then the loser would be the side whose morale collapsed first and collapsed completely, but there was no reason to believe that this would come about quickly. Under the circumstances the bomber theory envisaged a long war, and it was a central theme of British war doctrine that the German economy could not sustain one, therefore Germany would eventually lose. The German military had indeed anticipated a short war, but was catapulted into it years before they were ready by an impetuous and cavalier leader. It was their use of air support in Blitzkrieg, lightning warfare, that characterised their approach and it proved to be spectacularly successful in Poland and France where the enemy were overcome swiftly, and to some extent in Russia initially, but the longer the war went on the more their strategy was exposed and, in the end, their haste to combat would become their downfall. For Britain, when its bluff was called in 1940, it 'had not the wherewithal to carry [it's strategic bombing war] out'.[49] It would suffer as a result of a muddled doctrine that had, in panic, hurriedly shifted from strategic bombing, for which it lacked the rudimentary requirements, to desperate tactical defence – which it managed to cobble together just in time.

The Spanish Civil War was an invaluable testing ground for air doctrine. It was quickly seen that fast bombers were able to survive fighter attacks but slower machines, regardless of how well armed they might be, were a dubious proposition. Crucially, the Germans soon discovered that 'the success of every major offensive and defensive operation of the war was dependent upon air superiority and the effectiveness of that air power'.[50] Although France was not an active participant in the war, it was close enough to keep an eye on developments there. In particular, the initial success of the Soviet Polikarpov R-5, which was similar in many respects to the French Potez 25, gave pause for thought. The P25 was becoming obsolete, but the French were encouraged to look again at the concept of ground attack when ordering new aircraft.

Many countries watched eagerly from the sidelines to see air doctrine put into practice. The US Military Attaché in Spain was impressed with the strategic initiative and reported that the bombing of ports was 'sapping people's endurance and lowering their morale', and weakening the government's war-making potential.[51] The importance of ground-support operations was emphasised by the number of foreign observers who went to great pains to emphasise it in their reports. One Nationalist officer reported that 'the intervention of aircraft in ground operations exercised great influence, both material and psychological on ground troops'. The US Attaché reported that 'the only really new factor to appear in the tactical field since [the First World War] is the destruction and demoralising power of attack aviation'. The German war analyst General Karl Drum believed that close support operations were of 'paramount importance', while the French General Armengaud described aviation as 'the most potent weapon for ground offensives'. The Soviet commentator called aviation the 'decisive factor in modern combat'.[52]

Between 1919 and 1939 the development of European air doctrine had been essentially a debate between independent air action, which would create a completely new layer of military capabilities requiring a new and separate command structure, and air-ground support, which would remain an integral part of army and navy operations and control. Since the army and navy held all the reins of military power at the start, it was very much an uphill struggle for the advocates of strategic air power to have their voices heard, and when heard, listened to. Germany was alone of the great powers to give equal consideration to strategic and tactical air power and this was, ironically, in no small part due to the Luftkriegfährte having no legitimate existence after 1919, and therefore allowed to explore developments mostly on a theoretical rather than practical level. Others could take the financial risks of developing new aircraft while Germany looked on and took note. The internal debate over doctrine was influenced as much by geography as dogma. There had to be a balance struck between attack and defence. As a means of taking offensive action the strategic bomber was seen as the preferred option, but Germany's vulnerability to strategic bombing from across its borders with France, Czechoslovakia and Poland made defence also a consideration demanding equal attention. It was a matter of some importance to evaluate the threat in terms of numbers of potential attacking aircraft and their proficiency, and the Technical College of Berlin was assigned to collect data on this. Public debate was welcomed and aired in publications such as the *Air Defence Newsletter* and *The Siren*, and entered into with gusto by many prominent leaders, including von Seeckt when he became a member of the Reichstag.

MILITARY AIR POWER IN EUROPE PREPARING FOR WAR

The air forces of Europe had spent time, energy and resources in varying degrees to prepare for a war that seemed all but inevitable right from the moment the ink had dried on the Treaty of Versailles. The main question was when. Of the six European powers discussed in this book, three, Germany, France and Britain, were advanced industrial economies and three, Russia, Poland and Italy, were not. All would eventually come together in another catastrophic conflagration for which none were quite prepared, and each would suffer the consequences in its own way. For each of them, during the 1920s and 1930s, the growing threat of war played its own part in their political deliberations and their preparations for war were governed by their own ambitions and preoccupations.

Ironically, it was the two authoritarian regimes, the Italian fascists and the Soviet communists who allowed free debate within their air forces, and the two democratic states Britain and France who tried to impose a singular doctrine. Germany adopted an open-mind policy where it made great efforts to keep abreast of developments in theory, practice and technology in other countries and, through its Lipetsk testing facilities, shared much of its knowledge and experience with the Soviets. French military doctrine, which embodied tradition at the expense of innovation, was very much a top-down affair with the will of the commanders imposed and debate discouraged. While Germany, Italy and the Soviet Union were able to test out and, where necessary, modify their theories during the Spanish Civil War, France – and Poland, by virtue of its links with France – had taken careful note of events but had left it rather late to translate them into their own doctrines. Britain had already started to redefine its priorities in 1936 and accelerated that change after 1938, but little of what it did in that regard had been influenced by events in Spain. It had observed the war from an aloof distance and assumed that there was little to learn from what it saw as primitive forces squabbling over scraps.

Chapter 2

The Evolution of Fighter Aircraft during the First World War

'aviation is a fine sport ... but as an instrument of war,
it is worthless.'

General Ferdinand Foch, Allied Supreme
Commander in the First World War[1]

The concepts and applications of air power developed during the First World War remain the basis of air power strategies today. By the end of the war there were a number of specialised types of aircraft and the tactics which had been developed would become standard for future generations.[2] The essential character of the air war in 1914–18 was its technical nature as all sides strove for an advantage in the battle for air supremacy. Aircraft in service would either prove to be useful and effective, or they would quickly fade from the scene. The pace of the 'arms race' was such that even the successful types became redundant in little more than a year. The concepts of air superiority, interdiction and close air support were all introduced and explored, but many other hard lessons learned would be quickly forgotten.[3] The pace of technological change can be measured by noting how the short-range, underpowered machines of 1914, still very much playing second fiddle to the tethered balloon and the hydrogen-filled airship had, by 1919, become masters of the skies capable of crossing the Atlantic.

Dirigibles had gained a formidable reputation as passenger craft before 1914, but their military potential was still largely unexplored. While enormously impressive for their sheer bulk and air of menace, they were difficult to handle in all but the calmest weather and extremely susceptible to intense ground attack, especially when incendiary darts were introduced. At height they were well nigh invulnerable to attack from aircraft, but at lower levels they were 'sitting ducks'. When flying through cloud they would deploy a 'Goertz car' navigation basket suspended on a 1,000 metre cable and fitted with a telephone line for communicating with the mother ship. An observer in the basket, having a clear field of vision, would then guide the ship to its target. Britain had a number of smaller ones but it was the German craft designed and built by Count Ferdinand von Zeppelin which played the greater role in the First World War. These Zeppelins and, in lesser numbers, Schütte-Lanz dirigibles, had originally been allotted reconnaissance roles, but they began bombing raids over the London docks in January 1915 after British bombers had struck at their bases a few months earlier. They flew at heights up to 20,000ft which made them all but invulnerable to ground attack, but did little for the accuracy of their bombs, which more often than not killed civilians. Soon the British deployed aircraft to shoot them down in flames with incendiary bullets and the dirigibles, having no defence against that, were soon 'finished as a fighting service'.[4]

On the Western Front in 1914, aircraft on all sides initially achieved notable success employed as a natural extension of cavalry reconnaissance units. Given the advantages ground commanders gained from this they inevitably wanted to deny the same resource to the enemy, so both sides began by aiming ground attack at enemy aircraft and followed up by arming the pilots with hand-held weapons to challenge enemy craft in the sky and drive them off. This escalation saw the development of specialised aircraft with ever more elaborate guns, which became the first generation of fighters typified by the German Eindecker and the French Morane L and N pre-war designs that had been hastily modified for military use.

By the spring of 1916, machine guns had been incorporated into aircraft design, a development permitted by the advent of synchronised firing mechanisms, resulting in a growing number of casualties as fierce gunfights erupted in the skies, but still the main role of aircraft was intelligence gathering. There was, as yet, no appetite for sending out aircraft with the expressed purpose of challenging for dominance over a given area. However, the French commander, Joseph-Édouard Barès, the 'far-sighted and able organiser of France's Aviation Militaire', was soon to scale up from the lone patrol to employing aircraft in combination with others both for mutual protection and greater fighting strength. He established sixteen specialist fighter squadrons or 'escadrilles' with Morane-Saulnier aircraft.[5] When the British commander of the Royal Flying Corps (RFC) suggested something similar he was promptly given a flea in his ear by the army commanders who would have none of it at first, but he persisted and in July 1915, the first of the Vickers FB5 'Gunbus' fighters armed with Vickers machine guns arrived at the front to operate as a squadron.

The early aircraft, which had simply been modified sports machines, were soon exhausted by the rigours of combat and a second generation of fighters emerged as a diverse selection of biplanes, both pusher and tractor-types such as the FB5, the Nieuport 11 and the Fokker D.I, II and III. The pusher aircraft had its propeller mounted behind the wings with the engine located immediately behind the pilot. They were among the first powered aircraft types to fly and popular in Europe with Farman, Caproni and Gotha all having pusher engines. The type allowed for forward-firing machine guns without the risk of hitting the propeller. Their limitations, however, were soon exposed. They suffered from excessive 'drag' and wind resistance, but most of all they killed or maimed crews if the aircraft crashed on landing when the heavy engine would break loose and surge forward with catastrophic result.

This second generation of aircraft was designed from the outset to accommodate weapons, but still included many pre-war concepts. The RFC countered with their FB5 pushers having a second crewman as observer in the nose, equipped with a Lewis machine gun. It was the world's first custom-built fighter aircraft, introduced in 1915 with the all-fighter unit No.11 Squadron; with a maximum speed of only 70mph, it was initially a 'surprisingly effective aircraft'.[6] In the fast-evolving landscape of the air war, however, their usefulness was short-lived. Their slower speed was a disadvantage and overall they were soon 'hopelessly outclassed' by the Fokkers with their superior synchronised guns, which began to get the upper-hand all along the front.[7] The FB5s soon became obsolete and were phased out by the autumn of 1916. While the Allies had begun operating in squadron strength the Germans, who throughout the war used fighter aircraft primarily in defensive roles, were slow to adapt by grouping their fighters. It was not until after their chastening experiences at the Battle of Verdun that they came round to the idea of concentrating them in '*jagdstaffeln*' (squadrons).

The use of hand-held machine guns in single-seat fighters had the obvious disadvantage of being heavy and hard for the pilot to aim, as he also had to control the aircraft. The answer was the fixed forward-firing synchronised machine gun that fired through the propeller without damaging it and which was aimed by pointing the whole aircraft at the target. Two engineers, Franz Schneider in Germany and Robert Esnault-Pelterie if France, had patented devices for firing a machine gun through the propeller without hitting the blades before 1914, but while the cam mechanism they invented was sound, the lack of uniformity in the ammunition meant that neither worked successfully. The idea was taken up by the French firm Morane-Saulnier and developed by pilot Roland Garros before being finally perfected by the German Fokker company, whose Parabellum machine guns were more easily adapted than the French Hotchkiss.[8] The British came late to synchronisation, initially with their Scarff-Dibovsky, which was not a great success, but then with their 'C.C. Gear', which became standard fitting on all British fighters.

The first victim of synchronised machine gun fire was a German Albatros reconnaissance aircraft shot down by Garros in a French Morane-Saulnier L 'Parasol' on 1 April 1915. It was Germany, however, that perfected the mechanism and installed them in a number of Fokker M.5 monoplanes which became 'a disastrous factor' for the RFC when their reconnaissance aircraft suffered serious losses at the hands of Fokker pilots such as Max Immelmann and Oswald Boelcke.

The Fokkers had adopted the timeless tactic of attacking 'out of the sun' to avoid visual detection and had terrorised Allied reconnaissance aircraft, but now that the FB5 had arrived, the lumbering BE2c could be effectively escorted, although each one had to follow Trenchard's 'hard and fast rule' that it be escorted by three fighters in close formation and had to abort if any one of the three escorts was detached.[9] This had the obvious disadvantage of reducing the number of possible reconnaissance missions, given the small number of fighters available, but the saving grace for the Allies was that the Fokkers were not extending their dominance beyond their own lines, seemingly content to maintain a defensive posture. Trenchard saw that the answer was to organise his own fighters into large units and fly 'in close formation', but was wary of introducing the idea of massing aircraft for fear that the Germans would copy it and, with their superior aircraft, would be tempted to extend the boundaries of their aerial dominance by adopting a more attacking posture. As a compromise he organised his fighters into what became the bedrock of RFC fighter pilot training, and was to remain so with the RAF until 1939. This was the unit of four aircraft in line abreast, line astern or echelon. It demanded great skill, especially in echelon formation where execution of turns required total concentration and attention to the lead aircraft. It was the introduction of a new aircraft, however, that broke the stranglehold of the Fokkers over the battle lines.

The Battle of Verdun, 'an indecisive battle in an indecisive war' as historian Alistair Horne called it, erupted on 21 February 1916 and blundered on for a full ten months with no advantage to either side at the end. While the ground war resulted in stalemate, the air war revolutionised air strategy and tactics. French Army commanders demanded that the air units support ground operations, but the French air commander, Jean du Peuty, opted to employ his six fighter escadrilles in offensive, deep penetration missions. He was fully supported by Trenchard, who sent as many aircraft as he could spare to boost du Peuty's force of Nieuport 11s in their mission to 'seek the enemy in order to engage and destroy him'.[10] The French Nieuports, designed from the start to be combat aircraft, were a generation ahead of the Fokkers in design and had no trouble in penetrating the thinly defended German air space, forcing the German fighters into a desperate defensive battle and denying the German reconnaissance aircraft freedom to operate. This forced the Germans to innovate and create specialised fighter units operating in squadron strength, but still they did not stray from their own lines and showed no ambition to penetrate Allied air space. This, however, had the unexpected benefit of delivering into the hands of German aircraft designers many British and French aircraft which were shot down over German lines and whose technical secrets were instantly revealed. By mid-April, the French held dominion of the air over Verdun, even destroying the German Drachen observation balloons using crude air-to-air rockets.[11] The whole Verdun experience was solidifying Trenchard's enthusiasm for strategic air offensive, but the French air commanders yielded to the demands of their army to return their aircraft to ground support as the battle reverted to static stalemate.

Verdun, in the air at least, had proved to be a resounding success for the French, but the Germans learned from the punishment they had received and quickly revised their tactics. Britain and France took their successes as vindication of aggressive, strategic operations as a means of controlling air space and benefited from the experience of close cooperation between their two forces. The Germans, on the other hand, had recognised the deficiencies in their own methods and began concentrating their aircraft into fighter squadrons. This became apparent when the British launched their Somme offensive in July 1916 supported in the air by French Nieuports and the newly arrived FE2b pusher two-seater fighters. A third generation of aircraft, designed with the benefits of experience, was taking the stage. They were generally more powerful, better armed, structurally more robust and more aerodynamic than their predecessors. Typical of this generation were the German Albatros and British Sopwith 'families'. Initially the British fighters operated with impunity over the German lines, but when the Albatros arrived on the scene the picture changed dramatically. The German Roland CII was the first to challenge British dominance, followed by the Fokker D.I, D.II and D.III, then the Halberstadt D.II, D.III and D.IV. The Albatros D.II, a general purpose tractor biplane introduced in 1916, was powered by a 160-hp Mercedes engine. It had two fixed forward-firing Spandau machine guns and a top speed of 109mph. It began to prove its worth as its numbers grew and greatly improved the morale of the German pilots. This coincided with a reduction in the quality of training received by British pilots being rushed through as replacements for the 170 pilots lost in September alone.[12] The average life-expectancy of an RFC pilot in combat on the Somme front dropped to a frightening three weeks in October 1916. The Allies desperately needed better aircraft to counter the German aircraft, which threatened to extend their aerial dominance to above British lines for the first time. More than half of all RFC casualties were now coming down over British-held territory.

Fortunately, salvation of sorts came in the guise of the Sopwith 'Pup', an aircraft with 'superb handling characteristics [standing apart] as the finest flying machine of the First World War', and the French Nieuport 17 and SPAD S.VII, an aircraft of 'great strength and power', with its liquid-cooled 150-hp Hispano-Suiza engine designed by Béchereau and built by Blériot.[13] The 'Pup' was a single-seater tractor biplane fighter, with a single forward-firing Vickers or Lewis machine gun and a top speed of 111mph. It was introduced in 1916 as having pleasant flying characteristics and good manoeuvrability; it proved very successful, but soon its lack of power became evident when it came up against the newer German fighters. While Allied aircraft were still fitted with single Vickers machine guns, the Germans had standardised with the twin Spandau, and the French fighters, now less numerous than before, were not delivered in any significant numbers to the Somme battlefield until 1917. Trenchard called loudly for more fighter squadrons, which were provided by the Royal Naval Air Service (RNAS) in October.

The introduction of Albatros D.III and Halberstadt fighters meant that Germany once again 'stood poised on the threshold of air supremacy over the Western Front'.[14] However, it was not only the aircraft, but also the organisation of the German Air Force that brought this about. In October, the Kaiser decreed that all army aviation units be placed under the sole authority of the Imperial German Air Service (*Luftstreitkräfte*) commanded by Generalleutnant Ernst Wilhelm von Hoeppner. It did not have total independence from the army, but was well on the way to acquiring it.

The year 1916 opened and closed with Germany in the ascendant, but in between the Allies had gained the upper-hand. France emerged from the Verdun catastrophe with a new breed of fighter, the Nieuport, and a superior method of deployment in groups of squadrons. The British had fought for control of the sky with a tenacity demanded by Trenchard and had worked well with their allies as shown by the joint mission, including American crews flying with the French, to bomb the Mauser factory in Oberndorf, 230 miles behind the German lines, but by autumn the next generation of German aircraft, such as Jastas, had begun to claw back the initiative. With French designs superior to the British, Trenchard was not slow to place orders for Nieuports and SPADs, but a large number of Sopwiths were built in France under licence. Where the French had excelled, however, was in design of their new Clerget, Le Rhône and Hispano-Suiza engines.

Trenchard pursued a relentlessly offensive strategy, calling for an increase in the number of squadrons available to him and urging the British War Office to supply more up-to-date fighters before then RFC was 'hopelessly outclassed', only to find that labour disputes had halted production of the Bristol F.2A.[15] The F.2A was a two-seater tractor reconnaissance and general-purpose aircraft powered by a 190-hp Rolls Royce Falcon engine. It had a forward-facing synchronised Lewis gun and 'excellent handling qualities'.[16] The Bristol F.2B derivative was a strong and agile two-seater tractor fighter and reconnaissance aircraft with one, or sometimes two, moveable Vickers machine guns. It had a powerful 275-hp Rolls Royce Falcon engine giving it a maximum speed of 123mph and it was a 'very dangerous opponent'.[17] These were introduced in 1917 and remained in active service until 1930.

A new Allied ground offensive was planned at Arras in the spring of 1917 but delays in reinforcing the RFC unnerved the ground commanders, who foresaw air supremacy over the front passing to the Germans. Between September 1916 and March 1917, the total number of Halberstadt and Albatros aircraft in service along the front had risen from 32 to 398. In March the RFC lost 120 aircraft, half over their own territory. Trenchard was faced with sending his airmen in to an increasingly hostile environment, but the army demanded more and more reconnaissance. During March, 143 aircrew were lost, more than twice the February total.

When the Arras offensive was launched, Trenchard had 365 aircraft of which 120 were fighters, against 195 and 95 on the other side. The problem for him was that too few of his aircraft were third generation and could not prevail against the Albatros and Halberstadts, and British pilots were proving to be less well-trained and less prepared for combat than their German counterparts. The single machine gun that Allied fighters had was no match for the twin Spandaus. In the first four days of the offensive the RFC lost seventy-five aircraft in combat and a further fifty-six lost or damaged in accidents. One mordant wit claimed that new RFC pilots would 'survive [only] long enough for their replacements to reach France'.[18] With so many fighters assigned to reconnaissance and bomber escort, the numerical advantage of British fighters was irrelevant.

Meanwhile, there was growing interest in the application of air power in a strategic role. On the Eastern Front Igor Sikorsky's four-engine Ilya Mourometz heavy bomber was proving itself capable of defence against fighter attack, and in Germany Oskar Ursinus was building a twin-engine armour-plated battle plane which morphed into the formidable Gotha (Gothaer Waggonfabrik) bomber. With a bomb load of 1,000lb, three machine guns and a six-hour duration, the Gotha made its first raid on British targets when twenty-one of them flew from Ghent to strike on Folkestone on 25 May 1917, killing 95 people. Then on 13 June, seven Gothas struck on London killing 162 and injuring 432.

In response, Britain established the London Air Defence Area, with nine squadrons, including the Sopwith Pup and Camel, armed with twin synchronised Vickers machine guns, described as 'a fierce little beast'.[19] The Gothas were unwilling to face the swarm of fighters and resorted to night-time attacks against which the fighters, devoid of night-flying instrumentation, could do little at first. However, the defenders soon adapted and began shooting down the Gothas, even at night, a capability that was extended to the Western Front. The last Gotha raid over England was in May 1918 when they lost six shot-down out of twenty-eight. The cost of strategic bombing proved to be too high in terms of aircraft lost, but the Gothas had forced Britain to hold back a considerable number of fighters for home defence when they would have been of immense use in France at a time when the Albatros ruled the skies.

Throughout the spring of 1917, fighters had been primarily utilised in air-to-air combat to clear the sky and make way for heavier ground-attack aircraft, but thereafter they began to be used as a defensive screen against enemy bomber formations, and also as fighter-bombers against front-line targets. The Germans had introduced their Schlachtflugzug attack squadrons in response to RFC's use of fighters as ground-attack aircraft on the Somme. These had begun as sporadic strafing attacks carried out on the initiative of individual pilots and had not been as the result of any official policy. These developed into authorised 'hedge-hopping' sorties by Nieuports against enemy balloons, timed to coincide with an artillery barrage that suppressed ground attack in what was the first step towards a ground-attack doctrine. The Supreme Allied Commander, Marshal Foch, made it clear what the French approach was when he insisted that 'the first duty of fighting aeroplanes is to assist the troops on the ground by incessant attacks'. Soon S.E.5s were both strafing and bombing in low-level attacks, but although the damage caused to exposed targets was significant, the inherent danger meant that a 30 per cent rate of loss for a mission was not unusual.

The Germans had entered the ground-support role with a greater attention to safety with the Junkers J I (Möbelwagen) having 5mm chrome-nickel steel armour around the cockpit and fuel tank, but this came at a cost in performance characteristics. However, its twin forward-firing Spandaus and extra Parabellum machine gun facing back, made it a formidable attack weapon. Advanced Halberstadts and Hannover were introduced in 1918 to counter the large number of American aircraft now joining the war. German tactics emphasised the demoralising effect of ground-attack aircraft flying at less than 100ft on troops under aerial attack and learned important lessons from the way that air tactics were instrumental in halting the Cambrai offensive.

In 1917, the German fighters generally came out on top of any engagement and held sway over their own territory at least, where most of the aerial action took place. They concentrated all their effort on defence and were not tempted to go off marauding over enemy territory like the RFC did. Their era of dominance, however, was coming to an end as they began to lose technological advantage. The fourth generation of aircraft were coming through with more speed, better manoeuvrability and greater fire-power. During the second half of 1917, failure on the part of the Germans to take full advantage of their technological advantage and extend their superiority beyond the lines and strike at Allied bases was, perhaps, a mistake, because it allowed the RFC to maintain an offensive posture ensuring high morale among its pilots. It is doubtful, however, whether the Germans, even allowing for the clear superiority of the Albatros, ever had enough aircraft to dominate. These fourth generation fighter aircraft were more powerful with stronger bodies and sophisticated armaments capable of multiple roles. The best examples of this aircraft were the British Sopwith Camel and the German Siemens-Schuckert. Ironically, it may have been the success of the Albatros that delayed German plans for its replacement, and when the Allies introduced the Sopwith Camel, S.E.5a and the Bristol F.2B, it was too late to catch up. The Camel was a single-seater tractor biplane fighter with twin forward-firing Vickers machine guns fitted with a 130-hp Clerget rotary engine introduced in 1917. It was a difficult to handle but highly manoeuvrable aircraft which was very successful, although by the end of the war it had become obsolete as a fighter and was restricted to ground-attack roles. Only in the middle of 1918 did the Germans, with the Siemens-Schuckert D.III and the excellent Fokker D.VII, begin to claw their way back to parity, but by then the war was almost over. They even brought in a fifth generation of all-metal monoplanes during the final weeks, but all to no avail. Their failure to build on the clear advantage they held in the spring of 1917 ensured that they lost the air war.

It is asserted by writers such as Richard P. Hallion that lessons learned by air forces in the First World War were mostly forgotten by the 1930s. Britain's obsession with defence against the bomber during the period 1919–1939 caused it to train pilots to employ rigid attack formations at the expense of encouraging survival tactics when confronted by agile enemy fighters. The Cambrai offensive showed that a smaller number of good German fighters prevailed against a greater number of less capable fighters, but 1918 reversed the position when large numbers of third-level German fighters were produced but failed to maintain aerial dominance over the fourth generation Allied fighters operating in fewer numbers. Clearly technical superiority was crucial. All sides during the war built up a good understanding of what qualities made a good fighter aircraft, but their views were only slowly taken into consideration by the aircraft designers. Armament systems are an example of how even the Sopwith Pup, excellent in many other aspects, still only entered the fray late in 1916 with one single machine gun. Only in 1917, with the introduction of the Camel, had the British aircraft matched the Germans for firepower.

Chapter 3

German Air Power before 1939

'Our time will come again.'
Oberleutnant Herman Göring who, as commander of
Jagdgeschwader 1, refused to hand over his aircraft to the
victorious Western Allies on 11 November 1919.[1]

In 1919 the German Field Army's air arm, the *Luftstreitkräfte,* was emasculated under Clause IV of the Treaty of Versailles, but by 1939 the German Air Force, the Reichsluftwaffe, had become the most powerful and up to date air force in the world. Furthermore, at the start of the Second World War, it was the only major air force to possess a comprehensive and militarily effective air doctrine as an essential component of its operational philosophy.[2] This had been arrived at despite the economic and political upheavals of the Weimar Republic, when Germany's military capabilities had remained weak due to lack of investment and the intrinsic conservatism within the military High Command. Struggling to redefine itself after its defeat in 1918, but as yet unconstrained by the terms of Versailles, the German military (*Reichswehr*) had fiercely resisted any idea of an independent air force and battled to retain control of all air military services.

The towering military figure in the immediate post-war Germany was Friedrich Leopold (Hans) von Seeckt, head of the *Reichswehr*. He was a well-rounded, educated man who spoke fluent French and English and had travelled widely in Europe and India.[3] In military circles, he wielded considerable political power as 'one of the most influential military thinkers of the twentieth century',[4] and used it to further the interests of the army, especially in the area of rearmament, and the 'tottering semi-revolutionary regime' of the Weimar Republic.[5] His concept of wars fought and won by 'smaller, well-equipped armies relying on speed and manoeuvre' became the bedrock of German *Blitzkrieg* tactics in the Second

World War. After 1919, the German Chancellor Friedrich Ebert had given the army his full support in return for its cooperation in suppressing Bolshevik uprisings during four years characterised by a high level of political violence, but von Seeckt had little confidence in the government and favoured the establishment of a military dictatorship. However, he chose to stand aside from the abortive 'Kapp-Lüttwitz Putsch' in March 1920, when his army refused to open fire on two Freikorps brigades that had marched on Berlin to bring down the Weimar government after it had tried to disband them. Only a general strike prevented the coup from being successful and Ebert survived, but still needed the support of the army which had failed to support him yet had became a more potent force in German politics and 'a basis for support for anyone thinking themselves capable of managing the government'.[6] Ebert needed von Seeckt on his side and the army leader used his enhanced political power to advance the army's cause and aggressively pursue a policy of rearmament 'regardless of the cost'. After his troops had suppressed another attempt to bring down the government, this time the Hitler-Ludendorf 'Bierkeller Putsch' in 1923, von Seeckt was further empowered to the point where a military takeover had become a distinct possibility, but again he refused to step up and take responsibility and proved once and for all to be merely a 'political dilettante who played with the possibility of military rule'.[7] He retired from leadership of the *Reichswehr* in 1926 having achieved a great deal and 'accomplished the purpose of re-armament ... and left Germany with the nucleus of the finest army in Europe'.[8] His concept of modern warfare was encapsulated in an essay he published in 1929. In it he gives unequivocal support for air power as the 'key element of military strength', and the means of 'striking the centres of resistance of the enemy state'.[9] It had become, for him, 'the best counter-weapon to carry the fight to the enemy's country', and the charge that Germany had, after Versailles, been denied the means of defending its own population centres from such an attack was 'difficult to understand and even more difficult to answer'. He envisaged a new war as beginning with a simultaneous attack of the air fleets on the opposing air force to establish dominance of the air, opening up the opportunity to strike other centres of enemy power. He conceded that if both sides have similar air strength, a resolution will not be arrived at quickly. In that case it will be the side with greater 'moral powers of resistance' that would prevail.[10]

Of all the European nations after the First World War, it was Germany who had conducted the most thorough and comprehensive study of air power and had transformed its theories into a highly effective war doctrine by 1939. Forbidden by Versailles to have an air force, the army retained a shadow Air Staff within the army General Staff through which it retained the enormous body of experience acquired during the war in which it had fought every kind of air campaign: tactical, strategic, and ground support. As early as 1916, the German air service had acquired a centralised command which, even then, had tried to gain some measure of independence but had failed due to naval intransigence. At the end of the war, however, the German air service enjoyed special prestige as the only viable fighting force in the German military still capable of effective resistance. This gave them a strong case for independence that the other military services found hard to resist and allowed German airmen to feel no compunctions about creating theories and doctrines of air power that looked towards an unfettered existence.[11]

Denied an official air force during the 1920s, an air doctrine evolved thanks especially to von Seeckt's foresight, but because of conservative pressure and the obvious drawback of having no aircraft, this doctrine was dominated by army dogma restricting it to a subordinate role of ground support. It was to change, however, when the National Socialist German Workers' Party (the Nazi Party) came to power in 1933 with a clear ambition to create an independent air force, with an independent doctrine to govern its use, as a basic requirement of national defence and prestige. The main debate concerned the extent to which it should continue in a tactical role as an adjunct to army strategy, or create its own strategic role within the overall operational structure. The arguments on both sides had their champions but ambition was tempered by economic reality and compromise was the inevitable result. The war came too early for the Luftwaffe in 1939 and found it only mid-way through its development process, both materially and philosophically. It was to suffer the consequences of this failure nowhere more keenly than during the Battle of Britain.

During the First World War, the *Luftstreitkräfte* had gained a vast amount of experience upon which to build an air doctrine, having been 'an effective and formidable military force which had made tremendous strides in developing aerial technology and new concepts of organisation'.[12] It had gone into action with 'much better trained pilots' than the Western Allies and conducted almost every type of air campaign, including the first strategic air offensive designed to attack the morale of the British people, but overall it had been utilised primarily in support of ground forces. At the start of the war, military operations had been carried out mostly by single aircraft or flights of two or three in reconnaissance roles but by 1917, the two-seater Halberstadt CL.II and Hannover CL.IIIa aircraft were flying in squadron-strength in bombing and strafing attacks in support of infantry. These squadrons were soon combined in greater strength as *geschwader*, when three or four squadrons would operate as a unit, sometimes 70-strong, under a single commander. This was the first of many developments that inaugurated the concept of operational-level air campaigns.[13]

Ground-attack aircraft such as the heavily armed Junkers J 1 had been particularly successful at Cambrai in 1917, and during the 1918 German offensive. Alongside this, at a time when the German air force had the upper-hand on the Western Front, it extended its operations into strategic bombing using Zeppelin airships and Gotha V bombers. The period of German dominance was soon over despite the introduction of technologically advanced aircraft such as the Fokker D.VII, but the collapse of the German ground offensive in 1918 saw the German air force finish the war as the only branch of the armed forces that was still operationally effective, which may well have been the reason why the Allies ordered its eradication as a condition of the Treaty of Versailles. Despite losing the air arm, von Seeckt, 'a man of tremendous mental agility',[14] assigned 500 officers to conduct a thorough analysis of strategic air operations during the war in order to establish what lessons had or had not been learned.[15] On the strategic level they concluded that the loss of more than sixty aircraft on long-range bombing missions over Britain was a cost which outweighed the benefits, notwithstanding the fact that half the casualties were caused by accidents rather than combat. It had, in the analysts' view, not proved itself to be an effective means of forcing a major shift in enemy policy. Nevertheless, of a future war von Seeckt said,

> the war will begin with a simultaneous attack of the air fleets –
> the weapon which is the most prepared and the fastest means
> of attacking the enemy. Their target is, however, not the major
> cities or industrial power, but the enemy air force, and only
> after its suppression can the offensive arm be directed toward
> other targets.... It is stressed that all major troop mobilization

49

centres are worthwhile and easy targets. The disruption of the personnel and materiel mobilization is a primary mission of the aerial offensive.[16]

The army, for its part, was determined to retain aircraft under its control, operating exclusively in support of ground forces.[17] German military tradition incorporated the belief that the decisive battles of a war should take place at the outset, leading to short wars. In this scenario, ground forces were the key to victory and air power was to give itself over to total support of ground operations. The theory of strategic bombing, generally believed unlikely to bring about an early victory, was clouded with its concomitant sense of attrition in a protracted conflict which was not to be contemplated. The First World War experience had shown Germany that its geographical and economic situation would dictate its military strategy in a future war, and that it could not sustain another long war.

For more than a century, in Europe there had been a tradition of privately funded volunteer paramilitary armies lending their services to a variety of causes known as *Freikorps*. One such emerged in Germany after the war, made up of ultra-nationalist students and servicemen returning from the war. The character of this German *Freikorps* was one of resentment towards the men who had led them to defeat, overlying a deep hatred of communism. Demobbed soldiers and airmen, returning, disorientated and frustrated, from the war to a country ravaged by hunger, almost because they had little else to do, were easily drawn into the numerous squabbles all over Germany's eastern borders and even, led by Wolfgang Kapp and Walther von Lüttwitz, attempted and failed to launch a Putsch against the German government in March 1920, as mentioned earlier. Many men who would later rise to power with the Nazi Party, and many future Luftwaffe officers such as Bruno Lörzer and Erhard Milch, were active in the Freikorps at this time.

German factories continued producing military aircraft that had been ordered before the Armistice. These were commandeered by *Freikorps* air units and absorbed into the *Reichswehr*, but in November all that changed as Article 198 of the Versailles Treaty prohibited either the German Army (*Heer*) or Navy (*Kriegsmarine*) from possessing an air component, mentioning in particular the Fokker D.VIII. Article 201 demanded an end to military aircraft production, and Article 202 demanded that Germany hand over to the victorious Allies for destruction all air force equipment. At one time there had been thirty-five *Friekorps* air squadrons, but after Versailles they had all been ordered to disband as part of the demilitarisation of Germany. Even so, they continued to exist in different form as 'police' units (*Polizeifliergerstaffeln*) covertly supported by German President Ebert.

Versailles had also demanded that the 'German General Staff and all similar organisations shall be dissolved and may not be reconstituted in any form.' In order to get around this restriction, a cover organisation, the *Truppenamt* (Troop Office) was created to serve a similar purpose. This became 'a new slimmed-down professional highly-trained military establishment', and within this, von Seeckt set up an air branch headed by Major Helmuth Wilberg, a senior air commander from the war, and staffed by members of the professional officer corps, with a view to quietly monitoring the growing international armaments economy and taking note of technical developments in military aviation in other countries.[18] The central purpose of this branch was 'to put the experiences of the war in a broad light and collect this experience while the impressions won on the battlefield are still fresh'.[19]

Born in Berlin on 1 June 1880, Helmuth Wilberg, 'an energetic and clear-headed officer', played a vital role in the development of German air doctrine during the inter-war years.[20] He had been in the armed services since 1910 and became one of the very first holders of an Imperial Pilot's Licence (No 26). By 1917 he had been elevated to command over 700 aircraft, including von Richthofen's Fighter Wing. A mere captain in 1919, Wilberg would later end his career as General der Flieger. He would visit the United States in 1925 and inspect the Crissy Field installation of the US Air Corps in San Francisco. He might have been the perfect choice as first Chief of Staff of the New Luftwaffe in 1934, had it not been for his Jewish ancestry which left the way open for (the no less able) Walter Wever. He was, however, chosen to serve as Chief of Staff for German forces during the Spanish Civil War where he created 'Special Staff W', which collected and analysed the tactical lessons learned there. He was killed in an aeroplane crash near Dresden on his way to the funeral of Ernst Udet in November 1941.

Wilberg was considered to be a 'brilliant and innovative airman', who had considerable experience in ground-support operations and had on his staff Kurt Student and Hugo Sperrle, who would rise to prominence in the future Luftwaffe.[21] He surreptitiously ensured that senior Air Staff officers were kept informed through more than fifty small committees, sub-committees and study groups, and he assigned 180 officers with flying experience to be retrained in a 'shadow' air force, albeit one devoid of actual aircraft, to come up with a critique of the way Germany had used air power during the war and the way it ought to use it in the future. These officers were spread throughout the service and reports from them, printed under green covers, were designated 'informational documents compiled from foreign publications'. Numerous reports were produced considering air support, supply organisations, air unit organisation, combat tactics and technical developments both in Germany and elsewhere, and the findings incorporated into *Army Regulations 487, Leadership and Battle with Combined Arms*, the first part of which was put out in 1921.[22] The second part was published two years later and continued to emphasise the role of ground support. The first principle derived from the post-war critique maintained that Germany had made a major mistake in fighting with a defensive air strategy for most of the war. They had waited for Allied pilots to cross their lines before engaging them and although this was relatively successful, it forfeited initiative to the Allies and gave them air superiority over the lines. The report was instrumental in effecting a fundamental shift towards the doctrine of offensive air power. The air forces would achieve air superiority primarily by attacking the enemy air force on the ground and in its air bases. Enemy aircraft must be sought out and attacked, pushing them onto the defensive. Having gained air superiority, the primary mission of an air force would then become the bombing of vital enemy targets. This is essentially what the Luftwaffe tried but failed to do during the *Adlerangriff* stage of the Battle of Britain. What some see as the opening phase (the *Kanalkampf*) when convoys were attacked, played no part in this strategic campaign and should rather be seen as a familiarising process to get Luftwaffe crews used to operating over water. The Channel convoys were no more than a convenient target and had no strategic value for either side. The Atlantic convoys had been rerouted to the north of Scotland well before the Luftwaffe attacked. In his memoirs, Kesselring recorded that the operation against Britain did not start until 8 August 1940.

It is worth looking at the reports coming out of these committees in detail. One such presented by Major Streccius, the one-time Air Commander of the 18th Army, advocated small, mobile air units with twelve reconnaissance aircraft to be located close to the battle front, with all ground-attack aircraft retained further back to operate in mass formations under the direction of the army commander. Fighter tactics was another subject under the scrutiny of Sperrle, Student and Wilberg himself. They looked at the optimum number of squadrons in each fighting group, agreeing that it should be limited and consist of both single- and double-crewed aircraft. They advised that during operations, the group commander should be in total control and lead from the front. Heavy bombers were also discussed under the auspices of Captain Hermann Hoth, who became a Panzer Corps Leader during the Second World War. His report concluded that bombers had suffered excessive losses in daylight raids due to enemy fighter interception and so should henceforth be fitted with three or four heavy machine guns for protection, and have the capability of flying as high as 20,000ft. The main target of such bombers, Hoth believed, should be enemy supply lines and communications. Analysis of the last months of war concluded that the effectiveness of the air units had been reduced by shortages of fuel and trained pilots rather than aircraft. Traditionally, the German air force had trained its pilots to a higher standard than the Allies, but this meant longer training periods which, in the end, had led to pilot shortages.

It was a common view within Wilberg's department that German rearmament would come, and when it did the air force would take its place as an independent and equal branch of the armed forces. This idea was not opposed initially by von Seeckt or the senior army leadership, and this led to a consensus that air power should be developed independently of the other services although, crucially, bound to them by a doctrine of close cooperation espoused in Regulation 487. Notwithstanding its responsibility to support ground forces, this allowed free discussion of theories of air power which included a role for aircraft operating in ways to gain air superiority through offensive action, only taking on tactical ground support as a secondary role. The strategic role would be to force the enemy onto the defensive and follow up with the destruction of their military capabilities through bombing. This doctrine exposed the air force strategy of fighter-to-fighter combats during the First World War to have been a mistake and in future, priority would be given to the destruction of enemy aircraft on the ground in pre-emptive strikes to win air supremacy over the battlefield. During the Battle of Britain in 1940, confusion would reign over whether the German fighters should take on the British fighters in a war of attrition, or restrict their role to bomber escort.

Analysis of British bombing raids on German cities had shown that they had been launched at great cost, but the damage caused had been insignificant. There was, as a result, only minimal discussion of strategic bombing in Wilberg's committees. Any interest in strategic bombing was conditioned by the sense that it embodied the concept of a long war of attrition, and after the trenches, nobody wanted to go down that route again. Von Seeckt believed that, in a mobile war, an air force could create the conditions for a rapid and decisive victory by 'a simultaneous attack of the air fleets ... against enemy sources of power [including] major troop assembly points [as a] primary mission of the aerial offensive'. Wilberg endorsed the view and placed emphasis on operating the air force from forward areas to maximise the range, bomb-load and frequency of operations. By virtue of von Seeckt's initiative, during the 1920s German air doctrine was continuously updated according to the latest technical developments. An area in which he was particularly active was in developing close ties between civil aviation and the Ministry of Defence. When Wilberg was replaced by Sperrle in 1926, there was no slackening of the pace of research and technological development.

Hugo Sperrle, 'a big, heavy-jowled bear of a man', was born in Ludwigsburg on 7 February 1885.[23] He had been a competent, but not spectacular, reconnaissance pilot in the First World War but still managed to end the war as commander of all flying units in the German Seventh Army. After the Armistice, he had joined the *Freikorps* as an infantry officer but retained an interest in aviation and spent some time at Lipetsk in the Soviet Union undergoing advanced flight training. His career advanced steadily but not dramatically until, in 1934, he found himself in charge of the 1st Air Division in the (still secret) German Air Force. He was officially transferred to the new Luftwaffe on its formation in 1935 and was well placed to become one of its leading lights. After heading up the Condor Legion in the Spanish Civil War, Sperrle went on to command the bombers of Luftflotte 3 in the Battle of Britain. After the war he was tried and acquitted at Nuremberg on charges of War Crimes.

German commercial aircraft manufacture began even before the ink was dry on the Treaty of Versailles. Junkers produced the F-13 in 1919 and sold it to America as a transport aircraft, despite strong opposition from Britain and France. Sales of the F-13 grew but, when Russian and Japanese versions of the aircraft were equipped with bomb racks and machine guns, the Allies stepped in and closed down any further production.[24] This was overcome by transferring production to Danzig (now Gdańsk) outside the German Reich, under the control of Erhard Milch. The Dornier Company started production in Switzerland and Italy, while Heinkel set up factories in Sweden (Svenska Aero AB). Many of the civil aircraft produced could be easily converted for military use which prompted the Allies, at a Conference of Ambassadors in Paris on 1 February 1922, to put limits on the performance capabilities of all civil aircraft manufactured in Germany and called for manufacturers to report annually their output figures. France and Britain, in fact, doubted that the declared numbers of aircraft were accurate and furthermore suspected that covert production was taking place in the Soviet Union, but had no proof. On the surface, much of Germany's previous wartime aviation industry was closed, but factories opening up abroad clouded the picture.

Erhard Milch, a man of 'cherubic appearance [which] concealed a ruthless egoist with a justified belief in his own abilities', had been born in Wilhelshaven on 30 March 1892.[25] He was the son of Anton Milch, a Jew, but thrived in the Luftwaffe after his mother was coerced into swearing that his real father was a gentile, Kark Brauer. He was an artillery commander in the First World War but transferred to the air force in 1915 where he served as an aerial observer. In 1920 he left the armed services and in 1926 became managing director of the airline Lufthansa, with the avowed aim of creating a company 'free from the oppression of political force'. Whether this was his actual view at the time or whether it was a political statement, he was not averse to joining the Nazi Party in 1929 (membership number 123885) knowing full well what that meant in terms of political control. In 1933, he was appointed State Secretary of the Reich Ministry of Aviation (*Staatssekretär der Luftfahrt*) and, as an example of how much he had compromised, was personally appointed by Göring to be his successor should Göring die. Milch now utilised the huge resources of Lufthansa to provide training facilities for aircrews and research into aviation technologies, both of which were secretly designed to provide a basis for the resurgent German Air Force. He was instrumental in creating an ostensibly civilian infrastructure of air bases and facilities unequalled throughout Europe.[26] Within three years of his appointment there were thirty-six new bases with modern radio and landline communications, radio (blind-landing) and visual navigation aids and meteorological facilities. Milch had managed to cultivate a close relationship with Hitler and his entourage through his office and this caused Göring increasing unease. His jealousy of Milch's privileged access to the highest authority was easily fuelled by Milch's many enemies, who scorned him for his lack of military background and bearing, and who were quick to insinuate to Göring that Milch was actually becoming a threat to his position.

Civil aviation had been the one great loophole in the Versailles restrictions. The Reich Aviation Office had been licenced in 1919 to operate air transport services (*Deutsche Luftreederei*) in cooperation with the Dutch KLM airline, the Danish DDL and the British Daimler-Hire Company. By 1923 it had made 11,726 flights and had carried 13,927 passengers. In 1923, the German-Russian Air Transport Company began commercial flights between Berlin and Moscow. This permitted investment flows into German aircraft manufacturing companies such as *Junkers Luftverkehr*, who responded by increasing production. Eventually, government control of funds allowed Germany to force amalgamation of Aero-Lloyd and the Junkers Aircraft Company into a single entity, *Deutsche LuftHansa AG*, under the chairmanship of Milch.[27] On its formation, LuftHansa, with a 45 per cent government stake, operated the greatest air transport system in the world. carrying mail, freight and passengers with over fifty daily routes, some operated in conjunction with foreign airlines. The German government, besides their regular subsidies for air traffic, contributed the wireless and meteorological equipment and service to the air transport company. It also contributed generously to the expenses of exhibitions, research and experimental stations.

This was all done against the background of a 'moral malaise' in the country which seemed poised to succumb to a communist revolution led by the Spartacists.[28] The ruling elite had been crushed at Versailles and lost its symbol of power when the Kaiser abdicated. The German people, humbled by defeat and seething with discontent, were gripped by a sense of injustice as the country was being strangled by an economic blockade. After the fall of the Romanov dynasty in Russia and the establishment of a communist state, anything seemed possible. The Weimar Republic survived, however, but at the cost of uniting the German people in a spirit of vengeance against Poland, the country that had reclaimed Poznań and Pomerania, cut Germany off from its East Prussian heritage and had become the symbol of Germany's humiliation. To find a way of easing the external constraints, German negotiators wasted no opportunity to try and persuade the Western powers to show leniency towards them and put up a common front 'against [the] Bolshevism and disorder' threatening to engulf Poland and its neighbours. This idea was not viewed unfavourably by many, among whom the British Secretary of State for War and Air, Winston Churchill counted himself. Von Seeckt, however, did not trust the Western Allies and was prepared to reach an understanding with Soviet Russia to devour Poland, 'a mortal enemy of Germany'.[29] The Russians, for their part, did not trust von Seeckt, fearing that he might ally with Poland and launch an anti-communist crusade, but thought it prudent to maintain friendly relations with Germany at least until it had resolved its current war with Poland over their disputed mutual border. Throughout the Russo-Polish War, Germany publicly remained aloof but secretly sent military supplies to Russia and prevented French assistance reaching Poland overland. Polish victory, however, kept the communists at bay, which was very much in Germany's interests, but a Soviet victory would have served von Seeckt's purposes just as well by allowing him, despite Germany's weak military position, to enact his 'strategic plan for action against Poland', and grab back a large part of the lands lost at Versailles. As late as 1929, von Seeckt was still willing to discuss with Russian delegates, Radek and Krasin, a proposal to 'wipe out Poland'.[30]

Air Branch officers in the 'shadow' German air force sedulously worked to promote their cause and make ground forces aware of the potential uses of an air force for reconnaissance and air defence. This reaped rewards when the French occupied the Ruhr district in 1923. Germany had become insolvent under the dual burdens of insurrection and inflation that brought it to the brink of civil war and had defaulted on reparation payments. At the last moment the government instituted currency reform and negotiated new terms for reparations. The Soviet leader, Lenin, saw no benefit for himself in German reconciliation with the West and fuelled Germany's sense of 'monstrous injustice' at the hands of the French in an effort to further isolate Germany.[31] The German Reich President had been sufficiently unnerved by the French move to order mobilisation and authorised, in direct contravention of the 1921 Paris Agreement, the purchase from the Fokker factory in the Netherlands of 50 D.XIs and 50 D.XIII single-seater biplane fighters, considered to be among the finest of their day and powered by British 450-hp Napier Lion engines. The Fokkers had originally been ordered by Argentina and had Spanish lettering. When the Ruhr crisis abated the fighters went into storage in the Netherlands and were later delivered to the Baltic port of Stettin for transhipment to Leningrad. The aircraft arrived at Lipetsk in the Soviet Union in May 1925.

Lipetsk was referred to by the Germans as Wivupal (*Wissenschaftliche Versuchs- und Prüfanstalt für Luftfahrzeuge*) and had been made possible by the signing of the Treaty of Rapallo on 16 April 1922 which, despite German fears of communist insurrection within its borders, had established diplomatic links between Germany and Soviet Russia.[32] After the Treaty of Versailles and the stabilisation of the Soviet regime, both defeated Germany, and the political outcast Soviet Russia found it useful to identify common interests. Von Seeckt hoped to forge a common military front against Poland along with a collaboration in armament affairs. While the Soviets appreciated the benefits that might accrue from access to German technology, they were naturally embarrassed by cooperating with a capitalist power, albeit one weakened by defeat and emasculation. Von Seeckt secretly sent Oskar von Niedermayer to Moscow in the summer of 1921 to meet Victor Kopp establishing the framework for talks the following year when representatives of Germany and the Soviet Union met during the Genoa Conference in Italy in 1922.

On 16 April, they reached an agreement outside the Italian town of Rapallo at Santa Margherita Ligure, which was later formalised as the Treaty of Rapallo. The agreement noted that the two nations would renounce all territorial and monetary claims against each other as the result of the Treaty of Brest-Litovsk at the end of the First World War, and that the two nations were to engage in friendly relations. On 29 July, a secret clause was added whereby the Soviet Union was to provide heavy weapons and facilities for German military training, which was prohibited by the Treaty of Versailles; meanwhile, Germany was to conduct training for the Soviet military and to provide the Soviet Union with an annual payment. The Treaty of Rapallo was formally signed in Berlin on 5 November 1922. At the date of signing, a supplementary agreement was added to include similar terms of friendship between Germany and the Soviet republics of Ukraine, Byelorussia, Georgia, Azerbaijan, and Armenia.

The main strength of the Treaty at this time was political and symbolic but acquired an edge when, on 11 January 1923, the French occupied the Ruhr as compensation for Germany's failure to pay war reparations. This severely weakened Germany's western border and opened up the prospect of a French-Soviet alliance, which would effectively isolate Germany and make her vulnerable to further occupation by either or both. The Soviets had promoted the Treaty in the first place by persuading Germany that France had offered to abandon its long support of Poland to ally with the Soviets to prevent German recovery. Given the centuries of animosity and the crippling burden it had placed upon it at Versailles, Germany saw rapprochement with France as an impossibility. The Treaty was designed, not only to facilitate military cooperation but also to stimulate trade between the two countries, however, Germany was soon disappointed by the meagre level of exports the Soviets were taking up to 1928.

At the same time as the Treaty was signed, von Seeckt established a secret military liaison with Russia which was financed through the Reichswehr budget. Politicians had only a vague idea of what von Seeckt was doing and he was not a man who took kindly to inquisition. In exchange for use of the facilities at Lipetsk, the Germans gave Russia access to all technical developments resulting from their tests and included Soviet airmen in their training programmes. The first German commander of Lipetsk had been Major Stahr, who started out with a staff of 300 Reichswehr employees. Courses at Lipetsk offered elite, advanced pilot training in fighter tactics and ground support. Many of Germany's future Luftwaffe leaders trained there. Other bases were set up in Russia to experiment with gas (Podosinski, Tomka and Saratov) and tanks (Kazan). Junkers, Stolzenberg and Krupp all opened factories there. The Reichswehr set up a headquarters in Moscow to oversee cooperative ventures and 75 million Goldmarks, a huge sum that Germany could barely afford, was diverted to fund the scheme. When questions arose in the Reichstag about shady dealings, the interlocutors' attention was drawn to a 'common war aim', usually understood to be a reference to possible Russo-German action against Poland, which simply meant that they should look to the national interest and basically mind their own business.[33]

At Lipetsk, Russia was pursuing a clear policy designed to gain maximum military help in return for minimum political concession. They had been careful to negotiate separately with the German military and cooperation with them had progressed, albeit uncomfortably, but they resisted making any political and economic concessions to the German government. When Russia suggested a major increase in manufacture of heavy artillery, even the Reichswehr jibbed, fearing that such expansion would not go unnoticed by the West and undermine the whole 'Rapallo' entente. It was becoming clear that Germany was increasingly opening itself up to Russian blackmail by continuing the clandestine operations. There developed in Germany a sense that to end relations with Russia entirely would be 'impossible', but the agreement should be left to 'slowly peter out'. However, it was tacitly accepted that if the politicians did try to force the closure of Lipetsk, the Reichswehr would simply ignore them, double security and continue with their schemes anyway.[34] As it turned out, political opposition waned after 1926, amid fears that withdrawal from cooperation with Russia would simply allow the French to step into the void. The Reichswehr actually stepped up its activity in Russia to the point where, in 1928, Truppenamt Chief Blomberg was invited to observe Red Army manoeuvres.

The Locarno Pact of December 1925 had gone some way to stabilising German relations with the Western powers and loosened the economic constraints – but not the military ones – of Versailles. The Pact, which reinforced the validity of Versailles, was signed by representatives of Germany, Belgium, Britain, France and Italy. Border issues between Germany and France were resolved as French troops vacated the Rhineland, but it had the effect of weakening ties between France and Poland. It left the Soviet Union rather isolated politically which prompted a further effort to strengthen its ties with Germany, whose central position between east and west was becoming ever more significant. All in all, it was a successful diplomatic coup for Germany's Foreign Minister, Gustav Stresemann, and prepared the way for the renaissance of German military air power as all Allied air inspectors were withdrawn.[35] As an indication of Stresemann's diplomatic skill and his importance to German resurgence, a year after Locarno he had concluded the Berlin Treaty with Russia, which reaffirmed the Treaty of Rapallo and agreed mutual renunciation of wartime reparations and compensation. This took place at a time when the Weimar Republic, which had enjoyed neither political nor economic stability at the best of times, was veering to the right with the election of the authoritarian Field Marshal Paul von Hindenberg as President. Meanwhile, all was not going well for German economic interests in Russia. The Junkers aircraft factory at Fili, just south of Moscow, was threatening to close because neither the Reichswehr nor Russia were buying enough of its aircraft, but the Germans insisted that its demise 'must be avoided at all costs'.[36] In December 1926, after massive financial losses, Karl Junkers, hoping to extricate his company from the disastrous twenty-five-year agreement for Fili, leaked details of the secret plant to members of the Reichstag. On 3 December 1926, the scandal became public when the *Manchester Guardian* exposed 'Cargoes of Munitions from Russia to Germany'. The German government, which had been largely ignorant of (or unwilling to acknowledge) the illegal cooperation fell in disgrace after a vote of no confidence in the Reichstag.[37]

The Russians had asked Krupps to open a steel-making plant in Russia, fuelling speculation that they were intent on creating their own armament industry at Germany's expense. When Krupps, in the face of political (though not military) opposition pulled out, their place was taken by another steel manufacturer, Rheinmetall, and the Russians upped the stakes by insisting that it was a test of German goodwill and a preliminary agreement was signed in February 1930.

In the civilian sphere, emboldened by an apparent indifference on the part of the international community, German civil aircraft firms established other manufacturing businesses outside Germany. Dornier set up in Switzerland and Italy, Junkers and Heinkel in Sweden. The Svensk Flug Organization in Malmoe Linghamn, Sweden, was capitalised sufficiently with Swedish money to avoid the Versailles Treaty restrictions, but the French government accused it of mass-producing military aircraft for export to Chile. Within the Reich, too, moves were made to nurture the sort of skills that would be required in the event of Germany re-establishing an air force. Gliding clubs and sport aviation schools (Sportflug GmBh), which had not been proscribed, acted as training camps for future military pilots.[38] The Deutscher Luftsportverband, led by Kurt Student, ran large-scale courses from 1920 and eventually had a membership of over 50,000.

The concept of air power as the dominant factor in a future war was advocated by the Italian military theorist Giovanni Caproni and promulgated by Giulio Douhet in his book, *The Command of the Air*, first published in 1921, but not widely read outside Italy until the 1930s. Although he may well have been influenced by Guilio Douhet's theories, von Seeckt did not endorse the terror-bombing of cities, but he accepted that it would be an inevitable feature of any future war.[39] The influence of Douhet's book was widespread and underpinned much debate over air doctrine in the decade before the Battle of Britain. Douhet, however, had presented his powerful theories of air power dominated by strategic bombing, with little regard for the practicalities of its implementation in the face of modern air defence capabilities. He argued that the effect of bombing on the morale of a population was even more important than the material effect of damage, and would quickly lead to a breakdown of the social structure. It was generally held by his acolytes that the application of his theories of strategic air war would, in a future war, avoid a repetition of the stalemate and the slaughter of the trenches in 1914–18 and instead 'promise a quick, decisive and relatively bloodless outcome to warfare'.[40]

In his book *The Future of War and its Weapons* published in 1924, General Hans Ritter, who may well have been aware of Douhet's theories, saw modern war in economic terms where an 'entire homeland' had become the target. He argued that it was now 'morally acceptable' to use all means available to 'break the will of the enemy homeland'.[41] For Germany, the threat to its homeland seemed low given the dearth of heavy bombers in the air forces of surrounding countries, but prudence advised that it explore air defence measures, especially against poison gas attacks which were widely expected to play a part in any future war.

By 1925, German Air Staff within the armed services began to consider the strategic use of air power, even though the geographical position of Germany, the 'land in the centre of Europe' as Mary Fulbrook called it, meant that any future war would require an air force to act primarily in a tactical role in support of ground forces. However, since strategic bombing was seen as a way of avoiding trench warfare, it was thought wise to investigate the practical limits of such a doctrine also. A *Directive for the Conduct of the Operational Air War (Operativer Luftkrieg)*, which was secretly issued by Helmut Wilberg in May 1926 broke new ground by advocating the separation of the air branch into what was basically a tactical fighter/reconnaissance section and a strategic bombing section, although both would be directly subordinate to the military High Command.[42] The study stressed the different categories of targets and their relative importance in terms of how their destruction might influence a campaign.

Throughout the 1920, the 'shadow' German air force developed air doctrine through a regular programme of war games and conferences. The war games investigated not only air defence, but also strategic attacks on French war industries. Such a concentrated effort resulted in the creation of 'the best-informed air force in the world'.[43] As part of the Treaty of Rapallo, the Germans also carried out war games in cooperation with the Soviet air forces in 1926. One essential aspect of these war games was that, in contrast to the view held by many, there was no assumption that 'the bomber would always get through'. Enemy air defences were assumed to be tenacious and competent. Commanders were urged to always take a broad, inter-service view in which there was no place for an independent air campaign.

In 1926, all German civil aviation companies were merged, under the auspices of the Defence Ministry, into Lufthansa, with a fleet of 162 aircraft, which established a broad network of air routes across Europe under the guidance of Operations Director Erhard Milch. The airline invested heavily in night-flying and blind-flying navigation aids, which laid the foundation for further research into navigation aids such as the X- and Y-Gerät systems used by Luftwaffe bombers over Britain in 1940.[44] When Lufthansa ran into serious financial difficulties in 1928 as a result of a reduction in state subsidies, Milch appealed to the Reichstag Nazi Party contingent for help to restore aid. As a result of this, Milch made the acquaintance of Deputy Hermann Göring and forged a friendship that would have considerable consequences as Göring stormed to power beside Hitler.

Hermann Wilhelm Göring had been born in Rosenheim to wealth and privilege on 12 January 1893. His father had been a Governor of German South-West Africa, and the family owned castles and estates at Veldenstein in upper Franconia and Mautendorf in the Salzburgian Lungau. The young Göring is said to have been 'strong-minded', with 'great determination and energy', but 'seems to have been virtually unaffected by [the discipline of] school', which he attended only rarely and which left him with a 'contempt for all that was intellectual'. It was in the estates owned by his family that the young Göring acquired a fascination for the pageantry and chivalry of Teutonic Knights, such as the sixteenth-century Gotz von Berlichingen, which was to colour his personal life as he rose to power in his own right. As a youth he was also an intrepid and tough-minded alpinist. As an infantry officer, he was considered to be a natural leader. Later, as a flyer, his exploits earned him the Iron Cross First Class and the highest honour 'pour le Merite', after which he was given command of Richthofen's *geschwader* when the German ace was killed. In 1922 his political activism brought him into contact with Hitler, whose rhetoric impressed him and seemed to speak to his own ambitions for retribution for the humiliation of Versailles. He was quick to declare an oath of allegiance to Hitler and took part in the 'Beerhall Putsch' of the following year, when they made a pre-emptive but futile bid for power. Failure of the insurrection saw Hitler thrown into Landsberg Prison, and Göring wounded by a bullet from the Bavarian State Police.

In 1927, he was reacquainted with Hitler and once again became active in the movement, winning a seat in the Reichstag for the National Socialists. When the Nazi Party eventually gained control of the political apparatus after 1933, Göring was at the very heart of power and poised to evolve into the kind of folk hero he had so admired in his youth. Hitler appointed him as State Aviation Commissioner. Unlike Hitler, Göring was born into the conservative upper classes and could move effortlessly in their circles. He became a vital ambassador between the party and entrenched conservatism in the country. It was this socialising that Göring enjoyed above all else, but it left insufficient time or energy for the increasing number of administrative and leadership roles that he willingly accepted without due regard for the burden of responsibility that came with them. He eschewed detailed discussion about anything and refused to read lengthy reports, leaving policy detail to his subordinates. At the Nuremberg War Trials in 1946 he was indicted on four charges: conspiracy; waging a war of aggression; war crimes (including the plundering and removal to Germany of works of art and other property); and crimes against humanity (including the disappearance of political and other opponents, the torture and ill-treatment of prisoners of war, and the murder and enslavement of civilians). He was found guilty on all four counts but committed suicide before he could be executed.

The Locarno Pact had emboldened Germany to interpret Article 316 of the Versailles Treaty as prohibiting all aircraft from flying through German airspace. Britain, with its long-distance routes to India, was forced to compromise and sign a new Paris Air Agreement on 21 May 1926 which removed the restrictions on civil aviation manufacture within Germany and legalised the training of a limited number of Reichswehr officers in sport flying, but the much more profitable military aircraft production was still outlawed. By permitting German officers to train for a pilot's licence, however, the agreement had the effect of allowing Germany to begin creating a cohesive programme of military training.[45]

A year before, the German Army Command had established a new group, T2 V (L), bringing together all the disparate agencies associated with aviation headed, at different times, by Major Hugo Sperrle (considered 'capable rather than brilliant') and Major Helmuth Felmy, but still with lowly status within the army.[46] Sperrle had served as an air commander in the First World War and was said to have 'a firm grip of technical matters', while both he and Felmy were 'knowledgeable, capable, experienced and competent commanders'.[47] Felmy was a staunch supporter of the view that 'the strategic bomber would play the primary role in any future war', and would be called on to 'battle for the air against the military and economic sources of power of the enemy'.[48] Albert Kesselring was also involved in 1928 when he was instrumental in creating an Air Inspectorate to centralise all military aviation activities. It was not until 1932, however, that the work of T2 V (L) in shielding air activities from international scrutiny was recognised by giving its commanding officer the rank of General. It was still the case, however, that aviation was viewed by some as 'of very little practical effect'. Nevertheless, the branch was considered sufficiently important for the Defence Office to fund a 'four-year plan' for development, testing and procurement of aircraft and armaments at Lipetsk in the late 1920s under the tightest security.[49]

Back in Germany, in 1925, a lowly aircraft testing station at Rechlin am Müritzsee, just outside Berlin, had been elevated to the status of 'Testing station Rechlin of the Reich Formation of the German Aviation Industry', but kept under a strict security blackout. Lipetsk was still the main testing and training centre for aircraft and crews, but it was a huge financial burden on Germany and diplomatic relations with Soviet Russia, stretched uncomfortably to extract the maximum benefit to both parties, were far from cordial. From the German perspective the main benefit was that, given the nature of the Soviet regime, Rechlin was relatively well hidden from prying Western eyes, but the cost of transporting material to and from the Soviet base were becoming burdensome in the light of emerging alternatives. By 1930, it was becoming clear that the Soviets were benefiting much more than the Germans from Lipetsk and so, as soon as circumstances permitted, the Germans began transferring much of their research back inside their own borders. Within Germany, the fear of communist insurrection was making the continued bleeding of military technology to a potential enemy a risk too far. Naturally, the Soviets were anxious to continue accruing benefits from Lipetsk and made strenuous efforts, including veiled threats to confiscate all assets there, to persuade the Germans to stay. For the Germans it was a question of how to disengage with minimal losses. Felmy called for immediate withdrawal, but the German government was cautious and negotiated an agreement which allowed them to repatriate all moveable equipment with the exception of thirty Fokker D.XIII aircraft.[50]

When Rechlin had been expanded in 1925 a 'mobilisation calendar' had been inaugurated by the Reichswehr, setting out a programme of gradual development of the armed services. The air branch had its own trajectory within this plan which allowed for the eventual establishment of a number of squadrons, but struggled to achieve that with inadequate resources and its lowly status. The practicalities of creating these squadrons proved to be considerable and were only compounded by the loss of the Fokkers abandoned at Lipetsk.[51]

Of immense benefit to the air force had been the strength of German civilian aviation. In the late 1920s German airlines flew greater distances with more passengers than their French, British and Italian competitors put together. They accrued much experience of long-distance flying and navigation which, although not strictly convertible to military use, was an important source of knowledge on which the Luftwaffe could eventually draw.[52] A domestic aircraft manufacturing industry would be an essential component of any resurgent air force, but by 1929 there were only eight aircraft and four aircraft engine plants operating inside Germany with a level of technological development which was well below some other countries. The Wall Street economic crash of 1929 had seen American loans withdrawn from Germany, which heralded a huge rise in bankruptcies forcing three of these companies out of business with others such as Junkers barely hanging on. Only through increased state subsidies could any of them survive in the long term, but as a condition of any new contracts the government handed out, there was imposed upon the companies a blanket of the strictest secrecy. Military aircraft production was still forbidden but designs requested by the government were for three general types of aircraft: a long-range single-engine reconnaissance-bomber, a short-range reconnaissance aircraft and a single-seater fighter. Glaringly absent from the list was an aircraft for a purely bombing role.[53] All prototypes failed to meet specifications due to inadequate engine designs. This prompted the Transport Ministry to call for tenders to produce a 1,000hp liquid-cooled engine with high power-to-weight ratio, which ultimately led to production of the Daimler-Benz DB 600 engine which later powered the Bf 109 and the He 111.[54]

In 1929 Germany suffered a political setback when its 'chief architect of foreign policy' Gustav Stresemann died, which weakened somewhat the links that held Lipetsk together.[55] At the same time, the country was being dragged down by the world economic depression with millions unemployed.

Von Seeckt had retired from active duty, but as a member of the Reichstag his voice still resonated powerfully in German politics. His message was a precursor of Nazi doctrine by focusing on the harnessing of German cultural minorities in Eastern Europe to create a greater Germany. German-Soviet relations plummeted as Stresemann's loss was keenly felt and the 'Rapallo spirit' evaporated. It had always been a marriage of convenience between two culturally incompatible regimes, and the costs for Germany now outweighed the benefits both politically and economically. Russia, the junior partner in many ways, tried everything to keep the Germans at Lipetsk, but it was clear that the undercurrents of opposing philosophies were beginning to tear the liaison apart.

The Soviet base had been important not only for training but also for the development of air doctrine. Part of the role of instructors there was to write papers on tactics and strategy in the light of testing carried out with both men and machines in mock combat. An extensive manual was produced covering aspects such as formation flying, attack formations, air-to-air combat and ground support, as well as principles and guidelines for flight commanders.[56]

Elsewhere, developments in aviation accelerated despite the economic depression. There were advances in fuel technology to increase efficiency and power, and a move towards monoplane designs. All eyes were on new bombers introduced by the United States Air Force such as the Boeing B10 and B12 which had speeds equivalent to the fastest interceptors, and operating ceilings far above anti-aircraft gun range. Felmy was pessimistic about the ability of fighters to put up an effective defence against these new aircraft and championed the fitting of 20mm cannon to the Bf109 fighter to increase its fire-power and inflict considerably more damage than the standard rifle-calibre machine guns.[57] In 1932 he wrote a memorandum strongly supporting the idea of a bomber force to deter attack by France or Poland. Chief Technical Officer Wilhelm Wimmer backed this up with a powerful message, saying that fear of a strategic bombing reprisal would 'strike fear into the hearts of the enemy population'.

Very soon, aircraft production in Germany was scaled up, to the point where it was estimated that more than 7,000 aircraft could be produced annually, but this flew in the face of a myriad of difficulties including aircrew training, engine development and fuel production. The economic situation was dire, with Germany desperately short of foreign currency to buy necessary raw materials.[58] The army demanded the lion's share of any production capacity for their own requirements and was disdainful of any attempt to build up an independent air force, both for its drain on resources as well as purely prejudicial reasons. Industry was noticeably reluctant to invest in new production facilities to accommodate the air force because of uncertainty about its viability and also, where contracts were signed, because of rapidly evolving technology, plans for aircraft production lacked continuity and specifications were continuously upgraded, requiring expensive ongoing modifications to existing machinery.[59]

Prior to Hitler's rise to power in January 1933, the air section had, over a ten-year period, developed an air doctrine and training programme for its staff, and at the same time financed technological innovation and production capacity within the civil aviation industry, but it was not prepared for the scale of rearmament envisaged by the new leadership. Up to this point, military aviation, still under army control, was 'scattered among far too many agencies', but a growing admission of this precipitated the formation of a Reich's Commission for Aviation (Reichskommissariat für die Luftfahrt), which came under the control of Generaloberst Hermann Göring, by this time President of the Reichstag, who made no secret of the fact that he was strongly in favour of an independent air force. Göring had been appointed by Hitler, who was widely believed to be 'not fond of aviation in any form and [who] harboured grave reservations regarding its potential effectiveness in warfare'. It is here that we find the roots of Hitler's reluctance to become involved in the details of operations during the summer of 1940, when he had seemed to rely totally on Göring to lead Luftwaffe operations – which is not the same as saying that Hitler had total confidence in the man himself. Göring's political affiliations and naked ambition to promote the air force as an independent service also antagonised the army and navy staffs, who were unable to challenge his authority, but who would be ever reluctant to offer cordial cooperation; again, a feature that characterised events in 1940 when plans for the invasion of Britain were mooted.

On 9 February 1933 the new Nazi rulers of Germany, having walked out of the Geneva Disarmament Conference and withdrawn from the League of Nations, allocated forty million Reichsmarks for the creation of an air force, certain that it would be pliant and amenable under Göring's leadership. This new Luftwaffe would benefit alongside the traditional services as Hitler pledged to avenge the injustices of Versailles and create an economy

68

'devoted to rendering the German people again capable of bearing arms'. Göring brought in Milch as his deputy. Milch was a formidable organiser and 'a man of indomitable health and energy … tremendously ambitious, efficient…', but insecure and someone with a very 'thin skin' who was easily slighted. Brought in at the same time were Kesselring, an artillery officer, and Colonel Walther Wever, a staff officer who had been destined for the highest office.

Walter Wever was born in Wilhelmsort on 11 November 1887. He had served as an army officer on the staff of Field Marshal von Hindenburg and General Ludendorff during the First World War. A firm favourite of von Seeckt, Wever was promoted to Major in 1926. When he joined the air force in 1933, General von Blomberg lamented that the army had lost 'a future chief of the General Staff'.[60] Leutnantgeneral Nielsen said of Wever, upon his appointment as Luftwaffe's first Chief of Staff, 'His quick intelligence, his remarkable receptiveness towards the development of modern technology and his vast store of military experience soon enabled him to grasp the fundamental concepts of his mission.' Realising that the German military, especially the air force, was becoming increasingly politicised, Wever took the time and trouble to understand how the air force fitted into the Nazi philosophy, which saw the Soviet Union as its main enemy, and his own mission was to prepare for such a war. Unfortunately, Wever's prowess as an administrator was not equalled by his ability as a pilot. He had only learned to fly a year earlier and it was his inexperience that caused the crash which killed him in June 1936 when pre-flight checks, which would have been second nature for someone more experienced, were not carried out properly, causing his aircraft to crash on take-off at Dresden.

It was an indication of the growing importance of the Luftwaffe that the army should have agreed to Wever's transfer. There was now a powerful cadre of top quality General Staff officers in the Luftwaffe, including Wilberg, Felmy, Wimmer, Sperrle, Kesselring and Jeschonnek, but it was Wever in particular who would have a significant influence on the development of the early Luftwaffe.[61] The challenges faced by the new Luftwaffe organisation were immense, but Göring set about reorganising it. He had many contacts, both within the governing Nazi party and within the wider financial and industrial landscape, which ensured that massive resources were made available for the purpose. It was a bonus, too, that Göring, burdened with domestic political responsibilities, had little interest in the details of military aviation and so tended to leave all planning decisions to the air professionals while providing 'an inexhaustible supply of funds'.[62] It is worth noting here that Göring, as Reichs Minister, had tried and failed to purchase military aircraft from Britain, but the government did allow Germany, in spite of the Versailles restrictions, to buy two types of supercharged aero engines, especially designed for use at high altitude, characteristics of which were incorporated into the Daimler-Benz DB 601 that would later power the Bf 109 fighter. Questions in Parliament were fobbed off with the excuse that if Britain had not sold the technology, the French surely would have done so.

The 'tall, blue-eyed and strong-chinned' Prussian, Werner von Blomberg, was born on 2 September 1878.[63] He became head of the Truppenamt on 27 January 1927 where he was quick to appreciate new technology, especially air power, and studied how it would impact upon warfare in the future. Anxious not to draw attention to Germany's secret rearmament and catapult Europe into an arms race, Blomberg headed the German delegation to the World Disarmament Conference at Geneva in 1932. When he became Defence Minister in January 1933, Blomberg strongly supported an independent air arm and worked within the General Staff to promote its credentials under the man whom he had recently promoted to General der Infanterie, Hermann Göring, although he had expected to retain ultimate control for himself.[64] When Göring was elevated to Reichsminister für die Luftfahrt, he was still theoretically under Blomberg's authority, but given his standing in the Party and with Hitler in particular, Göring ignored such niceties and, although he had little interaction with the air services at first due to his political and economic responsibilities, he ensured that his candidate for Chief of Staff, Wever, was preferred over Blomberg's man, Erich von Manstein. Blomberg's enthusiasm for military aviation, however, was not affected by this rebuff and he was ever willing to support Milch whenever budgetary battles were fought. He even encouraged Wimmer's, ultimately abandoned, Ju 89 project against indifference bordering on hostility from Göring. In July 1936 it was Blomberg and not Göring who was the more enthusiastic when discussing Hitler's options in support of General Franco's rebel forces against the Spanish Nationalist government, especially when it was clear that it would be the Luftwaffe, albeit staffed by nominally 'volunteer' personnel, that would play the major role. When Hitler asserted in 1938 that his aim was to precipitate a European war in the search for 'Lebensraum', Blomberg was one of several leaders who strongly argued against it. This gave Hitler and Göring the chance they had been waiting for to rein in the German High Command, OKW. They plotted between them to have Blomberg removed and when they forced his resignation on 27 January 1938, Hitler assumed personal command of the armed forces. After the war, Blomberg, seriously ill with cancer, gave evidence at the Nuremberg War Trials and died soon afterwards.

Göring had argued since 1934 for large-scale rearmament, with arms factories and raw material production coming under direct state control; as Minister, Blomberg had rejected these proposals. Nothing daunted, Göring petitioned Hitler for a doubling of air strength against opposition from Blomberg and the President of the Reichsbank, Hjalmar Schacht, who adjudged Göring to have 'a complete lack of understanding of economics'. Göring apparently agreed with the latter when, in 1937, he admitted to being puzzled by 'complicated problems of economics'.[65] Furthermore, he eschewed detailed reports and tended to make decisions based only upon those aspects of an issue that he could understand, which often was the lesser portion of the evidence.

At this time, Göring's position was far from secure in a Nazi government not yet holding all the levers of power. While Hitler continued to include him in discussions about foreign policy and military planning, his only real platform was the air force, which was still a relatively minor department and he was treated with a modicum of contempt by such as von Neurath, the Foreign Minister, and with open hostility by Blomberg. It was the case, however, that Hitler needed allies in his struggle to wrest control of Germany from the grip of traditional forces, both economic and military, and it was in this context that Göring, with his aristocratic background, outwardly affable nature and important contacts, became more useful to him as a man who 'knew how to talk to these people', and had the strength of character to bring them into the fold. Furthermore, Hitler saw that the new air force, starting from scratch and without any military 'baggage', could become the most modern and outwardly impressive of the three services carrying the banner of Nazism into the future as he saw it. Nobody seemed better placed than Göring to head up that powerful new force. As a result, the air force, from the very outset, had an independent philosophy and overtly political character. Hitler did all in his power to support Göring when he petitioned, against significant opposition, for the resources to build it up and pull away from its dependence upon OKW for funding. While Hitler initially relied on diplomatic means to attain his political objectives, he understood the way in which an adversary's perception of Germany's military strength, especially the Luftwaffe, could be applied in a coercive manner, intending to overwhelm the opposition with a belligerent display of power. At this stage, the image of armed might was almost more important than true military capability. Numbers of bombers became more important than the types and characteristics of those bombers. German officials showed foreign dignitaries their aircraft and production capabilities in order to intimidate them.[66]

Even with Hitler's help, support for the new Luftwaffe was extremely difficult without more support from the economic ministry. Schacht had a conservative banker's affinity to financial orthodoxy which prioritised trade and fiscal probity over rearmament. An impasse was developing which Schacht sought to overcome by seconding Göring onto economic planning forums, hoping that his ineptitude, poor judgement and lack of expertise would undermine him and expose his 'amateurism'.[67] Göring, however, confounded Schacht by pressing for an acceleration in the process of rearmament which began to marginalise Schacht, especially in his relations with Blomberg. Göring then called on his many contacts in industry and the Nazi Party to build up an alternative economic strategy to oppose Schacht, whose conservative approach was increasingly frustrating Hitler's ambitions to free up the military budget. On 4 September 1936, Göring reported to the Council of Ministers that Germany's position vis-à-vis the Soviet Union placed it in 'imminent danger of war', and demanded greater state control over the economy. This reignited his political career as he was given 'a heavy office' of full power to set up a Four-Year Plan for the economy to prepare the country for war. He accepted the role, claiming that he was no expert but had been chosen as 'the plenipotentiary of the National Socialist Party'.[68] Schacht and Göring were now firmly espousing opposing economic strategies and, given the strong personality and inflexibility of both, destined to move ever closer to a decisive confrontation. Schacht eventually resigned as Economic Minister in November 1937 when it was clear that he had lost the argument.

Elevation to economic supremacy now allowed Göring to concentrate resources on the air force. Central to his plans for air power was Milch, a brilliant administrator and planner, who was 'probably the best man in Germany' to be state Secretary for Aviation when he had been appointed in 1933.[69] He had inherited a German aviation industry battered by the economic depression and he wasted no time in bringing it back to life by authorising an in-depth study of strategic concepts relating to the air force in the context of 'restoration of Germany's great power position in Europe'. Göring encouraged Milch to prise the air force from the army's grip and build on Felmy's concept of a strategic bomber capability. The tone of the final report was strongly influenced by an associate of Milch at Lufthansa, Dr Robert Knauss, who urged the creation of a large heavy bomber fleet as a strategically decisive weapon to create a protective shield over the country as rearmament was accelerated. Knauss claimed that Germany could build 400 four-engine bombers for the same price as two battleships. Such a bomber force would have political, diplomatic, and psychological impact way beyond its material existence, and would act as a powerful deterrent to any potential enemy who opposed Germany's rearmament by threatening them, in turn, with an indiscriminate strategic air offensive against their industry and population.[70] The report picked up on Douhetist philosophy of strategic air power but constrained it with anticipation of a 'preventive war' against Poland and France requiring a significant tactical contribution from the air force.[71] Milch tried to advance Knauss's principles and urged the construction of a heavy bomber force under the guise of legitimate civilian Lufthansa plans, but the cost of so many bombers, already burdened with the curse of underpowered engines as well as lack of industrial capacity, forced Milch to turn his attention to twin-engine medium bombers instead.

Under Milch's supervision, the air force made full use of many thousands of men who had been trained at Lipetsk and the gliding clubs. Lufthansa training schools were financed through the military as were new airfields. Civilian pilots, among them the future Jagdgeshwader 'experte' Adolf Galland, were sent on military training courses at Schleissheim where they attended lectures and were given many hours of combat aerobatics practice. Milch was a practical and cautious man who preferred gradual expansion of the facilities to ensure a sound and sustainable air force with high calibre personnel and first-class facilities, but political pressure from Göring and Hitler was never going to allow this 'petty pace' and his five-year programme of development was condensed into little more than one.[72] Factories were tooled up to meet requirements of revolutionary new aircraft as Milch's first production programme was put into gear on 1 January 1934 and private industry was encouraged to set up component divisions to supply parts. At this early stage it had been Milch's intention to concentrate on bomber production at the expense of fighters, but it was envisaged that the imbalance would be rectified in due course when the bomber force had reached a certain size. Aircraft design was, even at this early stage, of the highest quality with Heinkel He 111 and Dornier Do 17 bombers already in advanced stages of design.

While airframe manufacturers were falling into line behind government plans, aero-engine plants were struggling. Old rivalries persisted and prevented close cooperation in a national effort. Old technology also made mass production difficult, and the lack of skilled workers was always a problem. Where effort and will were positive there was still the problem of a shortage of raw materials and hard cash for imports. The Air Ministry had to browbeat and coerce businesses to support plans with guarantees of 'cost-plus' contracts with substantial profit margins.[73] The vast government subsidies meant that, in effect, many new factories, while operated under the auspices of established companies such as Heinkel, were 'de facto' state enterprises.

On 15 February 1935, the German Foreign Office, in an open admission of its having an air force, delivered a note to the British Embassy in Berlin stating 'the German Government is ready in principle to employ its air forces as a means of deterring disturbances of the peace'. The British responded by announcing a speeding up of its own rearmament programme. One month later the British Foreign Secretary was due to meet Hitler in Berlin to discuss London's concerns over German rearmament, but the meeting never took place. Hitler cancelled at the last minute on the pretext of having a cold. Shortly afterwards, he ordered military conscription in Germany and officially unveiled to the world a German Air Force which he claimed was already superior to the Royal Air Force.

Frequent public expression of British fears of growing German air power had revealed its vulnerability to propaganda which Hitler was not slow to exploit. For instance, when British officials were invited to visit German military establishments, Junkers Ju 52 air transports were fitted out with mocked-up bomb bays to imply that they had capabilities way beyond what was actually possible. Such public displays jolted British policymakers and analysts, who for years had downplayed German air power, but now seemed to accept, without question, everything the Germans said at face value.[74]

At Versailles, the Allies had specifically banned Germany from possessing military aircraft, especially the Fokker D.VII. But Anthony Fokker, the manufacturer of several successful German aircraft, including the D.VII, was among the first to aggressively circumvent Versailles restrictions. He and his company had hidden aircraft in barns and buildings throughout the German countryside, covertly put airframes on trains under tarpaulins and rigging that disguised the cargo and created diversions as the trains crossed the German-Dutch border into Holland. This was a successful deception that fooled the inspectors from the Inter-Allied Control Commission (IACC), designated by the Allies to ensure German compliance with the Versailles Treaty restrictions. IACC inspectors had little cooperation and spent a lot of time looking at facilities that had been warned in advance of their arrival.[75] The Army Peace Commission, a liaison group within the German Defence Ministry, obstructed the IACC's efforts at every opportunity and was completely successful in protecting the secrecy of the German-Russian joint testing centre at Lipetsk. As deception measures, German officers sent to train there were 'discharged' for the duration of their training. A customs office was established at Lipetsk to clear parts and schedule shipments away from normal points of entry in Germany that might be under observation, and aircraft were flown to Lipetsk disguised as 'mail planes'. The aviation staff was designated the 'Army Command Inspectorate of Weapons Schools' and immediately absorbed 120 former army and navy pilots into the newly established state-owned airline, Lufthansa. It did so through false job descriptions and secret training pipelines. After initial training at a newly established Commercial Flying School, the new pilots were brought to Lipetsk for specialised military training. Each year, the German finance ministry would collude with the military to falsify the budget to include inflated estimates and then divert the funds to Lipetsk.[76] While Britain and France may have had some inkling of the Russian connection, they were never in a position to furnish the proof that might have exposed it.

Commercial aviation was not restricted and so a Commercial Flying School was openly established to train crews for mail delivery, advertising, and sports, which in turn allowed for increased production of commercial aircraft, albeit with military potential. Germany was allowed to build high-performance aircraft to compete in air shows and set speed records. These aircraft designs would be the foundation for aircraft tested at Lipetsk and other facilities throughout the 1920s and 1930s. Surveillance was withdrawn in 1927 with the disbanding of the IACC, whose final report stated that 'Germany has never disarmed, has never had the intention of disarming, and for seven years had done everything in its power to deceive … the Commission appointed to control her disarmament.'[77] This left only the more closely controlled military attachés to try, without much success, to keep an eye on future developments.

Following the departure of the IACC, the Germans were able to rapidly construct airfields and other facilities in parts of the country less frequently visited. A budget of 10 million Reichsmarks was diverted from the Defence Ministry's public budget in secret and administered by a special branch of the Reich Audit Office that dealt with covert programmes. The rise of the Nazi Party brought about more aggressive deception to match this increase in activity. Though the commission was no longer a barrier to rearmament, the German government continued to take steps to ensure its covert build-up would remain undetected and quietly created the Central Bureau for German Rearmament in 1934 to coordinate what were, by then, numerous complex efforts throughout the Defence Ministry to increase Germany's military capabilities in violation of Versailles restrictions.[78] To try and stabilise its eastern borders, Germany signed a Declaration of non-Aggression and Understanding with Poland on 26 January 1934, but it contained no clauses and had the status of neither a Pact nor a Treaty. It simply declared that 'in no circumstances [will the signatories] proceed to use force in order to settle … disputes.'[79]

It was hardly a surprise to the world when Hitler officially announced the existence of the Luftwaffe on 26 February 1935, but its actual strength and composition was still not at all clear. The new Luftwaffe began to conduct large exhibition flyovers to impress both home and foreign observers. Dornier 17 aircraft with a very high specification were on display, but had been hand-built to a quality that could not have been replicated under mass production. Concealed by this masterly display of smoke and mirrors, the Luftwaffe had a ready-to-go comprehensive air war doctrine and an impressive new headquarters built on the site of the old Prussian War Ministry in the Liepzigerstrasse in Berlin, and boasted 800 operational aircraft. One of the primary goals of the fledgling service was to encourage German plane-makers to strive for 'a point of world leadership in capacity and technical excellence'.[80] It is not stretching a point to say that at this time Milch played a similar role for the Luftwaffe as that played by Beaverbrook for the RAF in 1940. Both men 'moved mountains' in the face of opposition and neither was particularly well-liked.

When the veneer of secrecy over German air policy was stripped away on 1 March, the newly formed Luftwaffe remained nominally subordinate to Blomberg, but Göring's primary allegiance was to Hitler, which put him in a unique position relative to other service chiefs. In disputes, Göring routinely insulted Blomberg by ignoring him and appealed directly to Hitler at every opportunity; despite the provocation, however, Blomberg remained professional throughout and ensured that the new Luftwaffe was afforded a good supply of first-class 'best of the best' officers from the army to create a 'tempestuous spirit of attack' within the new service.[81] Göring, on the other hand, gave less than his full attention to his role as Luftwaffe Chief, due, in no small part, to his many other responsibilities and preoccupations. As a result there was a certain amount of animosity towards him as a result of his aversion to 'steady, routine-type work'. His 'fits of enthusiasm and fruitful intervention' were followed by 'long periods of indifference and lethargy'. Nevertheless, he still had the energy to 'develop an entirely new service branch out of virtually nothing in defiance of formidable obstacles'.[82]

Wimmer was, alongside Milch, another example of 'the right man in the right place'. The dominant figure, however, was Wever, Luftwaffe Chief of the General Staff, whose compendious knowledge of technology and theory allowed him to develop a 'coherent and comprehensive doctrine of air power'.[83] In 1935, he had created a high-powered committee under Wilberg to formulate a Luftwaffe air doctrine. The result of their deliberations was Luftwaffe Regulation 16: Luftkriegführung (The Conduct of Aerial War). It not only stressed the primary importance of air power in an offensive role to 'break down the will of the enemy', but an ominously prescient paragraph that would come back to haunt Göring's legacy began: 'One can only be an air force leader who fully understands the demands of air warfare.'[84]

Just at the time when the Luftwaffe was stretching its wings and learning to fly, Wever had given it a stern reminder that it should not lose contact with ground forces and should at all times work 'in direct support of the army or navy' as required. Nevertheless, at the centre of this new doctrine was the sense that the Luftwaffe should be capable of taking on a strategic role, i.e. to launch attacks from the air designed to achieve a military victory all on their own; not to terrorise a civilian population, but to 'attack the sources of enemy [governmental, industrial and military] power'.[85] It does, however, advocate reciprocal action if German civilian areas ever came under bombing attack. Unlike the Nazi leadership, Wever eschewed the idea

77

of 'total war' and clearly laid out his ideas on the limits of warfare. Indeed, the concept of terror-bombing was tested by the Italian Air Force when it bombed Barcelona in March 1938 and was found to instil not so much terror, as a stiff resistance from the enraged civilian population.[86]

War games played a significant part in Wever's staff training and development programme which, initially at least, concentrated on scenarios involving France and Czechoslovakia and involved the Luftwaffe in both strategic and tactical roles. It was his objective to 'release [the air arm] from the straightjacket of tactical employment', and demonstrate to senior army officers that the Luftwaffe could operate on a strategic level.[87] He used the Reichswehr Winter War Games of 1934 in the Behrenstrasse during a simulated attack on France to strike deep into French territory and hit Paris and industrial centres with bombers. The assumption was that the French would sue for peace under such an assault, but the referees, not sharing Wever's optimism, thought differently. Wever challenged their assumption that the attacks would result in decimation of his bomber fleets, but his faith in strategic bombing, while still strong, had benefited from a dose of reality. The next year's war games saw him repeat his strategy, but with heavy fighter support for the bombers. This time he employed dive-bombers with devastating effect but, while making a point, was unable to alter the mindset of many Army commanders, who feared losing control of the air arm completely.[88] Göring was happy to allow the Luftwaffe to edge away from army control and after the war claimed at the Nuremberg War Trials that it had been his intention, right from the start, to prioritise the creation of an air force with strategic capabilities.[89]

While Wever is remembered as an advocate of the heavy bomber concept, he by no means ignored the ground-support role of the Luftwaffe, which was extensively explored in his war games and underwent significant development. He opposed placing air units under the direct control of the army, but to facilitate greater understanding between the services he arranged for air liaison officers, *FliegerVerbundungsOffiziere,* to be attached to army corps and act as forward intelligence. These officers, he believed, would play a vital role and he urged the highest attention be given to their training and communication skills to 'deepen our understanding of inter-service cooperation'.[90]

'Smiling' Albert Kesselring was born in Bavaria on 30 November 1885 and joined the German Army in 1904. While garrisoned at Metz, he had become interested in the idea of using balloons for reconnaissance purposes. He was forced into an arranged marriage which proved to be unhappy for him and resulted in his absorption in military duties. During the First World War he was decorated with the Iron Cross and transferred to the General Staff in 1917. After the war he served in various capacities within the armed forces and gained a reputation for his organisational and diplomatic skills. In modern parlance, he was a 'people person'.[91] At this time he developed an enthusiasm for right-wing nationalist policies and, in 1933, reluctantly accepted appointment as head of the Department of Administration at the Reich Commissariat for Aviation, having had his request to remain in the army turned down. In keeping with his new duties, and at the age of 48, he learned to fly. When Wever was killed, Kesselring was elevated to Chief of Staff of the new Luftwaffe, but although an able administrator, he lacked Wever's breadth of vision. His achievements in office included the creation of a parachute corps and a radical overhaul of Luftwaffe administration, but the central issue during his time as Chief of Staff was his feuding with Milch. As an opening shot across Kesselring's bows, Milch had demanded that Kesselring court martial the commander of the 3rd Training Group, Hans Jeschonnek, for the loss of a number of bombers which, Milch claimed, had been ordered to fly too low. Kesselring found the idea absurd and rudely implied that Milch should turn his attention elsewhere. He began agitating, with many of his colleagues on the General Staff, to have Milch's powers restricted to civil aviation, but he could not match Milch for plots and intrigue. Kesselring, a lifelong military man, admired Milch's exceptional knowledge and experience of the technical aspects of aviation, but was nevertheless disdainful of his lack of military background and command experience which, he felt, left him unfit for the high office to which he had been assigned for political reasons. Predictably though, Kesselring was soon worn down by Milch's constant machinations and requested a transfer at the earliest opportunity. He went on to command Luftflotte 2 during the Battle of Britain and later, after the war, was charged with, and found guilty of, war crimes. His death sentence was commuted to life imprisonment, but he was released in 1952 and died in 1960.

When Kesselring had stepped into Wever's vacant shoes with enhanced powers, Milch, who was an intriguer and manipulator of Machiavellian proportions and considered himself to be Göring's de facto deputy, bridled at being overlooked and the relationship with Kesselring soon became toxic. He had always been somewhat paranoid about his his Jewish background; fearing that at some point it would be used against him, he surrounded himself with sycophantic acolytes, a practice that was by no means uncommon in the Luftwaffe. Göring began to act against Milch by introducing constraints on his authority and power. When Kesselring grew tired of the incessant intrigue and resigned in 1937, it proved difficult to find anyone willing to take his place and work with Milch. Eventually Hans Jurgen Stumpff took on the job, but without enthusiasm. When it looked as if Stumpff was being given preferential treatment, Milch tried to resign but Göring, wishing to avoid scrutiny and embarrassment at his handling of the situation, at first tried flattery to mollify Milch and would not allow it, but to no effect. Nor would he tolerate Milch feigning illness as an excuse to return to civilian life – but he did suggest that he would have no objection to him committing suicide.[92] It was in the same year that Milch, together with Stumpff and Udet, made official visits to inspect the French Armée de l'Aire and the RAF, where they met Air Marshal Dowding. Milch boasted of Luftwaffe prowess and derided British radar research. His indiscretions cost him dearly as Göring finally lost patience with him and stripped him of much of his authority. In early June 1940, it was Milch who, when surveying the ruins of Dunkirk, was the strongest advocate of an immediate attack on the British mainland by securing the coastal airfields of Manston and Hawkinge and using them as a gateway through which to pour troops. Securing Dover would then open up a port for heavy armour. Had Göring been on better terms with Milch, he might well have responded in a more positive manner, but under the circumstances he dismissed the idea as 'nonsense'. Milch was arrested by the Allies on 4 May 1945 as he tried to flee Germany and was tried for war crimes by a US military tribunal in Nuremberg in 1947. He was convicted of participating in the ill-treatment and use of forced labour, the deportation, murder, extermination, enslavement, deportation and imprisonment of civilians. He was sentenced to life imprisonment in Landsberg Prison but had his sentence commuted to fifteen years imprisonment. He was released in June 1954 and died in 1972.

Kesselring had been propelled to high office at a critical time for Luftwaffe development. On 3 June 1936, Wever was returning in haste from a lecture given to cadets in Dresden to attend the funeral of the First World War hero Karl von Litzman; catastrophically, he failed to unlock the switch for the aileron controls of the Heinkel He 70 D-1 D-UZON before take-off.

The aircraft tried and failed to get lift as it reached the end of the runway. It crashed in flames with a full fuel tank, killing Wever and his crewman. Upon receipt of the news, Göring is said to have 'broken down and wept like a child'.[93] It was a tragedy for the Luftwaffe, but Wever had left it in 'excellent shape', poised to become a 'world-class air force with first-rate equipment'.[94] The death of Wever, who had really personified the modern Luftwaffe, left a gaping hole in the leadership that no single person was able to fill and which opened up the door to factionalism and in-fighting as rivals jostled for position to claim their patch of turf. Göring rejected Blomberg's preferred candidate to replace Wever and chose Kesselring instead. Milch disapproved of the appointment and set out to make Kesselring's tenure as difficult as possible. Kesselring, a 'highly-intelligent officer', was by no means a poor first replacement, but he lacked the authority to stand up either to Milch, who saw him as a barrier to his own aggrandisement, or Göring, who was starting to manoeuvre his personal friends, such as Ernst Udet, into senior positions for which they had neither aptitude nor credentials. As far back as September 1917, Udet had been with Göring and the von Richthofen brothers at a party to celebrate Bruno Lörzer's award of the Pour le Merite at the Bristol Hotel in Berlin.

Ernst Udet was born in Frankfurt am Main on 26 April 1896. He had been fascinated by aviation since his youth, joining the Munich Aero Club when he was 12, after building and crashing his own glider. He was too short to join the German Army in 1914 and so became first a motor-cycle despatch rider and then, after taking private flying lessons, joined the Imperial German Air Service as a pilot, becoming a *geschwader* commander and then a member of Baron von Richthofen's 'Flying Circus'. After the war he gained a reputation as a stunt pilot as far away as Buenos Aires and later appeared in several films for Universal Studios in California. He joined the Nazi Party in 1933 and researched the concept of dive-bombers with money provided by the party. In 1936, Göring brought him into the Luftwaffe in an official capacity as Colonel and Inspector of Fighter and Stuka pilots. He accepted the invitation without enthusiasm and, as he had feared, the administrative duties of his new post bored him. Only four months later he replaced Wimmer as Chief Technical Officer. Göring had never liked Wimmer and the appointment of Udet was pure cronyism. It was a spectacularly bad appointment. Udet lacked the maturity, patience and self-discipline for such a role and he developed an addiction for alcohol as a release.[95] It was not uncommon for his department staff to be unable to contact him for weeks on end, delaying important decisions or leaving them to be made by subordinates in his absence. Without leadership his department became 'a hotbed of in-fighting and political intrigue', exhibiting the worst of the characteristics that, to a greater or lesser extent, pervaded much of the rest of the Luftwaffe. After the failure of the Luftwaffe to subdue Fighter Command in 1940/41, Göring scapegoated Udet, who committed suicide.

The atmosphere of harmony and quiet competence that Wever had brought to the Luftwaffe was becoming polluted with politics and cronyism at the highest levels. It should be pointed out, however, that while the lower levels of administration were to some extent factionalised, it was the feuding at the top of the command structure in the Luftwaffe that threatened to do the real damage. Fortunately, the General Staff traditions that the Luftwaffe had inherited from the army gave ballast and ensured that the day-to-day business conducted by the middle management was still carried out with efficiency and professionalism, but it was difficult to create the sort of administrative coherence and strategic breadth of vision required in such a short time and with such inadequate leadership.[96]

In 1934, specifications had been published for a whole new range of high-performance military aircraft which included three heavy-bomber prototypes, nicknamed the 'Ural Bomber', capable of striking targets some 2,000km from base. Wever had supported the idea with a seven-year development programme, but for practical reasons only production of medium bombers got the immediate go-ahead. These bombers were the Dornier Do 17, the Junkers Ju 86 (later the Ju88) and the Heinkel He 111, while a new concept of the heavy fighter-bomber emerged in the shape of the Messerschmitt Bf 110. A new fighter, the Bf 109, was already in test flight by 1935. Development of the 'Ural Bomber' was held up until development plans could be set in place for the new more powerful engines required to cope with a ten-man crew, along with four machine guns and a 1,600kg bomb load. The nine-cylinder, radial, air-cooled Bramo 322 H2 engines of the original design, with its meagre 600 horsepower, did not even come close to being adequate. When a Dornier Do 19 prototype flew for the first time in September 1936 it turned out to be 'a tremendous disappointment'.[97] The Junkers Ju 89 prototype fared better, but was still poorly served by its Daimler-Benz DB 600 engines. Even Wever had started to lose faith in the whole heavy bomber programme before his untimely death, and although it still had support from Milch and Wimmer, who backed it as a long-term solution, it was in crisis until new engine technology was developed. Meanwhile, Wimmer had won support from Göring for a heavy, two-seater, long-range fighter to provide close escort for long-range bombers and carry out their own bombing actions, but on closer examination it became clear that no single aircraft could combine all these roles. A modified specification, however, saw development of the Bf 110 'Zerstörer'.

Kesselring initially carried on in Wever's footsteps, overlooking his latter-day misgivings with the heavy bomber concept, giving it wholehearted support despite the failure of early trials and, with Sperrle's encouragement, lobbied for a resumption of research into a second generation of four-engine aircraft that would overcome the failures of, and build on the experience gained from, the 'Ural Bomber' programme. What emerged was the Heinkel He 177 project, but the time lost with earlier models meant that there was no prospect of the He 177 coming off the production lines before 1942 at the earliest. Had it ever been built, the He 177 bomber would have been capable of travelling the long distances needed to strike decisively at the enemy's centres of power but, once again, its design was bedevilled by several technical problems. It required speed to escape fighter attack, long range to strike a distant enemy's centres of power, and the capability of flying at high altitude to evade many of the enemy's defences. Powerful engines, accurate bombing systems, and navigation and communication equipment were all crucial components of such an aircraft, and all integrated into an effective airframe. It was clear that something would be required to fill the bomber gap until 1942, so Göring authorised the mass production of a large fleet of high-performance medium bombers such as the Junkers Ju 88.

Over and above the problems of heavy bomber design and construction, the whole strategic bomber concept was clouded by the much smaller but intractable issue of poor horizontal bomb-aiming equipment. The Goerz-Vizier 219 and Loftfernrohr 7/7d were hopelessly inaccurate and even by 1937, the new generation of bombers could only place 2 per cent of bombs within a 200 metre circle from a height of 4,000 metres. An alternative bomb-delivery method was the dive-bomber, demonstrations of which had greatly impressed Felmy when watching Curtiss F8C and Goshawk F11C dive-bombing demonstrations on his visits to the United States. There were, however, grave concerns over the ability of airframes to absorb the stresses of diving at high speed, and the vulnerability of aircraft to ground fire when flying so low. Indeed, Udet was nearly killed when a prototype Heinkel He 181 dive-bomber in which he was flying almost broke up in a diving demonstration on 27 June 1934.[98] Ironically, it was Udet who remained an enthusiast and rescued the dive-bomber idea from obscurity when he took over from Wimmer as Chief Technical Officer, responsible for aircraft and weapons development. Wimmer had lost confidence in the heavy dive-bomber, and been urged to cancel plans for its development by Freiherr Wolfram von Richthofen who, in another ironic twist, would lead the specialist dive-bomber VIII Fliegerkorps in the Battle of Britain. Udet brought the programme back to life but by this time, through absence and over-indulgence in drugs and alcohol, had completely lost control of his department.[99] As a result, plans for the next generation of aircraft stagnated as critical decisions were deferred.

It was not only Udet, however; many in the senior administrative ranks of the Luftwaffe had little understanding of, or were even familiar with the fundamental concepts of, air doctrine. Only the rare exceptions such as Wever bucked that trend. Upon joining the Luftwaffe, he had immediately won the affection and respect of his colleagues. With his affable nature, he had been 'the only General Staff Chief who was able to get along well with both Göring and Milch'.[100] It was Wever who had changed Luftwaffe philosophy and started to create a sense of what an independent air service could achieve. He brought a new ethos and had laid the foundations upon which to build a unique tradition. It was not so much that Luftwaffe air policy underwent any fundamental change after Wever's death, rather that it lost a strong, charismatic, wholly competent and irreplaceable leader. The resulting power vacuum was quickly filled by the opportunistic Göring who, ever willing to dabble with no purpose other than to strengthen his own position, instead of calming things, simply took Kesselring's side and raised his status above that of his old adversary Milch – but not before Kesselring had seen the light and requested a transfer to remove himself from what, for him, was an unhappy situation. He had no interest in plots or machinations and just wanted to get on with the job which Milch, bloodied but unbowed, would now make as difficult as possible. Kesselring's brief to stay on the General Staff had begun with his reluctant transfer from the army in 1933 at Stumpff's insistence, and his time there had been uncomfortable as he tried to remain aloof from politics. His transfer to Luftflotte 1 in Dresden came as a relief, but during his final days he had achieved one notable accord with Milch when they had both agreed to cancel any further development of the first generation of Wever's 'Ural Bombers', the prototypes Do 19 and Ju 89.

When several top men such as Colonel Afred Jodl and Leutnantgeneral Franz Halder passed on the offer to replace Kesselring and work with Milch, it fell to Stumpff, who was eventually persuaded to take over. In a muddled attempt to sort out the administrative mess resulting from the Milch-Wever split, Göring divided the Air Ministry into military and civilian branches, putting Stumpff in charge of OKL (the General Staff Oberkommando der Luftwaffe), and Milch as head of the General Air Office as well as Inspector General of the Luftwaffe. Milch was incensed that Stumpff should have the greater role and offered his resignation, but Göring refused to accept it.[101] For his part, Stumpff was aghast at the 'power-grabbing' that was going on, but his attempts to bring some order to the command structure met with fierce opposition from Milch. The organisational chaos that ensued caused instability within the General Staff for some months until Stumpff, 'battered by infighting at the highest levels', stepped down and was replaced on the 1 February 1939 by Oberst Hans Jeschonnek.[102]

The Prussian Jeschonnek was born on 9 April 1899 and volunteered for military service at the age of 15; in 1917 he received pilot training. After the war he travelled widely in Europe studying aircraft development as part of von Seeckt's secret project. His knowledge and experience saw him promoted to Felmy's Air Inspectorate in 1928 and later as adjutant to Milch. He was 'an extremely bright young officer who impressed all who came into contact with him with his military bearing'.[103] He enjoyed rapid promotion in the early 1930s but seems to have grievously offended Milch, who tried to have him court martialled and might have succeeded had not Kesselring, in an early bruising encounter with Milch, championed his cause. Jeschonnek was unerringly hostile to Milch thereafter. When he was catapulted into the role of Luftwaffe Chief of Staff at an early age, Jeschonnek struggled to hold his ground in debate with subordinate, but older and more experienced, officers. While he had been appointed with the full and enthusiastic support of Göring, who was said to have welcomed Jeschonnek as a more malleable personality susceptible to manipulation and a foil against more conservative elements, he was scorned by the cadre of Göring's acolytes who surrounded the Luftwaffe leader. It was almost as if Jeschonnek had been put in place by Göring to 'neutralise' the office of

Chief of Staff as a source of resistance and aggravation. His stiff military persona had hidden an inner vulnerability which was inexorably exposed from the Battle of Britain onwards as the war became ever more protracted. His whole philosophy had been strongly influenced by Army Regulation 487, around the concept of a short intense war leading to rapid annihilation of the enemy, and by 1943, that was obviously not happening. He was acutely aware of his own contribution to failure, especially after crushing Allied bombing attacks on the rocket base at Peenemünde on the night of 17 August. The next morning a note was found next to Jeschonnek's body and the pistol with which he had shot himself: 'I can no longer work together with the Reichsmarschall.'[104]

Up until the outbreak of war, the organisational structure of the Luftwaffe continued to be 'full of compromises and thinly-veiled rivalries', with Milch and Jeschonnek high up on the scale of hostility towards each other, and Milch definitely not in Göring's good books.[105] In the few short years of its existence, not surprisingly given all of its structural issues and lack of tradition, the Luftwaffe had more than its fair share of reorganisation as it struggled to define its role in a country lurching ever closer to war.[106]

In 1936, extensive trials were carried out at Rechlin to assess the qualities of the new range of medium bombers coming off the production lines. Two of them: the Dornier Do 17 and the Heinkel He 111, were selected for further development. At this stage, the Junkers Ju 88 was not yet ready for inclusion in the trials. Fighter aircraft were given lower priority, but the Messerschmitt Bf 109, with its numerous radical ideas, was appraised alongside the Heinkel He 112, and preferred in spite of its manufacturer, Willi Messerschmitt, having a poor historic relationship with the Air Ministry. Milch had neglected the Messerschmitt's Bayerische Flugzeugwerke, one of the smaller manufacturers, having held a grudge ever since he was nearly killed in one of their BFW M.20 aircraft. Unsurprisingly, in the dive-bomber category, the Junkers Ju 87 was chosen ahead of the Heinkel He 118 in which Udet had almost been killed. Despite the potential of new aircraft and availability of new finance, the shortage of raw materials and technical problems with new models forced Milch to concentrate production, for the moment, on tried and tested – at times obsolete – types as an interim measure until newer models were ready to take their place.

At this pivotal moment for Luftwaffe development, the Spanish Civil War broke out. On 26 July 1936, Hitler received a delegation at Beyreuth from General Francisco Franco y Bohamonde, with an urgent request for air transport to get his Moroccan foreign legion troops across the Straits of Gibraltar to fight against the socialist government of the Second Spanish Republic. With his troops stuck in Morocco and all transport facilities under the control of the Republicans, Franco had appealed to Germany and Italy for help. Hitler immediately, and without consultation with his Foreign Ministry, promised assistance to pre-empt any Italian involvement. As early as 31 July, he sent twenty Junkers Ju 52 transport but, unwilling to be drawn into a war that might escalate beyond Spanish borders, he was careful to ensure that the aircraft were flown by 'volunteer Lufthansa pilots'. Six He 51s were assigned to act as escort to the transports.

Apart from political advantage, which Hitler was always swift to exploit, here was an important opportunity to put into practice all the military theories that had been carefully drawn up in areas such as leadership and commitment, as well as a chance for practical demonstrations of new equipment. All officers and men sent to Spain were instructed to keep complete records of their experiences and submit them for analysis to Luftwaffe headquarters in Berlin. Preparations were made for frequent visits to the combat zones by Luftwaffe headquarters' staff. Returning officers were to be assigned as instructors so that their knowledge and experience could be widely disseminated.

In what was an impressive and unprecedented action, the first German intervention was the transportation of more than 13,000 rebel troops and 270 tons of equipment from Morocco in the Junkers Ju 52 transports, flying under the Lufthansa flag, over several weeks in the summer of 1936 to relieve beleaguered forces around Seville, Granada and Cadiz in a move that transformed Franco's fortunes. The air-lift, carried out under strict security to avoid international repercussions, was given the codename 'Magic Fire' (Feuerzauber), and assistance was nominally rendered under a Spanish organisation, 'Hispano-Marroqu de Transportes Tetuan-Sevilla' to circumvent a formal agreement that European governments would not intervene in the war. This airlift of so many troops in such a short time was 'one of the decisive military operations of the ... war', and 'one of the most important developments in military air power'.[107] Initially, all other active participation by German personnel in Spain was discouraged, but inevitably 'mission creep' took over and it became necessary to formalise some sort of operational control. To avoid international condemnation, German aircraft had been designated as commercial transports, and crews, dressed in civilian clothes, had been 'volunteered' by their officers while others had 'resigned' from active service and been posted to the reserves before being sent. All were sworn to strict secrecy and sent to Spain ostensibly on a 'training mission' with the 'Union Travel Society' (Reisegeschaft Union) under the command of a fluent Spanish-speaker Major Alexander von Scheele.[108] The whole German intervention at this stage was essentially based on a personal understanding between Hitler and Franco.

Wimmer supervised the aid mission and Lieutenant Colonel Walter Warlimont joined Franco's General Staff as liaison on 1 October to coordinate military aid and act as military adviser. A few fighter aircraft and some heavy guns were sent as a second wave of materiel support. When Soviet forces entered the war on the side of the Spanish government, Hitler authorised the setting up, under the code name 'Winter Exercise Hansa' of the 'Condor Legion', a fully equipped and coordinated task force whose pilots were no longer 'volunteers' but Luftwaffe officers. Daily transports flew men and supplies into Spain from Augsburg. These German air operations in Spain were under the command of Generalleutnant Hugo Sperrle, who reported directly to Franco, with Lieutnant Colonel Holle as his Chief of Staff. German intelligence chief Admiral Wilhelm Canaris went to Spain on 30 October to discuss further assistance, with the proviso that German units must be led by German commanders. In addition, he made it clear that all German pilots, anti-aircraft and air communications units must be integrated into a German air force corps in Spain. The new Luftwaffe policy was to send only its most promising officers and crews to Spain, where they remained from three to seven months so that as many men as possible could gain valuable combat experience, but there were never more than around 5,000 at any one time. The usual tour of service in Spain was one year or less. All the prototypes of important aircraft later employed by Germany at the start of the Second World War were tried out in Spain.

Sperrle organised the 'Condor Legion' into bomber, fighter and naval air squadrons. There was a great deal of experimentation in all aspects of aerial warfare in this, the first test of Luftwaffe doctrine in action. Many of the Luftwaffe tactics developed in Spain went on to form the backbone of Luftwaffe operations during the Second World War. The Luftwaffe did not have it all their own way, however. When Franco tried to take Madrid, German fighters were unable to establish air superiority over Russian aircraft and suffered a collapse of morale. German bombers failed to hit the Russian air base at Alcala de Henares and losses forced the abandonment of daylight bombing raids.[109] Sperrle sent urgent requests to Berlin for more bombers which resulted in the arrival of Ju 87 dive-bombers under the command of, then Leutnant, von Richthofen, who became Sperrle's Chief of Staff in place of Alexander Holle. Sperrle and Richthofen did not like each other. Richthofen, whom Sperrle considered to be a 'ruthless snob', disapproved of Sperrle's 'coarse wit and table manners'. They were, however, able to work together in a professional and efficient way and Richthofen's popularity with Franco, stemming from their mutual contempt for communism, made him a valuable liaison tool. It was a bonus, too, that Richthofen was fluent in both Spanish and Italian. Back in Berlin he had been Udet's right-hand man and his transfer to Spain had left Udet rudderless which, for a man in his position, was a catastrophe.[110]

Meanwhile, the Soviet Union had sent forty-two Ilyushin-15 biplane fighters and thirty-one fighters to help the Republican forces. They proved to be technically superior to the Luftwaffe Heinkel He 51 aircraft, but the quality of German pilots more than compensated. The first Condor Legion aircraft arrived in November 1936 and, on the 26th, launched a concentrated attack of thirty-four Ju 52s, led by Sperrle himself, on Cartagena to try and disrupt the Soviet supply chain. Sperrle later led successful attacks on the city of Madrid, but it was only later, when the Luftwaffe officials finally realised the quantity and apparent quality of Soviet aircraft, that they decided to supply the Condor Legion with the new Bf 109 fighters and Ju 87 dive-bombers, after which the tide started to turn in Franco's favour. Early models of the He 111 and Do 17 as bombers and reconnaissance were also brought into play, with the He111 proving to be more efficient and reliable. All operations were bedevilled by poor intelligence resulting in bombing raids, ostensibly against troop concentrations in towns and villages such as Durango, killing many hundreds of civilians instead while the soldiers had moved elsewhere, and at Orchandiano, where German aircraft attacked 'friendly' rebel forces. The defending Basque Republicans had only a tiny air force which allowed the Nationalists to utilise their Spanish-crewed Heinkel He 51s, based at Saragossa, as ground-attack aircraft. A few of the first Messerschmitt Bf 109-Bs had also arrived but were only just being made operational. Taking advantage of the dearth of aerial opposition, Ju 52s and He 111s with SW.81s, operating singly, bombed the town of Durango in relays over a period of many hours on 31 March, which had a devastating effect on the defending troops.

Richthofen was quick to appreciate the value of air support for ground forces. His early antipathy towards the Ju 87, clearly stated in a memo of 9 June 1936 where he recommended abandonment of its development, changed to wholehearted support after seeing what a demoralising effect it had on enemy forces as a ground-attack aircraft.[111] Devastating combined bomber-fighter operations in support of rebels at the Battle of Brunete on 25 July were seen as a turning point in the war. There is no doubt that the best-remembered Luftwaffe action in the war was the infamous terror-bombing of the undefended town of Guernica, which killed around 300 civilians. The main bombing attack was by three squadrons of Ju 52 bombers, after which Bf 109 fighters sprayed cannon fire on refugees fleeing the town. The Spanish rebel commanders were incensed by the attack and insisted that their allies cease any further attacks on population centres.

As an example of the type of sophisticated military operation launched by the Germans, during the first week of July 1937, they made a spectacular coordinated attack on Spanish Republican forces at the Battle of Brunete, about fifteen miles west of Madrid. Messerschmitt Bf 109B fighters flew top-cover to maintain air superiority while Heinkel He 111 bombers attacked both strategic and tactical targets. At the same time, Heinkel He 51 biplanes flew in below 500ft, strafing and bombing troops and anti-aircraft batteries. The biplanes came in waves of nine-across formations, wingtip-to-wingtip, each carrying six 22lb fragmentation bombs and dropping them simultaneously. The resulting carnage demolished the morale of the surviving troops. So effective was the onslaught that by the time the Heinkels completed their runs, the attacking Spanish Nationalist troops were within hand-grenade range of the Republican defenders.

As the tide of war turned against government troops, the Condor Legion pilots won increasing dominance of the air. A dawn raid in Catalonia on 6 February 1939 saw the destruction of twenty-five Curtis and Rata aircraft on the ground, which effectively ended Republican resistance in the province. On 27 February, Britain and France officially recognised Franco as the leader of Spain, but the war was not yet over. German aircraft attacked Toledo and put the last Republican forces to flight. The war officially ended on 29 March and the Condor Legion returned to Germany a month later. During the war, the Luftwaffe had learned a great deal about the technical qualities of its aircraft and the most effective tactics in combat as well as giving invaluable experience to a group of pilots who would go on to play pivotal roles as Luftwaffe leaders during the Second World War.

Valuable tactical lessons learned during the Spanish Civil War were, however, to some extent balanced by erroneous conclusions concerning doctrine. German bombers and reconnaissance aircraft had often been deployed without fighter escort and had not suffered greatly as a consequence, which led some analysts to believe that well-armed bombers could defend themselves in daylight bombing operations.[112] Fighter ace Werner Lützow claimed, however, that 'slight losses' were the result of 'inadequate training and erratic leadership of enemy airmen', meaning that attention should be given to improving defensive armaments, a concept incorporated into the design of the Ju 88 which was still very much at the testing stage.[113] The Bf 110 had not been used in Spain and was therefore unable to benefit from combat experience. The Bf 109, however, showed the need for enhanced cockpit armour and heavier guns. Analysis of Spanish Civil War air operations shows that when Soviet Tupolev SB bombers were intercepted by fighters such as the Italian Fiats they were able to avoid loss, but it was a different matter altogether when they met the Bf 109s. On the other hand, the German Dornier Do 17 likewise got a wake-up call when confronted by Soviet Polikarpov I-16s. Observers noted that 'the peacetime theory of the complete invulnerability of the modern type of bombardment aeroplane no longer holds'.[114] German tactics of close air support were in evidence but these were in no way revolutionary, having been part of German air doctrine, albeit for many years in the absence of an air force, since 1917. Fighter-to-fighter encounters took place and showed clearly that the higher-performance aircraft had not gone beyond human endurance in their aerial jousting as some thought they might. Pilots still continued to function efficiently at high speeds and in the tight manoeuvres into which the enhanced performance of their aircraft took them without 'blacking out' under the g-forces.

Spain gave few opportunities to evaluate strategic bombing given the paucity of such operations, but tactical ground-support bombing was scrutinised and found to be very ineffective. The bomber Group KG 88 had seen action over Cartagena and Alicante, but most raids were carried out at night to avoid interdiction and this led to a realisation that crews, trained by day, were quite unprepared for night missions. Once this information was evaluated at Luftwaffe headquarters in Berlin, night navigation, instrument-flying and night-landing were given high priority in the training schedule. Where any bombing had been carried out, it was concluded that the most important consideration was for the bomber group to remain in tight formation, both in the approach to and over the target, to ensure maximum protection against enemy fighters. Where fighter escorts were deployed there had been severe problems of coordination, both in locating rendezvous points and maintaining effective contact during the mission given the disparity between cruising speed of the Ju 52s and the much faster fighters. The He 111s, when they came into service, were much better able to protect themselves from fighter attack and convinced Luftwaffe analysts that they could do so without their own fighter escort, therefore less emphasis was placed on bomber-fighter coordination than should have been the case. This was to have significant consequences during the Battle of Britain in 1940 when the Luftwaffe were forced to abandon daytime bombing. The experience gained in strategic bomber deployment in Spain was overall negative, except for a few positive results derived from night operations.[115]

The experience of tactical bombing, by contrast, brought a great deal of practical results. At first, ground support played a minor role, but that changed when the Nationalists opened their northern front in the spring of 1937. It was here that the ground-support tactics devised by von Richthofen, which came to characterise Blitzkrieg, were first employed. The first attack would be against enemy positions just prior to the ground assault, followed by attacks on specific pockets of resistance and reserve troop positions over several days. The bombers were required to be precise in their navigation and bomb aiming to avoid their own troops, something in which they were not always successful, but with experience came proficiency. Operations at Brunete were the first to employ fighter aircraft preceding the bombers to suppress ground fire and engage any enemy fighters in the vicinity, but in any case, the short time the bombers spent over enemy lines made it relatively safe compared to deep penetration bomber missions.

The most revolutionary new concept in air doctrine to emerge from the Spanish Civil War was undoubtedly the use of dive-bombers, an idea that had originated in the US, albeit against naval targets, and brought to Germany by Udet. At first the results of Ju 87 and Hs 123 bombing at Teruel was not encouraging, but again, it was simply a matter of experience overcoming initial failures. The concept of dive-bombing so gripped the Luftwaffe imagination that after Spain, dive-bombing characteristics became an important part of bomber design, the Ju88 in particular undergoing extensive modification in this respect, which may well have contributed to the unbalanced nature of Luftwaffe resources as it went to war in 1939.

Cooperation between air and ground forces in Spain yielded a wealth of new and extremely valuable experience.[116] At first, communications between the two had hindered progress, and resulted in a number of instances of bombing of 'friendly' forces, but once this had been identified as a major obstacle there was a focus on liaison and the development of an understanding by each of the role and methods of the other. The vast majority of fighter action had been in close support of ground attacks and it was no surprise that von Richthofen, in particular, was to add his powerful voice in support of 'close-support tactics at all costs' in future debate over air doctrine when he returned to Germany. His 'ruthless' approach and 'demanding' character allied to his reputation had given von Richthofen 'influence vastly exceeding his rank', and Jeschonnek was said to be 'unable to stand up to his dominant personality' as the Luftwaffe was led 'down the path of close air support at the expense of strategic aerial warfare'.[117]

The new generation of Luftwaffe aircraft that emerged in 1935 brought their own problems to the factory floor. Constant modifications introduced to keep up with the rapidly evolving technical developments caused delays as retooling was carried out. The more sophisticated production methods required an improvement in skills, but the already limited supply of qualified personnel was impacted by many being called up for military service. German propaganda glossed over these issues and even at the highest levels of command, the under-production of finished aircraft was not fully appreciated. The issue was somewhat ameliorated after the Anschluss when Austrian workers were drafted into the factories, and later the invasion of Czechoslovakia had a similar impact on production for the same reasons.

During Stumpff's time as Chief of staff, Göring had consolidated his position as head of the Luftwaffe with a number of radical administrative changes. Three offices were removed entirely from the Air Ministry and brought under his direct control. General Ritter Robert von Greim at the Personnel Office, General Otto Günther Ruedel at the Office of the Chief of Air Defence and Udet in the Technical Office now became 'vassal' departments. The debilitating factor was that none of the departments was of particular interest to Göring and he paid them little attention, which had the effect of 'cutting them adrift' from the main Luftwaffe organisation leading to 'command fragmentation and paralysis of many important functions'.[118] From a position of singular control enjoyed by Milch on his appointment, there were now five competing centres of power all subordinated to Göring. Udet's Technical Office was enlarged in 1938 to become the Office of Supply and Procurement responsible for aircraft and weapons development, procurement and supply to the Luftwaffe. It is almost beyond credence that such an office should have been allowed to operate under the command of Udet, a man addicted to 'wild parties, drunken sprees, drug abuse and womanising'.[119]

In early 1939, before Jeschonnek's unexpected elevation to Chief of Staff, OKL, the High Command of the Luftwaffe was separated almost entirely from the Reichs Aviation Ministry. This further marginalised Milch from operational matters and put the whole General Staff directly under Göring's control. Stumpff had been too weak to resist Göring's 'hoovering up' of responsibilities and suffered the ironic humiliation of being transferred to the Office of Air Defence which was under Milch, more, one suspects, for Göring's amusement rather than for any other good reason.

When he took up the reins on 1 February 1939, far from pouring oil on troubled waters, Jeschonnek had 'an overwhelmingly negative' influence.[120] Right from the start, he was bedevilled by the attitude of those over whom he had leapfrogged and who subsequently resisted his authority in small but not imperceptible ways. Being Wever's opposite in terms of affability and man-management and 'lacking an understanding of human nature', Jeschonnek struggled to earn the loyalty and affection of his immediate subordinates, many of whom were older and more experienced than he, that would have made his job so much easier.[121] His confidence was further eroded by none of Göring's immediate clique liking him, but in that regard he fared no worse than Milch, who was equally disliked by them. Men such as von Brautitsch and Teske, Göring's adjutants, would actually, on occasion, pass on Göring's orders directly to various commands, bypassing Jeschonnek completely. This was how the Luftwaffe functioned in 1939 and it begs the question of to what degree Hitler was aware of its dysfunctionality as he prepared for the biggest gamble of his life – up to that moment – by invading Poland.

Jeschonnek's main focus, one might almost say obsession, was on developing aircraft with dive-bombing capabilities in support of Blitzkrieg strategy. He was totally committed to the idea of a short war and brushed aside demands by Chief of the Luftwaffe Organisational Branch, Hermann Plocher, for 'a build-up in depth for both aircraft and personnel to ... replace losses in combat'.[122] Jeschonnek turned a deaf ear to Training Office demands for more pilot schools which were already short of staff, many of whom had been transferred to active units. There is no doubt that Jeschonnek's view was vindicated by the stunning successes of the French campaign, but it had deprived the Luftwaffe of the chance to build a strategic capability and it was this imbalance that was to prove so critical in the Battle of Britain. The crucial element of Blitzkrieg warfare was to probe for the weakest points of an enemy position then attack those points with concentrated force using all available resources including, according to Jeschonnek, all reserve units, in a drive to win a swift and crushing victory. In this he had been clearly influenced by Douhet's idea that 'holding forces in reserve exemplified the outdated and defensive thinking of surface commanders'. He did not expect, nor did he plan for, an extended war. He was 'putting most of his eggs in one basket', which was at odds with Kesselring and Sperrle's broader views. The longer any war went on, the more the Luftwaffe would be forced into a strategic role to attack the enemy at its industrial and military heart, at which point the lack of a heavy bomber would prove to be of significant importance. Udet shared Jeschonnek's enthusiasm for dive-bombers and indeed may have been the source of Jeschonnek's fervour in the first place, but his choice of designs to develop resulted in three types in particular that were quite unsuitable and failed to go into production despite heavy investment. Development of his heavily-armed ground-attack Hs 129 was particularly wasteful when it proved to be under-powered and unstable in flight. Even the Ju88, which was not a bad aircraft despite Junkers seriously overstating its performance when lobbying for the contract, suffered so many modifications that it was almost tantamount to a complete redesign, and serious delays due to Udet's insistence that a dive-bombing capability be built into the design. The delays resulted in far fewer Ju 88s being available to the Luftwaffe in the summer of 1940, in their primary role as medium bomber, than might have been the case.

The Anschluss in March 1938 had exposed weaknesses in the Luftwaffe system when it proved to be sluggish in what was a highly mobile military environment. As a consequence, Göring made more administrative changes which came into effect in early 1939. Air Fleets (Luftflotte) were created under leaders such as Kesselring and Sperrle. Each Luftflotte had at least one fighter wing (Luftgau), two bomber wings and a reconnaissance unit, with some having a dive-bomber wing also. Göring was able to conceal the weaknesses that had been revealed by ensuring that he, and he alone of Luftwaffe staff, was allowed direct access to Hitler. According to Hitler's Luftwaffe adjutant Nickolaus von Below, even Jeschonnek was never afforded private meetings with Hitler, which makes it clear that Hitler's understanding of all issues relating to the Luftwaffe only those that Göring was willing to give.[123]

On 18 February 1938 the Luftwaffe High Command had been asked to consider, for the first time, the possibility of war with Britain. Two months later, Generalleutnant Hans Geisler conducted a study which he and many others believed to be no more than a distraction from their other work. It is unfortunate for the Luftwaffe that more advantage was not taken of this opportunity to make a thorough study, when the issue of naval air power as a means of enabling maritime blockade might have been investigated, especially pertaining to the use of air-launched torpedoes. It is probably true to say that war with Britain was not considered very likely and the analysis and development of air power was carried out very much in the context of continental warfare.[124]

In late 1938, after the Munich Conference when it was clear that Britain was ramping up its armament production, Hitler commissioned a report from Felmy, which concluded that Germany was nowhere near ready to launch a war of annihilation against Britain. Bombers were unable to carry a sufficiently large bomb-load because the great distance to Britain's industrial heartland required maximum fuel at take-off. Only from bases close to the Channel coast in Belgium and Holland could effective bombing attacks be made. Felmy's final report, *Planstudie 39*, recommended an immediate air offensive by heavy bombers, which he assumed would be operational when the war started in 1942.[125] In response, Hitler demanded of Göring that he increase German aircraft production five-fold. Göring relayed this to his staff who, like him, realised the impossibility of such a thing; there is, however, no record of whether Hitler himself was ever made aware that his demands were way above anything that could be delivered, and that begs the question of what exactly Hitler believed the strength of the Luftwaffe to be.[126] Jeschonnek, almost alone of the General Staff and ever in thrall to Hitler, resisted calls to scale down the demands by announcing to the Air Staff that 'in my view it is our duty to support [Hitler] and not work against him'. In what must be one of the greatest feats of self-deception in the whole of the inter-war period, Jeschonnek persuaded Göring to authorise production of 500 He 177 heavy bombers. Both must have known it to be impossible but, no doubt, understood that it would placate Hitler. Stumpff and Milch raised the small issue of this extravagant ambition costing the equivalent of six years' total armament budget and the importation of 80 per cent of the world's fuel production. All must have left the room knowing that it was 'pie in the sky', and presumably was never referred to again.

Far from developing a long-term philosophy, the Luftwaffe was becoming a force that 'reacted to day-to-day political and operational pressures'.[127] Discussion of Luftwaffe capabilities at the highest level became dominated by numbers rather than type, and it was clear that the cost of manufacturing four-engine long-range bombers mitigated against their adoption as an integral part of production planning. The obsession with numbers of operational aircraft now also meant that production of spare parts was relegated to low priority, which would have an impact in a long drawn-out war, but Jeschonnek in particular was unconcerned, convinced as he was by the traditional concept that the application of maximum force at the outset would ensure a short, brutal conflict in which close support for ground forces would take priority over strategic bombing. It is worth noting that any long-range heavy bomber deployed by the Luftwaffe would still have been significantly constrained by the lack of efficient bomb-aiming devices and an inability to hit targets at night or in poor weather conditions with anything like pinpoint accuracy, even with the nascent X-Gerät navigational aids. The most that it could do was area bombing of large targets such as cities.

Re-armament was beginning to impact upon the German economy and not always in a positive way. Jeschonnek's unquestioning enthusiasm for Hitler's ambitious aircraft production programme flew in the face of Germany's critical shortages of raw materials between 1936 to 1938, and was exacerbated by the competition for scarce resources as widespread rearmament proceeded throughout all of Germany's armed forces. The price of raw materials was rising sharply on world markets just at the time that Germany needed to increase its consumption. Foreign exchange was in short supply because armament production reduced the amount of goods manufactured for export. Food imports had to satisfy the demands of a population now fully employed as factories drew in labour from the countryside. All in all, manufacturing hit the buffers in 1937 as production of aircraft fell by a quarter.

Notwithstanding the economic difficulties, aircraft production in particular was still impressive and Hitler was ever-ready to employ the Luftwaffe as theatre. In order to dissuade the French from interfering in Czechoslovakia militarily, he invited the French General Joseph Vuillemin to a display of Luftwaffe power in August 1938, which included a prototype Heinkel He 100 flying low over the airfield at 400mph. Vuillemin was allowed to overhear Milch say that a second production line was just starting up, when in fact only one example of the type ever flew and was soon abandoned due to fundamental design faults. The Frenchman was suitably impressed with the spectacle and gloomily, and rather presciently, declared that 'if war breaks out there won't be a single French aircraft left after fourteen days'.[128] Despite impressing Vuillemin with its apparent potency, in 1938 the Luftwaffe was seriously under-supplied with operationally ready aircrews for its expanding numbers of aircraft, not least because the flight training schools were starved of aircraft which had been supplied directly to operational units, which in turn, ironically, lacked crews to fly them. The Chief of Supply Services bemoaned the lack of reserve equipment and instigated urgent measures to rectify the situation, but circumstances weighed against him and little improvement was made.

In August 1939, economic realities together with a growing awareness that war was imminent, persuaded Göring, Milch, Udet and Jeschonnek to collectively curtail development and production of the Heinkel He 177 heavy bomber. Time was running out. Hitler's propensity to gamble politically and militarily at the highest level risked war with the Western Allies breaking out much earlier than the Luftwaffe had planned for. Long-term strategies were being subsumed by immediate short-term crises and while the Luftwaffe was undoubtedly the most up-to-date and potent air force in the world, it had neither the capacity nor the will to take the necessary steps to ensure that such a position of dominance would be preserved if the coming war became protracted.

The crucial issue for Germany was that it had embarked upon war in 1939 while the Luftwaffe was still in the early stages of a second five-year period of expansion and development, which had been designed to prepare it for war no earlier than 1943. On 1 September 1939, some squadrons still had obsolete equipment, lacked bombs and munitions, and others still needed more training to become fully combat-ready; overall, however, it was in much better shape than its potential adversaries and was 'by any standards an impressive force'.[129] It had experience and expertise in conducting ground-support operations which were founded upon sound doctrine and a very effective system of liaison and communications.

Strategic bombing doctrine was popular within the Luftwaffe, but remained a theoretical curiosity for the most part. It contained within it the proud concept of a war-winning capability, but was essentially flawed and destined to remain of secondary importance due to its lack of practical detail. All the old questions remained about what constituted the enemy's 'vital centres', what level of bombardment would be required to degrade them, in what order should the different categories of target be hit and crucially, did the Luftwaffe have sufficient resources at its disposal to carry out such a strategy? Despite its revolutionary X-Gerät and Y-Gerät navigation systems, bomb-aiming technology was not sufficiently developed to a similar level although strategic bombing continued to play a significant role in war-gaming right up to the start of the war.

Undoubtedly the great strength of the Luftwaffe was in its ground-support role. The fighter arm was primarily tasked with winning air superiority over the battlefield to clear the way for dive-bombers and light bombers, which would provide aerial artillery ahead of fast-moving Panzers. Experiences in Spain had encouraged designers to build ground-attack aircraft armed with cannon and protected to survive hostile ground fire. Air force officers had worked closely with ground commanders for a number of years so that each understood the capabilities and requirements of the other.

Ever since Versailles, Germany had seen France, Poland and Czechoslovakia as the main threat to its resurgence as a major European power. The Luftwaffe capabilities against these potential enemies were adequate, as history was to show, but when Britain refused to be cowed in 1940, the limitations of the Luftwaffe became glaringly obvious. It was drawn into a conflict for which it had not been prepared, either practically or doctrinally. It undoubtedly had a sizeable fighter force of outstanding quality, but its medium bombers could only operate effectively with fighter escort, and its long-range strategic bomber was years from deployment. Furthermore, its impressive numbers of front-line aircraft disguised the paucity of reserves and manufacturing capacity which would be of crucial significance in a long war. Air strategy had been formulated independently of aircraft development as priorities shifted.

The most controversial aspect of German air doctrine between the wars had been its abandonment of the heavy bomber projects, firstly because of the cost and technical shortcomings of the Dornier Do 19 and Junkers Ju 86, and later because of a peremptory decision by Göring to concentrate all production on existing medium bombers and fighters when catapulted into a European war for which the Luftwaffe was not ready. Another controversial issue was the almost total lack of development of a naval air arm which severely restricted German efforts to impose a naval blockade on Britain in 1939. Where the Luftwaffe excelled, however, was in its ground-support tactics as evinced by its pivotal role in the Blitzkrieg campaigns, but these became redundant in the context of Luftwaffe operations in the Battle of Britain.

The concepts of battlefield air attack were not created in Spain. They had been debated since the First World War but Spain was the opportunity, that Germany was quick to exploit, to test the ideas in real battle conditions. Some lessons were learned, some ignored, and some left unresolved. The performance and effectiveness of the Ju 87 in close air strikes and interdiction attack led calls for higher levels of production at the expense of other types, but its successes somewhat blinded its advocates to its deficiencies. Operating so close to enemy lines required it to have enhanced armour protection and a second crewman as air gunner, which inevitably reduced its speed and manoeuvrability. The idea of dive-bombing as the single most effective tactic in close air-ground assault was promoted by both Richthofen and Jeschonnek to the point where it was deemed appropriate to have a dive-bombing capability built into other types such as the Ju 88, which had to be heavily modified as a result. When the Luftwaffe came up against Fighter Command in the Battle of Britain, the Ju 87 suffered heavy losses due to its inability to defend itself against the high-performance Spitfire and Hurricane, and the Ju88 played only a minor role as a medium bomber due to delays in manufacture because of the many dive-bombing modifications it had to undergo.

Although the First World War had ended with Germany on the point of capitulation there had been no surrender in 1918, only an armistice, i.e. a cessation of hostilities. While its military had been emasculated by Versailles, the nation remained intact and viable, with ambitions and an urgent desire to regain its pride and status, both politically and economically. It was the way in which it set about doing that which stimulated reaction in the other European countries and essentially established the framework within which military developments took place. When Hermann Göring announced the existence of the Luftwaffe to the world in March 1935, it already had a fully developed organisation with self-contained operational commands (Luftflotten) comprising reconnaissance, fighter, bomber, transport, flak etc. While, like the air forces of other countries, the Luftwaffe had never fully reconciled strategic and tactical doctrine, it had managed to meld policy with evolving technology and test out theories during the Spanish Civil War from which it emerged with a clear view of the requirements of air power in a modern conflict.

Chapter 4

British Air Power before 1939

'We see no possibility for using aeroplanes for war purposes.'
Imperial War Office to A. V. Roe
(founder of the Avro Air Company) in 1909.[1]

The Committee of Imperial Defence examined the question of military aviation in November 1911 and recommended the formation of an Air Battalion, and that a flying corps be formed consisting of a naval wing, a military wing, a central flying school and an aircraft factory. On 13 April 1912 a royal warrant was issued establishing the Royal Flying Corps (RFC) which originally came under the jurisdiction of the Director of Military Training and had separate branches for the army and the navy. Major Frederick Sykes commanded the army wing which stayed within the RFC, but the Royal Navy, exercising its power and influence in Whitehall, separated its branch from the other two and renamed it the Royal Naval Air Service (RNAS). Thus a small core of enthusiastic officers was created with a purpose and ambition to investigate the potential of new aviation technology.

There was a long-standing military doctrine of naval power being applied against an enemy's trade and commerce to force them to bend to one's will by eliminating its capability to continue the fight, and so change its policy. As an extension of the same basic principle, British airmen believed, almost from the inception of air power, in the efficacy of strategic action, but crucially, in its capacity to be applied more comprehensively, more directly and quicker. [2]

During the First World War, one of the initial and most important uses of RFC aircraft was observing artillery fire behind the enemy front line at targets that could not be seen by ground observers. The obvious potential for aerial bombardment of the enemy, however, was not lost on the RFC, and despite the poor payload of early war aircraft, bombing missions were carried out. Aircraft were also increasingly engaged in ground-attack operations aimed at disrupting enemy forces at or near the front line and during offensives. While formal tactical bombing raids were planned and usually directed at specific targets, ground attack was usually carried out by individual pilots acting on their own initiative, or by small groups of aircraft against targets of opportunity. Although machine guns were the primary armament for ground attack, bomb racks holding 20lb Cooper bombs were soon fitted to many single-seat aircraft. Ground-attack sorties were, of necessity, carried out at very low altitude and were often highly effective, in spite of the primitive nature of the weaponry employed.

Brigadier General Sir Hugh Trenchard, a 'tall, broad-shouldered man with shaggy eyebrows and a deep voice', had been the commander of the RFC in France since August 1915.[3] His first ambition had been to join the Royal Navy like his grandfather, but he failed the entrance exam, and it was only with difficulty that he eventually managed to get into the army. He served in India and then in South Africa during the Boer War and afterwards spent seven years in Nigeria. When he was 39, he contemplated retirement but was persuaded to take up flying at the Sopwith School, which he took to with aplomb. This made him well placed to take the role of reorganising the nascent RFC at the beginning of the First World War. He took command of the No.1 Wing and a year later was given complete control of the RFC in France, serving directly under the BEF commander-in-chief. He imbued the RFC with a doctrine of incessant aggression which was set against the much more conservative approach of the German Air Force. During the Battle of Messines in June 1917, he ordered the British crews to fly low over the lines and strafe all available targets. Techniques for Army and RFC cooperation quickly evolved and improved; during the battle of Passchendaele, over 300 aircraft from fourteen RFC squadrons, including the Sopwith Camel, armed with four 20lb bombs, constantly raided enemy trenches, troop concentrations, artillery positions and strongholds in cooperation with tanks and infantry, but the cost to the RFC was high, with a loss rate of ground-attack aircraft approaching 30 per cent. In terms of how he deployed his air force, Trenchard's priority was ground support, which included reconnaissance and artillery coordination, and later encompassed tactical low-level bombing of enemy ground forces. Close support and battlefield cooperation tactics with the British Army were further developed by November 1917, when low-flying fighter aircraft cooperated highly effectively with advancing columns of tanks and infantry during the battle of Cambrai.

Right from the start, there were a number of factors at play in deciding the approach taken by the RFC and later its progeny, the RAF, when debating the revolutionary ideas of air warfare. The first, and indeed the most enduring, factor was the experience of the First World War. In 1914, there was little expectation within the armed services of aircraft having any significant impact upon the way wars were fought. They were seen, initially, simply as useful observation platforms for artillery, but gradually their utility was expanded when they proved to be effective in ground-support operations attacking enemy troop concentrations on or just behind the front lines. The aeroplane soon proved to have a further impact on the battlefield by exerting considerable psychological pressure on ground forces under attack in localised engagements. An RFC Staff Officer on the Somme in 1916 reported that German troops were 'seriously disturbed', and would 'crouch in the bottom of their trenches' when attacked by massed aircraft that would 'fly as low as 200ft and engage the enemy's infantry with machine gun fire … like buzzards who had fixed on their prey'.[4] Aircraft were also employed in close cooperation with ground forces by air commanders such as Major Trafford Leigh Mallory, commander of 73 Squadron, who was instrumental in developing ground support for the 4th Tank Brigade. This close cooperation between air and ground had seen notable success sufficient to impress Mallory's superiors by extending his command and role in ground support. Mallory later wrote *A History of Tank and Aeroplane Cooperation* and went on to act as commander at Old Sarum, and then most notably as Officer Commanding 12 Group in the Battle of Britain.

There were also the first signs of strategic deployment when Winston Churchill, First Lord of the Admiralty, ordered attacks on German assets well behind the battlefield lines of engagement. On 27 September 1914, in response to the bombing of Antwerp, Zeebrugge, Dunkirk, Calais and Lille by the German Zeppelin Z IX from Cologne, he sent out RNAS aircraft to bomb the Zeppelin sheds at Düsseldorf. Three further attacks followed with the Cologne Zeppelin sheds being bombed on 8 October when Flight Lieutenant Marix, in a Sopwith Tabloid, set Z IX on fire, Friedrichshafen on 21 November, and Cuxhaven, deep within enemy territory, attacked on Christmas Day 1914.[5] These raids were an attempt to destroy Germany's

Zeppelins on the ground where they were more easily located. In essence, they were a defensive act and as such they were successful, in that they damaged the Zeppelin programme enough to halt production for a while. However, they also galvanised the Germans into making good use of their Zeppelin fleet before it was destroyed by further enemy action and this prompted a series of Zeppelin raids beginning on 19 January 1915, when they took the First World War onto the streets of London. This led inevitably to the pursuit role in which fighter aircraft confronted marauding Zeppelins in air battles independent of the ground forces.

The German bombing offensive against London was the brainchild of Captain Peter Strasser, commander of the German Naval Airship Division, who was convinced that Britain could be crushed through air power.[6] At first, the Zeppelins raided in groups of four or five against negligible resistance, but soon Britain brought in night-time blackouts and started to pull together a defensive strategy. The raids got bigger, sometimes with spectacular results, as when nineteen airships raided in September 1916 and the citizens of London witnessed one of them exploding in flames having been struck by an incendiary bullet, the sixth Zeppelin to do so inside three months. The losses mounted and the frequency of raids diminished as the ships flew at greater heights above fighter aircraft ceilings, but the end was clear when eleven ships attacked London on 19 October 1917 in stormy conditions and only one returned unscathed. The age of the military Zeppelin was coming to an end, hastened by a self-inflicted catastrophe early the next year when five airships were lost in their sheds at Ahlhorn in an accidental explosion. Only Strasser continued to have faith, but on 5 August 1918, his ship with twenty-three crew was shot down in flames off the coast of Norfolk during a night raid. There were no survivors of what was to be the final Zeppelin raid of the war.

These attacks generated in the British political leadership a crisis of confidence in their country's ability to withstand them, and had the greatest consequences for the development of air doctrine in Britain. When two raids on 13 June and 7 July 1917 had caused alarm and outrage, a panicked government called for fighter aircraft to be withdrawn from France to protect the capital. Public outrage was clear when coroner's juries in London, convened to investigate deaths from the raids, brought verdicts of 'wilful murder' against Kaiser Wilhelm II.[7] The Zeppelin airships had begun their night-time bombing raids on industrial targets in Britain with impunity in 1915, but soon a makeshift defence system became so effective that the Germans changed to the faster and more manoeuvrable Gotha and Giant bomber aircraft of Kagohl 3, flying from Ghent. The Gotha raids, the largest of which contained forty-three aircraft, further enraged British public opinion and there were loud cries in the British press for revenge attacks against Germany.[8] A public meeting organised by the Lord Mayor at the London Opera House on 13 June 1917 demanded systematic and ruthless reprisals. It is difficult to overestimate the extent to which reaction to these raids on London cast a shadow over British air doctrine for the following twenty years. The British War Cabinet reacted to the raids by demanding a retaliatory raid by two RFC squadrons of No 41 Bomber Wing against the German city of Mannheim, relatively close to the French border. This was extended to include attacks against coal, iron and steel industries in Lorraine and Luxembourg, but crucially, avoided attacks against civilian targets for fear of German reprisals against French cities.

The British Army commander-in-chief, Sir Douglas Haig, and his Officer Commanding the RFC's units in France, Trenchard, now a Major General, were less affected by public hysteria and bluntly refused, at first, to send back fighters from France to protect the capital, saying that such a move would be 'a misuse of aircraft', but were unable to resist government pressure and were obliged to comply eventually.[9] To further assuage public opinion, the government set up a Prime Minister's Committee on Air Organisation to ensure 'that we should not be held up, in the adoption of measures to put our growing air strength to its fullest use',[10] and appointed a South African general, Jan Smuts, to study the problem. Smuts had been appointed by the Imperial War Cabinet having been elevated to statesman from rebel Afrikaner commander in the Boer War. He walked into a veritable storm as arguments raged between the Royal Navy and the Army over procurement and cooperation in air operations, a drama that was also playing out on the floor of the House of Commons between supporters of both sides. His report *Air Organisation and the Direction of Aerial Operations*, published on 17 August 1917, called for a separate air force made up of a combination of army and navy units acting independently to attack the heart of Germany under a single command and concluded that 'the day may not be far off when aerial operations ... may become the principal operations of war'.[11]

Smuts's exploration of air power led him to conclude that in order to avoid the devastation that aerial bombardment would bring about, there was an urgent need to avoid another war, which meant a swift reconciliation with Germany, a concept that the French vigorously opposed and which led to years of mistrust and suspicion between the two allies. He floated the idea of a League of Nations founded on 'principles of freedom and equality', that would 'criminalise' any nation that threatened to disrupt the peace.[12] It is ironic that bombing as a means of punishing such a rogue nation was justified as a way of restoring 'civilisation', or in the case of 'uncivilised' states or factions, a way of imposing 'civilised' values. As an indication of what measures were sanctioned to rein in recalcitrant nations, poison gas bombs were dropped by Allied aircraft on Bolshevik forces in 1919. Churchill was willing to employ extreme measures to halt the 'spread of Bolshevism', and had already sanctioned the use of poison gas in the Middle East against 'barbarian tribes'. In the summer of 1940, the British Cabinet, under his Premiership, sanctioned the use of poison gas as a last resort to oppose a German invasion of the British mainland. In 1918 the British government also had approved the use of bombers against Sinn Fein nationalists in Ireland, but a ceasefire was called before they could be deployed.[13] It was even possible that aircraft might be deployed on home soil as acute fear of revolution and civil war in Britain panicked the government immediately after the end of the war. Trenchard, with Churchill's approval, outlined the role that aircraft would play in the repression of any communist uprising.

The 'Smuts Report' 'sowed the germ of the seed of the vast British strategic air offensive in the Second World War [and was] the foundation on which British airmen would build a complete theory of warfare in the next twenty years.'[14] Smuts had become 'captivated by the vision of air power' and saw no limit to its future use. Despite Admiral Mark Kerr of the Air Board declaring that a first-strike of massed bombers would win the war, army and navy chiefs deplored the conclusions which put aircraft beyond their direct control, but politicians had been crushed by the failure of conventional forces to extricate themselves from the slaughter of the trenches and were excited by any development that gave hope of finding a new way of avoiding a repetition. The Prime Minister, David Lloyd George, acting on the recommendations of the Smuts Report, approved the creation of a new Independent Air Force (IAF) which conducted its first bombing raid, carried out by 41 Wing of the RFC, on 17 October 1917 against an iron foundry near Saarbrucken. He also ordered amalgamation of the RFC with the RNAS to form a new Royal Air Force.

41 Wing was thereafter expanded in size and re-designated No VIII Brigade RFC, but still consisted of only three squadrons by May 1918. No.55 Squadron, equipped with de Havilland DH.4 aircraft was the only day-bombing unit, while No.16 Squadron RNAS with Handley-Page O/100 heavy night-bombers and No.100 Squadron with F.E.2b bombers were the night-bombing component. By the end of the war, the Independent Force comprised nine bomber squadrons, four of which (5, 99, 104 and 110, each with eighteen de Havilland DH.4, DH.9 aircraft) were day-bombers and the others (97, 100, 115, 215 and 16, each with twelve Handley Page O/400s) were night-bombers. The sluggish DH.9, in particular, was quite unsuitable for strategic bombing with its troublesome engines. All aircraft struggled to navigate with unreliable compasses and the crews suffered from the extreme cold. Even if they located a target, the bomb-aiming equipment was crude and little better than useless and most crews released their bombs based on visual assessment. From mid-1918, these bombers came under increasing attack from German fighters, often outnumbering them by up to 3:1, and could not call on their own fighter escort given the unsuitability of available aircraft. Losses mounted to a staggering level, meaning some squadrons were unable to function due to crew shortages. Trenchard was forced to admit that his Independent Force did not have the strength to cause critical damage to the German war effort.

Lord Rothermere, 'a difficult and erratic personality who understood little about air power', was made President of the Air Council in November 1917 and took a strong political stance, calling for reprisals to avenge the murder of 'women and children'. The British War Cabinet, however, through its Committee on Air Policy, eschewed retaliation as a policy and restricted its aims to the bombing of German industry. Trenchard was recalled from France to become, albeit very reluctantly, Rothermere's Chief of Staff, and advocated attacks against German 'root industries', but rarely carried them out.[15] During his first month at the Air Ministry Trenchard repeatedly clashed with Rothermere. They were both strong-minded people with opposing views on the proper future use of air power. Trenchard had never wanted to leave the French theatre in the first place and took the opportunity to resign on the day that the RAF was founded. He had found the Air Ministry 'ridiculous and inefficient', and the Minister, Lord Rothermere, to be 'quite ignorant of the needs or workings of the Air Service'.[16] His main reason for resigning, however, may well have been his nostalgic hankering for the 'small self-contained staff in France', allied to his admission of being 'no good in an office' where he was frequently bypassed and overruled by the Minister. He was replaced as Chief of the RAF by Brigadier General Frederick Hugh Sykes.

With a mandate for a wider, more strategic application of air power, the Royal Air Force was born on 1 April 1918 to 'control and administer all matters connected with air warfare', specifically to prevent further German incursions and threaten retaliation against Germany in the event of future hostilities.[17] It was a rather inauspicious start. There were no fanfares or ceremonies to mark the day that the Royal Flying Corps suddenly became the Royal Air Force, only a brand new rubber stamp marked 'RAF' to block out the Royal Flying Corps heading on all new official documents. The changeover to a 'new service with its own doctrine, its own ethos, and its own material presence' would be rather more complicated.[18] By the end of 1918 it had 22,000 aircraft, including the technically advanced Sopwith Snipe, the Handley Page V/1500 and the de Havilland DH.9A distributed through 188 squadrons, but the Armistice saw it rapidly stripped down to a basic 371 aircraft in twelve squadrons. RAF personnel were signed up for a four-year period of service and transferred directly from their army or navy unit, but this was bitterly resented by the army and navy who vociferously tried to have the new service disbanded and agitated to bring aviation back under their control. The Royal Navy had long been Britain's imperial economic 'police force' securing its great trade routes, and the army its military arm enforcing political control on land. They had no objection to air power as such, only that there was, in their opinion, no compelling argument for its independence. Neither service was of a mind to have the upstart RAF take on any of their roles. Britain had, for centuries, externalised military violence, ensuring that all its great battles took place beyond its shores. It should, therefore, have been a wake-up call when the first crossing of the English Channel by an aircraft in 1909, with its implications of a military 'new age', implied that Britain would no longer have to 'go to war'; it was now possible for war to 'come to it', but ten years later the concept had still not penetrated the brick wall of army and navy intransigence.

Towards the end of the First World War, Sykes had been keen to take the fight to Germany 'day and night', and his new boss, the Air Minister, Sir William Weir, persuaded Trenchard to take on the role of General Officer Commanding of the IAF in France on 15 June 1918, tasked with carrying out strategic bombing raids over Germany. Sykes had not seen the bomber as fundamentally changing the principles of warfare, but having visited Italy before the war where it is possible that he came across the writings of Giulio Douhet, he did recognise its growing importance. Given the vulnerability of ground forces to air attack, Trenchard had recognised the importance of offensive air power, concentrating on air superiority and interdiction, but he also acknowledged the importance of strategic bombing of appropriate industrial targets big enough to be identified from the air. He was reluctant, however, to employ his aircraft in hazardous, long-range bombing missions believing the strategic role to be of lower priority and his resources too limited. He went so far as to call the idea of bombing of German cities a 'gigantic waste of effort and personnel'.[19] One of the main reasons for his view may well be echoed in the experiences of returning bomber crews, one of whom said, 'Experience has shown that it is quite easy for five squadrons to set out to bomb a particular target and for only one of those five ever to reach the objective.'[20] It was during this time, however, that Trenchard began to modify his views, take a more nuanced approach and formalise his concept of the aeroplane as an inherently offensive weapon, which might also have potential as a strategic weapon since, 'owing to the unlimited space in the air [the enemy cannot] prevent hostile aircraft from crossing the line if they have the initiative and the determination to do so'. Trenchard's 'unique single-mindedness bordering on stubbornness', allied to 'a policy of relentless and incessant offensiveness', was to characterise his approach from this point as one incorporating a belief in the need for air superiority as a first requirement, and only then allowing ground-support operations as a secondary role, but in an admission of the politically insecure status of the IAF, he insisted that 'operations conducted by bombing squadrons cannot be isolated from ... the operations of the army as a whole'.

Had the war continued beyond 1918, it was planned to form an Inter-Allied Independent Air Force to carry out large-scale strategic bombing of German targets. The British had developed, as part of this force, a 'super-heavy' Handley Page V/1500 bomber to operate from Bircham Newton against cities such as Essen and Dusseldorf, and even capable of reaching Berlin on a round trip of 960 miles, landing at Nancy. None of these aircraft ever flew over Germany and the IAIAF plan was never activated.

Trenchard had now completely changed his mind and come to believe that the aircraft was inherently a strategic weapon, unmatched in its ability to shatter the will of an enemy country through attacks on industry and, by extension, to have a devastating effect on the morale of workers living in the vicinity. He believed that 'long-distance bombing … ought to be vigorously developed', but conceded that under the circumstances of 1918, 'bombers had neither the range nor the mass to carry out effective strategic strikes'. Neville Jones, in his book *The Beginnings of Strategic Air Power*, sees Trenchard as an opportunist willing to modify his views in order to achieve an objective, but crucially, throughout the 1920s and early 1930s when his influence over the RAF was at its height, failed to keep abreast of developments in aviation. Under Trenchard's leadership however, strategic air power became the standard doctrine taught in RAF staff colleges between the wars and was fully supported by Trenchard's staff member John Slessor, 'the most intellectually gifted man in the group'.[21] The belief that air power could break the morale of enemy populations, which in turn would force the hostile government to sue for peace, is really an example of how an unsupported belief or supposition can become the basis of service doctrine. It is staggering to think of how such unchallenged assumptions permeated RAF official thinking right up to 1939, given that the very survival of the nation was almost certainly going to hinge on the soundness of its air power doctrine. Scot Robertson, in his book *The Development of RAF Strategic Bombing Doctrine*, describes the RAF approach to air doctrine as 'unintellectual and unrigorous'. Strategic air doctrine as adopted by the RAF, however, was not quite a slave to the Douhetian idea of acquiring total domination of the air, as shown by Slessor's remarks denying the possibility of achieving total control: 'Do not waste time pursuing command of the air, but commit yourself to achieve those local and temporary superiorities that effectively contribute to decisive results on the ground.'[22]

On 1 January 1919, the Air Ministry published a synopsis of Britain's air effort during the war, emphasising its strategic influence on the way future wars would be fought. Trenchard strongly endorsed the conclusions in the report, which stipulated the 'essential prerequisite for success in operations on land or at sea' to be offensive initiative and air superiority to allow 'freedom of action', and would be achieved only by 'a system of centralised command and control'.[23] The report went on to say that the most economical use of aircraft had been shown to be when they were concentrated in a single coordinated effort to expand the size and scope of the battlefield and exert pressure against objectives that neither armies nor navies could reach.

Clear strategic direction and unity of effort in the air, however, could only be possible where there was one central authority, a conclusion that was not going to please the other two services. Even so, the RAF's future as an independent service was not secure. Politicians, exhausted by war, were not anxious to give much thought on how to prepare for the next one. They would have dearly liked to relegate the whole military debate to much further down the peacetime agenda, and were not too interested in the military leaders who had failed them and who were now busy hauling themselves out of the administrative and operational mire of the war just gone.

At the end of the war, the air force was massively equipped with 188 operational squadrons, almost 700 aerodromes throughout the Empire and 290,000 personnel. Therefore one of the first tasks given by the government to the new Secretary of State for War and Air, Winston Churchill, was to reduce the burden of such swollen military expenditure now that the war was over, so that funds could be reallocated to rebuilding the economy. Churchill's views of the application of air power, articulated in 1917, were by no means revolutionary and saw air power as essentially tactical by assisting conventional forces to degrade 'the fighting power of [the enemy's] armies and fleets', and doubted its strategic potential, believing it was 'improbable that any terrorising of the civil population ... by air attack would compel the government of a great nation to surrender'.[24] High on Churchill's agenda was reducing the size of the new-born RAF, which was now in serious danger of being dissolved before it had even been properly formed. Thanks in no small part to Trenchard it only just survived, but its relationship with the other services was poor from the start and improved little over the next few years. Rothermere had resigned in April 1919, ostensibly on the grounds of ill health but in reality he had been pushed out of office over issues surrounding his general competence as Air Minister, and a year after leaving his post as Chief of Staff of the RFC, Trenchard was pressured by Churchill, who considered him to have 'outstanding qualities as a leader', to return as RAF Chief of Staff. [25] Trenchard accepted 'with a good deal of alarm', and was not optimistic that his second term would be any more successful than his first, but he had been out in the cold for a whole year and the opportunity to return to an active role was irresistible, especially now that Rothermere had gone. Trenchard was to establish a good working relationship with Churchill, but not before they had clashed over Churchill's view that the RAF should create for itself a completely new identity by creating new ranks within its service which would clearly distinguish it from army ranks. These were incorporated over his objections, but the much bigger question was how the RAF could continue to justify its existence staffed as it now was by 'a rapidly shrinking body of officers, men and women'.[26]

In its infancy, the new RAF had to contend daily with the 'unbridled hostility' of the army and navy, as well as the ambivalence shown by a government which was acting much like a parent unsure of how to handle a precocious new child threatening to disrupt the household. Much of the decision-making about the issue, however, was conveniently sidestepped by the government, which left the services to squabble among themselves and denied them funds by pleading poverty as the country grappled with the devastating economic consequences of the war. Hopeful that exhaustion and economic reality would prevent another major war for many years, the government adopted the 'ten-year rule' – which assumed that there would be no war for at least ten years. The idea was that this 'rule' would be readopted every year on a rolling basis with its unspoken assumption that since German rearmament was banned, there would be no need for the British government to expand the RAF and could introduce a drastic cut in the military budget. It was against this background that Trenchard was determined to find a role for the RAF that would justify its continued existence as an independent force. He argued that it was wrong to make any long-term decisions about the future of the RAF since no conclusions about its value could be drawn from the First World War experience, which yielded no conclusive evidence either way about its ability to expand the war zone, both laterally beyond the enemy lines and vertically into the third dimension, where exploration of its potential had only just begun. It must have time to show what it could do. While appeasing politicians by acknowledging the straitened economic circumstances, he also suggested a protracted timeframe to allow the RAF to conduct research and development into navigation, wireless telegraphy, photography and engineering, as well as to establish specialist training establishments. The long-term objective in Trenchard's mind was to create an air force capable of undertaking independent strategic operations, but this would have to take second place for the time being as the emphasis needed to be on the promotion of arguments that would persuade government to protect the RAF from incessant attacks by the army and navy, who wanted to see the back of it and reclaim its assets for their own use.

Despite his previous misgivings, Trenchard believed in the total independence of the air force, but realised that he had to tread carefully to avoid aggravating the army and navy so much that they would force its disbandment and reclaim air power for themselves. In reality his command existed in relative isolation, which did little to engender cooperation. When Churchill was made Minister of War in 1919, he was also given the Air Ministry and expected to combine the two departments. Sykes put the RAF on a collision course with Churchill by submitting a plan for a massively expanded air force to be deployed throughout the Empire. Churchill saw this as a provocation to the army, which might redouble its efforts to reclaim aircraft for its own uses, and did not want to see the RAF disappear before it had been given a chance to make its case; he had no intention of letting it become embroiled in high-profile arguments and sidestepped the issue by retiring Sykes and bringing back Trenchard, with whom he had served as a hussar and played polo against in India. It was a subtle move by Churchill, who knew Trenchard as a 'bureaucratic infighter' in his own mould; together they stood up to army chief Field Marshal Henry Wilson and navy chief Admiral David Beatty in exchanges that were at times 'stormy, bordering on rude.'[27] In an approach that was sure to appeal to government parsimony, Trenchard promoted the idea that the RAF could be a much more cost-effective means than the army of policing the Empire, but on a smaller scale than anything Sykes had suggested.

Trenchard made every effort to keep Churchill on his side and vehemently argued with all and sundry against any attempt to curtail the RAF. He circulated a memo urging the development of the air force to 'encourage and develop airmanship [and] Air spirit ... to make it a force that will profoundly influence the strategy of the future'.[28] Trenchard had taken on his new role with urgent enthusiasm and was clearly prepared to make the case for an independent RAF. In a dramatic shift of allegiance, Churchill, who came into his post with a clear mandate to cut the RAF down to size, had come to recognise it as a vital and, more importantly, relatively inexpensive means of maintaining order within the British Empire. Trenchard had developed a clear idea of how air power should evolve in a memorandum written in August 1919 in which he said, 'There can be no doubt that we must be prepared for long distance aerial operations against an enemy's main source of supply and Naval ports', and which was encapsulated in a White Paper presented to the British Parliament one month on from the Armistice by

Churchill, who had obviously been impressed by Trenchard's views. The paper incorporated ideas first espoused in an earlier memorandum which had looked at whether the air force should now be considered sufficiently independent to, where appropriate, conduct its own operations under air force command, quite separate from army or navy involvement. This, Trenchard argued in a tone distinctly different from that adopted two years previously when he had made the opposing argument, would remove the operational confusion of dual control. By emphasising the immediate relevance of the RAF and pointing out its clear economic advantages over ground forces in distant lands, Trenchard was slowly making the case for its existence and while there was, at this time, no case for creating a strategic bombing capability within the RAF, he had not entirely abandoned the idea. He was simply biding his time until the need arose, which he never doubted it would. Churchill repeated his support for Trenchard at the Cairo Conference of 1921, where Middle Eastern issues were discussed.

A consequence of Trenchard's legitimate (and some might say essential) sponsoring of the RAF as a policing tool to impress the British Treasury, was the way in which early air doctrine was informed by its actions. This was especially true in the Middle East, where most of those who would rise to leadership roles in the expanded RAF got much of their early operational experience in theatres where opposition to air power had been virtually non-existent. This proved to be at the expense of a wider vision that incorporated a strategic dimension to air power, and gave little in the way of guidance to the more central question of how to develop the aerial weapon for service against a first-class power in any future war.[29]

Tribal insurgencies along the British Empire's North-West Frontier gave Trenchard the chance he was looking for to illustrate the power of his air force. Although limited in numbers and quality, aircraft proved to be one of the greatest assets that the British possessed during this conflict. Not only did it allow them to extend their reach beyond the North-West Frontier of India and bomb Kabul, but it also enabled them to harass the retreating enemy and to break up tribes as they attempted to form larger groups prior to launching an attack. The ability of the British to project air power, even in small-scale raids, had considerable psychological effects on the enemy. This emboldened Trenchard to suggest that the frontier could be held by air power alone, thus significantly reducing the considerable cost of maintaining ground forces in the region. While this idea was rejected by the army, it sowed enough doubt to keep open the political debate about the future of the RAF.

The League of Nations in 1919, with its serving up of 'mandates', had shown itself to be 'the legitimisation of colonialism', and it was no surprise when a number of anti-colonial revolts broke out soon after.[30] Among those fomenting revolt was Said Mohammed Bin Abdulla Hassan, a 'holy warrior' who again stirred up a Wahhabi revolt against colonial rule in British Somaliland in 1919. The British Army, having failed repeatedly in the past to suppress his actions, was reluctant to launch another 'punitive expedition [which is] an enormously costly affair in lives and money, and drags on for months.'[31] Neither did they think sending in a few RAF aircraft would do much good; they were proved quite wrong when a single squadron of bombers caused such panic in the tribesmen that a small force of local troops was able to follow up and restore order, but perhaps this had as much to do with the fact that Abdulla Hassan had died of influenza as the actual bombing. The British Treasury was mightily impressed and knew a good deal when it saw one, so quickly allocated substantial funds to the RAF to take on responsibility for the security of Mesopotamia against Turkish ambitions in the region. The army scoffed at the idea and called for immediate withdrawal of all British forces from the area, but the government pressed ahead and later described the RAF operation as 'a conspicuous success'.[32] In Trenchard's own words, 'events in the near East and India have tended to show that, against a semi-civilized enemy unprovided with aircraft, aerial operations alone may have such a deterrent effect as to be practically decisive'.[33] The concept of 'police bombing' was born, and brought 'peace to white people and bombs to the colonised.'[34] Occupation of the ground was no longer a basic requirement of control. By establishing itself as an important element of imperial defence, the RAF had finally begun to stake its right to independence, but more than half of all air units were still under the operational control of the army.

Air control operations such as those in Somaliland began to cement the RAF's reputation as a reliable and cost-effective alternative to ground forces. Many of the future leaders of the service, such as John Slessor, would get their first command in these frontier skirmishes and their concept of air power was the result of experiences gained there. This skewed their perspective somewhat, given that successes were achieved in an artificial environment against an enemy who was incapable of mounting any effective defence;

lessons could not be applied in action against more sophisticated enemy. The effectiveness of strategic operations where aircraft were deployed independently of ground forces allied to the, still raw, memories of panic on the streets of London when the Gothas had spilled their ordnance, led to an exaggerated sense of helplessness against bombing and a vindication of the concept of the overwhelming power of the bombing aircraft, which 'cast a long shadow over considerations of British security and foreign policy'.[35] What the RAF strategists had failed to explain, or had chosen to ignore, was why success in the terrorising of poorly armed tribal forces should be taken as the basis for developing a theory of air power.

It may well be that the open hostility shown to the RAF by the other services helped it to forge within it a bond of camaraderie and a unity of purpose, but the way in which air units were dispersed did not make it easy. Many were sent to serve in the far reaches of Empire and a significant number of other squadrons were uncomfortably engaged in cooperative roles with the army and navy. Only four squadrons were assigned to the new Metropolitan Air Force in 1922, ostensibly as a defence against enemy attack. This was built upon a sophisticated system of air defence set up in 1917, consisting of multiple 'spotting stations' connected by telephone to a central headquarters in London. Telephones also kept this headquarters in touch with various airfields housing interceptor squadrons. These airfields, in turn, maintained contact with their airborne aircraft via wireless. This meagre commitment was justified on the grounds that there existed no immediate threat, a fact which also brought further pressure for disbandment of the RAF and its reabsorption into the army and navy.

Fighting a rearguard action against this almost overwhelming hostility, and in a desperate defence of his charge, Trenchard wrote: 'The nation that considers and develops its air forces as an auxiliary arm to the older services will suffer a rude awakening if faced by a nation [which has] developed its air power [as] a primary medium of war.'[36] The War Office missed no opportunity to appeal to the Treasury's parsimony by continuing to point out the (in its view) unnecessary extra cost of maintaining the RAF as a separate administrative layer of command. Trenchard had made his case in the most forthright manner by saying that the army 'cannot realise the value of mechanised appliances [and] think only in mere masses of men [and have] no concept of the value of speed and time'.[37] It must have worked because when the Committee on National Expenditure announced its review of military expenditure in 1921, it was clear which way the wind was starting to blow; the army and navy budgets were cut more severely in proportion to that of the RAF and where the RAF was cut, it was the army and navy cooperation squadrons that were axed.

The War Office seems to have given ground in late 1921 when Trenchard was able to negotiate a 'ceasefire' between the RAF and the other two services which guaranteed him twelve months' freedom from political attack by either, giving him a chance to stabilise his command. He used the time wisely by promoting the 'economic' case for the RAF to resolve foreign conflicts using the experience of Somaliland as evidence. He demonstrated how air power could be very useful in the vast expanses of the Middle East, which was becoming increasingly important to Britain with its navy, the bedrock of imperial control, now powered by oil rather than coal, making access to the oilfields in that region a matter of the greatest importance. While campaigns in Iraq, Afghanistan, India, Aden, Transjordan, Palestine, Egypt and Sudan were seen as neither 'grand nor glorious', they did make Trenchard's point and reinforced the hope that the RAF could survive its precarious early years; when news of possible instability in the post-war alliance broke with French threats to occupy the Ruhr, it was able to consolidate its position within British defence and foreign policy.

There had been a new government elected in Britain in 1922, and with it had come a new move to have the RAF abolished to save money. However, relations with France, for centuries the 'natural enemy' of Britain, had been uneasy since the Armistice, with trade and colonial issues bubbling to the surface intermittently, and when reports of a great and growing French air force unnerved the government, they began to view the RAF differently. After a government review and reappraisal of the European security situation, the RAF was now tasked with guarding against 'the strongest air force within striking distance'.[38] The French began threatening to occupy the Ruhr in response to German default on reparation payments but the British, who had a more sympathetic attitude towards Germany, saw the move as destabilising a European order that was slowly adjusting to post-war realities. While war with France was not a serious prospect, under the circumstances it was still not appropriate to see it stealing a march on Britain in any aspect of military development. This prompted the selection of France as the doctrinal enemy in theoretical defence studies and led to the design and development of short-range, light bombers with quick turn-around times which could operate under RAF fighter protection and would be suitable for conducting daylight attacks on Northern France, rather than on the longer-range targets in Germany and Italy which would be the targets for Bomber Command after 1939.[39]

While all this helped to assert the RAF's right to exist, it was still obliged to expend much of its energy not only in administrative 'turf wars' with the two other services but also in defending itself against influential non-service commentators, picking up on the public mood of insecurity in the face of the bombing aircraft, who felt they knew enough to make a legitimate contribution to the debate. The 'fundamental shift in Britain from confidence to insecurity about its defensive position was of major consequence during the inter-war years'.[40] The debate, however, did not prove productive since, as is often the case, advocates of one view or another tended to concentrate on those aspects that supported their position and ignore others. Concepts of strategic air power were undergoing a rapid transformation from theory into dogma and, in the process, avoided the sort of scrutiny that might have impressed the great Prussian military theorist, Clausewitz. The role of theory, he would have asserted, was to act only as a guide to illuminate the path towards uncovering fundamental truths upon which to build a doctrine.

What at first appeared to be a victory for Trenchard against the other two services now faltered, as the army and navy conducted a long campaign to undermine him and his still fragile service. Chief of the Imperial General Staff, Henry Wilson, complained about the RAF getting a leading role in the League Mandate of Iran in 1920 by saying that the Air Force was 'a wicked waste of money'.[41] Churchill, now Colonial Secretary, again faced Wilson's wrath a year later when he tried to extend the role of the RAF in the Middle East. 'Aircraft at present and for many years to come must act as an auxiliary arm to the Naval and Military Services and ... should be ... an integral part of these services,' Wilson argued.

Trenchard pressed on with his idea to create a small elite force that could form the nucleus for expansion should events demand it, but his budget was halved in 1921 and reduced further so that in 1923 it was no more than one fifth of what it had been four years earlier. Even at this level, the army and navy continued with efforts to purloin those funds for their own use. The RAF was, during those first few years, 'battling for [its] life against the forces of military reaction'.[42] Trenchard could see that in order to survive, the RAF was going to need a separate and distinct spirit and identity, and under his guidance a unique RAF ethos emerged. Close attention was paid to the training of personnel which was standardised initially at the Cadet College of Cranwell and then at staff colleges and technical colleges. These bit hard into the Air Ministry budget but Trenchard deemed the move essential to establish the legitimacy of the RAF, even if it meant a reduction in aircraft procurement. There was insistence on a broad education in all aspects of aviation and an urgent need, in Trenchard's view, to bring in a fresh generation of young airmen who had no residual attachment to either the army or navy and who would be imbued with an 'Air Force spirit'. Every RAF officer, whether flying crew, ground crew or administration, would be expected to be physically capable of flying in an aircraft. Officers were expected to have 'a high standard of courage, self-control and honourable conduct', and preferably a public school and university background.[43]

The world's first air academy was opened in 1919 at Cranwell to provide basic flying training, intellectual education, and to give a sense of purpose to the future leaders of the service. In April 1922 the RAF Staff College at Andover was opened as a parallel to the staff colleges of the army and navy. From its foundation and through the 1920s and 1930s, the staff college provided training to selected officers to prepare them for staff duties at the Air Ministry or at Command or Group headquarters. It articulated and disseminated the air power concepts of theorists such as Liddell Hart whose lectures emphasised the importance of a 'swift and powerful blow [to] bring the enemy state to a standstill'.[44] It is vital for an understanding of RAF doctrine during the 1930s to appreciate the influence that the colleges had on the men who would be making all the important future decisions, especially in the office of Director of Plans. Right from the start, Cranwell cadets were taught that 'due to industrialisation, the growth of democracy and trade unionism, people as a whole were now more directly affected by war [and] were more able than in the past to influence or even stop a war … It is now the will power of the enemy nation that has to be broken.'[45] Furthermore, their education included the instruction to 'carry out the decision of … government … even if such decision be repugnant to our own private conception of morality'. It was conceded that air superiority was an essential precondition for a strategic offensive but the difficulty in 'bringing the enemy to battle' was not easily overcome, except by threatening something vital to their security.

In July 1922 the RAF issued Doctrine Manual CD22 'Operations', which emphasised the need for air forces to cooperate with surface forces and destroy the enemy's morale, but first of all the enemy's air force must be subdued. All attacks, however, must be within the guidelines of International Law, against 'legitimate objectives', taking 'all reasonable precautions to spare hospitals and other privileged buildings'.[46] This was followed in 1928 with the AP 1300 Royal Air Force War Manual, which now saw air superiority as secondary to strategic bombing of selected targets which might include 'vital centres' of communications and transportation as 'the most effective contribution [towards] breaking down the enemy's resistance'. While such action would undoubtedly cause significant civilian deaths, there was 'clear water' between RAF and Douhetian doctrine which specifically advocated the bombing of population centres per se, but both incorporated the idea of the 'democratisation' of warfare, whereby whole populations were irrevocably involved.[47] A policy of indiscriminate bombardment was seen as 'illegitimate' and 'sheer unintelligent frightfulness', and was 'morally [and politically] indefensible [and] militarily ineffective', whereas RAF policy 'to terrorise munitions workers into absenting themselves from work' was deemed quite acceptable. The unspoken corollary to AP 1300 was a requirement for an in-depth understanding of the enemy's industrial and economic infrastructure, in other words economic intelligence.[48] This may well have been influenced by the particular vulnerability of London to reprisal attack, given its proximity to the European mainland.

In 1923 Trenchard fleshed out his ideas by saying, 'In the next great war with a European nation the forces engaged must first fight for aerial superiority [and] destroy the morale [of the enemy]. If we could bomb [them] more intensely and more continually than he could bomb us the result might be an early offer of peace.'[49] His idea was that an effective defence may prevent defeat, but only attack can bring about a victory; this meant having as many bombers as possible and as few fighters as necessary, which in Trenchard's opinion meant twice as many bombers as fighters.[50]

As tensions over the Ruhr subsided, Britain began to see France as less of a threat to peace in Europe. That country had been chosen as a theoretical basis for planning air policy simply because there had to be some yardstick against which to measure its capabilities, but now Britain scanned the horizon for other immediate dangers and saw none. The ten-year rule was in place and looked to be a sound policy, meaning there would be no requirement to prepare for war in the near future, which had the knock-on effect of creating a minor crisis with little guidance available as a basis for air planning. The Air Ministry had to discern operational needs without much idea of the role it might be called upon to play, and therefore what types of aircraft it would require. Only when operational objectives were formalised could it issue specifications for new aircraft and call for tenders. When a new review was called for in 1923, there had been two fundamentally opposed theories in play both emanating from First World War experiences. One saw the inevitability of bomber attack, with its corollary that the failure to make effective fighter interceptions of the Gotha attacks over London had given rise to a grim acceptance that there was no defence against the bomber. The diametrically opposed alternative, derived from the failure of the British bombers of the IAF in France to penetrate German defences without serious losses, was the equally disturbing conclusion that strategic bombing offensives were a costly business. The fundamental question inevitably asked was whether it was possible to put up a credible fighter defence against bombers and if so, what form would it take? The bombing lobby prevailed and was called upon to define the necessary characteristics of bomber aircraft; any specifications they came up with, however, were constrained not by operational ambitions, but by the limited size of hangers available to house them, and by the length of the existing airfield runways available for landing and take-off.

Having nailed its colours to the mast of strategic bombing, it would have been prudent of the Air Staff to turn their attention to testing theory on the road to doctrine and a better understanding of its nature, potential and vulnerabilities, but the level of inertia in the system saw slow progress to the point where, 'until two years before the war the operational and technical problems of strategic offensive had been neglected'.[51] It may be argued that the entire concept of strategic air war against a major power in mock battles would have been very expensive, disruptive and difficult to simulate, but having remade British defence strategy in the image of air power, the case for doing so was overwhelming. Not the least of the problems where large-scale exercises were carried out was the difficulty in designing them to test, without prejudice, not only the convenient 'low-hanging fruit' of conventional theory, but to give equal time and resources to reaching for the less immediate alternatives. For instance, the whole concept of air defence against bombing attack was thought to be 'a misuse of air power' and was consequently little explored beyond a grudging concession to political and public anxiety. What the Air Staff concentrated on was the counter-offensive, whereby overwhelming pressure was brought to bear on the enemy's 'centre of gravity', reducing its capacity to continue the war and it was this aspect that was the object of most attention. The impressive progress being made in the design of interceptors failed to penetrate the mindset of an Air Ministry dominated by bomber enthusiasts, and neither did the inability of bombers to find and hit their targets by day or by night shake their confidence.[52]

The Royal Navy had continued to make its case to have all air units working directly with the main fleet to be 'manned, administered and controlled by the Navy'. The matter came to the desk of Prime Minister Andrew Bonar Law who came down on the side of the RAF, but compromised by allowing operational authority of units on permanent secondment to naval vessels at sea to be put under the control of the Admiralty. This led, in 1924, to the establishment of the Fleet Air Arm.

Planning for the air defence of Britain assumed that any threat would come from the south or south-east and so proposed an 'air fighting zone' stretching from Cambridgeshire, circling London to Wiltshire, which would be given advance warning of attack by observation posts and sound locators all along the coast. It was generally accepted that this would give little chance of intercepting a mass bombing attack and so Trenchard placed equal, if not more, emphasis on creating a strike bomber force to take the battle to the enemy's airfields and factories. In January 1925, Air Marshal Sir John Salmond would be appointed commander-in-chief of a new command, 'Air Defence of Great Britain', which controlled all air defence units, but this command soon began to fade in importance with a slackening of political tension in Europe and postponement of French plans for an expansion of their Armée de l'Aire.

The coming to power of a Labour government in January 1924 had seen a new defence policy, with agreement on the need for a further eight squadrons and the setting up of the Auxiliary Air Force. Moves had also begun to transfer control of the Fleet Air Arm to the Royal Navy. A Conservative government followed in October 1924 with a promise to increase RAF strength to fifty-two squadrons. Churchill was made Chancellor of the Exchequer with further funding agreed for the RAF but with the proviso that the planned expansion of the service would now be slowed, ostensibly as a consequence of the signing of the Locarno Peace Treaty. Although by no means hostile to the RAF, Churchill thought it prudent to mothball Prime Minister Stanley Baldwin's promised expansion scheme. This brake on expansion was vehemently opposed by Trenchard, but he saw the inevitability of it and so chose to make best use of the pause on physical expansion by concentrating his efforts instead on building firmer foundations for the service and improving the quality of pilots and training programmes. This apparent benefit, however, soon began to evaporate as successive governments, encouraged by the Geneva Disarmament Conference and the League of Nations, kept rolling over the ten-year plan, which had the effect of putting off indefinitely any consideration of a fundamental reappraisal of British defence requirements.[53] The future of the RAF as an independent service was now confirmed and the Army and Navy were told by Prime Minister Baldwin to 'grow up' and accept it.[54]

With England's sense of defensive security laid waste the minute the Gothas had struck in 1917, a fundamental shift from confidence to insecurity was to dominate debate over defence policy throughout the 1920s. To the Air Staff, the position was now clear: strategic air power as a weapon of counter-offence was the key. They had, however, based this view on two markedly different experiences with limited application to a wider theatre of operations. The bombing of London had actually proved to be counter-productive for Germany at a significant cost, but the bombing concept persisted and was still retained as a component of doctrine on the basis of its perceived impact on civilian morale. The other was the apparently successful application of strategic bombing in the Middle East, which was taken at face value in Whitehall, thousands of miles from the action, and not properly evaluated against the circumstances under which victories were won against minimal opposition. Together these experiences fed into an unrealistic appreciation of the efficacy of strategic bombing, the general adoption of which, among other things, was justified by the assumption that 'attacks aimed at the sources as opposed to the manifestations of an enemy's strength … would produce much swifter and hence, in the end, more humane decisions'.[55] The true function of the bomber, in a strategic sense, was seen as being in support of an army by isolating the enemy on the battlefield from reinforcement and supply, and should not be used either in attack or defence on the battlefield itself, save in exceptional circumstances. Although many things would change during the 1920s, the fundamental essence of the theory remained unchanged and it became the role of the Air Ministry to translate that into doctrine for the application of air power. A number of theorists such as Liddell Hart and Colonel J.F.C. Fuller piled in with their own views. Fuller saw bombers making 'attacks [against] the civil population in order to compel them to accept the will of the attacker', while Liddell Hart imagined Britain paralysed with 'Whitehall in a heap of ruins [and] the slum districts maddened into the impulse to break loose and maraud'.[56]

While France and Germany designed their aircraft primarily to play a ground-support role in a mobile war, Britain, given its geographical separation and supreme disinclination ever to become embroiled in another continental war, had other priorities but failed to follow up with a comprehensive plan to support them. It yearned for disarmament, but lack of progress within the League of Nations and the subsequent collapse of the Geneva Disarmament talks in 1934 would make that impossible. Seeing the international order eroding under the weight of extreme politics of both left and right, Britain was reluctantly preparing to wage war at a distance but increasingly feared that it would end up fighting on its own doorstep. As a result, it tried to produce aircraft that might be effective in either scenario with predictable results. The most likely enemy, Germany, would have to be met with the counter-threat of Allied air power and face the destruction of its industrial base, not to mention a great part of its population, which was all well and good in theory, but where was the long-range heavy bomber that would bring this plan to fruition? The RAF had protected itself from internecine attacks by promising politicians that it had the semblance of a viable doctrine of counter-offensive and the politicians had, albeit uneasily, gone along with the pretence when challenged over the country's state of readiness for war. A typical occupant of the gap between two stools into which the Air Ministry fell was the Fairey Battle bomber which, with its underpowered Merlin engine, had neither the 'punch' for strategic bombing nor the 'parry' for nimble defence – and would not have had, even if fitted with the Griffon engine designed for it but produced too late. It was 1941 before the complex design problems of heavy, long-range bombers such as the Stirling, Manchester and Halifax bombers were overcome, and only then did the RAF have anything like the capability of backing up their words with action. As late as 1938, bomber production lines were still pouring out Battles and Bristol Blenheim medium bombers, obsolete before they left the factory floor, that would take such a pounding in the Battle of France in 1940.

It was the case, however, that while much effort was expended on developing the theory, far too little was applied to an understanding of the means of applying it through extensive exercises, with the result that dogma displaced doctrine. The most effective and productive exercises were in the form of expensive and burdensome full-scale operations involving large formations engaging in a mock battle, but these tended to be designed to test a pre-conceived idea rather than to explore the unknown. It is all too often the case that exercises expose the limitations of imagination and breadth of vision of their planners, rather than the discovery of hitherto unrecognised applications of theory or technology. As an example of this myopic approach, the concept of air defence against enemy bombing attack was thought to be a waste of valuable time and resources and, on the rare occasions it was contemplated, was essentially to simply placate politicians and calm public unrest over the bombing threat. The preferred approach to exercises was to explore the means of bringing overwhelming force against the enemy's source of power and drive it onto the defensive which, given that it was a reflection of enemy strategy, implied that success could only be achieved in a war of attrition by holding the better hand in terms of total air power. Since superiority of the RAF was the default assumption, the way that the exercises were designed tended to support the Air Ministry mindset. Blatant prejudice prevented any useful lessons from being learned. A 1931 exercise awarded victory to an attacking bomber fleet despite one judge claiming that 84 out of 112 attacking bombers had been destroyed. The expectation was that any degree of bombing would have an enormous detrimental impact upon the morale of the urban working class, which is indicative of the elitist mentality and jaundiced views pervading the Air Ministry at the time. It is clear that the air exercises conducted by the RAF were not allowed to challenge the Air Staff doctrine dominated by a belief in the effectiveness of bombing. The failure to test the doctrinal orthodoxy handed down by Trenchard was a major failure of policy.[57] The 'will to win' embodied in the RAF ethos was seen as the leading factor in a nation's ability to prosecute war. It was accepted as axiomatic that a nation's capacity to fight would disintegrate when ordinary life became impossible. The British Air Staff obviously still saw the civilian population as a primary target in any strategic air offensive.

It was unfortunate that, having gone to the trouble of setting up and playing out the war games, very few lessons were learned. This allowed dubious theories, in the absence of counter evidence, to be reinforced. No answer was forthcoming, for instance, to the question of how a bomber force would pass through hostile airspace without unacceptable losses. The choice of the most important targets was not addressed. Details of how the actual attack itself would take place; the approach, the sighting of the target, the accurate delivery of bombs, escape tactics, none were seriously examined.[58] Air Staff, who were so enamoured of the 'bomber will always get through' idea, saw little advantage to their careers by spending much time considering how to put up a defence against them. It may be argued that the relative 'newness' of the RAF denied it the depth of experience and philosophy required to seamlessly arrive at a nuanced, sophisticated and comprehensive doctrine, but in that regard it was no worse off than any other country. The way in which it tried, however, does differentiate it from Germany, for instance. Germany, having been denied an air force by the Treaty of Versailles, had drawn many of its Air Staff from the army, who had brought with them a rigorous approach to their roles; the RAF, being extant only since 1917, had the opportunity to recruit directly into the service and instil in their personnel an air force mentality which, because of the hostility from the other two services, set them apart. This undoubtedly engendered a superior attitude, especially given the RAF's preference for public school and university-educated recruits. The result was that air doctrine was arrived at internally and was both hostile to army interference and constructed by officers trained and commanded by men whose experiences of air operations had been, to a greater or lesser extent, of a strategic nature in the far-flung lands of empire.

In August 1937, a major exercise was carried out simulating a bombing attack on London – in particular, Tilbury Docks, Thameshaven oil storage depot and Fighter Command HQ at Stanmore. Training was essential for the many young pilots coming through the system, and so attacks were made both day and night; camera guns were used to record the accuracy of fighter attacks. Of course, it was not only the flyers but ground organisations that needed the experience. Unfortunately, most of the aircraft in the exercise were old types and the dynamics of engagement bore almost no resemblance to the real situations the crews would find themselves in three years later. A total of 176 bombers were ranged against 222 fighters. The bomber force was made up of Hinds (top speed 195mph), Gordons (136), Heyford (131), Hendon (143), Battle (257) and Blenheims (279), while the fighter force included Gladiators (210), Gauntlets (228), Fury II (223) and Demon (202) aircraft. Compare this with the Messerschmitt Bf 109 (365mph) and Bf110 (326). Essentially, the exercise was useful in testing the basic organisation, but the outdated aircraft gave little indication of how a real attack might play out. Another exercise conducted in July 1938 to test East-coast defences showed how difficult it would be for enemy surface-forces to approach the British coast without being detected from the air. By far the biggest exercise was a fortnight later when 945 aircraft, including Hurricanes and Spitfires, took part. All civil aviation was prohibited in the area for the duration of the exercise, which took place during almost incessant torrential rain, thunderstorm and fog. The format of the exercise was more realistically to minimise the effects of air attack, and closely resembled what would become the standard defence policy of Fighter Command two years later. This was centred around the 'control and command' system devised by Hugh Dowding.

Hugh Caswall Tremenheere Dowding had joined the Royal Flying Corps in August 1914 as a pilot on No.7 Squadron. He achieved command rank in France and had first clashed with Trenchard during the war over the amount of rest he felt his pilots needed and were not being given. After the war he was given a permanent commission in the RAF and served in Iraq and Palestine. Back in Britain, he became Air Officer Commanding Fighting Area in 1929 and joined the Air Council as Air Member for Supply and Research a year later. In 1936, he was appointed Officer Commanding of the newly created RAF Fighter Command and went on to lead Fighter Command through most of the Battle of Britain. He retired from the RAF in 1942.

Dowding had come into Supply and Research just at a time when specifications (F7/30) were published for a day- and night-fighter with an armament of four .303-in machine guns, a top speed of at least 195mph, a high rate of climb, and a landing speed of 55mph. The specification stressed the importance of a good 'fighting view' from the cockpit and suggested a low-wing monoplane design. The Chief of the Air Staff, Sir Edward Leonard Ellington, objected to the single-seater format with wing-mounted guns, preferring the two-man turret fighter with more flexible gun-aiming capabilities, but the single-seater was not abandoned and specifications were upgraded as technological breakthroughs occurred. This difference of opinion pervaded the Air Ministry right up until Munich when Dowding's preference for the single-seater held sway and the RAF was, just in time, supplied with Spitfires and Hurricanes in sufficient quantity to fend off the Luftwaffe during the Battle of Britain.

Once the underlying doctrine was accepted, the questions of navigation and delivery were considered. Too often the debate over objectives lapsed into generalities rather than specifics. Too little attention was given to identifying particular targets and investigating the ways and means of striking at them. It was almost as if the mere adoption of a strategic air doctrine was deemed sufficient to deter an enemy and deep study of its implications somehow intellectually suspect and undermining of the ethos of self-confidence within the service.[59] When it is considered that the answer to a question about air doctrine on the admission paper for Air Staff was heavily biased towards aggressive attack on enemy morale, it is no wonder that such a mindset pervaded the service.

A memorandum from Trenchard to the Chiefs of Staff Sub-Committee of the Committee of Imperial Defence in May 1928, outlining the idea of the RAF being able to defeat an enemy by attacking their industrial centres, met with opposition. The First Sea Lord strongly attacked strategic bombing as being 'a departure from the principles of war which cannot be justified by experience'. He argued that there was no evidence to support the Air Staff's claims that aerial attack on centres of production, transportation and communications would paralyse 'the life and effort of the community'. This hostility forced Trenchard to accept that cooperation between services was essential in war. However, he maintained that offensive bombing attack against industrial cities would be the crucial strategy in any future war.[60]

In 1932 the Air Staff estimated that Germany was capable of dropping 600 tons of bombs on London each day, despite there being no German military aircraft capable of reaching the British mainland. Nevertheless, the Home Defence Committee accepted the estimate at face value and gloomily said, 'It is obvious that the weight of attack ... is so great that even if unlimited money and resources were available it would be impossible to prevent heavy casualties and great destruction of property.'[61] The impact of these estimates on British official thinking was profound, clearly showing that the British Air Staff did not rigorously evaluate bomber capabilities, or indeed aircraft capabilities, as a whole. A stubborn refusal to face up to reality and look to the future meant that specifications issued for new aircraft owed much more to what had gone before, and designs lacked ambition to grasp the possibilities offered by technological advances. Retractable undercarriages were still thought a novelty well into the 1930s. Rather than solving the problems of improved aircraft stability and robustness to recoil if armed with cannon, machine guns firing .303 calibre rifle bullets were considered adequate. There was no systematic analysis of the destructive power of bombs in current use. Operational commanders preferred a bomber to carry a number of small bombs rather than one big one, and doubted the efficiency of detonators to explode the biggest bombs. The only bombsight in use required the aircraft to approach its target in a perfect straight trajectory at constant speed which, in real combat situations, was an open invitation to anti-aircraft gunners.[62]

There was no doubt that theories of the destructive power of strategic bombing on civilian and industrial centres had taken hold of Air Ministry imagination, but this cannot be entirely attributed to Douhetist influences since his works were not translated into English until 1933; it was probably the residual memory of death raining from the skies over London from German bombers in 1917 that motivated Prime Minister Stanley Baldwin's speech delivered to the House of Commons on 10 November 1932, in which he said,

> it is well also for the man in the street to realise that there is no power on earth that can protect him from being bombed. Whatever people may tell him, the bomber will always get through. The only defence is in offence, which means that you have to kill more women and children more quickly than the enemy if you want to save yourselves.

Words were one thing, but actions were another. The implication of the speech was that Britain had to pose a more serious bomber threat than a potential enemy, but it also contained the unspoken caution that to start a competitive arms race increased the risk of war, and war, in the end, was the only thing that could justify the huge economic burden of rearmament. Despite Douhet's growing reputation as an air theorist, the first article to appear in the official journal of the Royal Air Force was not published until 1933 and his book, *The Command of the Air*, was never required reading at the RAF Staff College between the wars. The future Bomber Commander, Arthur Harris, was contemptuous of any suggestion that the RAF was influenced by Douhet when he said that '[nobody] in the Royal Air Force had ever read a book by an Italian and much less been influenced by one'.[63]

A serious flaw in Douhet's doctrine, overlooked by many of his acolytes such as Billy Mitchell, Trenchard, Slessor and Alexander de Seversky, was that there was never any attempt to address the most fundamental issues of identifying the key vital centres of a country that would be targeted and the humanitarian, and indeed legal, issues that would flow from the resulting huge numbers of civilian deaths. Moreover, the debate failed completely to consider the question of which specific target sets within those vital centres: industries, transportation nodes, and command and control facilities, were most important, and what the order of priority was for striking them. Neither did it spell out the mechanism by which destruction of industry and the slaughter of working populations in the vicinity would translate into capitulation of a regime. There might be some justification for the idea that popular revolt in a country under bombardment might influence a democratic government, but the question of how an authoritarian leadership might be persuaded to change policy as a result of civil unrest went unanswered. On the issue of targets, air war now required fundamentally different types of intelligence regarding a country's industrial and economic structure and potential. Because intelligence agencies did not yet exist that could provide this type of information, Douhet's acolytes simply side-stepped the issue and resorted to vague and simplistic platitudes. Trenchard, for one, argued that all effort should be directed towards breaking the enemy's morale, but gave little detail about how this might be brought about. In 1928 he spoke of targets as 'centres which are essential for the continuance of the enemy's resistance', and left it to his staff to specify the detail.

Trenchard, now aged 56, was replaced as Chief of the Air Staff on 1 January 1930 by Sir John Maitland Salmond, 'an intellectual lightweight with an overinflated reputation and a proclivity for ... intrigue', under whom Air Vice-Marshal Hugh Dowding was Air Member for Supply and Research.[64] The next couple of years found Salmond frantically fighting against political pressure to reduce the RAF as a commitment to the International Conference of the Limitation of Armaments in Geneva, but the collapse of the Conference in 1932 brought him some relief. Britain had held back on military development in the hope that Geneva would guarantee peace in Europe, but Dowding was now acutely aware of the consequences of Geneva's failure in terms of European security, and set about bringing Trenchard-era practices up to date in the face of burgeoning technological developments and was determined to change 'the whole attitude of the service'. His new approach to procurement was that instead of specifying every detail of a new aircraft, he would ask for an aircraft to have the capability of performing at a level that was considered to be the ideal for a given task and would then leave all the detail to the designers. It was they who would consider how a fighter might be employed against bomber formations, and it was they who would design it to have such capabilities. Many on the Air Staff favoured a two-man crewed interceptor with moveable machine gun, discounting the fact that the pilot could not see the intended target, but Dowding preferred the single-seater fighter with forward-facing guns. Ellington, a firm advocate of the two-seater, replaced Salmond in May 1933 and overruled Dowding. The result was the Boulton-Paul Defiant, designed to fly in formation and attack enemy bomber fleets from below in blithe disregard of any fighter protection the bombers might have chosen to bring along, but since the range of German fighters fell way short of British shores at the time, such an objection carried little weight. Dowding was unable to prevent huge orders going through for the Defiants, but he did quietly press on with his own exploration of promising designs for single-seater fighters and ordered prototypes without consulting the Air Staff. At the same time, he issued a specification for a long-range heavy bomber, but did not pursue it in the face of Air Staff pressure who thought it 'unduly large'.[65] If nothing else, Dowding was pragmatic and this temerity on his part, in contrast to his efforts to expedite fighter innovation, put back the British heavy bomber programme by a number of years and left Britain, in 1939, without the means to carry out its avowed prime mission of strategic bombing. It must be remembered, however, that Dowding had never been popular within the Air Ministry, and had he persisted in annoying the Air Staff by pressing on with bomber plans which they disapproved of, he might well have been shunted off to an administrative backwater or given early retirement, and one can only speculate on what might have been the consequences of that for Fighter Command in 1940.

It has been asserted that 'British strategic air power doctrine was acquired in a fit of absent-mindedness' as it confronted the decline of its Imperial power and relative impotence to influence events taking place in continental Europe.[66] After Hitler became Chancellor of Germany in 1933, however, Britain began to wake up to the reality of a rising instability in Europe. The mood became darker and pressure started to grow for a change of defence policy. Churchill, who had previously opposed any increase in military spending as Chancellor, now became its most vocal advocate. Rumour, disinformation and propaganda made it impossible to know, with any certainty, what the strength of the Luftwaffe was when Göring announced its presence to the world in March 1935, but the clear assumption was that it was well on the way to becoming more powerful than the RAF. The German walkout from the League of Nations prompted Dowding to remove the weight limit on new bomber design to boost Britain's strategic bombing capacity and follow the example of US aircraft coming off the Martin and Boeing production lines but, as yet, there was no enthusiasm for loosening the purse strings at the Treasury for development of a heavy bomber. The government, however, was sufficiently unnerved to make the commitment in March 1934 that 'no nation would be allowed to out-build Britain in air power'.[67] In his book *The Shadow of the Bomber*, Uri Bailer suggests that in this regard, the government was overreacting to public disquiet and laboured under an over-estimation of German air power. It announced 'Scheme A', under which the RAF would see an increase to forty-two squadrons over five years, with the bulk of extra squadrons being fighters; this would take the total number of aircraft throughout the Empire to 1,304 by 1939. When the Treasury, and surprisingly the Air Ministry, quietly opposed this plan, its hollow rhetoric was swiftly exposed as bravado. While the Treasury simply said they could not afford it, the Air Ministry objected to such 'window-dressing' on the grounds that it was not prepared to see its elite force diluted by a hastily cobbled together bunch of air recruits, into which it would have neither the time nor resources to inculcate its philosophy and culture.

Little progress was made with Scheme A because of budgetary restraints and the less-than-cosy relationship between the Air Ministry and the Society of British Aircraft Constructors. Politically, the strategic bomber force was seen as the best deterrent to another war, a theory fully supported by the Air Ministry, but there was precious little sign of such convictions transforming into reality and Dowding was growing restless at the systemic opposition to change. In May 1935, intelligence reported that the Luftwaffe was well ahead of the RAF in aircraft numbers, causing a seismic shock to the foundations of British air doctrine. The political ramifications resulted in 'Scheme C', which was intended to calm public alarm by giving the appearance of a further increase in aircraft numbers – but in reality, allowed the Air Ministry to continue dragging its feet. Where front-line strength was increased it was by the production of more obsolete aircraft such as the Fairey Hendon and the Handley-Page Heyford. Training facilities up to 1934 had been adequate to meet the requirements laid down by Trenchard, but the proposed increase in squadron numbers would require a significant concomitant increase in personnel. Civilian flying schools were seen as the answer in the Dominions as well as at home, but while Australia and New Zealand responded positively, Canada would only agree to training a small number of pilots each year. Southern Rhodesia and South Africa also agreed to set up training schools under RAF control.

In the mid-1930s, the Chancellor of the Exchequer, Neville Chamberlain, did not have rearmament on his agenda. He saw 'financial and economic risks [as being] the most serious and urgent [and] other risks [would] have to be run'.[68] His idea of air power was as a 'cost-effective alternative to surface forces', but he carried deep psychological scars from the First World War and firmly believed that Britain must never be drawn into another European war. Military budget cuts in 1934, however, brought swift condemnation from the press and Parliament, forcing the government into promising that 'no nation would be allowed to outbuild Britain in air power', but little was done in practice to make good on that promise. Inflated British intelligence estimates of the number of Luftwaffe aircraft and the levels of production in Germany far outweighed anything Britain could match and made mockery of such a commitment, but the Air Ministry itself was not enthusiastic about expansion of its force, believing that an increase in personnel would dilute its prized professionalism unless done at a modest and carefully controlled pace. Churchill challenged the government and the Air Ministry over their proposed air expansion programme calling it 'tiny, timid, tentative [and] tardy'.

The official German announcement of the existence of its Luftwaffe started a flurry of political and diplomatic activity. Britain declared that it could never accept Germany's superiority of air power and invited Germany to enter a pact to limit European air forces. Hitler addressed the Reichstag on 21 May 1935 and seemed to offer some hope that he might agree to this, but when the Foreign Office sent a note to him in August to pursue the matter, they received no reply. Hitler later justified his opposition to the idea by saying that acceptance of limitations on the size of the Luftwaffe would result in the destruction of Berlin by the Soviet air fleet. When the size of the Luftwaffe became apparent after 1935, even allowing for exaggerated claims, British air policy was plunged into a state of acute anxiety. The idea that the RAF's threat of retaliation in the event of an attack by Germany was undermined by the growing disparity between their forces. As a consequence, the concept of defence against the bomber gained traction. The enemy now had a name and any air policy had to focus on that. A futile and meaningless government call for 'national will' tried to disguise the state of unreadiness in the country. With a flagging economy and no sign of recovery to allow for an increase in the defence budget, the cost of making bomber aircraft compared to fighters became a significant factor in encouraging the RAF to adjust its focus towards defence. By now it was clear that the idea of 'the bomber always getting through' was flawed. The performance characteristics of the new breed of interceptors coming through, or in the case of the Messerschmitt Bf 109 already extant, gave pause for thought.

Under pressure, the British government introduced a new expansion scheme for the RAF designed to assuage public disquiet, but its rhetoric disguised the slow pace of Air Ministry compliance. Expansion of the RAF now meant that for the purposes of efficiency, it would have to be broken down into four specialised commands, Bomber at Uxbridge, Fighter at Stanmore, Coastal at Lee-on-Solent and Training at Tern Hill. The Fleet Air Arm went under direct naval control in 1937. The Cabinet retained control of general strategy, while the Chief of the Air Staff was responsible for its execution and implementation of general policy. Air Officers at each Command would be given guidance but would have a large measure of independence in deciding how to achieve the desired objectives. The different Commands were sub-divided into Groups led by an Air Vice-Marshal or an Air Commodore with responsibility for all sectors within the group area. Fighter Command was set up on 6 July 1936 under, now Air Marshal, Dowding at Bentley Priory near Stanmore, although he believed his appointment to be a temporary twelve-month step-up to the post of Chief of the Air Staff.

The lack of clear air doctrine and the 'bewildering variety of expansion schemes' throughout the 1930s in response to the changing political climate on mainland Europe had resulted in a constant flurry of new plans, new aircraft, new systems and constant retraining which left Britain 'woefully unprepared to conduct [air operations] once war broke out'.[69] Manufacturing was inefficient at the beginning of 1936, with no less than fourteen different aircraft manufacturers building eighteen different types of aircraft. To meet new requirements, a great deal of retooling and retraining of staff was required, and raw material supply lines had to be established. The issue of flying personnel was addressed by more than a dozen civil flying schools being set up, while five new military flying schools were formed and training schemes were upgraded. Over a thousand new recruits entered the service as air expansion 'was being carried out with the utmost vigour and energy'.[70] A figure of 1,750 aircraft was authorised for home defence, with many specifications now incorporating the new technologies of monoplane design and metal bodies. To make up the numbers, however, many older types of aircraft had to be produced while facilities on the shop floor for the newer ones were put in place. Production was slow to improve with less than 1,000 aircraft produced in 1935. One problem was that the Air Ministry had never enjoyed a close relationship with aircraft manufacturers. Factories had been poorly served by the Air Ministry's vacuous promises of orders that never materialised and constant vacillation over designs which had not encouraged innovation, had given them little confidence to invest in the new manufacturing processes required for modern aircraft. The Ministry, for its part, had been unimpressed with the speed and level of factory output when orders had actually been placed. Now the government, under Secretary of State for Air, Viscount Swinton, had been forced to respond by financing the construction of 'shadow factories', introduced as a means of increasing production. At first, they were no more than extensions of existing automobile factories such as those at Austin and Rover who turned over production capacity to the making of parts for the Mercury aero engine, but later new factories were built at government expense specifically laid out for aircraft production. As for design specifications, in the absence of government funding advances were fortuitously made by private individuals for the early Schneider Trophy-winning Spitfire prototype.[71] The Spitfire and Hurricane appeared for the first time in public at the Hendon Air Display on 27 June 1936. Among the 150,000 crowd was Herr Kösters, the Heinkel aircraft company designer.

On 30 July that same year, Swinton announced the formation of the RAF Volunteer Reserve, designed to train 800 new pilots a year. Training centres were set up close to major cities all across the British Isles. Volunteers would be between 18 and 25 and sign up for five years. Flight training was given at weekends and pilots would receive £25 per year plus allowances. In the following year Hendon saw a crowd of 200,000, including the German Ernst Udet, head of the Technical Office of the Luftwaffe, greet King George VI and Queen Elizabeth. Meanwhile the Deputy Chief of the Air Staff, Air Chief Marshal Sir Christopher Courtney, had been invited to inspect aircraft factories in Germany where he met State Secretary of the Reich Ministry of Aviation Erhard Milch, who made a return visit a few months later with Udet and Luftwaffe Chief of Staff Hans-Jürgen Stumpff.

Dowding estimated that forty-five fighter squadrons would be adequate to meet any bomber threat from Germany, but the first training exercises carried out in 1937 were not encouraging. Even with the advantage of height and position, bi-plane fighters were unable to intercept the faster Bristol Blenheim bombers, but in the following year prospects were improved by the introduction of the first monoplane Hurricane fighters. Germany had encouraged foreign air forces to view its Luftwaffe displays and facilities, not only for the purposes of propaganda to give an inflated impression of its strength, but also to facilitate return visits by its own experts to get some impression of foreign developments in air power.

It was clear by 1936 that Germany had a vastly superior air force to Britain, which made mockery of the government's commitment to parity. Prime Minister Chamberlain's meeting with Hitler in Munich may have eased tensions, but the reality was that if Britain wanted to oppose German ambitions in central Europe it would be risking an onslaught by more than a thousand modern German bombers and would have only 760 fighters as a defensive screen, and less than 100 of those were modern Hurricanes. The fear of the Luftwaffe launching a massive pre-emptive bombing strike against Britain clouded Air Ministry deliberations. A flurry of special committees looked again at air defence policy. The sheer scale of the problem threatened to paralyse the Air Staff, but there was a move to reassess the previous default policy of strategic counter-offensive which was starting to give way to the concept of fighter defence.

The expectation was that in the event of hostilities Germany, who could not afford a protracted war, would launch a massive bombing strike in a bid to cripple British industry. This thought, while not comforting, at least allowed Prime Minister Chamberlain to promote the less expensive option of manufacturing fighter aircraft instead of bombers. The Air Ministry, however, was not giving up on bombers. They argued that domination of the enemy was achieved by having more bombers not more fighters, which may well have been a logical argument; the fact of the matter, however, was that the RAF simply had less, not more, bombers than the enemy and those they had were technically inferior and not in a position to 'dominate'.[72] The absence of adequate aircraft in both numbers and type, however, was not allowed to interfere with dogma and could not be allowed to undermine the supposed soundness of the theory. Slessor, now Deputy Director of Plans, and Deputy Chief of the Air Staff Sholto Douglas retained confidence in the ability of their new breed of fast bombers, which were at the design stage, to protect themselves over Germany against single-seater fighter interlocution, despite evidence from the Spanish Civil War that the Bf 109 had proved to be a formidable adversary.

Britain had followed events in Spain closely, not least because of the proximity to the conflict of Gibraltar and its close trading relations with Spain, but they also admitted they would have liked 'more red-hot information from Spain'. The Joint Intelligence Committee, because of its 'low opinion of the judgement and character of the Air Staff', formed a sub-committee JIC(S) to improve their flow of intelligence. It was seen as vital to collect as much intelligence as possible about German and Italian aviation but, unfortunately, innate prejudice and an unwillingness to accept evidence contrary to their ingrained opinions would minimise the benefits of their observations. On the ground, the lack of active agents meant that they could not find out about 'bombing effects' and struggled to 'get something useful'. The Foreign Office had 'consistently opposed' having anyone embedded at Franco's headquarters which meant that the British had no 'trained military observers'. When reports were filed, they initially highlighted deficiencies rather than strengths. The success of bombing was attributed to poor aerial defences, yet they still used this to support their own policy of reliance on anti-aircraft artillery, presumably inasmuch as it did not offer any 'admittedly incomplete' evidence to oppose it. On the other hand, their own preferred strategic bombing doctrine, they said, had not been tested, with 'air forces becoming very much tied to army tactical requirements', and so could not be refuted.[73]

As for the defence of their own realm, as far as they were concerned the Defiant was sufficient to stop the enemy bombers over Britain; it could indeed deliver a mighty punch in beam attacks from various angles, unlike the single-seater Bf 109 or Hurricane which could only fire forward. This view prevailed in the face of mounting evidence that German bombers were faster than the Defiant and would prove to be elusive targets, but with orders for 450 Defiants now with the manufacturer they had little choice but be optimistic. The Air Ministry argument for its policy was predicated on the fragile assumption that German bombers over Britain would be too far from home to carry fighter escort, as was the case for British bombers over Germany, but that balance of power would be mightily disturbed when German bombers started operating from French airfields after June 1940. Fortunately, orders would be placed later in 1938 for 1,000 Spitfires at Castle Bromwich, but delays to the Hawker Typhoon would mean that production of the Hurricane, fast becoming obsolete, would have to be continued in the meantime.

Dowding had been charged with looking at policy and strategy to address the problems of German air superiority. He assumed a German bomber force of 1,700 aircraft which required 'defence in depth' for the industrial heartland of Britain. The next government initiative was 'Scheme F', which promised to put Britain on a sound war footing with a front-line force of 1,750 aircraft, of which 1,000 would be modern bombers. It offered an increase in aircraft numbers for home defence at the expense of the Fleet Air Arm and Far Eastern forces. Having got over the hurdle of Treasury objections to expansion, however, there remained the problem of limited industrial production capacity over which all armed services had to compete with each other under a finite defence budget dictated by the Treasury. The Air Ministry, within this framework, argued forcefully for holding down expenditure on Far Eastern commitments and plans for an Expeditionary Force to mainland Europe in favour of an expanded strategic bomber force, which was the only thing that could stop German aggression. When Chamberlain became Prime Minister in May 1937, however, he adopted a conciliatory tone towards Germany and desperately tried to avoid a slide into war. A new mood of caution overtook Whitehall as he addressed the urgent need to restrain spiralling defence costs which he felt could only exacerbate the crisis and make the European political situation even more unstable.[74] As part of a freeze on defence spending, he advocated a strategy based upon air defence which he saw as the least expensive option to counter the threat from Germany. The Air Staff making an urgent grab for the largest slice of the budgetary pie now put forward 'Scheme J' and claimed that it required 2,331 aircraft for home defence, of which almost two-thirds would be bombers.

Then in December 1937, Sir Thomas Inskip, the Minister for Co-ordination of Defence, with Dowding's support, came out with a slick piece of sophistry backing up Chamberlain's position by rewriting history and suggesting that RAF doctrine had never actually been about delivering a knock-out blow to an enemy at all, but had all the time been designed to force them to resist the temptation to launch such an attack on Britain by threatening devastating reprisal. The idea of strategic air power delivering a quick victory had never been proven, he said, and had never really underpinned air doctrine. The way to defeat Germany would be first of all to survive any immediate attack, and then draw it into a long war in which Britain's superior economic strength would assure victory, a scenario that would clearly be a repetition of the First World War. There was absolutely no requirement for a bomber force to match that of Germany, since 'the decisive place and the decisive time for the concentration of our forces would be somewhere over our own territory at the outset of war'.[75] The Air Ministry was indignant that its most cherished beliefs were being denigrated and replied that such a strategy was a form of 'suicide'. The reality was that the doctrine of bomber deterrence, which had never actually been fully implemented, was being replaced by a doctrine of fighter defence for which there was no clear policy, let alone sufficient aircraft. One gamble was being replaced by another in a move that looked more like prevarication than decision. The point that Britain was avoiding here was the question of what it could threaten Germany with to deter an attack against Czechoslovakia or Poland. The Air Ministry had little to offer in this regard.

The rate of expansion of the German armed forces, in particular the Luftwaffe, and the resulting shift in the balance of military power, was something to which other countries had been slow to respond and subsequently unable or unwilling to match. The timescale for rearmament was such that for Britain to have been ready for war in 1939, it would have had to have given its full attention to a coordinated plan from as early as 1934, and that would have entailed putting the economy onto a war footing at a time before the Luftwaffe had even been officially unveiled. A policy of disarmament had seemed the prudent option in 1934, but this had given way to appeasement which then began to collapse after the Anschluss. All that was left after that was a desperate move to face the reality of war with time running out. Building up a strategic capability in such a short time was evidently impossible, leaving a hastily cobbled together air defence strategy based on fighters in a desperate hope that somehow, supported by the 'Dowding System' of command and control, they could hold off the bombers. Malcolm Smith summed it up by saying that because of a failure of integration of military, diplomatic and budgetary departments, 'the RAF went to war and won its most famous victory with a policy that made nonsense of everything the Air Staff had been teaching for the last twenty years'.[76]

The limitations across the whole spectrum of RAF aircraft in 1939 were apparent to all. The bombers were too slow, too lightly armed, too poorly protected, and carried too little ordnance to cause significant damage, while the fighters, swift and agile though they were, lacked the firepower required to bring down large numbers of bombers. New fighter and bomber aircraft in the advanced stages of design had all been delayed by obfuscation and technical problems. The Short Stirling bomber had a weak undercarriage (a fault incidentally shared with the Junkers Ju 88), the Avro Manchester was underpowered and required urgent modifications to its wings and tailplane, and worst of all, the Vickers Wellington, which carried the hopes of many, had to be completely redesigned after its disastrous first air trials. All bomber armaments and armour-plating had now to be upgraded in light of the prospect of attacks by the much faster Bf 109s; this increase in vulnerability of the bomber meant also that either targets had to be within the range of fighter escort, or raids would have to be carried out at night, which inevitably reduced the chance of hitting the target.

The inescapable conclusion is that the RAF as a whole never fully appreciated that the First World War could only provide a partial basis on which to build an air doctrine. Too early in its existence it had adopted the idea of strategic air power as an article of faith and had lacked the intellectual rigour and insight to subject its hypothesis to test and experiment. Lessons should have been learned from the way in which the massive strategic bombardment of Barcelona in the Spanish Civil War not only failed to break the will of the Catalonians, but stiffened their resistance, but these were completely ignored. The Air Ministry had even actively discouraged internal debate on the subject. An independent strategic role for the RAF was actually more than just a theory of air warfare, it was also a political weapon employed to resist the incessant pressure from the army to have it subsumed back under army control. In effect, only the RAF (went the argument) could prevent the sudden, catastrophic collapse of morale that would result from a devastating enemy bombing assault. This effectively hollowed out RAF doctrine. It had the appearance of substance, but no real content. All areas of development suffered as a consequence. Dogma effectively barred off whole avenues of inquiry, research and development. This was manifest in the belief, held for so long, that since the 'bomber would always get through', there was little point in wasting huge sums on trying to stop it and, working on the assumption that a similar conclusion would be arrived at by the enemy, there was little need to heavily fortify the bomber itself. This dogmatic approach meant that most of the exercises carried out to test RAF capabilities and potential lacked rigour and were designed by RAF planners with an arrogant assumption that their own views would be held with equal certitude by the enemy. The evolution of air doctrine within the Air Ministry may be best illustrated by reference to Thomas Kuhn's majestic work *The Structure of Scientific Revolutions*, in which he describes the way that tenacious allegiance to dogma by leaders who have based their careers on it, can only be broken by a sudden 'revolutionary' paradigm shift when the level of contrary evidence reaches a critical mass.

The fundamental flaw with RAF doctrine was that it was not really a doctrine at all. It was a theory held by officers who had never had the inclination or confidence to question it too closely and had never related doctrinal dogma to technological development, which would have exposed its weaknesses. In the early years of its existence, the RAF had been forced to fight to exist against army and navy hostility by emphasising its unique weapon of strategic bombing as evidence of its indispensability, but thereafter it failed to appreciate how development of fighter capabilities was undermining the concept. The Air Staff, however, were 'not inclined to view the concept of strategic bombing critically', which, had they done so, would have allowed the possibility of it maturing into something more like a doctrine.[77] The whole approach became one of how equipment policy, tactical development and operational planning were all undertaken with a view to how they fitted into prevailing dogma, rather than how they might advance a better understanding. Institutional rigidity meant that whole avenues of inquiry, research and development were closed off which, had the concept of defence against bombing attack been taken more seriously, or even considered at all, might have led to faster and better armed bombers being built. This was not a useful approach for either Bomber Command or Fighter Command, but Dowding did at least belatedly see the folly of it and it was only his last-minute drive to confront reality that made the difference.

In September 1938, the Air Council considered the legal implications of strategic bombing now that the theories upon which its doctrine had been built were nearing the point of application. Although Britain had never ratified the Hague Rules of 1923, Prime Minister Chamberlain insisted that his government would apply the principles of law with respect to aerial warfare. This meant that deliberate attacks upon civilian populations were illegal, military targets must be clearly identified by the bombers, and every effort must be made to restrict bombing to military objectives. The Air Ministry admitted that collateral casualties would be unavoidable, but actions must be rigorously restricted to unmistakeably military targets. Part of this approach was to avoid alienating US President Roosevelt, who had appealed for restraint. Chief of the Air Staff, Sir Cyril Newall, in a submission to the Air Ministry admitted that such a policy would not long survive the first shot of war, but Britain 'obviously [could not] be the first to take the gloves off'.[78]

Trust in the bomber ebbed after 1938 when it was clear that, as war loomed, RAF Bomber Command were not capable of delivering the sort of blow that would deter German aggression. When war was declared, the government was left with no alternative but to send an Expeditionary Force backed up by an Advanced Air Striking Force to support the French lines, and found itself becoming embroiled in another continental war which they had assiduously tried to avoid for the previous twenty years. The air component, however, would not be 'attached' to the army, but would operate as an independent force and 'there was no question of RAF units being on call to an Army commander'. So much for ground support, a role for which the RAF was neither trained nor equipped, but Douglas assured his army counterpart that they 'need not feel any anxiety'.[79] This despite fighter squadrons sent to France having to operate from front-line temporary airfields when they had been trained to defend fixed positions from well-equipped permanent bases.

For Britain and France, the scars of the First World War were slow to heal. Political and military leaders had been thoroughly chastened by the slaughter of the trenches and it was the fear of a repetition that drove their policies in the post-war decades. In the process of avoiding, as much as possible, consideration or debate about new dangers, military policies had become ossified and what appeared to be demonstrable truths arrived at in 1918 were not forensically examined. However laudable it was to work for peace, this had the effect of blinding them to new realities and, where some effort was made to move on, a reliance upon misconceived ideas took them down paths which were mapped out according to erroneous preconceptions. Britain, right up until the Czechoslovakian crisis, had prevaricated and done all it could to avoid being drawn into another European war. It was accepted that Germany would want to re-establish itself as a major European power and Britain, seeing no immediate threat of attack on itself or its Empire, was not unhappy about the prospect of a resurgent, powerful, militaristic German nation as a bulwark to Soviet communism. In terms of air doctrine, there seemed little need to refine any tactical ground-support capability given the ambition to avoid letting its army become involved in another continental land war. The strategic bombing doctrine of deterrence, to which it had become sturdily attached, not least because of the dominant and enduring influence of Trenchard, was the default option against which any alternative had to be matched and to do so successfully would need to entail a powerful set of arguments. There were dissenting voices, however, albeit muted at first, that had started to make inroads into the established doctrine after the German reoccupation of the Rhineland in 1936. It was beginning to dawn on the British Air Ministry that air defence might, after all, be possible and that their much-vaunted bombers were not going to have such an easy passage to Berlin, but there was still little enthusiasm to go public with doubts and expose their misconceptions to debate. It took the vision and determination of Churchill and Dowding to belatedly knock an isolationist government out of its lethargy and force a rethink of doctrine. They eventually forced the country to recognise the very real threat of German bombers over London once again and in so doing, persuaded the government to give serious consideration to a fighter defence of the realm.

Chapter 5

French Air Power before 1939

'This is not peace. It is an armistice for twenty years.'
French commander-in-chief Marshal Ferdinand
Foch commenting on the Treaty of Versailles.[1]

France came early to the table of air power theory with the writings of Clément Ader, an aviation pioneer who had built three 'bat-like' flying machines driven by steam power, the first one in 1886. Alongside his machines, Ader wrote a treatise describing three main types of aircraft: éclaireurs (scouts); torpilleurs (bombers); and avions de ligne (aircraft of the line). Predicting the role of an aircraft carrier, he even called for 'an airplane-carrying vessel [with] all the deck cleared of all obstacles'. His book went through ten editions and the French word for aircraft, 'avion', is attributed to him.

Throughout the First World War and during the two decades that followed, all the major European powers had acquired varying levels of experience in aerial warfare, but few had any clear concept of how to enshrine that experience in doctrine. France is an excellent example of how a failure to learn the fundamental lessons from the conflagration relegated it from the pre-eminent air power in Europe in 1918, to one that was destroyed in a matter of weeks during the German invasion in 1940. Its defeat then was the result of a senior military leadership having little understanding of air power and its capabilities. During the First World War, the French aircraft industry and aircraft engine industry had led the world in production and technical efficiency with the introduction of the first supercharged engine as well as the SPAD S.VII and S.XIII fighters and the Breguet XIV bomber and by the last year of that war, they had developed into a superb tactical force adept at supporting ground units with reconnaissance, artillery spotting, close air support, and interdiction attacks. They had even attempted to introduce a strategic dimension to their campaigns but the results were disappointing and did not encourage further exploitation.[2]

This French ascendency in 1918 had been built on a fine tradition. The French Army had first used a hydrogen-filled reconnaissance balloon, manned by Jean-Marie Joseph Coutelle, to great effect in the Battle of Maubeuge on 23 June 1794 and again on the 26th at Fleurus, making them one of the great pioneers of military aviation. They took to dirigibles with equal enthusiasm and the military had even invested in aircraft prototypes as early as 1891, but withdrew support after a few years of disappointing results. It took displays by the Wright Brothers in 1908 and a record-breaking 100-mile flight by a French Farman aircraft in 1909 to persuade the French Army to return to aviation research and buy two Antoinettes, three Farman biplanes and two Wright biplanes for trials to replace balloons as observation platforms. There was an immediate row between the Artillery, who wanted to retain aircraft for short-range observation, and Engineering branches of the army, who saw a wider, more independent role for aviation 'without limits'.[3] While the Engineers were the more vociferous in pleading their case, they failed to come up with any ideas of how aircraft might be used for anything other than artillery spotting, but managed to negotiate specifications for new military aircraft in 1913 which included two different types. A light, single-engine, single-seater observation aircraft and a larger twin-engine, two-seater reconnaissance type offered a modicum of scope for imaginative deployment.

An aerial arm of the French military was created as the 'Aéronautique Militaire' but operated totally within the confines of army control. Naturally the army looked at ways of integrating this new capability into its existing army doctrine and gave little thought to how it might create a new dimension to warfare. In 1914, it was still the tethered balloon which allowed ground forces to see beyond the immediate terrain and spy on enemy movements. These balloons observed the battle area in the vicinity and reported, via fixed line, to ground commanders on enemy troop deployment and movements, as well as acting as artillery spotters to identify targets. They had a certain vulnerability, however, when aircraft were deployed against them. On both sides, balloons were seen as easy targets for prowling aircraft to attack with hand-held guns or crude rockets and this in turn spawned a requirement for a defensive strategy, also provided by aircraft who would protect the balloon by challenging the enemy aircraft and forcing them to withdraw. It was then a simple realisation that aircraft could supplement or even supplant balloons by doing a similar job, but with less risk and greater freedom to operate over a wider area of the battle front as a sort of airborne version of the cavalry. The army's constant requirement for accurate reconnaissance intelligence persuaded it that military aviation should be developed exclusively to provide them with suitable reconnaissance aircraft and specialist fighters to protect these over enemy territory. Exhibiting a lack of imagination that would become familiar to Air Staff throughout Europe during the following years, the army decried any other employment of aircraft as a waste of resources.

Aircraft were soon to play a pivotal role in the trajectory of the whole First World War in a dramatic demonstration of what aerial reconnaissance was capable of. After the German attack on France in 1914, the Allied armies were in full retreat, falling back towards the river Marne. A German Rumpler Taube flown by Leutnant Hindelson dropped two small bombs on Paris as the city was threatened with encirclement.[4] Alexander von Klück, commander of the German 1st Army, then made a fateful change in his hitherto successful invasion plan. Instead of enveloping Paris from the west as originally prescribed, he turned eastward – risking its flank to a counter-attack from the south by the French Sixth Army. On 2 September, a French patrol captured a set of German documents, along with a map delineating the enemy's new line of march. The German Army's exposed right flank offered French General Joffre the opportunity he had been waiting for to counter-attack; he was prepared to take advantage of it but required confirmation of the German positions. There was no time to send out a cavalry patrol, so he asked for an aviator to volunteer and up came aircraft designer and manufacturer Sergeant Louis Charles Breguet. He flew with Lieutenant André Wateau as his observer in a new aircraft he had designed, called the AG 4 and given serial No. BR52. They took off over the German lines and confirmed the earlier intelligence. Follow-up flights by R.E.P. and Maurice Farman aircraft provided more details of the First Army's location and movements. Based upon that intelligence, Joffre initiated a massive counter-attack on 6 September instigating the six-day First Battle of the Marne, which stopped the German Army in its tracks and condemned both sides to static trench warfare for the next four years.

The success of this incident prompted an immediate expansion of military aviation, but confusion reigned when responsibilities for supply and operations were split between two men, Captain Joseph-Édouard Barès, commander of the 4th Army air units, and General Auguste Hirschauer, War Ministry Director of Aeronautics, who did not see eye-to-eye with each other and neither of whom had the final say. Things settled down when Hirschauer was replaced by a civilian, René Henry Besnard who was 'young, dedicated and affable, [having] all the qualities required to succeed in his difficult task', but he, much to the chagrin of the army, would prove more amenable to considering an independent role for aircraft. He supported some level of political independence for the air force, advocated large-scale production of aircraft using Hispano-Suiza-8 engines and hastened production of the multi-purpose Caudron G.4. Besnard soon became aware, however, of the same problems his predecessor had faced when negotiating with the aircraft manufacturers who had powerful political connections. When he accused Michelin and Voisin of delaying the introduction of new designs in an attempt to maximise profits from existing ones he came up against formidable opposition. There had always been a sense that aircraft manufacturers, along with other military industries, were profiteering from government contracts but opposing them was fraught with danger. Political and business vested interests plotted against him and found an excuse to have him removed after he was charged with failing to protect civilians during a Zeppelin raid on Paris in January 1916.

Barès was 'a progressive thinker and dynamic aircraft promoter who had flown in the Balkan Wars of 1912'.[5] Realising that the war was not going to be over quickly, he reversed many of his predecessor's actions and set about preparing industry and the flying units for a prolonged encounter. As an advocate of strategic aerial action, he saw German industries as a legitimate target, but forbade attacks against cities and civilian populations. His first programme of expansion called for sixteen long-range reconnaissance, thirty observation, three high-speed single-seater reconnaissance and sixteen bomber squadrons (escadrilles). Reconnaissance was the prime focus but Barès was keen to explore the potential for bombing and encouraged all reconnaissance aircraft to hoist a few well-aimed bombs at the enemy as they passed over their lines. While artillery spotting was never less than a vital role for military aircraft, it did not prevent them from slowly opening up new areas for battlefield intervention which built one upon the other to open up a whole range of possibilities.

By December 1914 the first bomber squadrons, made up of Breguet and Voisin pushers, went into service on the front line and by the spring four bomber groups had carried out raids on railway stations and industrial targets inside Germany. On 26 May 1915, eighteen bombers carried out a spectacularly successful raid when they flew 250 miles to drop converted artillery shells on explosives and gas factories in Luwigshafen and Opau. Enthused army leaders wanted to expand the bomber force even further and launch raids on the Essen armament factories in what would have been a classic strategic operation designed to debilitate the German war effort. In the meantime more large raids were carried out against blast furnaces at Dillingen, but aircraft losses were by no means negligible on these types of operations as Germany began to deploy fighter interceptor aircraft to bring the bombers down. Anti-aircraft artillery was set up also forcing the bombers to fly higher over the target which inevitably reduced the accuracy of their bombing, meaning that operations became less and less profitable from a military perspective. Strategic bombing, in practice, was in decline as bombers were found closer tactical targets along the battle front, but the concept remained attractive and was kept alive pending the development of more suitable aircraft. This was not the case with the army, however, who had lost its early enthusiasm for strategic bombing and now demanded that the aviation industry concentrate on the manufacture of more and better reconnaissance and fighter aircraft. As a result, there was little interest from industry in the manufacture of bombers. Barès requested a twin-engine, multi-crewed fighter-reconnaissance aircraft with heavy cannon armament, but it was the lighter single-seaters that proved to be more successful in combat as the French began to see some aerial dominance over the battle lines in 1915.

Roland Georges began flying in 1909 in a Demoiselle monoplane and quickly became a proficient pilot, entering several European air races. In 1913 he made the first eight-hour non-stop flight across the Mediterranean from France to Tunisia, during which he had to resolve two engine malfunctions. In 1915, he became interested in the problem of arming aircraft with machine guns. Previously such weapons had been hand-held or strapped to the fuselage in such a way that the bullets avoided hitting the propeller. A new idea had been to fix a cam to the propeller drive shaft to activate a machine gun firing mechanism so that it only fired when the propeller blades were outside the line of fire but the lack of standardisation in machine gun technology meant that the firing sequence was irregular, causing some bullets to misfire and hit the blades. Of course this was catastrophic for the aircraft so Garros came up with the idea of reinforcing the blades with armour so that if a bullet struck it would be deflected and cause no damage. This worked quite well for small calibre machine gun bullets but would require some rethinking as bullet calibres increased. For the moment, however, the system worked perfectly and he shot down a number of German aircraft before his Morane-Saulnier 'Parasol' aircraft was forced down over German lines. Fokker engineers examined it and copied the cam mechanism which they improved to work perfectly, allowing uninterrupted firing of a cannon without risking catastrophic damage. Synchronised guns were now fitted to all German Fokker Eindeckers which started to wrest control of the air space from the French. Since most aerial combats were taking place over German occupied territory, the French were not able to benefit in similar fashion from downed German aircraft. Their reconnaissance flights of antiquated pushers suffered badly at the hands of the newly fitted-out Fokkers and operations were no longer undertaken with confidence.

Barès urgently called for twin-engine, multi-seaters with guns facing fore and aft, but only got the single-engine multi-purpose Caudron G.4. Pilots were not at all happy with the way things were going and improvised by using the Nieuport 10 reconnaissance aircraft, one of the fastest in use at the time, as single-seater fighters with a fixed machine gun on the upper wing firing above the propeller. They had to stand up to fire it, but at least it gave them a fighting chance in combat with the Fokkers. A scaled down version, the Nieuport bébé, proved to be an excellent machine but Barès did not appreciate the significance of this development on the fighting front and persisted in his quest for heavier, multi-purpose aircraft. He was thwarted, however, by the manufacturers who had no facilities to produce the types he wanted and were unenthusiastic about investing in them, having seen a number of prototypes come to grief. It was pressure from the pilots at the front who made it clear that what they wanted to go up against the Fokkers was the single-seater nippy and aggressive fighter aircraft; they got one with the Nieuport 11, although in fewer numbers than they might have liked. These aircraft were concentrated on the Verdun sector against the German attack in February 1916 and deployed in squadron strength operating behind the German lines. The Germans set up barrier patrols but the Fokkers could not cope with the Nieuports. The reconnaissance missions, however, continued to take heavy losses simply because there were not enough fighters to protect them until the Nieuport 17 with its synchronised machine gun came on the scene, after which the tide began to turn in France's favour once again. Up to this point there had been insufficient numbers of German aircraft to challenge the French tactics of operating in group strength but when the main battle front shifted to the Somme a few months later, the French fighters became spread over a wider area and the Germans were better able to engage them on more equal terms.

By this time, the Germans had got their Albatros D fighters and had followed the French pattern of flying in packs, giving them parity even as the French introduced the SPADs with the new more powerful Hispano-Suiza engines. Barès had started to come round to the need for more agile fighters, but not sufficiently quickly and the factories could not produce enough. Army demands for more protection for their reconnaissance patrols which continued to take heavy losses without the required number of fighter escorts met with opposition from air force commander Colonel Paul de Peuty, resulting in a struggle for control of aviation along the Front. When Robert Nivelle became commander-in-chief of the French Army he replaced Barès with de Peuty, who began to impose his offensive fighter tactics over the protection role. When the 1916 spring offensive loomed, the fighter aircraft, numbering some 500 on each side, would be ready for a gargantuan air battle with considerably expanded forces.

Under de Peuty, the French air force had started to go its own way by sending out offensive patrols 'without restriction' behind German lines to hunt down and destroy enemy fighters, leaving their reconnaissance patrols pretty much to their own devices. This was not altogether successful since the German Albatroses were superior in many ways to the Nieuports and were able to avoid or engage them as they chose, according to whether they had advantageous position.[6] The French were thwarted and were achieving little. Their fighters were at a disadvantage in their preferred role of 'free hunting', while their reconnaissance aircraft were out patrolling without adequate protection. Germany was clearly winning the tactical war and French losses began to mount at an unsustainable rate. The French Army commanders furiously challenged de Peuty's tactics and were able to regain control of the fighters on the Front. His tactics had been too ambitious for the resources under his command.

The morale of the French air force in May 1917 had plummeted to an all-time low.[7] Poorly equipped and under-strength squadrons were still flying antiquated pushers, and the bombers did not dare to venture out either by day or night. Fighter deployment was still an unresolved issue. There were thirty-seven different types of aircraft on order. Only a little over half of all aircraft produced were reaching the front lines in combat-ready condition due to missing parts or poor fitting-out, and a quarter of those that did were of obsolete design.[8] The French Cabinet fell and the newly appointed commander-in-chief, General Pétain, shunted de Peuty back to his regiment (he was killed in action a few months later) and replaced him with Colonel Duval, who wasted no time in reining in the fighters to act more in line with army requirements. Duval 'did not have an aeronautical background' and was, consequently, expected to tackle his new role with an open mind.[9] He restricted production to only thirteen types of aircraft, of which a number were of new designs with more powerful engines, such as the Breguet XIV A2 and Salmson 2. Supporters of strategic bombing struggled to make their case to Duval who had appreciated the requirement for a day-bombing capability but, like Pétain, considered it to be a secondary role for bombers whose primary function was army support in combat areas. The main German industrial targets were considered too far away to be effectively bombed, but occasional attacks on rail communications behind the German lines would not be out of the question. In line with German expansion of their fighter force, Duval more than doubled the French contingent to eleven fighter groups with varying characteristics according to their intended roles. Unfortunately for him, he was let down in his campaign for parity by the failure of the Morane-Saulnier MoS 29 to live up to expectations, leaving him short of a reliable and effective fighter, but overall, numbers of efficient, high-performance aircraft were still rising. An updated version of the Breguet XIV was showing promise as a day bomber but it was never allowed to stray too far from the lines.

In July 1917, the German occupation of Lorraine and Luxembourg, where much of its iron was produced, and the coalfields of the border region, presented French strategists with an opportunity. If these areas could be isolated from the great industries of the Ruhr and Saar, then a

The glider in which the future famous Russian aircraft designer Andrei Tupolev made its first flight. (Alamy)

Aviators Wssewolod Abramovitch (1890-1913) and Russian princess Eugenia Mikhailovna Shakhovskaya (1889-1920). The two aviators were in an aircraft crash in 1913 in which Abramovitch was killed. (Alamy)

Above: Second Lieutenant Giulio Gavotti of the *Squadriglia di Tripoli*, dropped four small bombs from a German-built Etrich Taube on the towns of Taguira and Ain Zara on 1 November 1911. (Alamy)

Left: The French First World War pilot Eugène Adrien Roland Georges Garros. (Alamy)

Colonel Ludomil Antoni Rayski who became commander of the Polish Air Force days before Piłsudski's coup d'état in May 1926. (Alamy)

General Colonel Hans von Seeckt and Adolf Hitler watch Wermacht manoeuvres 1936. (Alamy)

Aircrafts on the secret Reichswehr flight centre in Lipetsk. They are most likely planes of the type Heinkel HD 40 ca. 1930. (Alamy)

Lord Trenchard (right) with Sir S. Hoare centre and Air Vice Marshal Halahan after the foundation stone of a new RAF College was laid at Cranwell July 1935. (Alamy)

dramatic reduction in war materiel production would surely follow. Rather than attack the industrial resources, which would inevitably risk a high level of civilian casualties and possibly provoke reprisal raids, the plan was to sever communications by striking with night bombers at the rail marshalling yards at Thionville, Woipy, Athus, Pétange, Conflans and Longuyon. This was a classic strategic initiative and might have had significant consequences for the German war effort but for a number of factors, not least of which was French Army indifference. Night bombing was never going to be sufficiently accurate even if the aircraft could find the target, which they often failed to do, and where the attacks struck home, bomb loads were insufficient to do much damage and repairs were swiftly made, given the large time lag between repeated attacks. Nothing could have better illustrated the enormous divide between the theory and practice of strategic air attack, but it seems to have had no discernible dimming effect on air strategists' enthusiasm for the doctrine. The failure of French aviation to apply strategic air doctrine would be repeated more than twenty years later by Germany, when the Luftwaffe made the exact same mistakes when trying to destroy RAF airfields.

When the Germans launched their spring offensive in 1918, there was no question of a strategic bombing response. General Foch declared that it was 'the first duty of fighting aeroplanes ... to assist the troops on the ground by incessant attacks with bombs and machine guns ... air fighting is not to be sought except so far as necessary for the fulfilment of its duty'.[10] The air force responded by demonstrating their versatility and potency as ground-attack aircraft and made a significant contribution to halting the attack but in doing so, by concentrating all efforts directly over the Front, had ceded control elsewhere. They were forced to sharply reverse tactics again in a bid to win back aerial superiority and in so, doing abandoned much of their ground-attack operations.

By the end of the war all French air units were employed in tactical roles, but still the army agitated for more control. They had planned to use a tank force with tactical air support had the war continued into 1919, but they never got the chance to test it in practice. Strategic bombing had never really had a chance to prove its worth either but the reason for that, the risk of significant losses, might well have cautioned its advocates to think again. It was this potential capability, though, that was the only real argument the air force had for maintaining and expanding its independence. The battle for control inevitably had consequences when it came to post-war aircraft design and procurement. There had been a political dimension to the debate right from the moment of the first bombs falling on Le Havre, Bourges, Lyon and Paris in 1915. Much more sensitive to public opinion than the military, the government had looked for protection against the bombers. Barès had wanted to bomb German towns in retaliation, but major French cities were much closer to German Zeppelin and Gotha airfields than was the reverse case, which quickly ruled that out. German attacks had continued against Nancy, Calais and Dunkirk through 1917, but in reality, the French did not have the strategic capability to retaliate.

The French government fell in that year, with the new administration claiming a say in how the air force was run. They started by demanding more effort in building a long-range bombing capability. New specifications for a medium and a heavy bomber were issued. Very much against the wishes of the French, the British launched bomber raids on German industry from French airfields which brought a reprisal raid by German Gothas on Paris on 30 January 1918 killing thirty-six, after which several more took place on and off for the next eight months. The Germans also had a long-range gun that could hit Paris. French defence against such attacks was almost non-existent. During the course of the war 3,000 French citizens had died as a result of bombardment and this fact was to influence air doctrine for the next twenty years. In general though, following 1918, France failed to learn the lessons that others would and did not grasp what capabilities tactical air power could bring to the battlefield.[11] Although there was a wide range of aircraft types in service at the end of the war, a disproportionate number were large multi-seaters which were not particularly suitable for ground attack or escort duties.

France had emerged from the war with her position as a world leader in military aviation seemingly secure for a generation, but only as long as Germany military resurgence was contained and this had seemed assured after Versailles.[12] The air force had introduced itself as a new addition to the military armoury, but had also gained a certain political importance as civil aviation was poised to make its mark on the world stage. An air mail service was established with government support on the understanding that the aircraft used must be kept in perfect condition and have certain characteristics that would make them easily convertible into war-planes in an emergency. The French government acknowledged its importance sufficiently to indulge the air force to the point of allowing it a measure of independence from army control, but only insofar as the ultimate authority remained with the land forces who insisted, even up to 1936, that the role of aviation was to provide security and 'allow the land forces to shield themselves from enemy power and to repulse attacks'.[13] In 1920 France set about establishing an aerial arm of national defence on a par with artillery, cavalry and infantry, with a special school of aeronautics set up at Fontainebleau and one for aeronautic engineering at Versailles. It continued, however, to be the 'poor relation', with its staff officers mostly having come up through the ranks and consequently treated with some disdain by the elitist army general staff, who resented the attention and public opprobrium afforded the 'upstart' flyers.

France controlled the largest air force and had initially, under pressure from the government for economies in military spending, been forced to trim its aircraft numbers, but air power became a measure of French resistance to any suggestion of a resurgent Germany and also a warning to Germany, if it defaulted on reparations payments, that French air power would not hesitate to force the issue. Even so, by 1921, reconnaissance units were about a third of what they had been two years previously and fighters also were scaled down, but bomber units remained at 1919 levels. Contracts made while the war was still going on meant that aircraft continued to spill out of the factories in significant numbers, so a great effort was made to export many of them to the nascent air forces of Poland and Czechoslovakia. France had no confidence in Versailles to restrain a resurgence of German militarism for long and tried to isolate it with the Franco-Polish Military Convention of February 1921, and later with treaties with Czechoslovakia and Romania. Relations with Britain were becoming frosty as France feared it was going soft on Germany and the US, which had not even signed up to Versailles, offered little support. They seemed more concerned with getting the German economy back on its feet so that Europe as a whole might benefit and hasten repayment of war loans to the US. This continuing instability in European relations persuaded the French to recharge their military budget, which included a reinvigorated air force.

Just like other countries, France set up an Air Force Inspectorate commission, headed by Colonel Paul Armengaud, to examine what lessons could be learned from the First World War. The final report concluded that bombing had been no more than a qualified success, especially when striking at targets beyond the range of artillery; the sheer number of enemy 'vital centres', however, argued against the expectation that aircraft could strike at enough of them to bring about a rapid change in the trajectory of the war. Ground attack was a role that a number of different types of aircraft could perform and there was no requirement for a specialised type in this area. An army contribution to the review concluded that the bomber was not a battlefield weapon. They still maintained that the primary role of aircraft was in reconnaissance. It was too early in the development of military aviation to expect a change in conservative army attitudes. While speculation abounded over the possibilities that might be opened up by air power, there was precious little evidence to support the vision and only vague ideas about how it could be applied in practice. Some effort was put into developing an air doctrine with publication in 1921 of *Instruction provisoire sur l'emploi tactique des Grandes Unités*, but few of its authors were airmen. It concentrated on army doctrine, emphasising ground advance in slow, methodical stages, covered by massive artillery support. These principles remained essentially unchanged throughout the inter-war period.[14]

As a result of wartime emergency production there were far too many French aircraft manufacturers in 1918 so many converted to other work such as automobiles, leaving only ten by 1920. Peace brought a sudden drop in military budgets with some departments, such as technological research, virtually ceasing to exist. Where possible, military and civil aviation departments were amalgamated, and both benefited. Huge quantities of First World War surplus was sold off under the French Minister Pierre-Étienne Flandin, despite the 'shoddy condition of much of the materiel'.[15] Many of the residual wartime military contracts were cancelled but new ones, especially for a new generation of Breguet bombers, Potez reconnaissance aircraft and Nieuport fighters, were signed in their place. There was no immediate requirement for them but, despite evidence that aviation technology was likely to make them redundant in a very short time, the government still went ahead in the expectation that they could be held in reserve to be called upon in the event of hostilities once more breaking out. It was a policy designed merely to prevent the military aircraft manufacturing industry from disappearing completely, and justified by the idea that as long as the German state remained intact it posed a threat to the security of France.

Flandin was anxious to ensure that the industrial base was not depleted to the extent that it could not be revived in the event of another war, but communications between the military and the governing elite, poor at the best of times, failed to bring the two sides together to view the problem from a common perspective. The problem as ever, was cost and public perception. The desire on the part of politicians to be seen to be doing something by a nervous population was offset by their desire to reduce expenditure and that, inevitably, led to a surfeit of numerous, sub-standard aircraft coming off the assembly lines. The practice of sharing contracts for a single type between several manufacturers placated business leaders but led to gross inefficiencies. The answer was supplied by Albert Caquot at the Air Ministry, who advocated reducing the number of aircraft types and consolidating production to a small number of companies at the same time as standardising parts which could be utilised over a number of types. Government funding of private aircraft manufacture was established to reduce the influence of the 'manipulative bankers of Paris'.[16]

Aviation, by its very nature, was most suited to aggressive mobile warfare, but there were few in the French General Staff who looked beyond a sound, static defensive policy. Aircraft were not only expensive to build but they required airfields and technical support. For them to be accepted as a major item in the defence budget would take more money and goodwill than anyone in government or military was prepared to give, especially the army, who were certain that they would face a constant battle to keep air units under their control and see their own funding cut if they didn't. The last thing they wanted was a maverick on the battlefield getting all the glory and eating into their budget while they toiled, rooted to the earth doing all the hard work. They were not totally opposed to aviation as such, after all, it had made a contribution to victory, but it would have to be of limited size, constrained to operate within an overall military strategy dictated by the High Command and definitely not go off fighting its own war in the air. Army commander-in-chief Pétain continued to maintain that attacking industrial targets would have little significant effect on front-line fighting and if the air force wanted to purchase aircraft to pursue such a policy, they could only do so when all army requirements for reconnaissance and fighter aircraft had been met. On a brighter note, by the end of the decade Hispano-Suiza and Gnome-Rhône had both developed new, more-powerful engines and new all-metal airframes began to appear as performance levels of new aircraft improved markedly.

The role of the air force would be determined by the type of aircraft at their disposal and it was here on the drawing board that the decisions were made about what the service would look like going forward. The number of different types was significantly reduced. There was still a place for small, specialised combat aircraft, but long-range reconnaissance was out and only one type of heavy bomber survived the cull. The emphasis was decidedly on tactical and not strategic capability. This consensus was not to last, however. Soon debate centred round development of a large BCR (bomber-combat-reconnaissance) multi-crewed, multi-role, heavily armoured 'destroyer' that would be able to hold its own in any confrontation and serve a number of different purposes. As a cost-cutting measure, one basic design could be adapted in a number of ways to create a range of aircraft able to carry out the different roles. When it came to designing such an aircraft, however, the problems multiplied. Balancing size, weight and performance proved to be almost insurmountable, primarily due to the lack of a powerful enough engine. Engine technology would prove to be one of the major restraining factors on aviation for at least the next two decades.

The army were not impressed and continued to order the twin-seat, single-engine, multi-purpose Potez XXV fighter-bomber and the light bomber and reconnaissance Breguet XIX for their own uses. All this was taking place against a background of a world-wide economic downturn in which funding for research was squeezed and production stalled. It was still the case, however, that French aviation was the envy of the world; as the Paris correspondent of a US newspaper wrote, 'Everything that is newest and up-to-date in French bombing planes ... can be seen in the sheds. Giant planes, mostly all-metal, or tiny wasps for reconnaissance or attack'. The US Air Attaché in Paris reported: 'Today France is the foremost military nation in the world [but] as the military power of France diminishes, it is considered essential by the General Staff that her air power increases.' On a cautionary note, the French air journal *Les Ailes* said,

> Under the cloak of sporting aviation, Germany is working
> hard upon schemes which will give her 2,000 young pilots ...

available for war. Germany is nullifying the Allies' restrictions over her aircraft construction by the establishment of great factories for the mass production of metal warplanes in Denmark, Sweden, Russia and Italy.

The piece referred to the Rohrbach works in Copenhagen, Heinkel in Stockholm, Dornier in Pisa and Junkers in Kiev.

When the French entered the Rif wars in 1924 on the side of Spain, aircraft were used against the Berber tribesmen in 'police actions' to clear villages and 'break the social and economic life', in a way similar to that employed by the French in Syria and Lebanon where they had bombed urban areas of Hamas and Damascus in an attempt to 'terrorise' the populations.[17] In the Maghreb, the Rif forces had inflicted humiliating defeats upon the Spanish and threatened to do the same to the French. Low-level ground-attack and bomber missions proved to be instrumental in turning the tide against the Rif and illustrated the usefulness of aviation in reconnaissance and ground support but the lessons, while significant doctrinally in terms of how valuable air supremacy was, could not inform the debate about security in Europe. Armengaud, who had commanded the 37th Aviation Regiment in Morocco, had been impressed with the results achieved by his aircraft but concluded that they should have been deployed much sooner and coordinated under a single command. 'Aviation,' he said, 'would best serve the war effort by concentrating rapidly and proceeding ... ahead of the army.'[18] In a prescient view that anticipated Blitzkrieg, he saw aircraft acting as ground support for fast-moving infantry when artillery was unable to keep up with the advance. He conceded, however, that 'aviation ... cannot achieve victory by itself'. Of more immediate consequence in terms of French air doctrine was his view that waiting for ground commanders to evaluate a situation and deploy ground forces while aviators 'champed at the bit', was to waste valuable time and miss opportunities. The solution was to allow the senior aviation commander to have command authority 'of all available air power'.[19] When it was their turn to contribute an opinion, the army accepted that aircraft had played an important reconnaissance role under certain 'special' circumstances, but it played down the overall air contribution to the campaign. It was all too easy for them to cite the unique circumstances of desert warfare to denigrate the achievements of aviation when unopposed. Despite the experience of Morocco showing that subordinating aviation to ground commanders proved impractical and inefficient in a fluid combat environment, the immovable object of army opposition had barely felt the breeze of change and 'the offensive power of the air force was entirely unappreciated or completely ignored'.[20]

For the French, the sight of German manufacturers turning out civil airliners in the immediate aftermath of Versailles might have been quite legal and in no way a breach of the terms of the Treaty, but it did not take much imagination to see that these were a mere technical step away from becoming bombers. Already in 1923, albeit in a blatant statement of propaganda, with Germany on the point of default of their war reparation payments to France, General Marie Émile Fayolle, Inspector General of the French Air Force, visualised dozens of civil aircraft hastily converted into bomber squadrons and threatening French cities with mass attack. There were few dissenting voices within the French government. Paranoia, traumatic memories of recent slaughter, a feeling that Germany was already a growing threat, the British apparent willingness to ease restrictions on Germany and a sense that public opinion must be assuaged, combined to create a national consensus that, whatever the reality of the dangers, a response was required. The 'Air Party' led by First World War ace Deputy René Fonck ensured that the threat from Germany and the Soviet Union was never far from the minds of French ministers.

After the war, capital had deserted the French aviation industry in preference to other manufacturing. The government, however, was determined to hold its dominant position among other nations with respect to aviation and created in the Ministry of Public Works an office of Under Secretary for Aeronautics, headed by André Laurent-Eynac, to regenerate its aviation industry and commerce, subsidise factories and airlines and develop aviation to a high degree, from the standpoint both of industrial production and commercial and military exploitation. Under this new office, all departments and the commercial lines were to submit their programmes to the technical service which, after study, would then submit them, in a technical form, to the aircraft manufacturers. Prototypes would be constructed and tested by the technical service. When satisfactory tests had been made, the different ministries would place their orders. At this stage the Fabrication Service assumed charge. This service supervised the manufacture of the materials and aircraft ordered at all stages of their construction, beginning with raw materials and continuing up to the final trial tests. The testing period of a design might be up to two or three years. The rationale for this was to aid the entire industry and prevent over-crowding any one firm with orders, but that would prove to be a double-edged sword for both parties.

Contemporary opinion throughout Europe was that there was no practical defence against sudden bomber attack on cities. Just like other countries, France chose the threat of retaliation as the best method of deterrence, but this policy required a significant expansion of its bombing capability, an ambition which inevitably foundered on the rocks of economic constraints and army intransigence. Only a fraction of the sixty-two bomber squadrons called for in 1921 ever saw the light of day. Night bombers, at first the poor relation, were now given some credence since, protected from any interference in their operations by darkness, they could be built with less armament and have less requirement for speed and so were a cheaper alternative to the fast, heavily armed day bombers. Fayolle laid out specifications which resulted in the excellent Loiré et Olivier LeO 20, but the Breguet XIX single-engine bomber, which proved to be a great export success and was manufactured under licence in several countries, was eschewed by France's own air force, leading to a severe downturn in Breguet's fortunes. These lumbering giants were clearly taking the air force down a strategic path but progress was slow and a reorganisation of air force administration was required to circumvent army resistance. The culmination of two years squabbling between four different ministries saw the creation of an independent Air Ministry in 1928 under Laurent-Eynac, who strongly opposed army interference and favoured strategic long-range bombing. He faced up to the immediate problems of ageing aircraft types, lack of modern aeronautical research facilities and the dissipation of energies through muddled doctrine. To encourage innovation in the industry, the ministry agreed to a procurement strategy in which they would pay, in advance, up to 90 per cent of the cost of any prototype that they considered worthwhile. While this, in theory, gave manufacturers confidence to do the research and development, it did nothing to speed up the flow of new aircraft types into service. Manufacturers, in the main, were not sympathetic to young designers with new ideas and were sceptical of innovation. Barès was brought back as Air Force Inspector against the fierce opposition of the army, but the case for an independent air force now had two powerful advocates and its time was coming.

Throughout the 1920s, specifications for French fighter aircraft had included a requirement for high performance at heights of 5,000 metres or above which had been influenced by First World War experiences where height was equated with advantage in fighter-to-fighter encounters. Slowly it dawned on the Air Ministry that this was having a deleterious effect on performance at lower altitudes where foreign designs were at their most effective. Manufacturers were encouraged to test out new designs against competitors in international races. Ambitious targets were set for 2,000-hp engines which, on the way there, produced the 12-cylinder Hispano-Suiza HS 12X and the 14-cylinder Gnome-Rhône 14K Mistral. Horizontal speed at medium altitudes was now the main consideration and attention turned towards low-wing monoplane design to maximise the pilot's field of vision. These characteristics would put French fighter design ahead of either Britain or German manufacturers, but the targets set for maximum speed lacked ambition and soon British fighters were reaching speeds above those demanded by the French specifications. New targets were set at regular intervals as new speed records were set elsewhere. Manufacturers became frustrated and struggled to keep up with the constant updates, but Morane-Saulnier responded by producing the M.S. 225 which in 1933 was 'without doubt the best fighter so far produced by the French', but it was still only on a par with the British Hawker Fury which had already been in operation for a whole year.[21]

While France had held its own in competitive civilian aviation during the early 1920s, military aircraft fell further and further behind because of bureaucratic maladministration. It was taking up to six years for aircraft to go from drawing board to service, by which time they were well out of date. Relations between government and industry were becoming soured as manufacturers preferred to deal with civilian airlines where there was greater stability of management compared with the ever-changing personnel and policies of government. Even so, production methods remained artisanal with huge reluctance on the part of manufacturers to invest in modern machine tools. French fighter aircraft designers seemed to hit a barrier in the early 1930s. Winston Churchill characterised this period as 'lotus years ... wasted in endless debate'.[22] There was some confusion over which aspects to prioritise over others. In order to have a chance of getting government contracts they paid careful attention to their requirements which, in large part, they interpreted as improvements in the pilot's field of vision. When the all-metal, open cockpit monoplane Dewoitine D.500 was chosen, it sent a signal to others. It was a very modern-looking design but still had a fixed undercarriage which caused drag and reduced speed, and had a section cut out of the wing to improve the pilot's downward view. The aircraft was extensively exported to Japan, the Soviet Union and Britain, but its performance was soon surpassed by fighters that were poised to emerge in Germany. Not only fighters but the German civil aircraft, the He 70 – which the French feared could easily be converted for military use – was faster than the D.500. The irony was that even a French bomber such as the Amiot E7 prototype was faster than the fighters being designed by the French for the interceptor role.

Pétain conceded that Barès could specify technical requirements of new aircraft, but only the army could make the final decision about which aircraft to buy. In time of war, they claimed, all control of military aviation would default to the army. The new Air Ministry found itself up against a War Ministry that was blocking its every move and preparing for a final showdown. Government was divided. Laurent-Eynac had seen enough. He resigned in December 1930 and was replaced by Paul Painlevé, an army appointee. The army seemed poised to regain the initiative, especially when Pétain was appointed in February 1931 to coordinate all air defence issues to mollify public disquiet. Pétain, however, had moderated his views somewhat in the light of developments both military and political. He had started to take the bomber threat very seriously. His status allowed him to advocate the creation of a French counter-strike bomber force without too much resistance from the army, who tried instead to create an air council with all three services having equal representation. Pétain would have none of it, but could not prevent the army forcing Barès out. It was a stand-off.

Prior to 1925, the primary activity of the French air force had been in supporting the army's ground campaigns, but soon there was a move to look beyond a subordinate role for aviation. Airmen were discussing the new ideas of Guilio Douhet which had appeared in the periodical *Revue Maritime* in 1927. French officers began publishing books and articles that commented favourably on Douhet's theories. An aviation journal, *Les Aíles*, translated a large part of Douhet's 1921 version of *The Command of the Air* and his stature as a military theorist provided French airmen with a legitimate excuse for promoting the idea of an independent strategic air force.[23] In his book, Douhet imagined a war between France and Germany in which the French air force, operating in a ground-support role, were outmanoeuvred by German bombers who attacked their airfields and bombed French cities, forcing capitulation. It was a fantasy devoid of empirical evidence but powerful enough, in the face of an elevated sense of foreboding, to force a review of French air doctrine. Even army theorists were conceding that perhaps the long-range bomber had a role to play after all. Armengaud piled in on the side of the strategic bomber, although he conceded that at the start of a war, after the first crucial strategic onslaught against principal transportation and communications centres and munitions depots, most aircraft would be required to give all their attention to ground support. He noted that German Lufthansa civil airliners, one small conversion away from bombers, matched the French bombers in numbers.

On another front, the Italian Duce, Mussolini, was known to be very interested in Douhet's theories. The pressure was building for a response, but although Pétain was sufficiently alarmed to advocate the construction of a 200-strong bomber fleet, he could not yet go along with full air force independence of action. He had moved away sufficiently from the idea of army control, but offered a bizarre compromise with the suggestion that the bombers should be controlled directly by the government. The army and navy made one last desperate effort to forestall the setting up of an independent air force but economic realities demanded compromise. Priority now had to be given to flexibility, not specialisation. All aircraft would be required to contribute to deep strikes on the enemy and many would also have to perform reconnaissance and even ground-support roles. Barès was again brought back into the fold and Painlevé retired through ill-health.

The political scene in France at the beginning of the 1930s was 'a spectrum of fancies and fears' torn between extremes of left and right.[24] Industrial strife was rampant and the population was gripped by pacifism and fatalism in equal measure. A critical moment had come for the air force and the man to define that moment was the 'youthful and ambitious professor of international law' Pierre Cot.[25] He was made Minister for Air in January 1933, but subsequent investigations showed that at the time he was actually an agent of the Soviet Union. With the new minister came a new name. The French Air Force was now called L'Armée de l'Aire and edged itself a little further down the road to independence. Cot brought with him a modernising zeal. He took an essentially disarmament stance, but this was tempered by a deep mistrust of Germany. His view was that an unscrupulous enemy might make a pre-emptive unprovoked attack, in which case all fighter aircraft from all services would have to be called upon immediately and all aircraft capable of a bombing role would be mobilised for a counter-strike – and this could only happen if all aircraft were under a single command. He argued that a defensive policy, as advocated by the army, would do nothing to help France's East European allies such as Poland, and if called upon to honour treaties in the face of aggression against any of them, only air power would be available. The army had to concede the point and agree to a further measure of independence for the air force, but they did not entirely give up their struggle to have overall control of it.

In 1933 also, French aviation received a boost when two French pilots, Paul Codos and Maurice Rossi, flew their Hispano-powered Blériot 110 monoplane 'Joseph Lebrix', from Floyd Bennett Field, New York, the 5,657 miles to Rayak in Syria to establish a new world record for distance. The 1,770 gallons of fuel made the aircraft's total weight 9 tons and it only just got airborne having used up the whole of the runway. Later the same year Gustave Lemoine lifted his Potez-50 biplane, powered by a Gnôme-Rhone K-14 engine, off the airfield at Villacoublay and broke the world altitude record, reaching a height of almost 45,000ft. This built on what was already a tradition of French aviation accomplishments. In 1930, Captain Dieudonné Costes and Maurice Bellonte had completed the first non-stop flight from Paris to New York in their Bréguet Point D'Interrogation in thirty-seven hours and eighteen minutes. The French could still be proud of their achievements, but such successes described above did little to inform the military agenda.

Air doctrine was fundamentally reformed to incorporate the concept of independent air operations alongside an expansion of resources led by Air Force Generals Victor Denain and Joseph Vuillemin. Independent action meant bombers. Nine strategic bomber wings were created under a single Air Corps completely outside army control. France had come round to examining a modern aviation concept but, alas, could only furnish it with outdated aircraft and view it through a prism of an outdated mentality that insisted on referring to the bomber units as 'heavy defensive aircraft'.[26] Cot was now able to make the decisions over which types of aircraft would equip each squadron, but the choices were limited. The LeO 206 and Blériot

127 were clearly redundant and quite unsuitable, but few new designs were on the table. The army still agitated for twin-engine, multi-seater reconnaissance aircraft while new bombers would be required to operate night and day with the concomitant requirement for heavy armament and a respectable top speed. Specialist fighters constituted a smaller and smaller proportion of the total air fleet. Economic considerations demanded that multi-role BCR aircraft were given the highest priority, but that flew in the face of the aircraft designers' inability to come up with ideas for such versatile aircraft. Larger aircraft meant fewer aircraft, which did not find favour in army circles, especially since the new aircraft envisaged, being designed primarily with long-range bombing capabilities, would be less than totally suitable for the reconnaissance and observation roles that were so important for them. The trend was irrevocably set for an increase in bomber numbers at the expense of fighters, cut by one third, and reconnaissance, cut by a half.

The 1934 specification for bombers met with little interest from aircraft manufacturers, who saw themselves struggling to make a profit from any contracts. Many, such as Farman, Amiot, Bloch and Breguet, preferred to prevaricate and cash in on existing contracts. Dewoitine and a few others were willing to gamble, but by 1937 only the LeO 45, an aerodynamically advanced but structurally complicated design, had made it to the runway – albeit well behind schedule.[27] Loiré et Olivier had been left behind somewhat by failing to abandon the biplane concept early enough, but made up for it with this new design powered by the experimental Hispano-Suiza 14AA radial 1,000-hp engine. Hopes were high for this aircraft, but test flights were quick to dampen expectations when the engines caused the prototype to vibrate violently soon after take-off; it only just managed to land safely. Cot was so convinced that the LeO 45 would be a success eventually that, to encourage development, he ordered twenty when he later returned to the Ministry, but engine problems persisted when another prototype crash-landed, both engines having failed.

Loiré et Olivier found that orders for their biplane LeO 206 heavy bomber dried up, and the LeO 208 which was under development had to be abandoned. A new company, Société des Avions Marcel Bloch, had met Air Ministry requirements much more precisely with their Bloch MB.200 all-metal monoplane with two supercharged 900-hp Gnome-Rhône 14K Mistral engines. Even this, however, was soon challenged by the, admittedly more expensive, Farman F.221. While the bomber seemed to be coming through, a design for a suitable multi-purpose aircraft continued to be elusive. The Air Ministry issued a new specification in 1933 which it hoped would make the job easier. That was doubtful, however, when the details were announced. What was required was an ultra-modern, fast, manoeuvrable, powerfully-armed, twin-engine aircraft capable of artillery observation, army reconnaissance, tactical bombing, strategic reconnaissance, long-range bombing, escorting and interception and a top speed of 217mph. Incredibly, at least four companies felt they could meet all these requirements. The Amiot 144, the Breguet 460, the Farman F.420 and the Bloch MB.130 were all submitted for consideration, but the order went to a design that had been submitted unofficially, the Potez 540.[28]

The whole concept of the multi-role aircraft had taken France in entirely the wrong direction. The requirements stipulated in the specification for heavy armour and multi-occupancy were incorporated in designs that paid little attention to aerodynamic styling, which was becoming more and more important with the development of more powerful engines and increasing speeds. The French exploited the extra power by building bigger but more cumbersome aircraft, while other countries were designing aircraft for speed. On top of this huge disadvantage, which the French were only beginning to appreciate, came the introduction of the 20mm Oerlikon S cannon with explosive shells, with which fighters could be equipped. This gave interceptors the ability to strike at bombers from a greater range than the bombers' machine guns could retaliate. Cannon had the disadvantage of heavy recoil which had to be absorbed if accurate aim was to be maintained, so if heavy bombers were to be equipped with cannon there would have to be significant reinforcement of its multiple gun positions meaning more weight and even less speed. The whole procurement strategy was thrown into disarray at a stroke. New specifications were published, but this time with speed as a major requirement. This did not seem too much to ask given that new air-cooled radial engines such as the powerful Hispano-Suiza HS 14AA were now coming through.

Expansion of the new Air Force was named 'Plan I', and had been agreed in principle in 1933 by the radical government of Edouard Deladier, though the funds were not released until July 1934, by which time Gaston Doumergue's conservative coalition government was in and General Victor-Léon-Ernest Denain was at the Air Ministry. Much of the funding remained unspent, however, due to Denain's unwillingness to support Cot's plan for the BCR. By early 1935, Denain used the unspent funds to order an extra 200 Bloch MB.200 and Potez 54 bombers, and then planned for a further 520 aircraft for which no funding had yet been approved. All to be delivered by the end of 1935. The plans were, of course, impossible. However much the aircraft manufacturers might have welcomed the orders, they could not possibly respond that quickly. In the event, the funding was not fully approved and orders were cut back. Industry's confidence in government, never great at the best of times, took another downward turn.

Political instability continued to dog the struggle for air force independence. In February 1934, Daladier's radical government fell and the new right-wing administration brought with it Denain, previously the Chief of the Air Force General Staff, as the new Air Minister. By this time, Barès had gone again. Many of Cot's initiatives were reversed, with bomber and fighter groups reverting to the direct army regional commanders.[29] One of the leading army doctrine theorists of the time, Lieutenant Colonel Charles de Gaulle, had little time for air power other than for reconnaissance and observation. Neither did General Gamelin show much confidence in the air force's ability to achieve air superiority, insisting that the primary duty of air power lay in protecting the army from enemy air attack. He said,

> Air superiority can only be achieved on the front lines and then only for limited periods. The role of aviation is apt to be exaggerated, and ... will more and more be confined to acting as an accessory to the army.

In fact, the army did come round to accepting the usefulness of aviation in a ground-support role as indicated by the 1936 *Instructions for the tactical deployment of forces*, but the air force had given little thought to how it might interpret those instructions.[30] Dive-bombers and specialist close-support aircraft were not on the Air Ministry agenda at this time.

Surprisingly, in view of the plans for a high-speed bomber, fighter specifications continued to be unambitious in terms of speed. Even when specifications nudged domestic types up to a new level, foreign aircraft had already passed the mark. There was little hope of advancement from Blériot who persisted with their biplane format, while Dewoitine prevaricated and messed around trying to get a few extra mph from the

D.500. Morane-Saulnier came up with the low wing cantilever M.S.405 with retractable undercarriage, which was a bit more modern in many respects but was still of plywood construction. Even though the M.S.405 had won the government contract, other manufacturers such as Bloch, who were not traditional fighter producers, were anticipating future trends by coming up with aircraft such as the MB.150 with performances above specification levels. The Bloch designers had obviously paid close attention to developments elsewhere and had come up with an all-metal aircraft with retractable undercarriage and enclosed cockpit, but this would not fly in service until 1937. The shortcomings of the MS.405 were thrown into sharp relief when it was compared with the British Hawker Hurricane which had just taken to the skies. The slow and steady increments in specification issued by the French indicated a lack of confidence in their manufacturers to make the 'quantum leap' that would take their aircraft to the front of the field again. Where they had called for an extra 30mph the competition had called for 50, and so each time the gap widened. If France was now relying on a fighter defence against bomber attack, it was failing to confront the reality of the situation, especially given the proximity of French industry to the German border which would allow them to deploy extensive short-range fighter escort for their bombers. The army, however, was comforted by the prospect of large numbers of aircraft ideally suited to support their ground operations, but it was not a solution for politicians, mindful of public opinion, who were still wedded to the concept of the retaliatory bomber strike as the ultimate deterrent.

Denain, 'a man who commanded respect with politicians and aviators alike',[31] looked across the Atlantic for inspiration and found it in the Martin B-10 and B-12 bombers, reputed to have maximum speeds far in excess of anything the current lot of Bloch and Amiot bombers could achieve. In the Soviet Union, French Hispano-Suiza HS 12Y-31 engines had powered the Tupolev SB-2 prototype bomber to almost 250mph. The new German Dornier Do 17, with the same engine, was almost as quick. The French Air Ministry now demanded equal performance characteristics from the next generation of designs. The folly of calling for multi-purpose aircraft was recognised and attention once again was directed towards a specialist long-range bomber fleet, with no requirement for it to be capable of tactical short-range duties.

When the Luftwaffe officially introduced itself to the world in 1935 it did not come as a total surprise, but what had been suspicion to the military now became reality to the public and, as such, required a response from politicians. The press was full of outlandish claims, fuelled by German propaganda, of devastation on an apocalyptic scale if war broke out. For the pragmatic, war between Germany and France was now almost a certainty, but just how soon it would start was the unknown factor. Denain's response was a bold vision of a new generation of specialised combat aircraft operating within a flexible framework, which he planned to implement within a four-year timeframe. All aspects of air power would be addressed, and all requirements accommodated.[32] Industry was told to gear up to produce 1,000 aircraft a year but while this was a reasonable ambition to meet an immediate threat, if war was delayed, the investment in what would by then be obsolete aircraft would be a scandalous waste. To ease the political pressure, France signed a Treaty of Mutual Assistance with the Soviet Union in May 1935 assuring each the help of the other if they were the target of unprovoked aggression. Militarily it was tenuous, but it sent out a message of assurance to the public and gave the French government an excuse for withholding much of the funding for Denain's ambitious plans. Manufacturers were dismayed at yet another government volte face and were further discouraged from making speculative investment in new aircraft designs.

Hitler made it clear in 1936 that he was planning to reoccupy the Rhineland militarily. Britain saw no good reason to oppose him, but France was facing the prospect of German troops now being stationed right on its border, and German airfields only a few minutes flying time from major French 'vital centres'. The French Army, trained and psychologically prepared for a defensive war behind the immense fortifications of the Maginot Line, could not and would not contemplate intervention. For them the policy was to make attack on the ground so costly an adventure for the Germans as to deter them completely, and to avoid provoking an air war. For the air force, the argument for bombing German cities in response to German troops marching through their own German countryside was not compelling. Half of its bomber force was grounded anyway waiting for spare parts or modernisation, and the remaining half had only two weeks supply of fuel.[33] Hitler's gamble was a political triumph for him and a humiliation for the French. Any expectation that Germany's ambitions could be thwarted by the threat posed by French air power was evaporating. It was the last time that the balance of air power would be in France's favour and a failure of imagination to see beyond the German smokescreen of propaganda blinded them to the reality of their own superiority which, had they retaliated against the German move at this moment, would have forced the Luftwaffe into a desperate battle for survival. The army also displayed a paralysing, almost insurmountable inertia in a time of crisis, which weakened their claims for control of aviation. What would be the point of building an air force committed to ground support in a war of rapid movement if the army refused to advance? It would simply leave the country without the means to launch a bombing counter-offensive to German attack, the prospect of which grew daily, at least in the minds of politicians and the public.

For years the French had failed to grasp the enormity of the technical revolutions taking place elsewhere under governments willing to invest in the future. Only now were they waking up to the reality. The Potez 540, described as 'everything and nothing', but which proved to be more of the latter than the former by its performance in the Spanish Civil War,[34] was coming into service, as were reconnaissance units which were now given dual-roles and renamed as bomber groups; groupes de bombardement. Now that the focus was on strategic bombing, the question of the bomber's ability to strike at targets from the sort of altitudes at which they would be operating came to the fore. In a mobile war bridges were prime targets, but time and again experience would show just how difficult it was to hit and destroy such a target. In 1935, trials had been carried out to test the suitability of existing bombers for attacking targets in dive-bombing mode. Not surprisingly, given the stresses put on airframes by high-speed dives, only the small Morane-Saulnier MS.225 single-seater fighter came anywhere close to being suitable and even that, with its single engine, was deemed too vulnerable to ground fire. The army bit back with a new demand for a reconnaissance-ground-attack aircraft with only a peripheral bomber role.

The army knew what it wanted, but the Air Ministry simply could not make up its mind what they wanted. There was no coalescing around a common ambition. The purse strings had been loosened but warring factions could not agree on specifics; one engine or two for fighters, one pilot or pilot and gunner, long-range or tactical ground attack, heavy bomber or dive-bomber, and all the time new benchmarks for performance were being set elsewhere. Between agreeing a specification and fitting out a squadron a whole generation of technologies could render an aircraft redundant before it left the ground. Playing catch-up was not an option with Germany now openly flaunting its mighty Luftwaffe, but with most of the major manufacturers heavily committed to Cot's multi-role aircraft there was little industrial capacity for manufacture of the new range of specialist aircraft which had not even seen the drawing board when there was another change of government and Denain was gone. Morale in the air force was low, with weak officers and a shortage of manpower. New aircraft types were demanding much more in the way of handling and maintenance. Pilots were getting older and less inclined to adopt modern practices, while not enough young men were entering the flight and engineering training schools. Cot had wanted to purge the service of 'dead wood' and revitalise it. In this he was successful to a degree, but the sort of changes he wanted would take many years to work through. The lost years could not be made up.

In June 1936, Léon Blum's left-wing Popular Front government had come to power and Cot was back at the Air Ministry. The remilitarisation of the Rhineland, begun in March, had galvanised the whole of Europe and threatened destabilisation of the military order. The whole of Denain's extended 'Plan I' was approved and rechristened 'Plan II', at a cost of 5 billion francs spread out between 1937 and 1941, but Cot's main contribution at this stage was the reorganisation of the squadrons, a more flexible command structure, mobilisation of reservists and a focus on long-range bombing capabilities. The old problems persisted when it was clear that orders for 700 aircraft a year, already a reduction from the proposed 950, proved to be beyond the capacity of industry to fulfil. The French public was being placated by Cot's pronouncements which 'went beyond the limits of decency' describing extensive rearmament, but the reality was that factory output was falling under the pressure of political turmoil and industrial disputes.[35] Industrialists, faced with radical government intervention, had gone into uncooperative mode at a time when public anger was rising at the lack of promised social reforms. The defence budget was leaving little scope for the government to carry out its domestic reformist agenda.

The army was incensed by losing control of its reconnaissance units, but the government had been shaken by the Rhineland crisis and quickly approved the introduction of a bombing capabilities to all air units now under direct air force command. Having raised the spectre of the German bomber to justify inaction over the Rhineland, the army could hardly complain when the government diverted resources to the air force bombing counter-offensive programme. They responded by backing aerial defence over strategic bombing in the hope that at least some of the fighters could come under army control. The air force did not object to an increase in the fighter force but suggested that if they were for army use, maybe the cost of extra fighters could come out of the army budget and not theirs. That was an argument that was not going to go far.

Cot pressed ahead with bomber procurement. His bomber of choice was the Bloch MB.210 which was adequate for the time but incapable of development in the way that, for instance, the German Heinkel He 111 was able to adapt to new technology throughout its operational lifetime. The tactical bomber now took second place to the long-range heavy bomber that was seen as the only credible means of deterring German aggression. Armament industries were nationalised in a move towards a war economy and Cot tried to exert more control but the manufacturers, having been stripped of their status, were in no mood to submit to what they saw as government bullying and resisted calls for the changes demanded of them. Amiot were working on their E7 bomber but frosty relations over disputed nationalisation compensation payments and arguments over which engines were most suitable slowed development. Cot responded by looking across the Atlantic at US aircraft as a possible alternative to domestic production.

1936 saw the eruption of the Spanish Civil War and suddenly a great deal of theory was to be examined under the spotlight of experience. France was anxious to be seen as neutral in the cause but Cot, with Blum's support, realised that if Franco's Falangists were successful, France would then be surrounded and threatened on three sides by totalitarian governments. Unwilling to come out openly in support and restrained by British pressure to stay out of the argument, they were forced to surreptitiously send aircraft and supplies to bolster the Republican forces by organising a fictitious sale of war planes to Saudi Arabia, Finland and Brazil, that found their way to Spain instead. In reality, however, this proved to be little more than a political gesture, given that the machines sent were virtually obsolete, of little military value and accompanied by almost no spare parts.

Once air forces were in action it was clear that ground-attack aircraft were making a big contribution to Republican victories, especially at Guadalajara in March 1937. Cot's team of General Phillipe Féquant, Armengaud and General Jean-Henri Jauneaud had been firmly in favour of building a strategic bombing capability, but a seismic shift was about to undermine their convictions and another U-turn in French air doctrine was imminent. Reports from Spain were effulgent in praise of the Soviet Polikarpov R-5 reconnaissance bomber and could not be ignored. While Cot did not totally abandon the strategic long-range bomber programmes, they were severely curtailed and the role of such bombers would henceforth include tactical close battlefield support. The army, however, still wanted the bulk of air power to be utilised in reconnaissance with fighter support and had no doctrine for close air support of ground forces but at least it was pleased that aircraft were now being reassigned from strategic roles. As the evidence from Spain continued to mount, the next French aircraft specification was issued for a high-speed, two-seater armed with cannon and bombs, capable of battlefield intervention. Douhetist theory was being quietly disowned by the French air force under Cot as tactical air doctrine became the order of the day. The problem for Cot was that, unlike the Germans, the French did not have any aircraft capable of, or capable of being adapted to, dive-bombing attack, and it had been this tactic that had so impressed French observers in Spain. Only time would allow them to fill that gap and time was running out.

At a stroke, the declaration of neutrality by Belgium in 1936 deprived the French of the option of stationing forces there, and opened up the potential for a German flanking manoeuvre beyond the Maginot Line. This forced the French Army to reconsider its position and start thinking in terms of a war of movement rather than static defence. They urgently called for heavy armoured divisions and thought hard about whether ground-support aircraft could also be part of a new defence strategy in combination with armour. More evidence from Spain showed that the common factor in every major breakthrough had been the large-scale intervention of ground-support aircraft.[36]

At home, Cot struggled with a number of unsatisfactory designs which started to look like a lost generation of aircraft. Engine design, in particular, was a nightmare for him with the Gnome-Rhône Mistral less than 100 per cent reliable and the Hispano-Suiza 14AA air-cooled engine outside the company's zone of expertise which had been built around liquid-cooled designs. Obvious improvements based upon foreign engine design could easily have been incorporated, but were ignored. A Bloch MB.150 fighter fitted with a Mistral could not even get airborne. The MS.405 remained the only option that looked anything like promising success and led to development of the MS.406 but again, structural problems made the new type difficult to mass-produce. By the end of 1937, neither the 405 nor the 406 prototypes had left the ground – and this at a time when the Messerschmitt Bf 109 was already in service.[37] When given the chance to test-fly the British Spitfire in June 1938, the French sniffed at the aircraft itself but asked immediately for the rights to manufacture the Merlin engine.

The MS.406 would be the most numerous of all French fighters available in 1940, but the delays in production meant that it was inferior to its contemporaries in the Luftwaffe and was already virtually obsolete. Its flaws were many, including defective weapons and radio, but most serious was the underpowered Hispano-Suiza 12Y-31 engine which objected to long periods at full throttle. The aircraft had a poor rate of climb with many features causing drag which reduced speed. They were only effective when in the hands of very good pilots.[38]

One of the main stumbling blocks to rapid and efficient production was the way that contracts were handed out. Production capacity was adequate, but contracts were awarded in small quantities. When 250 Bloch MB.210 were ordered, contracts went out to six different manufacturers. Each company had to create a new production process for a production run that might last only a few months, after which changes were required to accommodate the next model. Sometimes they would have to revert to a previous method if, subsequently, a repeat order for an old type came through which often happened to fill quotas when new designs were not ready. One aircraft production line had to be reactivated twice. Small production runs ruled out efficiency and pushed up unit costs. Despite these obvious flaws, Cot maintained that the French Air Force was second only to the Soviet Union, prompting critics to call him 'an illusionist'. The British made no secret of the fact that they had no confidence in him, calling him 'quite untruthful' and a 'disaster'.[39] Apart from their antipathy to Cot's politics, they were understandably nervous that their main potential ally against a resurgent Germany had no modern aircraft and no means of mass-producing any. At a time when the British were having to divert their affections, albeit very reluctantly, from strategic bombing to fighter defence, they were not encouraged by Cot's stubborn commitment to bomber production over other types. The French Army was no less frustrated with Cot. Few of his bombers were capable of providing the close air support they craved for their troops.

Cot and his air force chief, Féquant, had tried to expand Plan II in February 1937 by adding supplementary armament purchases requiring an extra 2.8 billion francs, but it was never approved. In a desperate measure to salvage his ministry, Cot retired a number of air force generals seen as not sufficiently modern in outlook and enforced administrative changes to streamline the service, but these measures met with resentment. Officers questioned his judgement amid fears for their own careers. He made himself very unpopular with both the army and the air force and was forced out of office in January 1938 to be replaced by Guy La Chambre, who 'knew nothing about aviation',[40] and brought in General Joseph Vuillemin, an ex-First World War bomber pilot 'of remarkable skill' as Chief of the Air Staff. Daladier, back in charge of the government and wanting swift action on rearmament, had been unconvinced by Cot's excuses and expected better from La Chambre, but the state of play in the Air Ministry shocked everyone. Both La Chambre and Vuillemin eschewed political machinations and intrigue and focused on the daunting task of putting the air force on a war footing. La Chambre offered an olive branch to the army by turning away from strategic doctrine and giving them back some control. This now allowed them to concentrate on working with them to source aircraft that could meet both their requirements. Vuillemin, a 'popular and highly respected figure',[41] bluntly described as 'derisory' the idea that the French bomber fleets were anywhere close to being adequate. There existed not a single day-bomber worthy of the name and there was only the Bloch MB.210 available to grope its way along in the darkness. Navigation equipment was such that pilots could only find their targets by following ground markers by day, and goodness knows what they hoped to find at night. On a visit to Germany to view their latest aircraft, Vuillemin morosely declared that in the event of war, the French bomber fleet would not last two weeks.[42] In a letter sent to La Chambre soon afterwards, he had clearly not recovered from the trip when he informed his boss that his fighters would not be capable of defending the reconnaissance flights and neither would they be able to protect industrial and civilian targets from attack. Civilian casualties, he predicted, would be huge. French intelligence supported his view.[43]

The Air Force General Staff, partly as a consequence of their antagonistic relationship with the army over control and procurement, had not absorbed the traditional organisational and administrative skills required of a military service which they might have inherited had their ties with the army been closer. They failed to establish efficient liaison and a meaningful working relationship with the country's manufacturing base. The dispersal of twenty-eight engine and airframe factories away from Paris to areas such as Bordeaux and Toulouse, beyond the scope of German bombers had, quite naturally, met with the reality of a dearth of skilled labour in the provinces. As a result, they fell further and further behind Germany in procurement of new aircraft. A new vision of rearmament shone through in a 'Plan V', approved in March 1938, only days before the Anschluss, increasing the front-line strength to 2,617 aircraft with a 100 per cent reserve by March 1941. This came with promises for a huge investment in modernisation of the manufacturing base, but the old niggling problems remained. Large increases in aircraft numbers were planned, especially in view of the recent German annexation of Austria, and many of the new aircraft would be fighters or dive-bombers in a move to reduce the over-reliance on strategic bombing as a viable deterrent. The planned expansion, however, when viewed against domestic production was quite impossible. The problems of labour relations and lack of investment in the manufacturing base were too ingrained to admit the changes required in the time available. Factories were simply not capable of gearing up quickly enough or finding sufficient skilled labour, even though industry leaders promised to speed up their research and development at modern establishments such as at Chalais-Meudon. There was a gaping hole in French fighter strength. To placate his critics, Cot had placed a huge order for MS.406s, but this was not going to work either because there were not enough Hispano-Suiza HS 12Y-31 engines to fit them out, despite imports from the Skoda factories in Czechoslovakia and Saura in Switzerland who were among a number of foreign firms queueing up to take advantage of France's plight.[44] The next option was the cheaper but less effective Bloch MB.150, currently undergoing engine redesign to boost its poor performance. Last of all was the stop-gap Caudron C.713, which was, in many respects at least, a generation behind other French fighters, let alone the new breed of Bf 109s. The reconnaissance and observation squadrons were the poor relations in all this and had been left behind.

La Chambre saw his immediate task as one of replacing the obsolete machines which hobbled his air force and to look for designs which incorporated all the latest features such as cannon, supercharged engines, retractable undercarriage and radios. Emphasis shifted again as Cot's strategic bomber force was split up and distributed among army divisions to act out a tactical role for which it had not trained. Still there was no consensus between air force and army over the most effective way to employ aviation. French air power ended up as 'the offspring of a couple who had never been well married', and conformed to the hopes of neither.[45] Cot's bomber and fighter corps were abolished, and all reconnaissance units were put under army control. Dive-bombers would make up a large proportion of new bomber fleets. All pretensions to having a long-range strike force equal to the Luftwaffe were abandoned. 'Plan V' was modified and may well have given France a chance against a German attack in 1941 if 'the [4,700] aircraft could be built, if they were good enough, and if the [40,000 ground staff and] crews could be trained in time to fly them'.[46]

La Chambre lacked confidence in French manufacturers and turned to the United States. Senator Baron La Grange was sent to negotiate for the purchase of 1,000 combat aircraft. Unfortunately, the US were reluctant to get too involved in European military affairs and surprisingly, were not much better placed to go into mass production quickly. It was also a shock and disappointment to find that the only fighter aircraft suitable for French needs was the Curtiss H-75 'Hawk', not quite what they wanted and not even available in any quantity, since factories were busy filling contracts for the US Army Corps. To add insult to injury, these Hawks would come in at twice the cost of the MS. 406, would have to be paid for in hard cash and shipped by neutral carrier at the buyer's expense. Given no choice, the French ordered 100 aircraft and 175 Wright R-1830 Cyclone engines without ever knowing when they would be delivered, and even invested in an expansion of production facilities to hurry them along. They had come off the wrong end of a hard bargain. Back at home, La Chambre only just survived savage attacks in Parliament for depleting precious gold reserves, investing in foreign manufacturing and denying work to French factories. Eventually, 316 H-75s were delivered, but the engines proved to be unreliable and few actually flew during the German attack in May 1940. The hasty deal for the Hawks had eaten up all of the 'Plan V' funding, so in

June a revision of the scheme was accepted which expanded the budget to accommodate extra aircraft to be ready within twelve months.

The Hawks came nowhere close to meeting the demand for fighters so a blizzard of paper contracts went out to French industry where, predictably, airframe production massively outpaced that of the Hispano-Suiza engines, around which most of the designs were built. Inevitably this led to the Air Ministry relying on aircraft such as the Caudron C.713 with its high speed but 'appalling' climbing performance, for which they placed an order of 200.[47] All in all, the Air Ministry had resigned itself to missing its targets for fighter production by quite a margin. Bomber production fared no better; modifications to the Bloch MB.131, needed to prevent it shaking itself to pieces in flight, made it so slow that it was hardly suitable even for reconnaissance, never mind bombing. Nevertheless, it remained in the plan. The Amiot 340 failed to meet specifications on a number of critical points, but optimism prevailed when the manufacturers promised modifications and it also remained in production. At least its engines were reliable. In the summer of 1938, there were serious problems with the performance of all bomber designs entering service.

When analysing the reasons for France's collapse in 1940, Pierre Cot blamed the French military for underestimating the importance of aviation. He claimed that French airmen were man-for-man, in morale and training, equal or superior to the German flyers. His, not uncontested view, was that the Morane-Saulnier 406 and Potez 63 were excellent pursuit and combat aircraft, if not quite up to the quality of their opposition, but the Dewoitine D.520, the Bloch 17 and the VG. 33 were somewhat superior to the German machines. His main arguments are coloured by his left-wing political views and clearly designed to pile much of the blame on the Daladier government, but his conclusion that the French lacked a clear understanding of modern warfare in the years up to 1940 is quite tenable. The General Staff were, if not quite anti-, then at least not pro-science. They failed to invest in research and development, preferring instead to rely on their 'war of position' doctrine, which was left standing by the German 'war of movement'. He cites, as an example of the conflicts which had existed all through 1937 between the Air Ministry and the Ministry of National Defence, a review in which Minister of National Defence, Marshal Pétain, the Chief of the Army General Staff, General Gamelin, and the Chief of the Navy Staff, Admiral Darlan, unanimously rejected the proposals of the Air Ministry and decided that 'there was no need to extend or modify the plans for the expansion of the air force'.[48] He rejects any idea that France was working at full capacity in the years 1937–40 to build up its air force, by reference to Air Ministry archive documents which show that 'The increase in productive capacity as represented by previous machine-tool purchases since the beginning of the year 1937 varies from 40 to over 100 per cent according to the companies [showing that] the aeronautical industry in 1937 was capable of producing more had it been asked to do so.' They go on to say that, 'The productive capacity of the French aeronautical industry can, without further plant expansion, satisfy a much greater demand than that which will exist in the near future.' If the Cabinet had asked for it, and had provided the necessary funds, the French aeronautical industry could have built the planes and engines that the French Army needed.

Manufacturing practices during the 1930s had been far from ideal but the problem, according to Robin Higham, was not the lack of finance but 'will, direction, and a sense of urgency to put the country in order for a modern war'.[49] There was a fundamental rift between industrialists who, holding essentially reactionary views, disdained politics and governments, who veered from one extreme to another in their transient manifestations, denying the conditions for a long-term coordinated air strategy. There was also the fraught question of labour relations within industry, which amounted to little more than mutual contempt between owners and workers who stubbornly eschewed any move towards finding common ground.

Since as early as 1918, French aviation had been controlled not by an appointed minister, but by a committee of forty-four members which operated, at times, more like a debating society than a functioning administration. Between 1 January 1930 and 3 September 1939, France saw twelve Prime Ministers, four of whom served two terms, and seven Air Ministers, three of whom served two terms. With each change at the top of the Air Ministry came new priorities and new directives. Huge orders were placed according to whichever concept the incumbent subscribed to, and well before these plans had seen fruition would come a change of focus and new plans to replace the old. Denain may well have been respected but he also had a reputation for being 'a military autocrat with a narrow mind', who knew nothing of technology.[50] He had put all his weight behind the BRC aircraft for which there had been neither prototypes nor facilities to produce it. Modification of other aircraft prototypes were sometimes asked for after production was already under way, forcing expensive retooling on the shop floor. Often the parts of a single aircraft type were manufactured by different companies meaning that any delay on the part of one manufacturer led to a delay in the entire production. Relations between manufacturers and government were soured by late payments and haggling over contracts. Cronyism saw massive contracts awarded to the private manufacturers Renault, Breguet and Amiot in 1938, which flew in the face of the fact that their product was inferior to that of the nationalised companies.[51]

When Germany marched into the Rhineland in 1936 to jolt France from its complacency, the air force was both tactically and strategically deficient.[52] None of their air doctrines was supported by a broad vision. Denain claimed that the main weakness stemmed from the air force's subservience to the army, but it had done little to flesh out its own strategic concepts. Cot tried to focus all efforts on the strategic bombing aspect and abandoned his previous enthusiasm for the BCR. The 1937 *Instructions* had a much greater emphasis on offensive action for aviation, but the army was still not impressed. Under Cot's leadership, a number of the reforms in organisation implemented by General Jauneaud had inspired the Luftwaffe to copy them and modify their air formations in 1940. Jauneaud had been shuffled into an administrative backwater by Vuillemin who 'disliked the ideas and personality of [the] young, intelligent and ambitious [Jauneaud]'.[53] France gave up their own ideas of air divisions at the very moment Germany began to apply them. In 1940 the French air forces remained dispersed and strung out. A thousand aircraft were left on the Mediterranean and 400 in the Alps, facing Italy, not yet a belligerent. Germany attacked France with 80 per cent of her total air force, said Cot, while 'We opposed it with only 40 per cent of an already insufficient air force.'[54]

The French Air Force, so powerful in 1918, had begun to lose its focus after Versailles. Unlike the RAF it had failed to break free of army control and was unable to define itself according to its own priorities. Lacking an independent voice at the highest levels of government, it was dictated to and had policy thrust upon it by governments and politicians that were mostly pre-occupied with internal strife, and none of whom stayed long enough to build the sort of culture and internal organisation that the air force required to thrive and grow. Not until Pierre Cot came into the Air Ministry in 1933 was the air force given the freedom to become L'Armée de l'Aire and start to define its own terms of existence. Yet where defence policy was discussed there was still too little time given to discussion of strategic air doctrine. France, it seemed, was going to ensconce itself behind solid border defences and resort to a 'war of position'. As a continental power vulnerable to aerial bombardment, it had little appetite for encouraging a strategic air war that could leave its cities in ruins, unlike in Britain where vital centres were far from German airfields. Moreover, French industry did not have a track record of profitable relations with government, preferring to focus its attention on supplying the private economy, and this resulted in stilted and stuttering programmes of military aircraft procurement which drained the system of energy and innovation. During the inter-war years there had been 'too much talk and too few decisions,' leading to disagreements and confused policy.[55] Cot had tried to modernise the aviation procurement programme but failed to get agreement for adequate investment. La Chambre did better when he came in, but was too late to undo all the damage in time before Germany struck.

Hubris and over-confidence contributed to lethargy and had been reinforced by a belief in 'static war'. Diplomatically, France had tried to hem Germany in by forming alliances with eastern European countries such as Poland, Czechoslovakia and Romania, but these were slowly undermined as Germany grew in confidence and power. Air doctrine was never sufficiently addressed, even after an independent air force was created because it was never able to break free entirely of army control and political machinations. Basically, they did not have a clear idea of what their role would be when war broke out and when it did, the army command became so distressed by its own failures that it was not able to give proper guidance to an air arm that could have contributed much more had it not lacked coordinated leadership.

The French defeat in 1940 is a complex, much debated and well documented event in which the French air force played a significant part. When Germany launched its Fall Gelb attack across northern Europe on 10 May 1940, the French were still obsessed with the bombing threat against its cities. While the German strategy was, to put it simply, a restatement about the importance of mobility in warfare, the French had adopted the radical, new, and essentially untested idea that strategic bombing would be the decisive factor. As a consequence they had an insufficient number of fighters to meet the Bf 109s and Ju 87s which combined so effectively with the Panzers to breach the Meuse defences at Sedan and outflank the

Allied defences in Belgium. It was clear by June 1940 that the French bomber fleet may well have been a powerful political and psychological weapon, both domestically and externally, but it had proved to be a 'paper tiger'. The rift between the army and air force, which had been ever present between the wars and never bridged, was very much in evidence in May and June, proving to be the dividing line between resistance and failure. The fighter force, split between army support on the front line and rear defence against the bomber threat, was never focused where it was needed. Reconnaissance aircraft with inadequate protection were driven from the skies by the German fighters, blinding the French forces on the ground. Abandonment of production of aircraft such as the (admittedly obsolete) D.520 and MB.174 in favour of the newer designs, untested and delayed, left the bomber fleets with insufficient numbers of either. The French air force contributed to the country's disastrous military collapse by failing to remember, and build on, its successes in the First World War and placed too much faith in radical and unproven theories.

Chapter 6

Polish Air Power before 1939

'The horse-mounted cavalry, once Poland's greatest pride, was still, in the late1930s, regarded as a decisive weapon, capable of bringing about a final victory.'[1]

Many of the issues influencing air doctrine between the wars were common to several countries but there were a number which were unique to Poland, not the least of which was that since 1795, its national identity had been subsumed and its lands occupied by the neighbouring powers of the Russian Empire, the Kingdom of Prussia and the Hapsburg Monarchy. Poles wishing to give military service had been obliged to do so by joining the ranks of one of their occupying forces, but the dream of Polish nationhood was reborn when the First World War saw the whole political structures of Eastern Europe undergo huge changes, through revolution and collapse of empires. Since Napoleonic times, the Poles, without tangible evidence, had somehow seen France as a crucial ally in the fight to restore nationhood. The fact that France had remained aloof from Polish attempts to escape the Russian yoke in 1830 and 1863 and was, during the First World War, an ally of Imperial Russia, failed to dim their faith. During that war, Poles in the German and Austrian armed forces fought Poles in the Russian forces but by the end, alliances had changed as France now saw a united, independent and autonomous Poland as a potential new ally in Eastern Europe. So much so that in June 1918, it encouraged the formation of a quasi-governmental National Polish Committee and a Polish Army division under General Haller to be set up in Paris, and a new Franco-Polish alliance was formed which would shape the trajectory of Polish air power for two decades.

The Polish people had taken to aviation in a big way right from when the first heavier than air machines left the ground. As early as 1909, the Aviator's Circle (Koło Awajatów) had attracted enthusiasts and prompted the opening of a flying school at Mokotów Field. Poles were among the first to receive pilot training in the nascent air forces of their partitioning powers, and many of them had joined the Austrian-sponsored Polish Legions of the Imperial and Royal Air Troops, all of which engendered a nationalist fervour that lobbied for a separate Polish Air Force (PAF). Polish airmen were prominent within their respective regions. Major Gustaw Maciewicz was even commander of the Russian 7th Squadron at Osowiec in 1911. Later, during the First World War, large numbers of Polish pilots were enlisted in the air services of Austria, Germany and Russia where there was a 1st Polish Air Detachment at Minsk under the command of General Jósef Bowbor-Muśnicki.

Józef Klemens Piłsudski had been born on 5 December 1867 in the Zułów estate to wealthy industrialist Józef Wincenty Piłsudski and Maria Billewicz, who came from a family of nobility. When his father's business empire collapsed, the impoverished family moved to Vilnius. As a student, Piłsudski became involved with revolutionary movements and was arrested. Brought to trial he was found guilty and sentenced to five years internal exile in Russia. When he returned to Vilnius he joined the Socialist movement, travelled abroad to London and supported the Polish struggle for independence. He was arrested again in 1900 and charged with operating an illegal press, but feigned insanity and was sent to the Warsaw insane asylum – from where he escaped a year later. He fled to London then returned to continue his subversive activities. During the Russo-Japanese War he travelled to Tokyo via New York and San Francisco where he tried to establish links with Japanese Intelligence, swapping information about the Russian political and military situation in return for money, but there was little cooperation. When the Russian Revolution broke out in 1905, Piłsudski joined anti-Tzarist groups and organised arms dumps for use in the eventual liberation of Poland. In 1906, he tried to establish links with Austrian intelligence to further the aims of Polish independence, but opposed forces who wanted to unite Polish lands in a confederation within Russia. When the First World War broke out Piłsudski fought with Polish troops in the Austrian army against Russia, during which time he unilaterally announced the formation of a National Polish government and became the unofficial 'commander-in-chief of the Polish Army', which he hoped would stimulate moves for independence, but most Poles saw his movement as 'a group of irresponsible rabble-rousers'. Nevertheless, he gained recognition for astute tactics against the Russian troops and his reputation grew; he was arrested again in 1917, this time for urging Polish troops to refrain from taking an oath of allegiance to Germany, which only served to boost his status as a patriot. When Bolsheviks fomented revolution in Germany in November 1918, the German Army, desperate to prevent German and Russian revolutionaries from joining up, released Piłsudski in the hope that he could rally Polish forces to create a barrier between the two. As a result, local centres of Polish power were established which eventually led to the creation of Polish statehood. On 11 November the Polish Supreme Council officially named Piłsudski as Supreme Commander of the Polish Army.

Eager for any sign that captured the sense of Polish national ambition, flyers came to see an independent PAF as a beacon of nationhood. In 1916, Janusz de Beaurain suggested the formation of an all-Polish squadron under the leadership of Piłsudski, but he was not particularly interested in aviation so de Beaurain looked for another route and began enthusing fellow Poles in the Austrian aviation school he attended. de Beaurain had been born on the 25 December 1893 in Warsaw, to Karol and Zofia, née Kosmowski. He was a graduate of the L'viv polytechnic and in 1916 joined the Austrian Aviation Officers School to train as an aviation observer, after which he served on the Italian front. He was part of the group that captured Lewandówka airfield from the Austrians on 2 November 1918 and the next day he was given command of the 2nd Air Combat Squadron, taking part in the first Polish air combat on the 5th. By March 1919 he had been appointed as Chief of Staff of the Air Force Command, and in May of that year the position of the Deputy Inspector of the Air Force. When Poland later fell to the Germans in 1939, he fled to Romania and then to France, eventually arriving in Britain in September 1940. In December 1943, he was called up for active service and joined the staff of the Polish commander-in-chief on 1 January 1944. After the war, he settled in Scotland and died there in 1959.

In 1916 a Polish Society for Aerial Navigation was secretly formed in German-occupied Warsaw with the intention of training and politicising Polish flyers. The Germans, however, were quick to uncover it and closed it down. By contrast, in Russian-occupied Poland, all-Polish aviation units were welcomed, but they struggled to organise in a country now ravaged by revolution until Captain Zgmunt Studziński exploited the political confusion to grab a quantity of arms and equipment and form the '1st Polish Aviation Unit' at Mińsk, albeit with a single Nieuport fighter aircraft.

Soon afterwards they commandeered two trains carrying dismantled Russian Nieuport and Morane aircraft, which were quickly reassembled. The unit was short-lived, however, as German forces advanced on their base at Bobruysk and threatened to sweep it up. Rather than surrender their machines, the Poles destroyed them and fled, many to France to join General Haller's Polish Army there.[2] At Odessa, another group of Poles were able to form an aviation unit of nine aircraft, which were dismantled and concealed from the Russians.

Józef Haller von Hallenburg was born on 13 August 1873 in Kraków which, at the time, was part of the Austro-Hungarian Empire. He joined the army after graduating from university but resigned in 1910 'in order to serve the country in some other way until [my] Homeland needs me'. He took up a post in education, organising agricultural, farm and dairy courses. During the First World War he joined the Piłsudski legions and was given command of an infantry regiment tasked with preventing Russian advances through the Carpathians. German forces there threatened to wipe out his command, forcing him to flee to Moscow where he became head of the Polish Army Commission. He travelled through Murmansk and ended up in France, where he took charge of Polish army units which came to be known as the 'Blue Army'. This force eventually numbered some 100,000 men and was deployed on the Ukrainian front where, again, they were accused of waging anti-Semitic pogroms. He had opposed the signing of the Brest-Litovsk Agreement in 1918, fearing that an end of fighting against the Soviets would reduce the chances of creating an independent Poland.

The October Revolution in Russia led eventually to the signing of the peace Treaty of Brest-Litovsk, which had a direct bearing on Franco-Polish-Russian relations. The lengthy negotiations that preceded the signing of the Treaty allowed German troops to advance deep into the ethnically Eastern European heartlands, resulting in national movements in this area to declare their independence. On 3 March 1918, the new Bolshevik government of Russia, on one side, signed a treaty with Germany, Austria-Hungary, Bulgaria and the Ottoman Empire on the other. The Baltic States of Lithuania, Latvia and Estonia were ceded to Germany with all signatories recognising the independence of Ukraine. It was a temporary measure that was annulled by the Western powers at Versailles in the following year. Although Poland was not represented, the Russian negotiators, on its behalf, vehemently defended its right to independence, a stance not unrelated to Poland's geographical position between Russia and the West. It was, however, ceded to Germany. It was only after Versailles that Polish independence was granted, but that laid bare the question of where the Russian-Polish border lay. German imperialism had triumphed and Soviet helplessness was exposed. The Bolsheviks denounced the Treaty of Versailles and began an advance into the borderlands, where they clashed with local Polish self-defence units and regular Polish troops. Hostilities, which began in January 1919, are generally taken as the beginning of the Polish-Soviet war, although war was not officially declared by either side.

The promise of nationhood being restored to the Poles was a great incentive, and with the help of the French, the independence movement gained traction as more Polish units were formed; as quickly as they emerged, however, many were swallowed up again by the German advance. Haller had been commissioned by the French President to form a Polish Army in France, and it was agreed that it should include an air force. Polish pilots from many countries made their way to France to join up. The French provided Haller with seven combat squadrons, comprising more than 100 aircraft, complete with training facilities at Dijon and Pau. Initially they were manned by French airmen, but they were progressively replaced by Poles as the squadrons were moved to Poland in the spring of 1919. When French military aid was withdrawn from Poland, the Aviation Squadron of the 4th Division, under Colonel Ludomił Antoni Rayski joined General Haller's 'Blue Army' at Chernovtsy.[3]

Ludomil Antoni Rayski, born on 29 December 1892, was the son of an impoverished nobleman who had served as an officer in the army of the Ottoman Empire. He attended the Lwów Polytechnic at the same time as Janusz de Beaurain. He volunteered for the Piłsudski legions in the First World War but was conscripted instead into the Ottoman army and wounded at Gallipoli. Once recovered, he volunteered for flying duties with the Turkish Air Force and served with them until demobilisation in January 1919. His experience gained him command of a Polish air squadron against the Soviets and then, with Poland facing a drastic shortage of capable pilots, was given command of the Kościuszko Squadron. After the war he returned to his studies but remained an active aviator, becoming famous for extraordinary endurance flights. This caught the attention of the authorities and he was sent for specialist training and later was appointed deputy to

Francois-Léon Lévêque. He became de facto commander of the Polish Air Force days before Piłsudski's coup d'état in May 1926.

In the chaos of 1918 as military structures, weakened through long years of conflict, fell prey to the febrile ambitions of once subjugated peoples and lost much of their control, soldiers, sailors and airmen began drifting back to their native lands. Once there they formed ad hoc groups and turned their efforts towards purely national goals. Where there had been continental war now there was localised conflict as borders became 'negotiable'. Empires were struck from the map and new countries emerged. On 5 November, just a week before the Second Polish Republic was legitimised, military aircraft flew their first combat mission under the Polish flag.

By late 1918, the Poles were confident that the Austrian and German empires were collapsing making the restoration of their country's borders a very real possibility. Austria, however, had organised Ukrainian elements in their armed forces to create a buffer zone in Galicia to separate them from the Poles. Ukrainian troops occupied Lwów, but Polish airmen occupied the nearby Lewandówka airfield. The first ever combat recorded by the new Polish Air Service (Lotnictwo Wojskowe) was that of 1 Eskadra Bojowa a week before independence was announced. Pilot Lieutenant Stefan Bastyr and observer Lieutenant de Beaurain took a Hansa-Branderburg aircraft from Lewandówka airfield on 5 November 1918 and dropped three 15kg bombs on forces of the Western Ukrainian People's Republic before strafing them with machine gun fire at Persenkówka Station.[4]

The Polish Air Services were eventually established in November 1918 when personnel from air units of all partitioning powers were brought together in a somewhat uncoordinated pattern of declarations. Lieutenant Colonel Hipolit Łossowski, a former commander in the Russian forces, seized Mokotów Field, which by now included not only a landing area but buildings, a training school and extensive repair facilities.[5] The taking of Mokotów Field was essential for establishing a basis upon which to build an air arm. Elsewhere, Lewandówka airfield was occupied, Rakowice Field at Cracow and Przemyśl Hureczko likewise. The previously German facilities at Ławice air station at Poznań, and the Zeppelin hangar at Winogrady fell into Polish hands along with others at Toruń, Bydgoszcz, Grudziądz and Puck, yielding up numerous German aircraft. Rakowice alone held thirty-six Oeffag-Albatros and Brandenburg aircraft. In a move, later considered to be a vital development in the formation of the PAF, twenty-six fully operational aircraft were captured at Ławica in the former Prussian region. Occupied by about 200 German soldiers, the air base was stormed on 6 January 1919. German Gotha bombers flew from Frankfurt an der Oder to destroy the airfield buildings, but failed to penetrate the air defences. An aircraft hangar in nearby Winiary yielded up more than 300 airframes alongside a number of two-seater aeroplanes such as LVGs, Rumplers, Albatroses and Halberstadts and single-seater fighters such as Albatroses and Fokkers. As well as the aircraft, there were also several dozen aircraft engines, spare parts, ammunition, aerial bombs, on-board weapons, field hangars, cars, motorcycles, carts, photographic equipment and also some balloon paraphernalia. While Ławica became the assembly point for all Polish aviators in the region of Greater Poland (Wielkopolska) and brought a measure of organisation, the aircraft, unfortunately were of very poor quality with many of them only 'suitable for a museum'.[6] A shortage of trained pilots was partly alleviated when an appeal was met by a number of Polish veterans of the German Air Force who had remained after the German retreat, but there was still a dearth of leadership quality. French influence was in evidence when the Squadron BR66 with mostly French crews and a French commander, Captain Gontran de la Perelle, moved to Ławica from Warsaw in response to increased German-Polish tensions.

Personnel flocked back from their units in Austria and Russia to join their new national air service, but many were not familiar with the types of aircraft on offer. There was an acute shortage of trained observers and navigators, and even when a training school was established it could not find sufficient instructors. The Polish Ministry of Military Affairs gave financial incentives to war veterans and private pilots to join the service, but the parlous state of the machines and the lack of familiarity with them led to numerous fatal accidents. It was only the arrival of Haller's French units that saved the PAF from catastrophic disintegration.[7] Poland, at the time of the arrival of Haller's army between April and June 1919, was facing hostility along its borders from Russia, Germany, Lithuania and Czechoslovakia. Piłsudski, a man with 'a profound distrust of democracy' and who found Party politics 'repugnant' was installed as Polish Head of State in November 1918.[8] He hated anything Russian, admired Germany's sense of order and discipline and, despite his worship of Napoleon, 'resented the paternalistic attitude of the French government towards Poland'.[9] After Versailles, against the entreaties of the victorious Allies, German troops withdrew from positions in Eastern Europe and allowed the Russians to advance into Poland.

Evolution of the PAF was a 'bottom-up' operation which gathered pace as the different districts freed themselves from foreign control. Operations were chaotic, with units often going into action without specific orders. Different regions even adopted different markings for their aircraft at first, until December 1918 when the white and red check, the personal emblem of Lieutenant Stefan Stec, was officially adopted as the insignia of the PAF. More aviation groups were created with concomitant training schools and airfields. These were quickly organised into three groups and rushed off to see action in eastern Galicia under the auspices of a new Air Section (Sekcja Żeglugi Napowietrnej) led by Lieutenant Colonel Łossowski. By the end of the year, the Supreme Command had created two separate offices, an Air Forces Command (Dowództwo Wojsk Lotniczych) under Łossowski, and an Air Section of the Ministry of Military Affairs run by Colonel Aleksander Wańkpwicz. The following April saw Air Forces Command re-designated as the Air Forces Inspectorate, responsible for training and support services and a new Air Command (Szefostwo Lotnicze). In this way a measure of order was brought to a somewhat chaotic structure and laid the foundations of a much more stable air organisation. It was still not a very inspiring group though, described by one as 'a group of enthusiasts who did not even speak the same technical language', but with nationhood eagerly anticipated, differences were overcome. Numerous minor conflicts broke out all along what would be a contested border and gave them a common purpose.[10] Four more squadrons were added in early 1919 and again, they were sent East. Łossowski began to suffer from a chronic illness (he died in 1925), lost some of his vigour and was replaced at the Air Forces Inspectorate by General Gustaw Macewicz. At the same time, Major Jan Stachowski took over from Wańkpwicz at the Air Section. The whole Polish air organisation received an enormous boost in January 1919 when French-sponsored units were incorporated, along with substantial financial credit arrangements from the French government. Polish airmen went to France to attend training schools at Dijon and Pau, after which they returned to Poland as part of seven squadrons of the excellent Breguet XIV A2/Br, together with Salmson 2 A2 and SPAD S.VII fighter aircraft which had been supplied to General Haller by the French.

Polish air units saw a great deal of action against Czechoslovakia and Ukraine in 1919, and Lithuania in the following year, but the most intense combats were with Soviet Russia over the Polish-Russian border around Vilnius, Bialystok, Ternopil and Lwów after German forces had abandoned the areas. In contrast to the slaughter of the fixed entrenched positions of the First World War, the Russo-Polish War, which erupted in 1919 when the newly reformed Polish nation battled against Russian forces over the disputed border between them, was characterised by dynamic mobility, the concept of which informed the development of Polish military doctrine thereafter. Despite there being 'no base for air power' in the new republic, Poland had benefited from 'some modest advantages which had an impact on the development of aviation'.[11] The Russian squadrons had been disbanded by the Germans after the signing of the Brest-Litovsk Treaty in March 1918, but some Polish-manned units remained intact. They escaped to form an air wing of the 4th Rifle Division under Brigadier General Lucjan Zeligowski.

In early March 1919, the Ukrainian offensive started on the eastern borders of Poland. The 2nd Combat Squadron engaged Ukrainian forces advancing on Lwów, which the Poles were determined to hold. As Polish ground forces gained the upper hand there with air support, fighting broke out all along a wider front but air support weakened due to the rapidly deteriorating state of the aircraft and the bitter winter weather. Come February, however, the Ukrainian forces launched a new attack on Lwów with superior forces and air support. The Poles countered as the weather improved and a new milestone was marked when Lieutenant Stec shot down a Ukrainian Nieuport fighter in the first recorded single-seater 'dog-fight' victory for the PAF. Along a rapidly changing front, aircraft had to be moved by rail to reach the sectors where their support was most needed, while the Ukrainian air units seemed reluctant to attack Polish troops and risk engagement with Polish aircraft. The Ukrainian front was stabilised in May, but the French and British, who had bankrolled the Polish and now feared that any further defeat for the Ukrainians was politically awkward, called on them to halt a planned attack to drive the Ukrainians back. French commanders and air crews among the Polish forces were ordered to withdraw.[12] French officers and pilots had joined as 'volunteers', but were allowed to act only on orders from France and so many were soon replaced by Polish personnel. Only French technical advisers remained to help with organisation and development.

The PAF was also intensively engaged in conflicts that had erupted all along other border regions. In September 1919, the 1st Squadron was moved east to Babruysk, where it was engaged with Bolshevik forces on the Lithuanian and Belarusian fronts, bombing communication nodes and supply lines, as well as armoured trains at Zhlobin and Rahachow. The unit changed its name to the 12th Air Force Squadron, and shortly afterwards to the 12th Intelligence Squadron, after which it provided air support in the battle of Šacilki. The 2nd Greater Poland Air Force Squadron attacked armoured trains and bridges along the Babruysk–Zhlobin railway line.

Czech forces, acting in contravention of the Czech-Polish Agreement of November 1918, advanced at Cieszyn. Soviet revolutionary troops had taken Wilno in the north-east and when Haller moved units to counter these threats, the Ukrainians took advantage by launching a new offensive which was quickly halted and withered away. This allowed the Poles to reinforce the Soviet front and drive on Minsk with air support. In a bizarre twist, the Ukrainians now asked for Polish assistance to hold its own frontier against the Soviets, but Poland's Western backers saw no advantage for themselves and vetoed the idea, although this did not prevent combined Czech-Polish action towards Kiev in the spring.

Maximum air power had been deployed against the Ukraine in April when aircraft were used in the absence of ground forces at Svietlahorsk, but soon the old problems emerged again. Commanders were forced to cut back on missions owing to the 'fatal state' of their units, one of which existed only on paper and others reporting severe shortages of spare parts.[13] A hiatus ensued as commanders waited anxiously for the arrival of new aircraft which were 'expected at any moment'. The Air Force 'teetered on the brink of collapse'. Fortunately, the opposing forces had similar, if not worse, problems of supply and serviceability, but when the Soviet forces entered Poland at the end of July the PAF was down to thirty serviceable aircraft. The PAF was facing mounting problems owing to the great disparity of aircraft types and the difficulty in getting spare parts to keep them operational. To make up for this the Poles purchased thirty-eight Albatros D.III single-seater fighters from Austria and a number of others from Germany – albeit through clandestine channels, but the Poles needed more, much more. It was estimated that they needed at least 300 new aircraft with full ground-support facilities.

Notwithstanding its disparate origins, the nascent PAF had acquired a vast experience through First World War operations and quickly brought it all together to create 'a rich basis for theory'.[14] At once, influential voices called for the establishment of an independent air service supported by a home production capacity to provide security. During the First World War, Lieutenant Colonel Jerzy Syrokomla-Syrokomski as commander of an air regiment, had been shot down, wounded and made PoW by the Germans. In November 1918, he joined the Polish Army with the rank of major. He was also involved in journalistic and social activities and had been the editor of the newspaper *Orędownik pod Jasnej Góra i Ostra Bramy* (published in Warsaw in 1906–7), publishing poems in its pages under the pseudonym 'Almokorys'. In 1913, as a pilot, he published the article 'Platowiec as an intelligence officer and combat unit', and in 1918 in the *Bellona* magazine he published the article 'Aviation as an independent type of weapon'. In this article he emphasised the importance of the role of the future PAF as an independent force. In 1919 he was one of the founders of the aviation journal *Polska Flota Napowietrzna*, the first aviation journal published in independent Poland. The '1st Aviation Competition', held in Poznań in 1919, was organised on his initiative and that of the editorial office of the journal 'Polish Aircraft; it was the first air and sports show and competition in independent Poland.

The result was a mixed bag of machines at the end of 1919 which struggled to remain operational, and those squadrons that managed to maintain some level of technical efficiency lacked skilled pilots. To make up the shortfall, foreign nationals from Germany, Italy, Russia and France were signed up.

In the spring of 1919 a young American captain named Merian Cooper was visiting Poland as a member of the American Relief Administration, an American humanitarian mission in Europe following the First World War. Cooper presented to Polish commander-in-chief Jozef Piłsudski an idea to recruit a group of American aviators to fly with Polish forces in recognition of the contribution of Polish soldiers such as Tadeusz Kościuszko and Kazimierz Pulaski in the American War of Independence in the late eighteenth century.

This volunteer unit became the Kościuszko Squadron. They flew a mix of Albatros D III fighters, Italian Ansaldo A.1 Balilla and Breguet XIV light bombers. The Polish military hoped to recruit more US citizens of Polish descent for a second squadron and set up the Polish American Air Group as a recruiting organisation.

Given the go-head, Cooper went to Paris and found nine American pilots, Major Cedric Fauntleroy, Lieutenant George Crawford, Captain

Edward Corsi, Captain Arthur H. Kelly, Lieutenant Kenneth Shrewsbury, Second Lieutenant Edwin Noble, Lieutenant Carl Clark, Lieutenant Edmund Graves and Lieutenant Elliot Chess, ready to go immediately to Poland. They were given Albatros D. III (Oef) fighter planes and instructed in Polish air operations tactics. Fauntleroy took command of what became the Seventh Air Squadron. Cooper was shot down on 13 July 1920 and spent nearly nine months in a Soviet POW camp, from which he eventually escaped. American pilots fought with the 7th Fighter Squadron established on 21 December 1918 and were active in Eastern Małopolska. The American volunteers who arrived in Lwów on 16 October 1919 were commanded by Major Cedric Fauntleroy. Sixteen Americans went on to fight in 1920 against Semyon Budyonny's Soviet 1st Cavalry Army, and again during the Battle of Zadwórze on 17 August 1920.

The Seventh Polish Fighter Squadron, also known as the Kościuszko Squadron, played an important role in the history of the Second Polish Republic during the first years of its existence, while also strengthening the bond between Poland and America. The squadron's origins date back to 7 November 1918, a few days before Poland officially regained independence.

In February 1920, fighting broke out with Russian forces over the disputed border in which Kościuszko Squadron was involved. By late spring, flying Italian Ansaldo A.1 Balilla fighter planes, which, due to the poor quality and defects, were referred to as the 'flying coffins', the squadron conducted its first strikes against the formidable Soviet First Cavalry Army, also known as Budyonny's Cavalry Army. Captain Cooper took over the command of the squadron from Major Fauntleroy, who took on the leadership of a newly formed air squadron and became commander-in-chief of the Polish Second Army's aviation.

Lieutenant Crawford took over as commander when Cooper was shot down and made PoW. In total, three American pilots died while fighting for Poland during the 1920 conflict, while many more sustained wounds. These American volunteers would go on to gain official recognition for their role in the war, with many receiving the highest Polish military decorations such as the Virtuti Militari and the Cross of Valor. During the Second World War, Polish pilots flew with the Royal Air Force. Many were scattered among different squadrons but a number were recruited to the new 303 Squadron, which carried the Kościuszko insignia and served with distinction – especially during the Battle of Britain.

At the beginning of 1925, the Kościuszko squadron aircraft were replaced with SPAD S.61s and then in the spring of 1925, a new number was given to the Escadrille; between 1925 and 1928 it is referred to as the 121st Fighter Escadrille. Another change of numbering (the last one) took place on 14 August 1928. In the spring of 1933 the unit received the modern, all-metal Polish-made fighter aircraft – the PZL P.7. In 1935 they also received the PZL P.11, a new type which later saw combat in September 1939 at the beginning of the Second World War, fighting against the German invaders. By that time the Escardille had been transformed into the 111 Fighter Escadrille, which took part in the defence of Poland as a part of the Pursuit Brigade.

Obviously, the Poles were not happy about relying on foreign nationals to fly their aircraft, but had little choice when it came to instructors. With some urgency, they set about creating new pilot training facilities under the direction of Captaine Carl Marie Francois vicomte de Vergnette de Lamotte, one-time commander of the legendary French Escadrille 23, and operated them under the control of another Frenchman, Major Mauger de Varennes earning it the title of 'French Pilot School'.[15] Training was rigorous but pilots were much better prepared afterwards before being whisked off to the Russian front. The multi-national make-up of the trainees, especially those who had seen action, allowed them to contribute a range of experiences which were put to good use at the Superior Pilot School (Wyższa Szkoła Pilotów) at Ławice Field. Not only pilots but mechanics and support personnel, including civilians, were given extensive training also. Syrokomla-Syrokomski, with the blessing of the Air Service, used his connections to the periodical *Polish Air Fleet* to write stimulating articles and place advertisements in an effort to attract recruits.

Qualified pilots who went into action saw plenty of it. There had been intense fighting in eastern Galicia in the autumn of 1918, where air units were heavily involved, and then in the Russo-Polish War. Few squadrons were fully equipped to take part, but those that did were mostly employed as reconnaissance and communications units, while some bombing operations were carried out against fixed positions. Air operations were described as 'ramshackle', despite the best efforts of the flyers.[16] Radios were virtually non-existent, as were cameras for surveillance and aircraft soon began to suffer from lack of maintenance, especially the older types. Some squadrons became completely depleted of operational aircraft despite the 'black magic' efforts of 'resourceful and energetic' ground crews.[17] By 25 July 1920, twenty Polish combat squadrons had only thirty-one serviceable aircraft at their disposal.[18] Fortunately, the 500-mile-long front over which the Polish and Russian forces competed was such that only rarely did opposing air units face each other. Each enjoyed almost total freedom of aerial action, which gave them little in the way of experience on which to draw when composing a comprehensive air doctrine.

The main contribution of the air elements was in surveillance and communications over the vast disputed areas where Polish air power proved to be considerably more effective than their opponents in all respects. A winter of diplomatic activity brought a lull in fighting and a chance for the Air Ministry to concentrate on raising the status of the air force to a level equal to the cavalry and infantry as administrative structures were put in place. Operations were scrutinised to inform the debate over new aircraft design. There was a call, which went unheeded, for strike aircraft to be organised into independent units, but there was a general acceptance that new bombing squadrons would be needed and it was hoped to use the huge Friedrichshafen GIII and Gotha GIV aircraft for the purpose, but the lack of spare parts for some aircraft prompted Macewicz and Vergnette to take the German machines out of service and rely more on the French Breguet and British Bristol types, for which parts were more readily available. This was a reflection of the overall poor condition of aircraft, with many of the 150 or so available being 'weary and sub-standard relics [whose] expectation of service life [was] exceedingly short'.[19]

With the advent of a new campaign season in the spring of 1920, the first manual was produced on air-ground cooperation. The use of aircraft in support of ground forces during the Russo-Polish War added an important dimension to the fighting and had significance for future military operations.[20] Although the Soviet Air Force was numerically stronger, its airmen were significantly less experienced than the Polish flyers and most Polish casualties were the result of ground fire or accident, rather than at the hands of Russian pilots. Operations were of such an ad hoc nature, with few enjoying sound planning or having clear objectives, that neither side developed a well-thought-out air doctrine beyond a vague idea of aircraft performing a variety of roles in support of ground forces. As in the Ukrainian campaign, both Polish and Russian aircraft enjoyed almost uninterrupted freedom from enemy aircraft which did not require any special tactical expertise on the part of pilots. In general, Polish air strikes were rather more coordinated, but the lack of air-ground communication once the aircraft were flying put significant constraints on their efficiency. The greatest success of Polish aircraft, and the one that made the most telling contributions to the war, was the breaking of the morale of Soviet infantry and cavalry with bombing and strafing attacks. The Polish retreat back to Warsaw during 1920 was made less debilitating by air attacks slowing the Russian advance. Eventually Piłsudski's forces were able to regroup and counter-attack, but he had little time for aviation and made little effort to use it effectively. In any case, there were never enough aircraft to make the sort of decisive interventions that could turn a battle.

It was a huge relief when the new Bristol fighters started to arrive, albeit without instructions on how to assemble them, but pilots were sent into action before they had been given sufficient time to familiarise themselves with the controls and aircraft flying characteristics. The refreshed units, nevertheless, provided significant support for Polish forces around Warsaw by scouting Soviet positions and raising panic behind their lines by attacking troop columns. No more than a dozen aircraft had halted a whole Soviet division of Semyon Buddeny's cavalry which was stopped in its tracks at Lwów.[21] Experience of the Russo-Polish War encouraged development of an air doctrine based primarily on tactical air-ground cooperation. Indeed, Piłsudski placed no great importance on air power over and above its army-support role of reconnaissance and communications and tended to see it as having no great relevance in warfare. He generally eschewed doctrine at all levels, preferring the Napoleonic concept of war as an art form. This resulted in the air force, almost by default, placing 'overemphasis upon developing front-line support aircraft'.[22] It is agreed that the PAF made a substantial contribution to Polish success in the war with the Soviets, but its operational efficiency was patchy and owed much to the quality of leadership at squadron level.[23] Under intense combat conditions in a volatile theatre, training of crews was almost impossible and most had to learn 'on the job'.

By the end of the summer, Soviet forces were in full retreat all along the Eastern Front after their defeat in the Battle of Warsaw, but when a cease-fire was agreed on 12 October 1920, the Poles were obliged to withdraw to borders well behind their advanced positions. Even before the signing of the Treaty of Riga in March 1921 which ended the Russo-Polish War, many

Polish air units had been demobilised at the behest of a beleaguered treasury, but the Minister of Military Affairs, General Kazimierz Sosnkowski, pressed for the retention and upgrading of twenty-five squadrons. Poland had been constrained, however, in its drive to economise on military spending by its signing of the Franco-Polish Military Convention on 21 February 1921 which committed France to provide material and technical support for Poland in the event of it being attacked by either Russia or Germany. France and Poland had strengthened political ties in the nineteenth century, having found a common enemy at that time in the new German Republic. They combined economic trade with a mutual defence pact aimed not only at Germany, but Soviet Russia too. Both feared that Germany would seek a revision of Versailles, by force if necessary, and both saw that any such move would be to their detriment. Poland had a large army and France wanted it to stay that way. Polish agricultural products would be traded for French military technology, but only on the understanding that Poland maintained thirty-five infantry divisions and eleven cavalry brigades as a bulwark against Soviet aggression. The Treaty guaranteed Poland a military alliance with Europe's dominant army and gave it access to investment capital and surplus war materiel while an accord with Romania gave it access to import routes should the German border ever be closed. This year also saw the issuing of the first set of 'Air Force Instructions' (Regulamin Sluzby Polowej) by Major Jasinski. These instructions were informed by French thinking and based primarily on the experiences of the Russo-Polish War.[24]

The Russo-Polish War had generally been fought with 'very poor or obsolete equipment ... on both sides', with 'great deficiencies in command'.[25] Both sides had enjoyed almost total freedom of air operations, but where air power was deployed, the Poles enjoyed considerably more success – although not without combat casualties, which were almost all the result of ground fire. Little was done to investigate the employment of squadrons in specialised roles. Under army command, they were usually used in a variety of ways depending upon prevailing circumstances giving them a multi-purpose character. Air Force commanders had no opportunity to expand their experience within a limited operational environment and tended, going forward, to form their opinions according to this narrow view. Since many of them would go on to play leading roles in the development of the PAF, it is clear that doctrinally it was constrained from the start.

Essentially, the PAF never had a chance to show what it could be capable of, and so was not able to impress upon the Polish military mindset the extent to which air power had the potential to revolutionise warfare. This had an impact not only on the way the Polish military developed its doctrine over the following twenty or so years, but left it in ignorance of how a potential enemy might do so.

After the ceasefire of October 1920, the PAF had a chance to take stock. The deficiencies it found in both numbers and facilities meant that there was no 'acceptable basis for healthy development of the service'.[26] The country that had been at war for every minute of its short existence was in an 'appalling financial situation' and desperately needed some respite to find its feet. Economies were essential and the PAF was right in the firing line for a severe cut in funding now that the country was finally at peace. An order of 18 January 1921 reduced it to thirteen squadrons, each with no more than four or five serviceable aircraft. To sugar the bitter pill the demoralised staff were promised that, as things improved, so the squadrons would be built up to full strength by 1925.

France and Poland had signed a treaty of political alliance on 19 February 1921, which was backed up by a military convention, subsequently followed by an economic agreement in February 1922. The Treaty bound both partners to concert action in the event of unprovoked aggression upon either. The convention put real teeth into the Franco-Polish understanding by stipulating immediate mutual assistance in the event of German aggression. It also bound France to take measures to check Germany in the event of Soviet aggression towards Poland.

Early Polish air doctrine envisaged three main uses of air power: pursuit to attack ground units and enemy aircraft, bombardment to destroy the enemy's military preparations, and reconnaissance, all of which were to be employed in support of ground forces. At this point, air power was seen as little more than a modern equivalent of cavalry, albeit with greatly enhanced capabilities. Before air doctrine could be advanced to any appreciable degree, however, it was necessary to transform what was essentially the 'detritus of war' into a modern military service.[27] Work started on creating the promised 'excellent, but small Air Service'. The first units were primarily comprised of two-seater reconnaissance aircraft which were attached to army divisions, but financial constraints continued to dog the process and only a small number of squadrons were formed. All types of equipment and materiel was in short supply in Poland itself, but the country did not have the foreign currency to buy from abroad in any great quantity and so tried instead to encourage Polish industry to turn to military production. The only company to offer any prospect of building aircraft was E. Plage & T. Laśkiewicz of Lublin, who pledged to produce up to 200 Ansaldo A.300-2 and 100 Ansaldo Balilla, but owing to a shortage of skilled labour and 'chaotic and inefficient methods of production', no more than about 12 per cent of their order book was ever fulfilled. When aircraft did come out of the factories, many were found to be of poor quality and the Fiat A.12bis engines, imported from Italy, were notoriously unreliable. Only 120 aircraft were produced before the government terminated the contract.[28] Another factory was opened under French-Polish management with orders for 300 airframes and 600 engines, but it never began production. Meanwhile the Poles begged surplus machines from German and Austrian stockpiles which had been confiscated by the victorious Allies under the Treaty of Versailles, but their pleas were ignored. The only way left open was to buy foreign Albatros D.III machines from such as Österreichische Flugzeugfabrik AG (Oeffag), although production, even here, was limited by the level of finance made available by the Polish government and was uncertain depending, as it did, upon the goodwill of the Allies – which was capricious at best.

The French stepped in once again to rescue the plot when the French general Francois-Léon Lévêque was made commander of the Department of Air Navigation (Żeglugi Powietrznej) in 1923, taking over from Maciewicz. The US *Aircraft Year Book* of 1924 reported that 'French manufacturers and French aviators are practically in charge of the Polish Air Force.' Lévêque brought to the chaotic Polish Air Ministry a calm, methodical approach and its 'first rational basis for proper development and expansion'.[29] His appointment was accompanied by a huge French armament loan which allowed him to set about restructuring the Polish aviation industry. With a freedom only possible when spending somebody else's money, he ordered 150 Potez XV-A2s two-seater army cooperation biplanes, seventy Harriot HD 12 and 14s trainers, and purchased licences to manufacture more of the same in Poland by new aircraft manufacturing concerns. 'Samolot' would build the Harriots and PWS (Podlaska Wytwórnia Camolotów) the Potez. With no engine plants in Poland, Lévêque was forced to buy 1,500 Lorraine-Dietrich W-type engines from France. Another joint French-Polish enterprise, 'Francopol', was created and given orders for 2,500 airframes and 5,600 engines to be supplied over a ten-year period. Lévêque, however, cancelled the contract amid swirling rumours of corruption. The strong French influence exerted over Polish aviation at this time meant that French doctrine, with its emphasis on close cooperation with the army, tended to dominate within the PAF and the aircraft procured tended to fit into this pattern.

Lévêque's appointment was short-lived as national pride demanded a home-grown leader and they got one in Włodimierz Ostoja-Zagórski, 'a good Pole, very ambitious, extremely intelligent and gifted'. Zagórski had been one of the founders of 'Francopol' and, upon his appointment, refilled its order book. When the first SPAD S.61 aircraft came through, however, they were found to be extremely unsafe and the Farman FG.60 Goliath were already obsolete. Only the Potez-54 were any good. The contract for home-produced aircraft was never fulfilled.[30] General Władysław Eugeniusz Sikorski, the new Minister of Military Affairs and keen advocate of French-Polish cooperation, brought in a new concept of air doctrine and, with Zagórski, created a new vision and energy 'to transform Poland into a major air power'.[31] More huge French contracts went out for 250 modern Blériot-SPAD S.61 fighters which had already been rejected by the French Air Force having become notorious for their numerous crashes. The 250 Breguet 19 bombers made of aluminium alloy were better, but the thirty-two Farman F.68 Goliath bombers were getting a bit past their prime. The contracts became mired in (not unwarranted) accusations of corruption, with Zagórski coming under scrutiny for his financial connections to 'Francopol'. His whole enterprise had been ill-conceived and its shortcomings amply illustrated by the fact that Poland lacked trained pilots to fly the vast number of aircraft so peremptorily ordered, lacked the proper facilities to house them, and lacked properly trained technicians to service them. As a result, although Poland had an impressive air force on paper, squadrons of airplanes were left outside in all weathers unused and rusting away. Of the many aircraft that were procured under the new arrangements, a large number were out-of-date war surplus which the French had been only too pleased to off-load, and the thirty-two Farman bombers had neither crews to fly them nor hangars big enough to accommodate them when they arrived. Polish industry had, however, benefited from contracts for aircraft and engines manufactured under licence from France and financed through foreign loans that the government had been forced to take out.[32]

Władysław Eugeniusz Sikorski, along with Piłsudski, had been active in several underground organisations before the First World War which promoted the cause of the independence of Poland from the Russian Empire. The two often found themselves on opposite sides of arguments, but were able to work together for a short time to further the Polish cause. Sikorski led Polish troops in the Polish-Ukrainian War and later in the Russo-Polish War. On 1 April 1921, he was appointed as Chief of the Polish General Staff with a clear ambition to keep the military out of politics. He was briefly made Prime Minister in 1922 but resigned on 26 May 1923, after which he returned to the military. He refused to back Piłsudski's coup d'état in 1926 and was relieved of his command after it succeeded. He spent the next years in France before being appointed Polish Prime Minister in exile on 30 September 1939. He died in an aircraft crash in 1943 in circumstances that were long considered dubious, but no incontrovertible evidence has emerged to suggest that it was anything but an accident.

Ostoja-Zagórski had been born in France into Polish nobility. His mother was from the House of Romanov. He served in the Austro-Hungarian Army before being appointed as Chief of Staff of the Polish Legions in 1916 over the objections of Piłsudski, who felt that Zagórski was too much wedded to the Austro-Hungarian Empire. As the war turned against the Empire, however, Zagórski turned against it and ended the war as Vice-Chief of the Polish General Staff, but that was short-lived and he was sent back to take up a field command in the Russo-Polish War. In 1924 he was brought into the Air Force in the War Ministry. In this role he purchased a large number of French aircraft through the Francopol company, in which he was a shareholder, but there were insufficient numbers of trained personnel and infrastructure in Poland to make use of them. The growing rift between Poland and France had undermined Zagórski's position. Neither did his prospects improve when his old adversary Piłsudski sweep back into power by ousting Sikorski in a coup d'état in May 1926. Zagórski had refused to support him and was subsequently arrested in April 1926 on charges of corruption in relation to his Francopol dealings and put in Vilnius Prison. Zagórski had found himself on the wrong side of history. Never brought to trial, he was released and last seen in public boarding a train from Wilno to Warsaw, ostensibly to attend a meeting with Piłsudski. He disappeared completely amid speculation that he had been murdered.

Notwithstanding Ostoja-Zagórski's murky dealings with the French aviation industry, he was instrumental in the implementation of significant reorganisation within the PAF in an attempt to modernise it by replacing general-purpose air regiments with specialised fighter and bomber regiments with new internal structures that augured the beginnings of a strategic air power concept. To mark the transition all units were given new numbers, which did not go down all that well with veteran flyers who already had an emotional attachment to their squadrons and felt the change to be a break with their traditions.

The way in which Polish air doctrine continued to reflect French policy was evident in 1924 with the issuing of a further set of 'Interim Regulations Pertaining to Air Force Organisation' (Tymczasowy Regulamin Formacii Lotniczych), which elaborated on the functions of all types of units but especially bombers, which were seen as having the potential of operating as an independent strategic force. The concept of single-purpose squadrons (eskadra) was introduced for the first time. Fighter squadrons would have six to ten aircraft, bomber squadrons eight, and general-purpose reconnaissance and communications squadrons, ten. A total of six Air Regiments (Pułk Lotniczy) were created with thirty squadrons, and to ensure that there were sufficient trained staff to man all these new squadrons the Flying Schools at Grudziądz, Poznań and Bydgoszcz were expanded.

In 1925, meanwhile, the political landscape changed in a way that was detrimental to Poland. The major European powers except Soviet Russia met at Locarno to formalise the post-war territorial settlement and normalise relations with Germany. An uneasy entente was formalised between Poland and France in October 1925 with the agreement on the Locarno Treaties which stated:

> In the event of Poland or France suffering from a failure to observe undertakings arrived at this day between them and Germany, with a view to the maintenance of general peace, France and, reciprocally, Poland, acting in application of Article 16 of the Covenant of the League of Nations, undertake to lend each other immediate aid and assistance, if such a failure is accompanied by an unprovoked recourse to arms.

There was a guarantee of Germany's western border, but its border with Poland was left open to 'arbitration'. The Pact was a diplomatic triumph for

Germany's Foreign Minister Stresemann, who was awarded the Nobel Peace Prize, ensuring more stable relationship with both Russia and the West, but despite the Polish-French guarantee of security built on the alliance created in 1921, it left Poland in limbo and was a public humiliation for Polish diplomats becoming one of the contributing factors to the fall of the Grabski cabinet. France and Poland had signed a treaty of political alliance on 19 February 1921, which was backed up by a military convention, subsequently followed by an economic agreement in February 1922. This Treaty had bound both partners to mutual support in the event of unprovoked aggression upon either, but Locarno undermined this concord and led to a worsening of relations between Poland and France. Poland feared that the deep-seated hostility between Germany and France 'seemed to have given way to a spirit of friendly cooperation' when Germany agreed to join the League of Nations in 1926. Piłsudski would later say that 'every honest Pole spits when he hears this word Locarno'.

During the two years of Zagórski's leadership the PAF 'made the biggest and most startling leap forward on the whole inter-war period'.[33] This was done against a background of stagnation within the Polish economy and a general European movement towards disarmament and reduction of military budgets. Poland, however, was very precariously positioned between regimes not inclined to respect its borders and it needed to establish a credible defence policy. This at a time when the Polish government was wracked with parliamentary instability and factionalism which threatened anarchy in the country. Zagórski was ever mindful of the external threat and his work to strengthen air defences left Poland with 'the second largest and best-equipped air power … on the continent of Europe', albeit one that had been built up with French finance, French aircraft and French-inspired doctrine.[34] Polish pilots were among the best trained anywhere in the world, the state-owned aviation industry was producing original designs and airfield development was well advanced. Despite this, and Rayski's drive for transition from foreign to home-design and production, the PAF had made little progress towards independence from the army and remained little more than an auxiliary service.

In May 1926 Piłsudski came out of his three-year retirement and forced President Wojciechowski to dismiss the government. Piłsudski imposed his conservative, authoritarian views on the Presidency of the Polish Republic and his appointment to replace Zagórski at the Air Ministry, Rayski reversed decisions to form new elite fighter and bomber regiments and emphasised the role of air units as reconnaissance and liaison only. When Piłsudski ordered that 'aviation is to serve only for reconnaissance', the Air Ministry was firmly 'slapped down' and demoted to become only a minor adjunct of the army, which reduced its combat value and had a significant effect on its structure.[35] Some officers who were unable to accept this and agitated for an independent service were not tolerated and were soon purged from the PAF. All indigenous aircraft manufacture was taken over by the state which, for a time, seemed to spur productivity, but many aircraft types still relied on foreign engines manufactured under licence from the British. When the reduced home demand for aircraft created a surplus, the extra aircraft were sold abroad. The Francopol factory that had received such a large order from Zagórski was riddled with corruption and inefficiency, producing only two completed aircraft and not a single engine; this prompted Rayski to cancel the contract, liquidate the company and sell its premises to the Czech Skoda concern, transferring manufacture to a new company, CWL (now called PZL Państwowe Zaklady Lotnicze). The SPAD fighters were a huge disappointment. Despite more than thirty coming off the factory floor in 1927, they suffered from considerable structural weakness and were quickly abandoned. In desperation, Rayski turned to the Czechs with their Skoda works to supply Avia BH-33 built in Poland at the Skoda-Polska factory. The lack of good fighter aircraft plagued the PAF for many years until the high-wing, all-metal monoplane PWS-10 was produced.[36]

The new politics introduced by Piłsudski, whose cabinet 'shaped their military doctrine on experiences in the Russo-Polish War' and 'appeared to show a singular lack of enthusiasm and understanding for aviation', led to a reorganising of the whole command structure of the Polish Armed Forces, whose character changed little over the next decade.[37] There was now no place for a specific aviation section in the General Staff which, given its low profile and the lack of interest shown in it by his superiors, allowed Rayski to take total control of aviation and impose his views. General Stanislaw Ujejski was the most senior of a number of aviation officers who were invited onto a Special Experimental Commission, the purpose of which was to conduct theoretical and practical studies upon which to establish the rules for the use of aviation in field conditions. Thus began a process of rationalising of management and administration of the air services and the creation of a unique Polish air doctrine designed specifically along national lines.

Sergiusz Abżółtowski's mother was Russian and his father, a Polish general in the Russian Army. During the First World War he had served as an observer in the Russian 2nd Destruction Aviation Division, and in 1917 he trained as a pilot before commanding the 5th Destructive. In 1918 he volunteered to join the Polish Army in France but returned to serve as head of the PAF on the Central Front in the Russo-Polish War, after which he was appointed Deputy Chief of Polish Field Aviation. He became a celebrated military aviation theorist but was purged from the military after 1930 because of his Russian heritage. He died in mysterious circumstances in 1939.

Abżółtowski and General Sikorski contributed to the debate over the role of the PAF in a new periodical *Air Force Review* (*Przeglad Lotniczy*), as French influence waned and the PAF began to create its own ideas, which placed emphasis on the strategic role of an independent air force. It was their report of 1931, 'Regulamin Locnictwa', the culmination of three years' work, that formed the basis of Polish air doctrine, emphasising 'front-line support', upon which the country went to war in 1939. Major Marian Romeyko was a lecturer in aviation tactics at The Higher Military School who had travelled widely on numerous occasions, to study Italian, French and Czechoslovak aviation. In 1936 he published an important book, *Aviation Tactics* (*Taktyka Lotnictwa*). There has been much debate over the influence of the men over Polish aviation. Cynk claims that it was limited owing to the unpopularity of Abżółtowski, Sikorski and Romeyko with Piłsudski's reactionary government over their progressive views.[38] Peszke, however, disputes this assertion and argues that the positions held by Romeyko and the long-term influence of 'Regulamin Locnictwa' indicate that they never fell out of favour. Cynk seems to agree that although they were not held in high esteem, 'there is no evidence that progressive-thinking officers were discriminated against'.[39] Proponents of strategic air doctrine saw military exercises over a number of years which explored the practical effects of the bombing of railway lines to disrupt communications and troop movements. Simulated attacks on Polish cities were also carried out to ascertain what damage might be inflicted on an enemy should Polish aircraft bomb enemy cities.

In Poland, as in other Eastern European countries, there was no great industrial tradition on which to build. Engineers had to be trained, higher educational establishments had to be created, factories fitted out with modern metallurgical machine tools had to be built and money had to be found to pay for it all, but Poland in the 1920s and 1930s was not seen as a safe bet for foreign investment. Up to 1930 Polish military aviation had been built primarily on French doctrine and equipment and it was only in 1931 that Polish PWS-10 single-engine fighter aircraft were coming into service and the revolutionary all-metal PZL P7 with a Bristol Jupiter VII F engine was not far behind. A new era began, however, starting with the organisation of the Skoda engine plant and the PZL airframe factory, the purchase of a licence and the production of Wibault fighter planes, Fokker communication-bombers, Wright and Lorraine Dietrich engines, and the manufacture of Puławski fighters. The PAF started to modernise its outlook with more attention to safety brought about by changes in training, ground infrastructure, tactics and functioning of the air force. Plans were laid for the next generation of twin-engine, two-seater ground-support PZL Jastrząb fighters to replace the P7 and P11 single-seat fighters, which were left behind by the rapid technological advances after 1934.

All this had taken place within a framework of aggressive government action to control aviation manufacture. Some companies such as PWS were quickly brought under government control, but others resisted. The Samolot company was one such, but teetering on the brink of bankruptcy, its factory was devastated by a fire leaving it in dire need of government aid – which was bluntly refused, tipping it over the edge into insolvency. PWS had crippling cash-flow problems forcing down its market value. In both cases the government eventually stepped in to pick up the remnants of these companies at knock-down prices, effectively nationalising them. The manufacturers E. Plage & T. Laśkiewicz of Lublin were given orders, but after the company had put in major investment to retool for the work the orders were abruptly cancelled, driving this company also into bankruptcy. When the government took over the plant, production was immediately fired up again.

At the start of the 1930s, Poland had about 800 first-line combat aircraft, half of which were in reserve. The much-admired PZL P7 all-metal monoplane fighter designed by Sygmunt Puławski, with excellent all-round visibility and its Bristol Jupiter VII F engine, had made the PAF the world's first air force entirely equipped with all-metal monocoque fighters. This, however, proved to be a high point of Polish military aviation. During the rest of the 1930s, it slowly lost ground against other air forces. When new aircraft were introduced to replace types which were rapidly becoming redundant, they were insufficient in number and somewhat behind the curve in performance characteristics. Even the P11 which came into service in 1934 was pretty much rendered obsolete only a year later when the Luftwaffe unveiled their Messerschmitt Bf109. Poor decisions were made when the requirements of modern air power were overlooked in favour of prejudice and a conservative mindset. When a replacement for the P11 fighter was chosen, it turned out to be an all-purpose, twin-engine, two-seater, unrealistically expected to operate both as a dive-bomber and interceptor. The elimination of a pure fighter from the aircraft mix was 'suicidal'.[40] The P.23B Karás, which came into service in 1934 after much redesign to accommodate a third crewman, proved to be underpowered and too slow for deployment in close-support roles. At a time when most European countries were waking up to the growing threat of war and developing aircraft to modern standards, the Poles were in 'an era of utter stagnation ... in the worst equipment situation for almost fifteen years.'[41] Training of crews, however, continued to be a high point in the PAF at centres such as the vast, well-appointed establishment at Dęblin, which offered three-year training courses.

Piłsudski died in May 1936, leaving the country as a dictatorship without a dictator. When German troops reoccupied the Rhineland unopposed, it was clear that Poland could no longer rely upon French assurances of military aid in the event of an attack by Germany. However, the French, still anxious to prop up Polish military power as an ally against a resurgent Germany, did agree to provide a new major loan of two billion French Francs to finance Polish rearmament. This money was channelled through a Fund of National Defence designed to modernise the Polish armed forces and create an industrial base to make Poland self-sufficient in military equipment.[42] Half of all the money, however, was for the direct purchase of military equipment from France, since it would take some time before Poland, starting from a much lower level than other European countries, could establish an industrial base for manufacture of home products. There was nothing in Poland remotely comparable to the German Krupps or the British Vickers manufacturing giants. In a purely political gesture, almost 5,000 million zloty was theoretically allocated to a six-year military budget, but it was soon clear that the government was neither willing nor able to live up to the commitment and the promise was watered down by extending the period of investment to ten years instead. The government clearly 'regarded [the PAF] as an extravagant auxiliary army service of dubious operational value', and was simply unwilling to afford it the attention it desperately needed in a rapidly deteriorating and increasingly dangerous European political landscape, declining 'to face up to the realities of the changing military scene.'[43]

In total, seventy-eight air force squadrons were envisaged, but the whole could not be guaranteed before 1941 at the earliest. Spending on the air force was less, under the new budgetary regime, than was the case in other European countries and events proved it to be quite inadequate to serve the country's needs.[44] In 1936 there were only thirty-three squadrons, seventeen light bomber with Potez 25 and Breguet 19, thirteen fighter with P 17 and PL 11, and three heavy bomber with Fokker F.VII. Many of these aircraft were at the end of their useful lives, however, and in need of urgent replacement by more modern machines. The requirement for bombers to be able to impede a German advance east of the Oder river as demanded by the General Staff was laudatory but quite unrealisable. It is clear that military and political leaders were espousing doctrine devoid of any sense of responsibility for, or realistic expectation of, its implementation. As an example, Rayski called for a total of almost 900 aircraft by 1942 at a cost substantially exceeding the whole of the French four-year loan in 1936. When confronted with the impossibility of executing such a plan, Rayski chose to prioritise bombers and reduce the overall numbers by cutting out some fighter production.

The Polish cavalry played a major but poorly understood part in the narrative of September 1939 and remained the pride of the Polish armed services; still considered to be 'a decisive weapon', it consumed one fifth of the military budget between 1935 and 1939.[45] During that period the PAF was allocated one tenth of the same budget. Nothing could better illustrate the 'contemptuous attitude towards the air force'. By comparison, the French spent fifteen times more, the RAF some thirty times more and the Luftwaffe almost a hundred times more. The overall commander of the PAF was responsible to no less than six different authorities and had very little say in development, budget or methods of use in war. It is hardly believable that a new skeleton Air Staff formed in 1937 did not consult the aviation commander, and did not even make known to him their decisions until the last minute. When the aviation commander wanted a new aircraft he had little idea how that aircraft would be used when it came into operation a few years hence and so could not issue a detailed specification to the designer.

There is no doubt that in terms of quality some, but not all, Polish manufactured aircraft were the equal of any produced in other countries in the early 1930s, as evinced by the number of their successes in international aerial competitions, but this was not matched by administrative efficiency in the Air Ministry which had two sections that failed to cooperate in the manner required of a military organisation preparing for war. The General Staff, under the strong authoritarian control of Edward Rydz-Śmigły, controlled all military planning including the Air Force section under Ujejski. They wanted to avoid 'a harmful separation of military aviation with its own war doctrine'.[46] Air Ministry ambitions for an independent role were strongly opposed by the Army faction and by Rydz-Śmigły who ordered that in the event of war, Józef Zając at the Air Force Inspectorate would assume command of the Air Force. He had tried to organise air staffs into each army command but also retained some fighter and bomber squadrons to act independently. The main weakness was in the small number of fighter squadrons. There had been very successful aircraft designs which had proved to be a match for any at first, such as the PZL 7 and PZL 11 and the export version PLZ 24, but they were no match for the new generation of fighters coming out of the German factories. When the war came, the PAF proved to be a whole generation behind the Luftwaffe, and the best fighter they had, the PZL 24, continued to be exported right up to July 1939 as a desperate measure to finance the Polish military-industrial base.

Zając had been an infantry officer without any knowledge of aviation when he was appointed to the Air Inspectorate in 1937, but this had not prevented him from 'pronouncing judgement on the most fundamental and intricate technical and operational problems facing the PAF'. One of his first decisions, based on his 'astonishing conclusion' that Poland did not need bombers, was to discontinue production of the P37 Łoś, 'the most modern aircraft in the PAF's armoury [and] one of the finest bombers extant'.[47] He advocated a purely defensive (i.e. tactical) air force and held the somewhat optimistic view that Poland did not need a twin-engine medium bomber because their allies, Britain and France, would provide the strategic arm. His firm opinion was that 'creation of a strategic bomber force [was] a needless waste of effort and money'.[48] He was, however, greatly concerned at the lack of fighter units, especially given their 'excellent morale and competence', and urged every effort to upgrade equipment and facilities. Peszke claims that Zając's apparent antipathy towards home manufacture of bombers was a natural consequence of the provision made in existing budgets for the purchase of foreign types which allowed the shortfall to be made up. Poland tried to buy British Hurricanes and French Morane-Saulnier aircraft which they hoped to sell on and replace with bombers, but negotiations stalled. Britain was not ready to lose any fighters, but they did allow the Poles to utilise credit facilities to take on some of their outdated Fairey Battles, which the Poles had to accept as an alternative to nothing at all.[49] While the lack of aircraft was a significant issue, it was the shortage of crews, especially bomber crews, that characterised Polish lack of readiness for war. Adopting a policy that would prove sound in other theatres at other times, the PAF assigned extra crews to each squadron on the basis that combat was more wearing on people than machines. This, naturally, reduced the number of fully manned squadrons and led to the demobilisation of some older bi-plane squadrons.[50]

There was substantial overlap between the sections run by Zając, Rayski and Ujejski, leading to lack of clear demarcation lines between departments. Administrative duplication, inefficiency and rivalry resulted. Zając, in direct opposition to Rayski's views, was of the opinion that Poland's primary weaknesses in aviation were its outdated fighters and its poor communications and navigation equipment, both of which were essential for an effective bomber force. Belatedly, the General Staff seem to have had a sudden change of heart and decided that they did want a single-engine, single-seater fighter after all and ordered the P.50 Jastrząb (Hawk) with the British-built Mercury VIII engine, which proved to have unreliable carburettors, and British-made landing gear, which was much delayed. A modified version with a Bristol Taurus III engine was better, but never saw service before the Germans struck on 1 September 1939.

The story of Polish aircraft production in the 1930s shows clearly why the PAF was in such a parlous state. Development of new models was two years behind schedule. When orders of older types were fulfilled, factories sometimes lay idle as designs for new types were argued over. Often where newer aircraft were produced, they were exported to meet the government urgent requirement for foreign currency. Far from painting a picture of steady improvement in PAF operational readiness, in November 1938, Zając wrote a report bemoaning the fact that the new home-produced aircraft promised in Rayski's plan would not be ready before 1940 at the earliest and urged procurement of foreign fighters in the meantime to counter the imbalance with bombers. Rayski complained that he had been given insufficient authority and inadequate funding to carry out his work and resigned in March 1939 to be replaced by General Władisław Kalkus who supported Zając's ideas, but time was running out. Rayski's policy of home production together with emphasis on a strategic capability had proved to be disastrously wrong and their lack of hard currency left them little chance of putting things right quickly. Zając had ordered 300 Jastrząbs but was forced to call a halt to production because of numerous problems. Complete modern fighters could only be bought from France, but could not be supplied before 1940.

All through the 1930s it had been assumed that the greater threat to Poland came from Soviet Russia and 'all works were conducted in accordance with directives of the High Command to prepare for war in the east', but when the Germans marched into Prague in March 1939, Poland hurriedly mobilised its Western garrisons.[51] Money was thrown at Kalkus to prepare the air force for war. All exports of Karaś PZL43A aircraft to Bulgaria would be stopped, but only as a last resort. A new air base was established at Brześć to house a bomber brigade. Training programmes were stepped up. The British Prime Minister Neville Chamberlain, in the House of Commons on 31 March 1939, said:

> I now have to inform the House that ... in the event of any action which clearly threatened Polish independence, and which the Polish Government accordingly considered it vital to resist with their national forces, His Majesty's Government would feel themselves bound at once to lend the Polish Government all support in their power. They have given the Polish Government an assurance to this effect.
>
> I may add that the French Government have authorised me to make it plain that they stand in the same position in this matter as do His Majesty's Government.

On 23 August Poland, along with its Western allies, was shaken by the Molotov-Ribbentrop Pact between Germany and Soviet Russia. Two days later the British government signed the Agreement of Mutual Assistance with Poland, which contained promises of mutual military assistance between the nations. Talks with France and Britain held through the summer of 1939 at one point included the prospect of stationing French heavy bomber squadrons on Polish soil. Tension mounted as Luftwaffe reconnaissance aircraft became increasingly prevalent in Polish air space but were invulnerable to attack because of their altitude. Poland now feared imminent attack, but its plans to meet a German invasion were based upon the optimistic assumption that any such move would be met with a French attack on Germany's western borders. In desperation, Kalkus tried to buy foreign aircraft, but by now his main suppliers were reticent to comply, being more concerned with retaining their major assets for home use. Britain did actually agree to supply a small number of Hurricanes and thirty obsolete Fairey Battles as part of their Mutual Assistance agreement, but the aircraft were never delivered. The French promised sixty Amiot 143M twin-engine bombers, but again these failed to arrive in time. The US offered aircraft with credit to purchase but the price was too high and anyway, the aircraft were designed to use 100-octane fuel which was not available in Poland. Only the French came up with a few Morane MS406s, obviously on the assumption that even the smallest extra pressure on Germany's Eastern Front would be that much less against them in the West. Polish home-production became chaotic as directives came and went, with the result that 'equipment deliveries in 1939 were the lowest for 5 years'.[52]

The German-Polish Agreement of 26 January 1934, signed by von Neurath and Lipski, had promised 'a lasting peace [as] an essential pre-condition for the general peace of Europe', but crucially included the text: 'can then be denounced by either Government at any time on notice of six months being given'. In October 1938, German Foreign Minister Ribbentrop offered to renew the agreement with the codicil that Danzig be annexed by Germany. Poland refused and Hitler unilaterally rescinded the pact on 28 April 1939. The PAF was mobilised for war on 23 August. It had 392 serviceable aircraft of which 158 were fighters, and faced a Luftwaffe with 3,652 first-line aircraft.[53]

In September 1939 there was no actual document stating what Polish Air Force Doctrine was, nor was there official guidance on what role was envisaged for aviation and what were the expectations of it. It was simply assumed that aircraft would operate under army control with bombers intervening at the battle line in support of ground forces, enemy airfields would be attacked and enemy rail and road communications targeted. These broad instructions were constrained by a directive to 'prevent [inadvertent] bombing of enemy civilian or private property'.[54] For too long, aviation in Poland had been regarded as an ancillary army service and its fate had been decided by high-ranking army officers who had no understanding of the air arm and usually did not share the views of air commanders. At no time was air policy discussed in terms of how it was linked to war aims, and where instructions were formalised, such as in the *General Directives on the Use of Aviation* issued in April 1939 by the General Staff, the document had received only limited circulation before 1 September when the German offensive was launched.[55]

Chapter 7

Soviet Air Power before 1939

'The creation of an aviation industry in backward Russia was
to be a long and difficult task'[1]

It is clear that Russia recognised the military potential of aviation very early
by the fact that the War Minister, General D.A. Muliutin, had set up the
Commission to study the military potential of balloons and dirigibles in
1869. By 1895 balloons were being used regularly in manoeuvres and had
a permanent place in the Russian military at the start of the Russo-Japanese
war in 1904.[2] The first authentically recorded powered manned flight in
Russia was by Baron Alexis Van den Schkrouff, who flew a Voisin at Odessa
in July 1907; a year later the All-Russian Aero Club was established at the
Kolomyazhsky Hippodrome in St Petersburg as the pre-eminent flying
school for aspiring pilots. Branches were quickly set up in Rostov, Kiev,
Sevastopol and Moscow. The world's first Aerodynamic Institute had been
in existence since 1904 at Kuchino near Moscow under the mathematician
and engineer, Nikolai Yegorovich Zhukovski, who had already set up the
first wind-tunnels in Europe in 1902 with his student, and future aircraft
designer, Andrei Nicholayevich Tupolev. The Russian Army was interested,
but clearly did not know what to make of aircraft and hedged their bets by
saying in the War Ministry Annual Report of 1908, 'in general they are not
suitable for military purposes [but] in the future they will, nevertheless,
play a tremendous role in military affairs'.[3]

The geography and military history of Russia demanded that its main
military effort be concentrated on land forces, but by 1909 the powered
aircraft had captured the imagination of a generation of young army
officers who, despite official War Ministry preference for dirigibles, had
been encouraged to become 'air-minded', and began to view aircraft as
the natural extension of the horse in a reconnaissance role. As a result of

this enthusiasm, the War Ministry acquired five Wright biplanes and a few English Bristol aircraft and established military schools for pilot training at Sevastopol in Crimea, and at Gatchina near St Petersburg.[4] As an example of the way that ideas about aviation had been taken up in Russia, in 1909 the great aviation pioneer Igor Sikorsky, who at the time worked for a railroad manufacturer, built his first helicopter, and Aleksandr Aleksandrovich Porokhovschikov built a military aircraft with an armour-plated cabin. A French firm founded the Duks plant in Moscow, a Gnome et Rhône engine assembly plant was set up alongside it and the Russi-Ballit factories built French aircraft under licence. A small native 'Kalep' aero engine plant started up the following year in Riga.[5]

The Grand Duke Alexander Mikhailovich, who had headed the 'Committee for the Strengthening of the Naval Fleet by Voluntary Contributions', found himself with surplus funds at the end of the Russo-Japanese War and used them to obtain foreign aircraft from France and the US and hire instructors from the French Bleriot and Voisin companies. With these resources he was granted permission from his cousin, the Tzar, to create an aviation branch of the military in 1909. His enthusiasm was boundless and upon receipt of the machines he declared: 'Victory in a future war will be impossible without an aerial fleet.'[6] By 1911, aircraft were taking part in army manoeuvres and civilian air shows as interest in them grew at the expense of dirigibles.

In mid-1912, operational control of the armed forces was transferred to a council of defence with the 'Aviation Division of the Chief Administration of the General Staff' directly responsible for aviation (now called the Imperial Russian Air Services) similar to the way it was done in France, indicating the huge influence that the French had on Russian aviation at this time. While some aircraft were bought in, there were attempts to fire up a domestic industry when Sikorsky, now fully employed in aviation and breaking new ground, designed and built the successful three-seater S-6 Biplane and then a four-engine 'Grand' bomber with a wing-span of 28 metres, the forerunner of all multi-engine aircraft, both of which were mass-produced during the First World War. The 'Grand' was especially remarkable in that it was capable of transporting sixteen passengers in 'luxurious' surroundings.[7] The military, however, were not particularly imaginative in their use of aircraft despite the relatively large number available to them in 1914. Neither did the obsolete designs encourage confidence as machines built for novelty rather than endurance quickly became unserviceable when the fighting started, after which they were repeatedly required to operate with urgency. The government, having seen all the other countries in the war adopting aviation with increasing enthusiasm and using them in novel ways, were convinced that they also needed to explore air power. They imported French and Italian aircraft, both to give experience to their flyers and to stimulate domestic production. Unfortunately, given Russia's agrarian and overwhelmingly uneducated population, where factories were set up to produce aircraft on home soil, the lack of a skilled workforce slowed progress and often resulted in poorly constructed machines. The main problem was the lack of sufficiently powerful engines which could not be manufactured domestically, so a number of Farman aircraft were bought in from France and the US. This was no more than a stop-gap measure and not really a solution because of the drain on foreign currency and, more importantly, the Russians were generally fobbed off by the sellers with older types or inferior models no longer considered suitable for their own use; unfortunately, in time of war, it was a seller's market.

The Imperial Air Force was reorganised in early 1915 along the same lines as the British and French with special bomber, fighter and reconnaissance units set up to provide support for the ground forces, but the units generally were short of trained pilots and maintenance staff. All this, together with the high number of aviation accidents, did not do much to change the army mindset about the utility, or lack of it, of aviation units which were already considered to have 'no significance [as a] branch of weaponry'.[8] Furthermore, the air force lacked recruits since it was not seen as the sort of service that capable, ambitious military officers would want to stake their careers on when the cavalry was still seen as the acme of military calling. That left only the few real enthusiasts to try and fill the ranks of fliers. Among these, fortunately, was the Grand Duke Mikhailovich, but even he was not able to advance the cause of independence for the air force. It was difficult enough for Russia to find skilled technicians and resources to build aircraft, but the rapid advances meant that machines, insubstantial at the best of times, became worn out very quickly and required a sustained effort to keep them flying. By 1916, the majority of Russian aircraft were unserviceable and domestic production was at a virtual standstill. The reliance on foreign parts was a major feature of Russian aircraft manufacture and this inevitably proved to be its Achilles Heel when the Central Powers' blockade cut off supplies. French visitors scoffed at Russia's first home-built aircraft calling them ' ridiculous contraptions … as solid as barges'.[9]

Generally, the performance of the Russian air force in the First World War was poor and certainly inferior to other nations.[10] It was never in a position to gain even limited air superiority on any front. The statistics of aerial combat make it abundantly clear that 'The Russians could not gain even a temporary ascendancy.'[11] Baron Manfred von Richthofen, who flew with the German air force on the Russian front, confidently and arrogantly reported that 'compared with flying in the West, flying in the East is absolutely a holiday'.[12] Overall, the Imperial Russian Air Services were unable to make much of an impact on the fighting along the Eastern Front where aviation had, in reality, been little more than a sideshow. Sikorski's 'Grand' bombers were being fitted with machine guns for defence, but little thought was given to the possibility of them operating in a strategic role beyond strict army controls despite operating at squadron strength under Major General M.V. Shidlovsky and dropping more than 2,000 bombs. In 1916, as a result of experience and observation of enemy activity on the Western Front, it was decided to create a fighter force specifically designed for escort duties to reconnaissance aircraft and to interdict against incursions by enemy spotters. Commander Voevodsky set up the first fighter force but it clearly had much to learn and usually came off second-best in any fighter-to-fighter engagements with the Germans, not least because of their inferiority in construction and maintenance.

Russia did not have the resources to sustain involvement in a long war and soon the numbers of available aircraft dipped alarmingly due to attrition and poor maintenance but all through the war the greater problem was the shortage of experienced – or even qualified – pilots, despite further schools opening in Odessa and Moscow. The small number of trained pilots, slow to increase due to the low level of technical background of recruits, was often less than the number of serviceable aircraft which, in itself, was on the low side.[13] Notwithstanding the impressive increase in the number of aircraft factories in Moscow and Petrograd employing some 10,000 men, production of new machines simply could not match the attrition rate, primarily due to the shortage of materials as a result of the economic blockade imposed by Germany and the reluctance of foreign manufacturers to provide specialist technical advisers. While Russia was still very reliant on foreign machines such as Morane Parasols and SPADs, Sikorski, with the help of German investment, had come up with a modified version of his 'Grand', the (Russo-Baltic Wagon Factory) Ilia Muromets, a four-engine reconnaissance-bomber, which was in full production. However, there was no way of speeding up supplies of new machines to the front, given the hopeless production capacity, and the rate of technical advances was such that by the time they flew in anger most aircraft were already obsolete. The problem of obsolescence applied equally to many of the aircraft bought from France causing 'bad blood' with the French, who were thought to be taking advantage by getting rid of their older models (some of which had already seen action on the Western Front) to Russia while they equipped their own air force with the latest models. Memories of this dispute echoed down the years creating a general distrust of French intentions during the inter-war years.[14]

Under the Tzar, Russia had simply lacked the social and economic foundations on which to build an air force. Unlike traditional armed forces, it required technical expertise and, especially in the field of engine production, sophisticated industrial facilities, communications and workforce. Pre-revolutionary Russia with its feudal structure, uncompetitive industry and poorly educated citizens offered few of these. The social unrest in evidence everywhere, together with a growing antagonism towards the ruling classes and general malaise within society as the war dragged on, made progress impossible. It was not helped by official lukewarm enthusiasm for aviation within a Defence establishment that saw 'no significance [in] this branch of weaponry', and the Grand Duke Mikhailovich himself could make no headway in promoting the potential of strategic air power at General Staff Headquarters.[15]

A notable contribution to the history of Russian military aviation at this time were female pilots who were among the first aerial combatants. A 25-year-old Russian princess, Eugenie Mikhailovna Shakhovskaya, was awarded her pilot's licence in 1912 and had travelled to Italy where she volunteered to fly with the units operating over Tripoli but was rejected. Upon returning home she applied directly to the Tzar for permission to fly with the Imperial Russian Air Service and was allowed to fly reconnaissance missions. Shockingly, she was held captive and repeatedly raped by her male colleagues and when she tried to flee she was arrested and tried for treason. Eugenie, benefiting from the chaotic revolutionary times, avoided incarceration and later, during the Bolshevic purges, she became addicted to hard drugs and served for a time as an official government executioner. In 1920 she shot her assistant in a fit of madness, at which point she was also shot dead. Nadesha Degtereva served in the Russian Air Service by disguising herself as a man and flew two-seaters on numerous reconnaissance missions. On a mission in spring 1915, she was wounded in the arm and legs in a swirling dogfight, but was able to fly back to her base. Her gender was revealed when she was taken to the hospital for treatment and she was subsequently prevented from taking any further part in the air war. Lyubov Golanshikova, who had gained fame in Germany by flying with Anthony Fokker in 1913, was a test pilot during the war but flew a Voisin on at least one reconnaissance mission. When the Bolsheviks came to power in 1918, she trained pilots for the VVS Red Air Fleet (Voenno-vozh-dushnie Sili) and continued flying combat sorties against Poland. When the Russo-Polish war ended she travelled to New York, where she worked as a taxi driver for the next forty years.[16]

When the Bolshevik Revolution engulfed Russia, the air force received a serious setback along with most other military sections. Some of the most capable engineers and designers were imprisoned and others, such as Sikorski, fled the country and ended up in the United States, where they made significant contributions to that nation's aviation during the following two decades. Up until this point, Russia, despite the prevailing anti-scientific establishment, had achieved a great deal of recognition for its outstanding research in such fields as aerodynamics and mechanics, having pioneered the earliest work in the field of rocket propulsion using liquid oxygen and hydrogen as propellants.[17] After the November Revolution, however, production of aircraft virtually ceased as many factories were damaged during fighting. Within the air units factionalism was rife with personnel split on political lines and many of the officer ranks driven out, or in the case of Shidlovsky, shot by revolutionaries. The political leadership was torn between destroying the military, which had been a tool of the Tzar, and preserving it to challenge counter-revolutionaries and defend Russia's borders against German and Polish encroachment; by the end of 1917 the College for the Administration of the Aerial Fleet had been set up to restore some semblance of order and resume aircraft production. A number of active squadrons were reformed but the aircraft were hopelessly outdated. Revolutionary fervour saw the air arm renamed as the 'Workers' and Peasants' Red Aerial Fleet', and the nationalisation of all aircraft factories just in time

221

for the civil war which erupted in the wake of the Bolshevik revolution. The new body urgently needed a leader and got one in A. V. Sergeev but, as before, all air services remained firmly under the control of the army.[18] The problem of establishing a workable air force under conditions of revolution then civil war, and war with Poland, at the same time as warding off attacks by Western powers at Murmansk and Archangel cannot be overstated. The Bolsheviks first looked to Germany to help build up its air force and internal aerial transport system but foreign investment would have to compete for scarce resources in an economic environment where 'Bureaucratic excess and inadequate coordination were characteristics of the period.'[19] This road would not be easy; although the Treaty of Brest-Litovsk had been signed on 3 March 1918, there was still open hostility between the two over disputed borders all across Eastern Europe.

By May 1919 the basic air unit was six machines of various types according to availability, each one attached to a rifle division. Supply and maintenance problems continued to dog the service with up to three quarters of the whole air fleet unserviceable due to redundancy, poor maintenance or lack of spare parts. Factories were seized by the workers from their owners and reorganised along lines dictated by the communist government, but this inevitably caused delays as new management structures were put in place. In addition, many factories were in areas embroiled in war and were relocated where possible. While the Duks and Krasnie Letchik plants, among others, had once again started building Nieuports, SPADs and De Havillands, the numbers of aircraft coming out of the factories was way below requirements. The reasons were simply that 'many unskilled workers were employed, tools and techniques were improvised and production management was weak'.[20] Most effort went into the more practical task of refitting older machines by cannibalism where necessary. In these early years the Soviet Air Force was comprised of 'almost exclusively foreign fuselages and ... foreign aircraft engines'.[21] Meanwhile, in an attempt to jump-start domestic production, a research centre, The Central Institute of Aerodynamics and Hydrodynamics (TsAGI), was set up in Moscow under Zhukovski and Tupolev, which became the centre of Soviet aviation development for many years to come, and from which would emerge practically all of the country's industrial team leaders between the wars. Despite such problems, however, the Bolsheviks were able to build up a small air force of some 400 aircraft, albeit many of which were virtually obsolete, and initiate a post-revolutionary programme of aircraft manufacture based upon foreign designs and reliant upon foreign engines.

The new Soviet leader, Lenin, saw aviation as a key component of Bolshevik power and prestige, both within and without the country, and 'urged the development of the Soviet aviation industry by all possible means'.[22] The Imperial Air Service would be reformed under the communist banner with a radical philosophy and a level of scientific and technological expertise to challenge that of any other country but initially Lenin said, '[we] can only maintain ourselves in power by appropriating all the cultural and technical experience [of] progressive capitalism'.[23] Both France and Germany offered help, anxious no doubt to offload war-surplus, but Russia was in the throes of civil war and later, war with Poland which further degraded its air power. During this time, aircraft took a part in actions against the Germans and Romanians, the Czech troops along the Trans-Siberian railroad, the White Finns, against Moslem, Ukrainian and other rebelling nationalist and political groups. They were also employed against Allied forces, particularly those of the United States and Great Britain and their White Russian allies in the Archangel area, the British in the Trans-Caucasus and Trans-Caspia, the French in the Ukraine, in the Crimea and along the Black Sea, the Sea of Azov and the Caspian Sea. The wide range of terrains and extreme distances over which the air units operated posed special problems of maintenance and logistics. During this time, the new Soviet Air Force had adopted a strategy of concentrated air power with three or four squadrons operating under a single command in support of ground troops, especially against the anti-Soviet 'White' forces at Perekop in November 1920.

As a result of these campaigns, aviation leaders began to develop an air doctrine including tactics, command and organisation, as well as training and equipment needs, but the actual performance of Red air units during the Polish campaign was summed up by an official US government report as 'not indicative of aptitude, extraordinary courage or good equipment'; the failure was attributed specifically to a shortage of spare parts.[24] There grew a firm commitment to developing effective ground-attack capabilities as the fundamental role of aviation. Although the strategic potential originally demonstrated by the bombers was never realised, the Soviets did not lose sight of it. However, German influence was creeping in whereby the rapid concentration of fire-power on the ground assisted by aviation and the employment of reserves at the crucial juncture of a battle became a hallmark of Soviet military doctrine. There had been very little experience of air-to-air combat to inform doctrinal debate and so the emphasis was heavily biased towards reconnaissance and ground attack in support of land forces. Battlefield air support rather than strategic bombing was the main thrust of development. Training for air fleet personnel was expanded at the Zhukovski Academy in Moscow, the Yegor'evsk Theoretical Flying School and the Serpukhov School of Air Combat but they initially had a 'small, poorly educated student body'.[25] As well as these established institutions, new training facilities were opened at Kiev, Sevastopol, Odessa, Omsk, Borisoglebsk and Tashkent, where young flyers from India and Afghanistan were among the student body. Politics, however, became a major consideration and the organisation of the VVS was determined as much on political imperatives as it was on sound air power doctrine, with political indoctrination an important part of the training syllabus.

When demand for aircraft increased dramatically during the Russo-Polish War, and home-production due to the ravages of revolution diminished, the government looked to imports from Holland, Italy and Britain, but foreign currency was desperately short and few countries were prepared to offer credit. The only one to show any interest was the other European pariah, Germany, who had little to lose after the war. Germany had established relations with the communists before the revolution, and even funded arms purchases, in the hope that a successful revolt against the Tzarist regime would ease the pressure on its Eastern flank, allowing German troops to be reassigned to the West. When Lenin came to power there was already a diplomatic channel open and Germany had even begun giving military aid to the communist regime as early as 1918. All this was taking place at a time when both countries were actually, albeit temporarily, facing up to each other over border disputes in the Ukraine. It did not, however, prevent trade agreements being drawn up within months of Lenin taking control and there were exchanges of military personnel, including Air Staff who, in Germany, would be humiliated by being stripped of their aircraft at Versailles.

A region of buffer states, with political boundaries imposed by Versailles, between the two pariahs of Russia and Germany largely ignored long-standing cultural, ethnic and national orientations and created political instability all across Eastern Europe. After Versailles, Russia and Germany, both fearful of the new Polish state with its huge army and centuries-old grievances, saw advantages in continued collaboration. Rather than give up aircraft to the victorious Allies as ordered, the Germans had chosen to destroy many of them, or leave them behind as they retreated from Ukraine to be picked up by the Soviets. Other aircraft, engines and spare parts that Germany had been ordered to hand over were illegally exported to the Soviet Union through neutral countries instead.

Domestic aircraft production started up, at a modest rate, in 1920 at the Duks plant in Moscow (State Aircraft Factory (GAZ) No.1) and the Krasnie Letchik factory in Petrograd (State Aircraft Factory (GAZ) No.3) which made Nieuports and SPADs. Progress was slow for many reasons, not least of which was the acute shortage of skilled workers and equipment. The one hope for improvement was assistance from Germany, which had skilled aircraft engineers and technicians who were redundant as a result of Versailles. It was clear that both countries could benefit from closer cooperation. There had been sporadic military and technical liaison between them since 1917 which had survived confrontation over the Ukraine, but which was severely tested by the collapse of Germany in November 1918. This was quickly renewed, however, in 1919 when German military aid played an important part in Bolshevik defence on all fronts. By the end of 1920, Germany was providing limited material and technical support to the Soviet aviation industry.[26] On 6 May 1921, the two countries signed an official trade agreement under which Germany would help Russia to develop its industrial base. Initially it was hoped to set up an aircraft manufacturing centre in cooperation with the state-owned Albatros Flugswerk, but the Russians were not interested in the old wooden Albatros, they wanted the metal-constructed aircraft made by Junkers. Hugo Junkers had already opened negotiations with Russia over the establishment of a commercial airline in 1920, but the aircraft they had hoped to use were confiscated in Hamburg by the Allied Control Commission, acting in compliance with the terms of Versailles, forcing the company to the point of bankruptcy. The new trade deal which was agreed by Germany was a lifeline and, indeed, probably the only thing that prevented Junkers from folding altogether. A private deal was struck and a secret agreement was signed between the company and the Soviet government on 6 February 1922. Under the terms of the agreement a provisional production facility would be set up at Fili near Moscow where Junkers would provide tools and technology to train Russian engineers and mechanics and build a repair shop for the conventional wooden-structured

Russian military aircraft. Junkers was contracted to 'remit to Russia with the shortest delay possible 500 new aircraft, Junkers type, with the corresponding amount of spare parts'. which would be built at the industrial plant of the RBVZ (Russko-Baltiiskii Vagonnyi Zavod) at Fili and at the St Petersburg-based Russo-Polish Automobile Plants, as well as at Kharkov, Taganrog and Rostov, on the understanding that 'the Army of the [Soviet Union] will have the possibility of fully utilising the production of the ... factories'.[27] Only at this point did the potential for a truly domestic aircraft industry begin to emerge, albeit one based firmly on foreign designs, which would see growth and development sufficient to sweep the Soviets to the forefront of military aviation during the next decade and beyond. The Fili plant became known as the State Aircraft Factory (GAZ) No.7, and Junkers technicians were transferred to it from their plant at Dessau. The total cost for both programmes was calculated to be around 1,000 million Reichsmarks, which would be provided by the Reichswehr. Hugo Junkers had not been at all enthusiastic about investing in the Soviet Union despite the dire state of his company, but he was assured that the whole enterprise would be underwritten by the German government and half the aircraft produced would be available for sale outside Russia. He was persuaded that it would allow him to develop his military expertise, technical testing, and production in areas from which he was disbarred by Versailles. The German military commander Hans von Seeckt saw these factories as the best hope Germany would have of equipping an air force in the event of another war with France. In turn, the Soviets hoped to increase their military industrial production cheaply, gain access to German technology, and train hundreds of new engineers.

Work started there on producing Junkers Ju20, Ju21, F13 and JuG1 aircraft and Jumo-L-5 engines. Foreign engine plants making Gnome Rhône and Hispano-Suiza models started up, but production levels were extremely low until things improved a little with the introduction of German engineers and technicians sent, with the secret consent of a small number of leading German ministers, to continue development of its own military-industrial base made moribund under the constraints of Versailles. At its peak there were more than 1,100 personnel working at Fili, but the relationship between Junkers and the Soviets quickly soured when the Soviets claimed that the aircraft produced were below acceptable standards of performance. Furthermore, they objected to the many components which were manufactured in Germany at Dessau and shipped to Fili for assembly, thus depriving them of the transfer of production know-how. The project was proving to be an unhappy experience for Junkers.

French and Belgian occupation of the Ruhr on 9 January 1923 was not entirely unexpected given Germany's default on reparations and France's frequent threats, but it sent shockwaves through the German military who feared it might embolden Poland and Czechoslovakia to encroach on her eastern borders. In response, the Reichswehr reinforced diplomatic channels to Moscow and sought closer military cooperation despite Soviet support for communist insurgents trying to foment revolution within Germany. Foreign Minister Gustav Stresemann opposed such a move but von Seeckt ignored him and continued with plans, which he now pursued with increasing secrecy from his political masters. The total ban on military aviation imposed by Versailles meant it was exactly that on which any covert activity would concentrate. This, however, was no more than an extension of a programme that had been running since 1921, in which German Army officer trainees had been sent to the Soviet Union; it was the introduction of air trainees, however, that prompted development of a dedicated air training facility. Allied inspectors were active within Germany trying to uncover any illegal military activity, and though they were generally inefficient and easily misled, they managed to act as a deterrent to large-scale breaches of the Treaty terms. A base deep within the borders of communist Russia, an international outcast with impenetrable borders, was a perfect place to set up testing and training centres well away from prying eyes. Germany and Russia were politically strange bedfellows, but in military terms they saw great mutual benefits from cooperation and looked around for a suitable site.

Lipetsk, 300 miles south-west of Moscow on the Voronezh river, had good rail access, a large empty factory space and was sufficiently remote from population centres to offer the ideal solution. The joint Soviet-German training centre set up there was the brainchild of von Seeckt and the Soviet Karl Berngardovich Radek, who had been imprisoned in Germany for fomenting communist insurrection in 1918 and had subsequently established contacts there with several influential German political and industrial leaders. The Soviets saw Lipetsk as a means of acquiring technical knowledge and developing its military aviation, and for Germany it was a way of circumventing the restrictions on air power imposed upon it at Versailles. In 1924, sixty German instructors and 100 technicians established a testing and experimental flying station there under the rubric 'Fourth Squadron of the Red Air Force'.[28] Runways were laid down and a full range of administrative, maintenance and storage facilities were installed. Fighter and fighter-reconnaissance aircraft were based there, many having been transported by rail through Leningrad, together with instructors who were civilian contractors from the German national airline Lufthansa, and paid in US dollars.

Lipetsk, of course was in contravention of the Treaty of Versailles and may well have had serious consequences for Germany had the French been able to find any tangible evidence of its existence to solidify their suspicions. As a consequence of the secrecy surrounding the mission, von Seeckt used considerable portions of the Reichswehr's 'black funds', financial resources hidden from the German government, to subsidise these programmes.[29] The cooperation begun at Lipetsk inaugurated an immutable relationship between the German and Soviet approach to air power and the Soviets clearly strove to model their air doctrine on the example of Germany. They benefited from witnessing all the theory that German pilots had been taught in Reichswehr classrooms being put into practice, especially tactical doctrine where all the focus of attention was on providing ground support.

The Lipetsk experiment was never going to run smoothly, given the cultural and political differences between the participants, but it was hoped that pragmatism would prevail in the best interests of both. It was not long before the first cracks started appearing, however, when the first Junkers Ju21s from Fili were delivered to Lipetsk and found to be sluggish, awkward in flight, and landed at an uncomfortably high speed. In order to maintain the training schedules it proved necessary to bring in other Heinkel aircraft from outside the country which, apart from adding unnecessary costs, was of little benefit to the education of Russian engineers. Inevitably the tension and mistrust engendered by the contradictions inherent in the arrangement made working relationships between Russian and German personnel, who worked in separate areas of the base and were forbidden to socialise, difficult to say the least. Stresemann now gave his full support to the project, but fearing diplomatic mayhem if it was ever uncovered by Britain or France, insisted that no active listed German officers should attend courses in Russia. At the same time, he realised that the whole venture was time-constrained and could not remain covert forever, so advanced plans for training facilities to be established inside Germany to take on many of the responsibilities for training airmen, thereby slowly reducing reliance on Russian cooperation. The German contingent at Lipetsk was led by Captain Martin Fiebig, who lectured at the Moscow Academy for Air Commanders. As part of his duties he organised war games for Soviet officers during which he was critical of their enthusiasm for strategic bombing; a role for which the Soviet air force was singularly ill-equipped. The several hundred Soviet airmen who trained at Lipetsk were therefore strongly influenced by the German ground-support theories, at least until such times as their own service had been sufficiently modernised by Lapchinski's programme of Tupolev TB.3 bomber mass production.

A few years later when Stresemann died in 1929, the Lipestk project and von Seeckt would lose a valuable ally and Germany lose its respected and influential foreign policy supremo. A political power vacuum ensued in which the German Army, at a time before the air force had got independence, attempted to restore its control of aviation by forcing the withdrawal of air personnel from Lipetsk to rejoin army units. Allied intelligence agencies who had long suspected the existence of Lipetsk, started to openly refer to 'unspecified' German activity in Russia which was threatening to embarrass Germany diplomatically. This, together with the burdensome cost in a time of financial turmoil worldwide and the expansion of domestic facilities at Rechlin, further eroded the rationale for retaining the Russian base. Activity began to reduce from 1930 onwards, as one after another of the training programmes closed down. Russia was being viewed more as a potential enemy and the risks inherent in sharing military know-how were growing; 1932 saw a dramatic reduction in activity at Lipetsk which infuriated the Russians who still had much to gain from cooperation. It was simply a matter of the Germans cajoling the Russians and preventing a major bust-up with them while they tried to negotiate their way out of the deal and repatriate as much equipment as they could before the final showdown.

Meanwhile, a joint German-Russian civilian airline, 'Deruluft Airways', had been set up in November 1921 and had begun commercial flights between Moscow and Königsberg a year later with Dutch-built Fokker F.III aircraft. Companies such as Heinkel, Dornier, Rohrbach and Fokker followed Junkers in establishing commercial ties with Russia as it tried to modernise its communications infrastructure.[30] The rail system in Russia, already inadequate before the revolution, had become neglected and run-down during the war years, which prompted interest in civil aviation as a means of communication over the vast distances between cities. Significant funding was given to the development of air links but they were still totally dependent on imported aircraft. Dereluft had opened up a small number of internal routes, flying Junkers F 13 and W 33 aircraft, as well as the link to Königsberg and a study was carried out to determine the shape of a network of air routes to cover the whole country. 'Dobrolyot', a joint stock company in which Junkers had a stake, was established to help develop the country's air fleet in the areas of airmail, cargo and passenger lines, and expansion of the domestic aircraft industry as a whole. As part of its remit, it oversaw the construction of airports and weather stations. The Germans hoped, through its stake in Dereluft, to develop civil air routes across Eastern Europe from Sweden to Turkey and eventually to Japan and China through Soviet air space.

At the same time as civil aviation was flourishing, Russian military aviation was struggling with shortage of raw materials, financial constraints and a lack of skilled labour. Although there was an abundance of aircraft types, old and new, the many different engines in use in the new VVS posed a logistical and maintenance nightmare. The limited domestic manufacture of poor quality engines due to the paucity of skilled workers and lack of modern designs, was seen as wasteful of resources. There was progress on the design front, however, as new Soviet aircraft such as the 'Komta' bomber powered by the imported 240-hp Fiat engine had started coming out of the Duks plant as early as 1920, and a year later the Tuploev ANT-1 with a British Blackburn engine followed. Nikolai Nikolievich Polikarpov actually designed fighters which incorporated advanced characteristics that were later picked up by Heinkel and the American Curtiss company and incorporated into their own aircraft. Tupolev later brought out the R-1 attack bomber, copied from the British de Havilland 9A with an American 'Liberty' engine, of which 2,000 were manufactured over the years. Although the Soviet leadership was supportive of its air force it showed little appetite for expansion, even though tension simmered along the Polish border and the fear of war was never far from their mind. They took comfort in the vastness of Russia and lack of industrial targets in a largely agrarian society, which, its leaders surmised, made air attack by a foreign power unlikely. Attacks on civilian centres, given the Soviet leadership's casual acceptance of their expendability, seems not to have been a concern. Any advance in aviation technology would be on the civilian side and, for the moment, the military would have to live off the crumbs from that table.

It had been hoped that the industrial aspects of the working relationship with Germany would lead to a growth of technical and managerial competence and create the framework of a Russian aircraft manufacturing capability, but the requirement of threefold cooperation between the two governments and German aircraft manufacturers proved to be elusive. At Fili, Junkers had been contracted to supply the skilled labour and technical know-how, while Russia provided the raw materials and unskilled labour force, but the deal had been undermined by disputes between Junkers and the Soviet government who threatened to stop taking any aircraft until they were given full access to technological production processes. Junkers threatened to halt investment while the Reichswehr cancelled an order for fifty Junkers Ju 22 single-seater fighters for use at the new Lipetsk training facility, which had proved unfit to fly, and instead bought Fokker D.XIII from Holland. Production at the Fili plant ground to a halt in March 1925 when all German funding ceased and all the Junkers technicians returned to Dessau.

In early 1924, Mikhail Frunze, known to have creative and unorthodox views, took over from Leon Trotsky as Soviet Commissar of War and boosted investment in aircraft production but militarily, it continued to play a minor role employing only 2 per cent of military personnel. Frunze was anxious to change this and end Russia's 'aeronautical illiteracy'.[31] by adopting offence as the primary role of aviation. With the emergence of domestic aluminium production, all-metal aircraft became possible promising release from reliance on foreign imports. A major sticking point was that, along with even the most advanced industrial nations, Russia was unable to overcome the technical difficulties in the manufacture of high-powered engines. Frunze tackled this head-on with insistence on driving up technical proficiency of the workforce and improvements in machine tooling. He understood that to achieve the goal of self-sufficiency in military production, huge industrial complexes would be required with tens of thousands of workers. It was not lost on him that as a result, there would emerge a substantial military-industrial complex which would become an essential part of any future war effort – and that would make it a target for enemy attacks, especially factories close to the Polish border around Leningrad. This, of course, was an admission of the future importance of strategic air doctrine but he did not advance such a theory and continued, publicly, to deny that aviation would play a decisive role in a future war. Frunze was an early victim of Stalin's purges when he was assassinated in 1925 and was replaced by Marshal Mikhail Tukhachevski, 'one of the most original and influential military theorists of the twentieth century'.[32]

Tukhachevski developed the theory of the 'deep battle', which dominated Soviet doctrine until the Second World War. The basic concept was air support for the breakthrough of motorised forces deep into enemy territory and follow up with paratroops dropped behind enemy lines to seize headquarters and supply bases. Tukhachevski always saw aviation not as a subordinate or an independent entity, but as an integral part of a joint military. In Field Regulations set out in 1936, he specified detailed roles of ground-attack aviation, fighter aviation, and light bombers – the air force's first objective being the annihilation of the enemy air force, which would then free air power to act decisively against enemy columns and reserves in the approach and pursuit phases of the battle. As for strategic bombing, he believed that, together with airborne troops, it could prove decisive in war. He saw that technological developments would bring with them new opportunities and new concepts which should be grasped with vigour. He was supported by General A.N. Lapchinski, a future Chief of the Air Staff, who had written a book in 1920 lauding the military aircraft as 'a new, independent factor of war', and laid the foundations of what would become the world's largest strategic bomber fleet – but he would not go on to espouse Douhetist doctrine, preferring instead to see aviation as part of the 'interaction of all arms … supporting the ground battle'.[33] At a time when the Soviet air force consisted of little more than obsolete aircraft left over from the First World War, Lapchinski laid the theoretical groundwork for the creation of what would become the world's largest strategic air force by the early 1930s.

As domestic aviation slowly expanded its horizons to Ukraine and central Asia, an aviation trust, 'Aviatrest', took control of aircraft production which, at this point was a mix of state-owned and private concerns and was manufacturing both civil and military aircraft. Lenin had made a tactical retreat on the domestic political front by allowing private industry to continue in direct contradiction to communist principles since 'everything must be set aside to increase production'.[34] Only by foreign trade, either through purchase of aircraft or by acquiring foreign expertise, could the aircraft industry advance. This was never going to be an easy ride, however. Cooperation at Fili and elsewhere had collapsed and Junkers had gone by

1927, having suffered massive financial losses after the last K30 had been delivered, despite the promised reimbursement from the Reichswehr of their original investment being withheld to prevent them from abandoning Fili.[35] Only 218 aircraft in total had come off the production line between 1923 and 1926.

Politically, the relationship between Russia and Germany, lukewarm at the best of times, was cooling. As time went on, neither remained the outcast from international affairs that they once were and their need for each other became less and less. Germany signed up to the Locarno Treaties in 1925 and joined the League of Nations a year later, leaving the Soviets feeling somewhat abandoned. While the political divide started opening up and business ventures stumbled on, the need for military cooperation was still real and it was this, and only this, that held the 1922 agreement together. In fact military ties were strengthened, interchange of personnel increased and training schedules were expanded. Germany was not yet ready to openly flaunt the terms of Versailles with France, the most vocal of the Allies, still showing belligerence and threatening to punish violations, but Germany was certainly planning for the day that pressure from Britain and the US would force France to back off and allow it to return to some sort of normality. When that time came, Germany would be ready to reclaim its status as a military power and its air force would be at the forefront of that rehabilitation – and for that to happen it would need to have its airmen trained to the highest standards. For political reasons the Soviet pilots at Lipetsk had not been encouraged to socialise with the German personnel and had been kept strictly apart. This was not conducive to building trust and friendship and meant that the Soviets did not benefit from the exchange as much as they might have done. Germany was, no doubt, content to get the most out of the arrangement, with a free hand to experiment and test new machines and ideas while giving away as little as possible to what they suspected might one day be a mortal enemy.

By the time of the Fifteenth Communist Party Congress in 1927, the Soviet Union was poised to launch an industrial revolution committed to heavy industrial production, from which aviation manufacturing was set to benefit. Commercial aviation promised rapid communication between the population centres across the vast Russian lands and the air force would empower and add prestige to the modern state that Soviet leaders were trying to build. As part of the industrialisation of the hitherto agrarian state, Soviet engineers were becoming sufficiently confident to start taking over from the Germans at Lipetsk and by 1927, had advanced to the point where they had 'acquired an exemplary system of all-metal construction … and an excellently equipped engine construction workshop'.[36] After a mere four years into the supposed twenty-five-year contract with Junkers its dissolution was almost complete, with a Soviet takeover of the factory nearing completion. Even though commercial and military cooperation had foundered on the rocks of Soviet duplicity, both sides had every reason to continue with the arrangements at Lipetsk. Germany had no other option if they wanted to continue with their covert development of military aviation, and for their part, the Soviets were sure that their 'relatively quick progress' was due primarily to 'assistance from German military and technical personnel'.[37] Senior Soviet officers would continue to receive training with the Reichswehr in Germany right up until 1933, but the rise to power of the fiercely anti-communist Nazis ensured that this would not be allowed to continue. Meanwhile, the Soviets had launched their first Five-Year Plan in 1928, one aspect of which was for aviation to 'rid itself finally of foreign dependence', which Stain claimed it had done by 1933 but, in terms of engine production at least, that was something of an overstatement.[38]

Under Frunze, Soviet military aviation had begun to develop a doctrine of aggressive ground support with only the merest hint of a strategic capability. It was still bound by the dictates of the Red Army High Command, which fitted in well with the doctrine inherited from the German connection favouring tactical operations, and anyway, the economic limitations placed on it by the government denied it any chance of purchasing heavy bombers or manufacturing in quantity domestically. Frunze was also called upon to sort out the conflict between the Chief Directorate of the Air Force who would have liked a little more independence and the Red Army military district commanders under whose control military aviation operated and who had no reason to loosen its grip. There was little enthusiasm for initiative in the communist state, where Air Force General Staff were obliged to operate in accordance with directives of the Red Army General Staff which was, in turn, constrained by political ideology. The political grip tightened on the air force as more and more command positions within its ranks were taken up by Communist Party members, and its activities, both operational and in research and development, were closely monitored by the secret police.

One of the priorities of the Soviet hierarchy, both to reinforce its internal doctrine and promote security along its borders, was to inculcate communist ideology in its neighbours. As part of this strategy, in 1923 they had helped to establish an air force in Afghanistan by supplying aircraft, building airfields and by establishing a civilian air link to Kabul and Tashkent. These initiatives were opposed by the Western powers, both on commercial and ideological grounds, which forced the Soviets to rein in their bid to export communist ideology to the region. However, the exercise had taught the Soviets about the importance of air power as an effective political tool externally, and this helped to increase government interest in aviation and boost the level of aircraft production as part of the massive programme of industrialisation about to start under the first Five Year Plan introduced in 1928. At this stage, Soviet Aviation was at a very low point, operating with a motley collection of mostly foreign aircraft, many obsolete, which were poorly maintained;[39] it could only improve.

In 1923, almost all aircraft in the VVS had been imported from other European countries and were of redundant design but slowly, domestic production started to take over and the growing strength in numbers was evidence of the status enjoyed by the air force in the Soviet political hierarchy by 1928. More specialised types were taking over from what had been multi-purpose reconnaissance aircraft. Soviet designers were coming into their own. Tupolev had produced the I-4 and was working on the TB-3 and TB-4 heavy bombers, Grigorovich came up with the I-2bis fighter and Polikarpov a whole range of two-seater ground-attack aircraft, while Mikhail Mil was experimenting with helicopters. Unfortunately, as elsewhere in Europe, engine design was holding back development, not least because of the Soviet backwardness in metallurgical sciences, its lack of machine tools and a shortage of aluminium and copper. By the end of the first Five Year Plan, most Soviet aircraft were still powered by foreign engines.[40] When production did expand, quality was sacrificed at the altar of quantity. Things changed for the better in the early 1930s, however. Zhukovsky had died in 1925 and Tupolev had branched off from TsAGI to establish his own department for experimental design of multi-engine bombers, while Polikarpov had specialised in the design of fighters which equipped, almost exclusively, Soviet fighter units up to 1939. An early success of the Tupolev's organisation was the TB-1 (ANT-4), the world's first all-metal, twin-engine bomber. This was followed by the TB-3 (ANT-6), a four-engine bomber with a substantial payload and great range, carrying a crew of eight and eight machine guns; an aircraft in the true strategic sense. Polikarpov, meanwhile, had built the excellent I-15 and I-16 fighters that would go on to play a major role in the Spanish Civil War.

In 1925, in an effort to create a powerful air fleet, more than 7 million gold roubles had been contributed toward strengthening the VVS, but most of the subscriptions had been deducted from workers' salaries and had made the organisation somewhat unpopular. The Soviet Air Fleet in July numbered ninety-eight squadrons of twelve machines each, but much of this was on paper only and the Russian Air Programme called for buying 1,030 new aeroplanes, of which 500 were to be built in Russia, chiefly by the Russian Junkers Company now under almost total Soviet control, 330 to be ordered from the Fokker Company and 200 from a number of Italian firms.

One area in which then Soviets had been particularly successful was in encouraging young enthusiasts to take up flying. As early as 1923 a society called 'Friends of the Russian Air Force' had supported the establishment of many glider schools and assisted in the training of technicians. Their efforts proved particularly successful given that almost all their pupils had to be trained from scratch with minimal resources. These young men were much more willing than the veterans to learn new skills and explore new technologies. One of the significant benefits of cooperation with Germany was the development of training programmes for Soviet aviators. Trainees were selected at an early age to attend military schools and then moved on to one of more than twenty technical colleges, where they were inculcated with concepts of unity, solidarity with Soviet doctrine, and nationalistic pride. Professional standards were enhanced at flying academies by superior living standards and recreational facilities, alongside tuition from the best aeronautical designers and technicians and access to the most modern aircraft. All of this education was further enriched by contact with the best German instructors and airmen who passed through Lipetsk and Soviet Staff officers were sent to Germany to study theory at the Reichswehr Academy.

At the start of the second Five-Year Plan in 1933, with Hitler coming to political prominence in Germany, the Soviet industrial programme turned more towards war production and its air force benefited accordingly. General D. Walter Schwabedissen, who joined the German Air Force in 1933 and previously had twice visited Lipetsk, summed up the state of Soviet military aviation at the time as follows:

> thanks to foreign support and its own strenuous efforts, the Soviet government had succeeded, despite numerous difficulties, in building up a new force from nothing; numerically, this force had to be considered a power factor although it had not yet achieved the standards of efficiency common to other major military powers.; in addition, the need for outside assistance had been overcome in both the military and technological fields, and the road was open to complete independence.[41]

The number of tactical units in the VVS at this time is difficult to gauge. Some were designated as existing before there were any aircraft available to equip them, and others were publicly denied to present the Soviet Union on the world stage as a nation seeking peaceful coexistence with the West. When they began buying aircraft from the US after 1930, there were already a plethora of different types in service from half-a-dozen different countries, but the real benefit of US trade was in engine technology. As a result of the worldwide economic depression, there was no shortage of companies in the capitalist world ready and willing to trade with the Soviet Union at this time despite ideological differences, and many were willing to offer very favourable terms of trade (it brings to mind Lenin's oft quoted phrase to the effect that the Western capitalists would compete to sell Russia the rope with which it would, in turn, hang them). After this though, domestic production started to improve. All types went into production, including the giant TB-3 bombers and even seaplanes. Numbers of personnel had continued to increase alongside aircraft, with many of the brightest young technicians attracted by the prestige, social and economic benefits that went along with membership of the air force. The number of students in aviation schools multiplied five-fold between 1926 and 1931, despite the entry qualifications being the highest of all the military academies.[42]

During the 1920s, the Soviet Union was almost constantly in conflicts which involved its air arm. As well as the suppression of internal revolts in Uzbekistan and Tajikistan, where mass bombing of civilian areas was carried out, a short war against China in 1929 gave flyers some experience of combat. In Manchuria, the VVS operated against a barely credible opposition when it bombed towns such as Suifenho, Manchuli and Chalainor without interference, while Japanese bombers struck at civilians in Chinchow and Shanghai. Soviet instructors accompanied aircraft sales to countries in central Asia where they were trying to foster friendly relations and export communism. The Mongolian Army was given ten aircraft with full supporting personnel in an attempt to prise it away from Chinese influence. Aircraft were also sold to Persia, with full training given to indigenous recruits. Civil air links were planned to allow international air travel across Soviet air space after Junkers had agreed to carry out an aerial survey of the intended routes as part of their Fili deal, but only the Berlin-Moscow route flourished, although Teheran and Constantinople were opened up to air travel in a small way.

When the 'People's Commissariat for Heavy Industry' took control of the aircraft industry in 1932, it had grown to the point where there were more than thirty large aircraft and engine factories. The number of employees had risen tenfold in places. From the start, the Soviets had employed a sophisticated design strategy which was now further supported by a number of research, technical and educational institutes staffed by university graduates and polytechnic students who were encouraged to specialise. The abandoned Junkers factory at Fili now employed some 4,000 workers using the fine German equipment left behind to build all-metal, multi-engine aircraft. Some factories were already being planned or built further east, away from areas that might be overrun or might come within the range of bombers in the event of war with Poland or Germany. The stockpiling of raw materials became government policy, again with war in mind, which did not help the production figures but aircraft numbers coming out of the factories were well above 1,000 for each of the five years of the Plan. Most domestic production now specified simple construction, ruggedness, limited instrumentation and ease of maintenance. Technical developments included constant-speed propellers, high-octane fuel and supercharged engines. Engineers had visited the Douglas aircraft factories in the US and obtained licences to manufacture the DC3 as the Li-2.

In 1935, the first Soviet heavy bomber force was created as a result of pressure for an independent strategic capability, but there remained the assumption that such units would only operate in accordance with wider parameters set by the ground forces and in close cooperation with them. There was no suggestion that they might independently attempt the systematic destruction of an enemy's war-making capabilities in the true Douhetian sense. Of more interest to the Red Army command was the possibility of aircraft such as the TB-3 delivering airborne troops behind enemy lines. Indeed, a special force, the AON, was set up and tested in military exercises when 600 paratroopers were deployed at Kiev in 1935 under the eyes of foreign military observers and again during exercises at Byelorussia the following year.[43]

Following on from its diplomatic split with Germany, the Soviet Union was looking for allies in the face of Nazism in Germany and Fascism in Italy. Joining the League of Nations seemed a logical step, but the response of that organisation to Italian aggression in Ethiopia and the German remilitarisation of the Rhineland was so flimsy that it could not be relied upon to safeguard Soviet interests should it be attacked by Japan, Poland or Germany. They appealed to the US and other Western countries for reciprocal student exchange facilities in aviation and aircraft manufacturing but they received little encouragement. Then, in 1936, it became clear that German and Italian military aid was going into Spain in support of General Franco's Nationalists as they rebelled against the left-wing government. All major powers had agreed publicly to keep out of the conflict but after German and Italian interference, France made tentative moves to avoid having a third fascist regime on its doorstep by supporting the Spanish government, although was very wary of getting too involved for fear of escalation. The Soviet Union had no such qualms and saw a chance to prolong the Spanish war as a means of diverting German attention away from Eastern Europe. Like the Germans, who had sent their military aid in the guise of 'volunteers', so the Soviets operated under the mantle of the 'International Brigade' of left-wing sympathisers who went to fight. Soviet tanks, artillery and aircraft covertly arrived in October 1936, along with a group of Red Army specialists, to fly and maintain the aircraft, but the Red Air Force at no time showed any enthusiasm for integrating into the overall Republican military structure.[44]

The Soviets sent Polikarpov I-15s (Chaika) and I-16s (Rata) fighters, Tupolev SB-2 (Katiuska) bombers and Pilokarpov R-5 (Rasante) light bombers under the command of Colonel Jacob Smushkevich. The I-15 single-seater biplane was not the newest of the Soviet fleet but was still one of the best fighters in operation at that time, with only the Fiat CR.32

able to match it. The I-16 was newer and faster but less well armed than the Chato. The 'Komsomol' squadron of SB-2 Katiuskas had fast, twin-engine all-metal bombers which were, at first, sufficiently well armed to operate without fighter escort, but that would change when the Condor Legion Messerschmitt Bf109 was introduced. As many as 300 Soviet pilots served in Spain and were generally held to be among the most effective of all combatants, but Soviet tactics and operational efficiency was not of a high standard compared to their opponents. They tended only to offer air support to those units of the Republican forces who fought under an overtly communist banner in an effort to force the Republican government to follow Soviet policy. Right from the start it was clear, as evidenced by the significant presence of the NKVD secret police, that a further major Soviet policy objective was to exert maximum political leverage to increase communist influence in Spain. The Spanish air force commander General Kindelán was often left in the dark about how many Soviet aircraft were available to him and at which airfields they were located. He described Soviet air doctrine as 'excessively theoretical [paying] little attention to protection of their own troops and focused instead on the airfields and population in the rear … but did not cause much damage due to lack of intensity'. The Italian Fiats, by contrast had concentrated on 'the destruction of the enemy fighter force'.[45]

The Spanish Civil War was exploited by the Soviets as an opportunity to test its aircraft under actual wartime conditions.[46] The Soviet intervention now ensured that Republican forces would not be quickly overcome and a protracted conflict was in the offing. It was also clear to the Soviets from their first involvement in the battle for Madrid that neither would the Nationalist forces be easily defeated and this somewhat altered their war aims, which were now to prolong the conflict in order to keep German attention focused well away from Eastern Europe. On a practical level, the Russian pilots tended to fight their own battles where they chose and paid little heed to the general direction of the Republican operations, and their participation. They were much more concerned with testing their aircraft and tactics in combat conditions. The most effective use of Russian air power in Spain was seen in direct support of ground actions, employing a mix of different aircraft types in groups of between seven and fifty. Very low altitude strafing and bombing proved to be quite effective but in retrospect, the Soviets lost an opportunity to explore the advantages of air power as an independent strategic element, because they had a limited capability of interdicting lines of communications and had chosen instead to engage forces in action along the combat front. They committed very few of their early long-range bombers to this theatre and had little success in using them. It can be said that, in this respect, they were again following tactics learned from the Germans.

German assessment of the impact of Soviet air power in Spain was not particularly flattering, citing an awkwardness in operational thinking and inadequacies in general staff training. Among the detailed criticisms were: lack of flexibility (not surprising given the authoritarian doctrinaire political environment), lack of originality, failure to concentrate power and a tendency to dissipate forces. While Soviet airmen were said to be of excellent quality and performed well in defence of their own territory, they were 'timid' and rarely ventured into enemy airspace. Estimates vary, but 800–1500 Soviet aircraft altogether operated in Spain over the three years of the conflict.[47] The very manoeuvrable Soviet I-15, the 'excellent' I-16 fighters, with their hand-cranked retractable undercarriage and open cockpit, and the SB-2 bombers made up the bulk of the Republican air force. At first, they operated individually, but soon began operating in flights of four and then in squadron strength, but their tactics were inferior to the Germans and combat leadership was weak.[48] The I-16 fighters were by far the best aircraft flying in Spain in early 1937, until the Germans introduced the Messerschmitt Bf109-E and began to dominate the air war. Thereafter, what few bombing missions the Soviets had carried out were discontinued and the SB-3s were restricted to ground-attack operations. The tide was turning inexorably in the Nationalists' favour and Soviet aircraft, unable to compete for air space, were progressively withdrawn. The most effective use of Russian air power in Spain had been seen in direct support of ground actions. The Soviets, however, lost an opportunity to explore the advantages of air power as an independent strategic element and committed very few of their early long-range bombers, poorly equipped with navigation aids and often lacking radios, to this end. They used low-level close air support extensively, showing a more mature and nuanced understanding of the battlefield support role, but were forced to withdraw their lumbering Tupolev SBs to a safer high-level bombing role after some losses. An American observer said: 'The Russians are the only ones to have developed any special attack aviation.'[49] The Germans had only belatedly become interested in low-level high-speed ground-attack tactics after their early air component proved unsuitable for air-to-air combat.

It is worth noting in detail, what a German observer had to say:

> The Soviet air Forces ... revealed fundamental weaknesses in their command, organisation, training and technical performance. These weaknesses they were unable to remedy in spite of their pronounced aggressiveness and flying ability ... and ruthlessness of their command methods.
>
> The Soviets learned a lot in the Spanish campaign ... particularly in operations, formation flight, training ... and the importance of the ground-attack arm, which they developed to a remarkably high standard. False conclusions led them to forego the development of an effective bomber arm and thereby forfeit an opportunity for strategic air war.[50]

Meanwhile, a few thousand miles away, Japan was threatening to expand into Manchuria, northern China and Inner Mongolia. The Soviets initially had over 1,000 aircraft supporting General Vasily Bliukher's Far Eastern Army, but with the increase in tension in 1937 this number was boosted to 2,000. As with Spain, the Soviets saw advantage in having their potential foes embroiled in other conflicts and so piled in to bolster the Chinese, hoping to tie the Japanese down for a while. When the tiny Chinese air force had been quickly disposed of by the Japanese, the Soviets shipped aircraft 3,000 miles to the east by truck, unwilling to risk them over the vast distances without adequate navigation. Soviet pilots operated alongside Chinese trained to fly the newly arrived aircraft and dealt an early blow by decimating Japanese bombers attacking Wuhan. The Soviet I-15 and I-16 fighters fared much better against the poor Japanese fighters than they had against the Bf109s in Spain. The Soviet intervention might be considered a success, since it gave pilots valuable combat experience and tested aircraft in war, but it was against a decidedly inferior opponent and offered little in the way of preparation for the war that was to come in Europe.

The first Five Year Plan of 1928 had laid the foundations of the ultimate victory of the VVS over the Luftwaffe in what the Soviets would call 'The Great Patriotic War' of 1941–45. The second Five Year Plan of 1933 saw a further increase in aircraft manufacture and the introduction of fine aircraft such as the I-15. By 1937, there were around 2,500 front-line aircraft in the VVS, over half of which were bombers. As a result of the plans, the VVS had grown steadily in size and capabilities, having first flirted with Douhetist doctrine by building a fleet of heavy bombers but subsequently adopting a more strategic policy after its experiences of the Spanish Civil War. It was also a war that had exposed the vulnerabilities of the Soviet I-15 and I-16 fighters, which had been as good as any aircraft flying until they came up against the Messerschmitt Bf109. The failure of their bombers to make any sort of impact in Spain convinced the Soviets to concentrate on tactical air-support doctrine when designing the next generation of aircraft. Their prime asset in this role would be the Ilyushin Il-2 ground-attack aircraft designed in 1938 and brought into service in 1941. They had a three-to-one margin of superiority in numbers of aircraft when Germany launched Operation Barbarossa in June 1941, but lost almost one third of their fleet, still on the ground in forward airfields, in the first few hours of the attack.

The significant failures of Soviet military aviation before 1939 may be itemised as:

- Inadequate production of light bombers and reconnaissance aircraft.
- An over-emphasis on manoeuvrability rather than speed and fire-power in their fighters.
- An over-confidence derived from their successes during the early stages of the Spanish Civil War, despite their I-15 and I-16 fighters proving inferior to the Bf109.
- The catastrophic effect on leadership and aircraft design as a result of Stalin's purges.

The last point is key, because no study of Soviet air power in the 1930s is complete without mention of the great purges instigated by Stalin. The air force was particularly hard-hit. Initially, military structures had been completely altered with the introduction of post-revolutionary 'citizen' councils, but pragmatism had forced the slow reintroduction of a conventional military hierarchy. This was not to survive the murderous political upheavals of 1937 when a commissar system was brought back under direct control from Moscow. Clearly Stalin saw the air force as a threat to his power, and while he very much wanted to retain its military capability, he also wanted to eliminate the command chain that he believed had come between his own authority and the actual service. Stalin's strong personal interest in aviation began in 1933 when he praised the development of an aviation industry as one of the major accomplishments of the first Five-Year-Plan. On 28 April 1933, at Stalin's initiative, the Soviet government designated a yearly festival, Aviation Day, to be celebrated every 18 August, and this became a major holiday in which there were ceremonial appearances by the leadership. He publicly associated himself with all the major achievements in Soviet aviation and urged his flyers to 'fly farther than anyone, faster than anyone, and higher than anyone'.[51]

During the early part of the Spanish Civil War, German aviation had been taking the offensive and by the Battle of Brunete in July, it was clearly gaining control of the Spanish skies. This early success of Soviet fighters encouraged the idea of superiority and quelled calls for newer fighters. That was to change, however, as the Germans reclaimed aerial superiority with the introduction of advanced Bf109s and dive bombers, and made improvements in the speed and armaments of their aircraft and adoption of tactics to counter the advantage of the I-16. The Soviets sent far more fighters to the Republicans than the Germans sent to the Condor Legion to aid Franco, but quality made the difference. It was becoming clear that continued Soviet participation in the air war was increasingly dangerous to Soviet military prestige. In June 1937, the British Air Attaché in Moscow reported Soviet bombers were clumsy and vulnerable to attack, and Soviet fighters were not up to the latest foreign standards in speed and manoeuvrability.[52] Domestically, the advantage of German fighters in speed was also demonstrated for all to see at the Zurich International Air Show on 26 July 1937.

It might be argued that the Soviets learned the most from Spain. They had concluded that light bombers could not be expected to operate in hostile skies without fighter protection. On the issue of close air-ground support, they realised that communication was the key to coordinated effort. The importance of air attack in support of ground forces became a central tenet of Soviet air doctrine, holding that 'air-land battles ... begin in the air and end on the ground'.[53] It was clear to all that strategic bombing from height was extremely difficult to carry out with even moderate accuracy, and the destructive power of bombs on buildings had been greatly exaggerated.[54]

It is probable that Stalin was not fully apprised of the changes wrought when the Bf109-E was introduced, but in early 1938, as the war turned increasingly against the Spanish Republicans, he was certainly aware of the situation and reacted, first of all, with a search for scapegoats. In June 1937 Tupolev, the designer most closely associated with long-distance record attempts, made a fateful admission. He noted that the ANT-25 was five years old and already outdated by contemporary aviation standards. He was arrested and imprisoned on charges of espionage after a visit to the US, but was allowed to continue his work while in prison. Aleksandr Sergeyevich Yakovlev, a noted Soviet engineer and chief of research and development, noted that

> Stalin reacted very painfully to our failures in Spain. His dissatisfaction and wrath were directed against those who quite recently had been considered heroes and who had been showered with richly deserved honours.[55]

Yakolev also bemoaned the

> fascination of some of our tacticians with the Douhet doctrine of the 'omnipotence of strong bomber air fleet,' the existence of which would supposedly give the country a decisive military superiority.... The influence of the Douhet doctrine on certain of our aviation leaders in the 1930s was expressed in the overestimation of bomber aircraft and the clear underestimation of other types of aircraft.

It was, however, a dangerous time to buck the trend, and those military specialists and technical experts who saw the need for change were unable to alter the basic direction of Soviet policy being restricted by the norms of party discipline and intimidated by the purges. The designer K.A. Kalinin was shot when one of his experimental designs crashed, killing four Communist Party members. In March 1937 Tukhachevsky was arrested and executed. Lapchinski followed soon after. Air Force Commander Yakov Alksnis, who had dared to sound a public warning in August 1937 about the need for faster military planes, was arrested on 23 November 1937, charged with setting up a Latvian fascist organisation, and shot on 28 July 1938. His deputy,

245

Vasily Vladimirovitch Khripin, was arrested three days later and executed the following year. Commander-in-chief of the Leningrad Air Command, I.A. Lopatin and General R.A. Muklivich were also executed. By 1939, almost three quarters of all senior air force officers had been murdered. For the entire decade preceding war, it was the overbearing influence of the only two important design organisations run by Tupolev and Polikarpov that ensured mass production of those aircraft most likely to please Stalin with the biggest propaganda impact, rather than those demanded by the military requirements of the day.

Chapter 8

Italian Air Power before 1939

'I decided today that I would try to drop bombs from the
aeroplane.'

> Second Lieutenant Giulio Gavotti of the Squadriglia
> di Tripoli, dropped four small bombs from a
> German-built Etrich Taube on the towns of
> Taguira and Ain Zara on 1 November 1911.[1]

As early as 1909, the Italian King Victor Emmanuel III had been
mesmerised by Wilbur Wright's demonstration flight on the outskirts of
Rome and started a fascination in the country for aviation that culminated
in the establishment of the Italian Air Force, Regia Aeronautica, as a
separate service on 28 March 1923. In 1910, the Italian Parliament had
debated the desirability of leaving military aircraft construction in the
public arena and concluded by allocating 15 million lira for the creation of
an air fleet, Flottiglia Aeroplani.[2] The Libyan campaign of 1911–12 and the
First World War accelerated the process. New operational requirements,
dictated by trench warfare, such as tactical reconnaissance and artillery
spotting, vied with new ideas such as aerial bombing, and brought to life an
air arm that incorporated, in embryo, all air missions conceptually defined
to meet the future. A command and control system based on the principle
of centralised planning was strictly related to the more fundamental idea
of the unified command of all air resources. Alongside the practical, the
basic elements of an air power doctrine began to emerge which reached out
beyond current technology to embrace ideas of monumental consequence.
It was accepted that the creation of an independent air force required a
unique approach in which doctrine and technology would go hand-in-
hand. The close bond between technology and doctrine would very soon
become evident in the emergence of radio-telegraphy for communications

between the aircraft and ground forces, and improved cameras for detailed images of enemy positions.

One of the earliest and most important Italian aircraft manufacturers was Caproni who was building his own machines in 1910, as well as Blériots under licence. In 1914 he patented the world's first monoplane fighter with a machine gun on a high pylon to fire above the propeller. This was developed into the Ca.20, which was built under licence by the French and flew in the First World War in 1916. A number of Capronis were sold to Britain also. Caproni bombers were flown by Italian airmen against Austria-Hungary and the firm continued to design and build aircraft for the Regia Aeronautica throughout the inter-war years.

Aircraft had been assigned to the army in 1910 but with little preparation and little understanding of what they would do with them. When early manoeuvres exposed the woeful training of pilots and frailty of the machines, airships were immediately brought in to replace them, but in the Battle of Tripoli during the Italo-Turkish War (1911–12) when Italy tried to prise Libya from the Ottoman Empire, aircraft were again called up to perform a reconnaissance role as well as artillery spotting and even bombing missions. Captain Carlos Piazza flew the first reconnaissance mission from Tripoli to Aziz in a French Blériot XI, and the first bombing mission was carried out by 2nd Lieutenant Giulio Gavotti, who dropped four 4.4lb bombs from his Etrich Taube aircraft on the towns of Taguira and Ain Zara, having first pulled out the pins with his teeth.[3] These early bombs were followed by crude 'fragmentation' bombs which caused little damage, but as one observer noted they had 'clearly shown that air navigation provides a terrible means of destruction [and will] revolutionise modern strategy and tactics'.[4] This brief conflict brought into focus a number of weaknesses in concept and operation much more quickly than manoeuvres ever could, leading to a significant increase in knowledge and improvements in equipment and tactics, such as the need for reliable air reconnaissance and the dangers posed by ground fire; there was no suggestion at this stage, however, that the air arm might have an independent existence. The Turks had not had any aircraft to deny the Italians freedom of the skies, but it was understood that in a more challenging environment, such as a European war, air space would be much more fiercely contested and air superiority would be required to provide freedom of action to one's own reconnaissance aircraft and to negate the same capability for the enemy.

It was still the case within the military establishment, however, that air warfare and air doctrine were generally considered to be little more than subjects for academic discussion. The aircraft was considered merely as a means to expand the radius of action of the cavalry in its traditional reconnaissance and search for contact operations. In 1913, however, some politicians, such as Marco di Salluzzo, were calling for an independent air force with 'excellent pilots and officers' ready to make Italy 'the first nation with a well-organised, well-trained and flourishing [air] fleet'.[5] Unsurprisingly, this was resisted by General Albert Pollio, Chief of the General Staff, who did not wish to see any of his budget hived off to an organisation operating outside his control and was successful in limiting any extra expenditure on 'expensive and useless' aircraft. Regulations in 1914 stated: 'Aircraft can effectively support both long range and short range reconnaissance thanks to the capability to observe from above but these machines are still under development and therefore the few hints that are given for their use have to be considered as a rough reference.'[6]

At the start of the First World War the Italian Army (Regio Esercito) had eight squadrons (squadriglie) of Nieuport and Bleriot monoplanes for close air support, and three squadrons of Farman MF1912 biplanes operating from fixed airfields. By the end of the year, however, the MF1912 were replaced by Farman MF1914s fitted with the 100-hp Fiat engine, and thirty Caproni Parasol monoplanes. Reconnaissance units had twenty Voisin biplanes powered by the Canton-Unnè 130-hp engine, whereas combat units flew Caproni and Macchi Parasol monoplanes for artillery spotting. The relatively large number of aircraft was not supported by adequate crew numbers, however, which were well below those required. Furthermore, prospects were not improved when the new military aviation chief was announced as Major General Giovan Battista Marieni, a man who 'knew very little about the air force'.[7]

Now that Europe was at war, Italy increased funding of the air force with ambitions to raise seventy-two squadrons by 1917. The Corpo Aeronautico Militare was established as a separate branch of the Italian Army on 7 January 1915. It was organised in a General Directorate of Aeronautics (Direzione Generale d'Aeronautica), which was part of the War Ministry, having two separate commands for airships and aviation, and the Aeronautics Central Institute (Istituto Centrale Aeronautico). The Aeronautical Construction Establishment (Stabilimento Costruzioni Aeronautiche) was part of the airships' command while the Military Aviation Technical Directorate (Direzione Tecnica dell'Aviazione Militare) came under aviation command. Budgets were increased in 1915 to expand the air force with machines from companies like Savoia (Farman), SIT (Voisin), and Caproni e Macchi at a rate of fifteen aircraft each month.

On 23 May 1915 Italy declared war on Austria-Hungary and an Aeronautical Services Office (Ufficio Servizi Aeronautici) was established within the Supreme Command under General Luigi Cadorna on the Isonzo front. In the First Battle of the Isonzo, aircraft were used not only to identify enemy positions and to attack active batteries and approaching reinforcements, but also to direct artillery fire. It was soon realised that to increase the number of squadriglie and to equip them with new machines was not enough; an efficient air-to-ground communications net also had to be organised, with wireless-receiving stations spread out along the front line to relay air observers' firing data to the artillerymen via dedicated telephonic lines. By the time of the second Battle of Isonzo some two weeks later, the first airborne wireless transmitting stations had come into operation after which Morse code messages could be transmitted a distance of a few tens of kilometres.

The obsolete monoplane aircraft were eventually withdrawn from front-line service, and starting in June, a Farman MF1914 squadriglia was deployed at Asiago, in the Trentino sector of the front. On 20 August, the first two Caproni Ca.1 trimotors, powered by 100-hp Fiat A.10 engines, carried out their first bombing mission against the airfield at Aisovizza in retaliation for an Austro-Hungarian raid on the city of Udine. The Italians were keen to avoid collateral damage, since most urban targets within range at this time were Italian cities then under Austro-Hungarian rule. A true fighter component was created in the 8a Squadriglia using Nieuport Ni.10 twin-seat biplanes and Ni.11 monoplanes. In the third Battle of the Isonzo, five squadriglie d'artiglieria conducted tactical reconnaissance and front-line surveillance; radio-telegraphy was now commonly used, and cameras vertically installed in the fuselage allowed for precisely mapping enemy positions.[8]

In 1915, Italy deployed the first ever aircraft designed solely as a 'strategic weapon' for bombing in the Caproni Ca.1.[9] It was to be under the direct control of the Supreme Command and used for mass attacks as far as the number of available aircraft would allow, operating mostly at night, in order to avoid anti-aircraft artillery, against targets which could have 'a relevant effect on the overall conduct of military operations'.[10] This required further technological innovation such as a lighting system for the airfields as well as specialised training in night-time navigation. At the time, aircraft-versus-aircraft engagements were still episodic and inconclusive, and even the agile and fast Nieuport biplanes were not the best of the fighters since their Lewis machine-gun was installed on top of the upper wing in order to fire outside of the propeller arc, which caused significant problems in the aiming process. Technology provided the answer in early 1917 with the Nieuport Ni.17, built under licence by Macchi, which was to be the first Italian fighter equipped with a synchronised machine-gun.

From May to December 1915, the aeronautical industry, although plagued by organisational difficulties and by a shortage of qualified manpower and raw material, produced 424 aircraft, including forty-two Macchi Parasol, and 606 engines. All aircraft, with the exception of twenty-eight three-engine Caproni and a few Aviatik derived from a German model, were of French design. Expansion continued during 1916, notwithstanding the continued difficulties of manufacturers. Even though orders for bombers and fighters were placed in large numbers, with the building up of a strong bombardment component which was unique to Italian aviation, reconnaissance and artillery spotting were of the greatest interest for Supreme Command, being so important in trench warfare, and three more artillery service squadriglie were established in March to partially cover the mountain sector of the front.

In early 1916, Austro-Hungarian aircraft struck at Rimini, Ravenna and Milan, causing some collateral damage and casualties, prompting the Supreme Command to order a retaliation raid against the railway station of Lubiana. On 18 February, ten Capronis took off from La Comina and Aviano armed with 200 kilograms of bombs, but crucially without fighter escorts, and were badly mauled by two Fokker fighters with their synchronised machine-guns. Following these raids the Capronis were fitted out with a second machine-gun mounted in such a position to cover the tail sector, and the standard crew was set at four men: two pilots, one observer and one gunner. In the coming months, the Capronis hit the railheads at Ovcia Draga and Kostanjevica and the depots at Lokvica and Segeti.

Italian aviation had claimed the initiative with a significant level of air superiority that Italy would maintain till the end of the war, losing it only for a few weeks at the end of 1917. The bomber component was now to be used for more ambitious goals than battlefield interdiction and counter-aviation, and on 1 August 1916, answering a request from the Regia Marina, twenty-four Capronis headed for Fiume, bombing the Whitehead torpedo factory, the Danubius shipyard and the oil refinery. Anti-aircraft fire was not an obstacle, and even though a bomber was shot down by a gunboat on the way home, the raid was a clear success and had a great impact on Austro-Hungarian public opinion.

The increasing importance of the fighter arm saw the Caudron G.3, the Farman, and the Voisin replaced with more advanced machines, but still falling into the tail boom, pushing-propeller pattern with the Savoia-Pomilio SP.2, an Italian designed two-seat aircraft that had the same layout as the Farman. At the end of 1916, Italy had forty-six squadriglie in the front line, and in spite of the shortage of raw material, mainly steel and alloy, managed to replace French models with aircraft of Italian design. Many designs, however, were failing to incorporate the most up-to-date technologies. The new Caproni triplane bomber would prove to be too cumbersome, but the more powerful variant of his biplane the Ca.3, equipped with three 150-hp Isotta-Fraschini engines was slow to emerge.

The Supreme Command was still in direct control of the bombing force and some fighter and reconnaissance squadriglie deployed between Udine and Pordenone but within this context, the reconnaissance component was organised in squadriglie d'armata (army squadrons) under the direct control of army headquarters. Its task was to keep under surveillance the enemy's rear-guard and lines of communications. Squadriglie di corpo d'armata (corps squadrons), under the tactical control of corps headquarters, operated up to a depth of 15–20 kilometres from the line of contact, performing battlefield surveillance, enemy trench system surveys, mapping and artillery spotting.

In February 1917 on the Italian, Albanian and Macedonian fronts, there were twenty reconnaissance squadrons equipped with Farmans, Voisins, Caudrons, seven squadrons of Nieuport Ni.11 fighters, five air defence Farmans and SAML squadrons, twelve Caproni Ca.1 and Ca.2 bomber squadrons. Most squadrons were due to convert to up-to-date aircraft, with the Savoia-Pomilio replacing the Farmans, the Voisins and the Caudron G.3 in the reconnaissance units, the 110-hp Nieuport Ni.17, the 80-hp Nieuport Ni.11 in the fighter units, and the 450-hp Ca.3. The aircraft industry struggled to keep up with the demand.[11]

Artillery service squadrons sent their two-seaters with fighter escorts to reconnoitre long-range targets such as choke points, logistic terminals, command posts. Together with reconnaissance squadrons they kept the battlefield approaches under continuous surveillance. Reconnaissance two-seaters and fighters, together with the Caproni bombers, launched massive raids on the enemy rearguard on 23 May on the Carso plateau, and on the 25th north of Gorizia, between the Bainsizza plateau and Monte Santo. It was the first time that Italian aviators were directly involved in battle, but from then on, ground-attack sorties became an intrinsic part of planning. Attacks lacked accuracy, but the morale of Austro-Hungarian troops was badly eroded. Even with Brandenburg KD.1 and Albatros D.IIIs of German design, the Austro-Hungarians were unable to seriously threaten the Italian bombers with their machine-guns and Nieuports and SPADs on escort duty that were raiding logistics centres and railway stations day and night in the rear of the Isonzo front.

The number of Ca.3s available allowed the Italian Supreme Command to consider targets more in line with a pure strategic use of air power such as the mercury mines at Idria, which were bombed on 7 and 28 July and the main Austro-Hungarian naval base at Pula on the night of 2 August. Twenty Capronis dropped six tons of bombs over Pula, but intense anti-aircraft fire damaged ten bombers and engine problems forced three more to make emergency landings once back in Italian territory. The raid was repeated the following night, with twenty-seven bombers dropping nine tons of bombs, and again on the night of the 8th by twenty-five with eight tons of bombs. Pula continued to be the focus of strategic attacks through September and October, but always at night. Remnants of ships sunk at Pula during the autumn and winter of 1918 still littered the harbour floor a hundred years later. Striking at Austro-Hungarian industrial centres was quite out of the question, given the mountain barrier screening the targets and their location deep inside the Austro-Hungarian Empire.

Some 150 miles distant from Gioia del Colle airfield in Puglia, Cattaro naval base was a secondary target, but the number of available Capronis was dwindling. In autumn 1917, Italian aviation was relatively well-balanced with numerous reconnaissance and observation squadrons, increasingly vital for trench warfare, and supported by a fast developing fighter arm and flanked by a bomber arm that, although not very large, had shown the capability to hit well beyond the front lines.

The deteriorating weather now came into play as the Austro-Hungarian forces, with German air support, massed for the twelfth Battle of Isonzo, better known now as the Battle of Caporetto.[12] Initially, there were fierce air battles with significant losses but as the Italians fell back, their aircraft had the upper hand over German aircraft which were constantly having to relocate their operating bases. This did not last, as Germans began taking over abandoned Italian airfields and became much more active on the battle front. Italian losses began to mount alarmingly but they had, by now, eight French and five British squadrons of reconnaissance units in support, yet still they were forced back on the defensive until the Battle of Istrana on 26 December, when German aircraft attacking that airfield had eleven aircraft shot down by Italian and British fighters which stabilised the situation somewhat in Italy's favour.

The Battle of the Solstice and the Battle of Vittorio Veneto in 1918 had shown that Italian aviation was able to make the best of its technical and organisational superiority acting in line with modern concepts of air power. It carried out a clearly conceived programme of air-to-ground cooperation, but an important contribution to this success came from the ability to mobilise industry to achieve the expansion required by the air arm. Although Italy depended on France for its fighters throughout the war, the Italian industry was able to licence-build most French models and was able to supply reconnaissance aircraft and bombers of domestic design in large numbers and outproduce the Austro-Hungarian aeronautical industry.

The story of Italian aviation in the Great War proves the direct link between technology and doctrine, and the right relationship between them created a well-balanced air force that could perform the tasks assigned in the best possible way within the context of close air-to-ground cooperation. It was clearly understood that a fighter was to be a fast and agile single seat machine, equipped with a couple of synchronised machine-guns, and thrown into the fray in massed formations, while the reconnaissance aircraft had to rely on radio-telegraph and photography to carry out its mission, but that was only possible in a local context of air superiority. Winning air superiority was therefore fundamental to winning the artillery battle and to providing the essential liaison duties between troops and headquarters. Air-to-ground and ground-to-air communication systems were still in their infancy, but wireless technology pointed the way forward. Meanwhile, the great attention paid to bombing enabled the strategic dimension of air power to emerge, even though technology did not yet have the answers for payload and armament, as well as radius of action.

In view of his association with one of the fundamental concepts of air doctrine, it is worth looking in detail at the life and career of Giulio Douhet and in so doing consider his nemesis and (in Italy at least) equal in terms of influence, Amadeo Mecozzi. Much opinion throughout Europe about aerial warfare in the 1930s was founded on the work of Giulio Douhet, the 'arrogant and quarrelsome' author of a 1921 book *Command of the Air*, championing air forces as the pre-eminent players in any future war.[13] Douhet was among the first people to think deeply and write cogently about air power and its role in war, methodically and systematically elevating an idea to a level of abstraction that could be considered a theory. Basically, his idea was to win command of the air, neutralise an enemy's strategic 'vital centres' and maintain the defensive on the ground, while taking the offensive in the air.[14] Clearly Douhet was a visionary. With only the scantiest empirical evidence to go on, he brought into being the whole concept of strategic air war. By sheer imagination, he also recognised the necessity of air supremacy, or what he called 'command of the air' – all this before Italy had even entered the war in 1915.[15] Douhet, however, vastly overestimated the impact of conventional bombing and ignored the use of aircraft in other roles. His vision was decidedly flawed, but the significance of visionaries lies not in the details but in the stream of thought they set in motion. Douhet's contribution to strategic air doctrine between the wars, however, remains debateable. Peter Gray claims that it is 'far from clear if [Douhet] had more than a second- or third-hand influence'. Robin Higham says that his influence in Britain, at least, was a 'myth'.[16]

Giulio Douhet was born in Caserta, near Naples, on 30 May 1869. He was commissioned into the artillery in 1888 at the age of 19. Soon after, he attended the Polytechnic Institute in Turin and continued his studies in science and engineering. Assigned to the General Staff as a captain in 1900 he made a detailed study of the Russo-Japanese War of 1903 and wrote several papers advocating mechanisation of the Italian Army to compensate for its inherent weaknesses in manpower and natural resources. When Italy built its first dirigible in 1905, he immediately recognised its revolutionary possibilities in military technology and was also seduced by Wright's demonstration flight at Centocelle, even getting his photograph taken alongside the American pioneer. Within a few years, with the advent of aircraft, he advocated the creation of an independent air force and predicted that:

> the skies are about to become a battlefield as important as the land or the sea.... Only by gaining the command of the air shall we be able to derive the fullest benefit from the advantage which can only be fully exploited when the enemy is compelled to be earth bound.[17]

A further declaration by Douhet in 1910 is worth reproducing in detail, given that it directly opposes his later pronouncements:[18]

> No bombardment has ever proved decisive, except when directed towards cowards ... dropping bombs on a city from an airship would be a useless and barbaric act ... The conscience of a man of my century tells me that there are methods it is impossible to use honestly, even in the event of war ... we should not even envisage launching an action against defenceless cities. This would be an act of such barbarism as to revolt the conscience of the civilised world.

In 1911 Italy had gone to war against Turkey for control of Libya in a war that saw aircraft used for the first time. Amazingly, most of what would become the traditional roles of air power employment were identified and attempted during that very first year of aerial combat. The following year, Douhet was asked to write a report on the meaning of the Libyan War for the future employment of aircraft. His report included the comment that although some people thought the primary role of aircraft was reconnaissance, he believed that aircraft should be used for high altitude bombing. In 1912, Douhet assumed command of the Italian aviation battalion at Turin and soon wrote *Rules for the Use of Aircraft in War*, one of the first such manuals in any air force, but he had obviously gone much further than his superiors were willing to sanction and all his radical references to aircraft being used as 'weapons' were officially redacted before publication.

He started out with an intense campaign of essay writing which soon gained him a reputation as an irascible, outspoken and opinionated commentator on all matters of aviation. His main argument, and the one that brought him into direct confrontation with his immediate superior, Colonel Maurizio Moris – a keen dirigible advocate – was for the formation of a new, independent air service with its own budget and chain of command, which achieved some success in 1915 with the formation of 'Corpo Aeronautica Militaire'. In 1914, he had written an article in which he predicted that modern war had become total war and would be very long and costly, but his tone clearly suggests someone with pacifist sensibilities when he states:

> the nation that takes up arms to impose its will on the nations among whom it lives [commits] a criminal act. Militarism ... is barbarous and uncivilised; it is repugnant to the developed man.

Later that year, however, he seems to have undergone something of a change of heart when he wrote that Italy should build an air force whose purpose was 'to gain command of the air' so as to be able to 'attack with impunity any point of the enemy's body'.[19] He became so incensed by the Italian Army's incompetence and lack of preparedness that he frequently wrote to his superiors, suggesting organisational reform and increased use of the aeroplane. He even wrote a memo to his superiors saying that 'a bomber force should drop one hundred tons of explosives on Constantinople each day until the Turkish government agrees to open the Dardanelles to Allied shipping', which earned him a reprimand.[20] Clearly, Douhet was conflicted between an abhorrence of war and a concept of how it should be fought. A generous interpretation might be that he believed that by making war so all-encompassing of the population, and of such ferocity that it threatened the end of civilisation, it would force its abolition for all time. This was not so far-fetched, given that the idea of aerial bombardment being legitimately employed by a supra-national power with the aim of preserving human life would become a reality many years later with the formation of the United Nations. In 1914 he was in trouble again when he ordered a three-engine bomber from his friend and fellow enthusiast, industrialist Giovanni Caproni, without proper authority to do so and for that the Army exiled Douhet to an infantry division at Edolo, near the Austrian border.

In frustration he began writing to government officials criticising the conduct of the war and noting that:

> we find ourselves without a reserve, in a crisis of munitions, with all our forces engaged in an offensive already halted, with the rear threatened by old and new enemies, exposed to being attacked at any moment and overcome decisively in the shortest moment.[21]

He must have really upset somebody high up in the ranks because as a result of his remarks criticising the Italian General Luigi Cadorna he was arrested in September 1916 and court-martialled for:

> issuing false news ... divulging information differing from the official communiqués ... diminishing the prestige and the faith in the country and of disturbing the public tranquillity.

He defended himself by saying that he had obeyed the law, which 'imposes upon us not to hesitate when we feel the duty falling on us to achieve a common good'.[22] The court found him guilty and he was sentenced to a year in jail at the fortress of Fenestrelle and a fine of 170 lire. Meanwhile, the Italian Army continued to blunder when, in October 1917, they suffered a catastrophic defeat at Caporetto.[23]

After his release, the mood had changed, and people began to take note of what he had said and started to believe that he might have found a new way of avoiding the gruesome land battles of recent memory. Defence budgets had been heavily reduced, which took a toll of any and all plans for military development, but there was ample scope for theoretical debate. Douhet was not only exonerated, but appointed Central Director of Aviation at the General Air Commissariat. This body was tasked with centralising, streamlining and providing the air services with materiel and personnel. When he took up his position, Douhet confirmed that the basic criteria were still valid: to ensure an unchallenged domain in the air and create a bomber force that could effectively advance the victory through repeated and massive raids into enemy territory. New designs and new production facilities promised much, but Douhet saw it as being fundamentally flawed not only because it envisaged too many different types of aircraft, but also because it missed what was, in his view, the true nature of air warfare. At the Commissariat he worked with his old friend Caproni, who had recently been instrumental in helping a US mission led by Colonel Raynal Bolling and Major Edgar Gorrell develop a US air doctrine and, incidentally, buy several hundred Italian bombers to be built under licence in the US (a contract which, as it happens, was never fulfilled.) Douhet and Caproni impressed the delegation with ideas of 'battle planes' destroying an enemy's arms factories, making it incapable of continuing the war.

The emphasis on heavy bombers had seen doctrinal disputes over the years with Douhet and Caproni underlining the need for a fleet of strategic bombers that could destroy the enemy industrial base and cripple enemy morale, annihilating their will to fight. It was an interesting view, but one that did not fit easily into the military situation as it stood at the time. His first report, *Using the Air Arm* (*Impiego dell'Arma Aerea*), boldly claimed that the air arm, by its very nature, was an offensive weapon and was to be used as such to win the air war and only then pursuing other goals, of secondary importance, which can be easily achieved once air supremacy is obtained. The idea to use the fighter to win air supremacy was inherently wrong, since the fighter was essentially a defensive weapon. Instead of fighters, the need was for a 'battle plane', something like the new SIA9B, which would be well armed and fast to go ahead of the bomber force and clear the sky of enemy aircraft, leaving the door open to strike at industrial and population targets with the aim of destroying both the enemy's capability and will to fight. One significant problem was that the SIA9B and Caproni Ca.5 bomber were still some way from overcoming technical problems.[24] These revolutionary ideas were far removed from the immediate preoccupations of the air service and clearly of no practical use in 1918.

Among Douhet's early writings was a short novel entitled *Come finì la grande guerra. La vittoria alata* (*How the Great War Ended. The Winged Victor*), which took its main theme as an independent air arm acting independently of ground forces in which,

> Over one hundred important towns served by important railroads or main roads were on fire and encased by poisonous clouds which, carried by the wind, sometimes brought trails of death and terror.

This book was never published, and neither were his military reports well received, so when it was clear that nobody, except a press eager for sensational stories, was interested, Douhet took umbrage and resigned his commission in June 1918, freeing himself to express his views without restraint. The air force would have to stumble on as best it could without him, with outdated aircraft and conservative doctrine putting strategic bombing well down the list of priorities. Soon his writings included blatant criticisms of the government and the debacle of Caporetto, into which they had launched an investigation. The findings exonerated Douhet and not only reversed the court verdict but promoted him to general. He was now seen as a military theoretician of some standing.

In 1921, after another scathing assault on the reputation of General Cardona, Douhet wrote *Il Dominio Dell'Area* (*The Command of the Air*), published by the War Ministry and officially endorsed by General Armado Diaz, which Thomas Hippler described as a coherent articulation of his philosophy. The book has been hailed as the first holistic doctrine on air power, with its powerful advocacy shifting the 'centre of gravity' of air war to the enemy home front with a campaign of massive strategic bombing. He followed this up with a nine-page memorandum to army General Alberto Bonzani strongly advocating an independent air arm, but Bonzani was not receptive to the idea and when he achieved deputy commissar status within the air force, he failed to acquire for the service the funds necessary to achieve Douhet's goals.

Much has been made of the influence Douhet had over air doctrine between the wars, but it should be borne in mind that initially he was not well known outside his native land. His book was not widely read although it was the subject of debate within Italy. A reputation had started to emerge, however, when a short extract from his book was received by the US War Department Military Intelligence Division in March 1922, and a translation of the first few pages was received at the Air Services Field Officers' School in 1923. The US publication *Aircraft Year Book* took note of Douhet's influence and stated that when the new office of the Italian Commissioner of Aeronautics was formed in 1923, Mussolini had 'the assistance of General G. Douhet, internationally known for his work *The Command of the Air*'. The second edition of his book, in which his theories had become more extreme, gained a much wider readership however.[25] The first French translation was in 1932, but the first article to appear in the official journal of the Royal Air Force was not published until 1933. Furthermore, *The Command of the Air* was never required reading at the RAF Staff College between the wars. The situation in France was a little different because French airmen were followers of aviation developments in Italy, and in 1933 the magazine *Les Ailes* published a partial translation of the book. French air leaders, specifically Generals Tulasne and Armengaud, were receptive to his ideas. In 1935, Colonel P. Vauthier wrote an analysis of Douhet's theories titled *La Doctrine de Guerre du General Douhet*, which further elucidated the Italian's theories and disseminated them to a wider audience. In fact, the accounts of Douhet that began appearing in British and American periodicals about this time likely were based on the French works rather than the original Italian. German military leaders were even more receptive to new ideas than were the French. Because of their failure in the First World War, they made a point of closely monitoring foreign developments. Although *The Command of the Air* was not published in German until 1935, it appears that Hitler was initially taken with Douhet's ideas, but his influence did not extend to the Luftwaffe as a whole and the official doctrine with which it entered the war focused on army cooperation rather than strategic bombing. Douhet had his earliest and greatest influence in America – but even there it was not great. In 1922 the Italian air attaché wrote about *The Command of the Air* in *Aviation* magazine, and Billy Mitchell later admitted that he had had a meeting with Douhet. While Mitchell was a great aviation theorist, he was not a prolific writer and although he may well have been influenced by Douhet in the 1920s, there is no reason to believe that he was a major conduit for his ideas across a wider audience outside the US.

In his essay published in 1943, the US aviation expert Edward Warner defines five essential elements of Douhet's theories:[26]

   i) The first requirement of an air force is to gain air superiority in time of war.
  ii) The prime objective of a strategic air attack should be the cities and industries of the enemy nation.
 iii) The enemy air force will be defeated by attacking airfields and aircraft factories.
  iv) The ground forces will hold the defensive positions while the air force strikes at its vital centres.
   v) The heavily armed bomber must be capable of defending itself against enemy fighter aircraft.

Douhet appears to have been not so much enamoured of the aircraft as such, but fascinated by the idea of a third dimension in which to wage war; in his view, this significantly reduced the importance of ground forces. The vastness of the air space into which conflict now reached out seemed to eliminate the very concept of defence. If defence as such was to be considered, it could only be on the basis of 'attack being the best and, indeed, only defence'. The crucial importance of air power meant that a country which lost control of its airspace had to endure whatever air attacks an enemy chose to inflict upon its airfields and aircraft industry in what Douhet referred to as 'destroying the eggs in their nest'. The lack of any defensive measures allowed Douhet to envision a rather peculiar scenario in which opposing air forces studiously ignored each other while flying past to destroy the other's airfields and factories.

In this regard, Douhet was one of the first people to realise that the key to air power was in its strategic use through pinpoint targeting, because although aircraft could strike virtually anything, they should not attempt to strike everything. One had to identify the most important objectives: industry, transportation, infrastructure, communication nodes and government buildings, and hit them most forcefully. An ominous addition to the list of targets was 'the will of the people'. Douhet knew that this made for 'total war' in which 'all people were combatants', but tempered this with the assertion that the very command of the air and the threat it posed would force capitulation, obviating the need for such actions. All this would be achieved without the air force having recourse to any tactical role. The first edition of his book recognised the usefulness of auxiliary aviation, but in the 1927 edition he described it as 'useless, superfluous and harmful', and should not be considered as a component of air power at all.[27]

More important than Douhet's concept of 'terror-bombing' was the idea of a wholly independent air force that did not have to rely on support and funding from the other armed services, which would inevitably dilute its potency by insisting on a substantial tactical component; this may have been more appealing and actually more important in the way that Douhet's reputation was evoked within air ministries throughout Europe. While Douhet's air force would have bombing and combat aircraft with similar performance characteristics they would, effectively, both be deployed as a single force in the pursuit of the bombing objective. Indeed, the perfect solution would be to combine the two into a 'battle plane' carrying both bombs and defensive machine guns. The one area where he conceded some leeway was in the requirement of reconnaissance aircraft to scout for targets and report on the results of bombing. In any war, it was necessary employ massed air attack immediately in a 'first strike', which meant that a country not ready for war would be forced to capitulate.

There is no doubt that Douhet's first edition was recognised by a small but influential coterie of other theorists and his writings in the mid-1920s, which expanded on the theme, slowly extended the range of his influence, but it was eschewed by those who had the power to implement its ideas. He spent the last years of his life defending his theories in the pages of the Italian Air Force journal *Rivista Aeronautica*, which allowed him to expand on his ideas, but generally, caused him to retrench behind his theories which he stubbornly refused to modify in any degree.

Any analysis of Douhet's theories centres on the idea of the extent to which air power can be decisive in war, and the conclusion must be that its effect is dependent upon too many other factors. By taking the approach that he did, Douhet was blinkered to the advances made in doctrine and technology within other arms of the military, which led to him to underestimating the limits that this would place on air power. His concept of total war overestimated the effect of bombing on civilian populations, many of whom proved to be immensely resilient, resourceful and defiant in the face of direct attack. In the absence of any empirical evidence, he was also over-optimistic about the level of destruction that could be wrought, especially given the small bomb-loads carried by aircraft in the inter-war years. While trying to break free from the shackles of historical analysis of warfare, Douhet ironically welded his theory to an expectation that a future war would be conducted along similar lines to the one just gone.

Mussolini, who had joined the Italian Aviation Federation in 1919, had been very much taken with the idea of air power as a cornerstone of fascist ideology with its futuristic avant-garde 'brutalist' imagery, and had recommended Douhet to be the new Commissioner of Aviation; the appointment was rescinded after behind-the-scenes objections, prompting Douhet to later revise his second edition in 1927 claiming:

> During all those years I had been trying with all my might to
> drive home the realisation of the importance of air power, but
> all my efforts met defeat at the hands of military authorities
> and government bureaucracies.

263

The 1921 edition had been augmented by a new section but Douhet, somewhat chastened by his incarceration, was careful not to ruffle too many feathers – especially since funding for the air force at the time was heavily dependent on the Italian Navy for instructors and facilities. He wrote:

> in order to accomplish anything practical and useful for my country, I had to be careful not to oppose too strongly certain notions firmly held in high places. Therefore, I was forced to emasculate my thought, confining myself to indispensable fundamentals, and wait for more favourable circumstances before presenting my ideas in full.[28]

Although Giulio Douhet is virtually the only name generally associated with inter-war Italian aviation, the Italian military produced other notable aviation theorists whose influence, in Italy at least, surpassed Douhet's. The thesis of *The Command of the Air*, which urged the development of a strategic air force that would strike decisively at the enemy's homeland, might have found popularity in Europe, but Douhet's home country by no means accepted it uncritically.[29]

Amedeo Mecozzi was born in Rome on 17 January 1892. As a young engineer at the outset of the First World War, he joined the air force pilots' school. During the war, he became one of the most distinguished Italian fighter pilots with six victories. After the war, he conducted experimental flights with several new aircraft.

Douhet's powerful and controversial ideas enshrined in his work *Il Dominio Dell'Area* were heavily criticised by Mecozzi. He argued that 'command of the air' by an independent air force was not possible, that strategic bombardment of civilians was unacceptable and the idea that an air force, independent of the other armed services, could achieve victory in war was simply wrong. Mecozzi published his own ideas in professional journals to challenge Douhet, but many have yet to be translated from the Italian. There is strong evidence to suggest that the theoretical basis of Italian air doctrine owes as much to Mecozzi as Douhet – if not more.

Although Douhet had yet to publish his book in December 1920, Mecozzi responded to his many articles published in military periodicals by arguing not that Douhet's ideas were necessarily wrong, but that they were impractical and his grand designs for air power were fanciful and unachievable. He brought to the argument a flyer's perspective, as opposed to Douhet as an artillery officer who scanned the sky while firmly anchored to the ground. Douhet had a cold-blooded approach in which a pilot was simply a component of a bomb-delivery system, but for Mecozzi, a pilot was a living, breathing person. Unlike Douhet, Mecozzi had a sound technical knowledge of aircraft and their capabilities.

Air Marshal Italo Balbo claimed to be a follower of Douhet and praised him regularly, even writing a preface for the 1932 edition, although he tended, in practice, to support the 'assault aviation' ideas of Amedeo Mecozzi, who had established the first ground assault group within the air force by 1931. Italian Foreign Minister Count Galeazzo Ciano, Mussolini's son-in-law and a rival to Balbo, characterised Balbo as 'a poor intellect, large ambitions, completely treacherous [and] capable of anything', yet praised him after his death as 'exuberant and restless ... a decent fellow [able to act with] decision and daring'.[30] Mussolini feared him as a 'buried mine that could explode at any time', but valued him as 'one of fascism's most glamorous and competent leaders'. When Mussolini had won power, Balbo, although equally committed to fascism, had opposed his 'royalist' ideas, but nevertheless was appointed to high rank in the new Italian Army. In 1926, Mussolini appointed him as Under Secretary in the Air Ministry. As would later be the case in Nazi Germany, military aviation had become popular with the Fascist government as an emblem of its modern outlook and revolutionary ideals. The aircraft signified technological revolution and an air force, operating independently to exert Italian influence well beyond its borders, was a powerful symbol of progress and fascist power. The air force quickly gained its independence under Mussolini and was given a substantial budget. At an air display over Rome in 1924, Mussolini had looked up to see 300 aircraft in flight and declared 'We must have enough planes by next year to hide the sun!' He dissolved the Air Ministry and took personal change of a new department combining military and civil aviation.

Balbo prepared the ground for claiming credit by first of all denigrating his predecessors for leaving him a 'disastrous situation', where the air force was 'the least ready of the services'.[31] Now he could demand a sizeable budget as well as make the most of the hundreds of aircraft, the existence of which he had denied. In his post, Balbo was responsible for both civil and military aviation, travelled widely and quickly gained a worldwide reputation as a flamboyant pioneer of Italian aviation. There is no doubt that the Aeronautica Italia was in poor shape when Balbo took over and he planned to rebuild it from the ground up, but he pleaded in vain for more funding. 'We are moving among giants' he told Parliament in 1928, comparing his budget with that of France as he bemoaned Italy's lack of air-mindedness and pointed out its vulnerability to air attack with its huge coastline and easy access for bombers to its cities. While Italy's military aviation at the end of the 1920s was not too dissimilar to those of other countries, it was the way that different countries developed in the 1930s that would determine their readiness for war in 1939, and in this regard, Italy did not preform well.

The newly formed air force academy opened in 1923 had been grafted onto a naval facility at Livorno on the shores of the Ligurian Sea and initially the commander, naval Captain Giulio Valli, had to rely on officers transferring from the army and navy, few of whom chose to do so, especially if they had good prospects where they were. Prospects for the academy were significantly improved in 1926 when it was relocated to the Royal Palace of Caserta close to Naples, at which point it was successful in recruiting many more university graduates with appropriate engineering and mathematics degrees. While the academy appreciated the pressure Douhet exerted for an independent air force, it was reluctant to adopt and teach his strategic bombing doctrine. Elsewhere, however, Douhet was lauded as a 'Maestro' by the publication *Rivista Aeronautica*, which published much of his writing between 1927 and his death in 1930. These essays continued to attract venomous responses from many sides, including Mecozzi, who saw Douhet's ideas as fanciful at best and horrifyingly unethical at worst.

Douhet's popularity with the general public, however, persuaded Balbo to take his theories seriously and in so doing, improve his own public image. He adopted three specific Douhetian principles: independence of the air arm, a first-strike capability, and massed fleets of aircraft, and set about redefining the Aeronautica in these terms. He had not, however, lost sight of Mecozzi in all this. Balbo was careful to hedge his bets by also making it clear that Mecozzi's theories of tactical air power would be given equal consideration declaring to an English newspaper that there was 'virtue in both'.[32]

For fifteen years after Douhet's book was published, *Rivista Aeronautica* carried numerous articles and much correspondence about his theories, which came under fire from Mecozzi and others, who vehemently opposed strategic air power, with its unspoken threat of waging 'war against the unarmed' and whose preference was for 'assault aviation' employed in close support of ground forces. It is fair to say that some of Douhet's ideas were only half-formed and not particularly well argued, as might be expected of a revolutionary idea, but it gave Mecozzi plenty of targets to aim at with his criticism. While Douhet was a pure theorist, Mecozzi relied very much on empirical evidence to support his arguments.

Mecozzi argued for a substantial air reserve available to interdict at critical points in a battle and suggested that zoned air defence, which Douhet had denigrated as irrelevant, could well play an important role. While Douhet had urged immediate separation of the air force from army and navy control, Mecozzi argued that the air force should be split into three parts with a strategic bomber force balanced by a naval air arm, necessary because of Italy's extensive coastline, and the remaining units, the bulk of the air force, supporting the army. His much less radical views found favour with politicians and senior military men alike and he became the bulwark against which Douhetist philosophy banged its head in vain.[33] Douhet, however, remained a popular figure in Italy and it was not good form to attack him or his theories outright, and given Douhet's fascist credentials, many senior air force officers, while not exactly endorsing Mecozzi, were not openly hostile and were quietly sympathetic to his concepts.

It is ironic that Douhet, an artillery man, should give his total backing to air power while Mecozzi, a flyer, should advocate a role for aircraft more in line with that argued for by the army. To follow Douhet's arguments to their logical conclusion, Mecozzi argued, would be well beyond the capacity of Italian military budgets to achieve and the best that could be hoped for was to develop an air force capable of contributing to the sum total of all the armed forces operations. Air power could only ever be a contributing factor alongside other armed services and any insistence upon total independence would provoke a response from the army and only result in losing what little it already had. Douhet's idea that Army and Navy budgets should be progressively reduced to finance a burgeoning air force would be totally counter-productive. When Slessor later says, 'Let us mass together air and ground forces in the place and at the time that are decisive ... While the air force inflicts decisive damage on the enemy, we should not allow the enemy to inflict damage on our sea and ground forces', he is echoing Mecozzi's views. Furthermore, Mecozzi argued that the idea that 'aerial warfare admits of no defence' was flawed, and that the Italian Air Force should create a sophisticated air defence force of fighter groups and artillery to protect specific areas. His views of warfare were more nuanced than Douhet's, accepting that whether in the air or on the ground, battles were complex events which often defied logic and the outcome of which was dictated by many factors. It was simply naïve to think that one single factor could outweigh all the others.

Mecozzi wrote: 'To achieve command of the air is as much Douhet's legitimate aspiration as mine, but it is also the enemy's aspiration. Douhet always forgets this.'[34] He accepted that it might be possible to win temporary command of the air, but believed that this could never be more than temporary when confronted with a powerful opponent. In other words, air power might give sufficient temporary advantage to allow other forces to make significant gains, but it could not be an end in itself. At other times, simply denying air superiority to the enemy might prove to be decisive in a defensive scenario.

In his two books *Aviazione d'Assalto* (1933) and *Quel che l'Aviatore d'Assalto Deve Sapere* (1936), Mecozzi clearly describes his belief in a mixed air force comprising fighter, ground attack, and bombers with small, light, fast, and agile multi-role aircraft able to fly very close to the ground in order to conduct air-to-ground attacks. Douhet, by contrast believed that very large, long-range bombers capable of fighting their way to the heart of the enemy state were the only truly useful aircraft which would destroy high-value targets, particularly at the very beginning of the conflict. Mecozzi did not accept that such aircraft would survive the hostile enemy air space without substantial fighter cover. Interestingly, he believed that every action is tactical at the time it occurs and may only later be defined as strategic or tactical in terms of its effect. An air strike might at first appear to have solely tactical consequences, but the cascading effects might ultimately affect the outcome of the war. Mecozzi argued that the air force must identify and prioritise targets such as enemy armed forces already deployed, rather than potential forces, in order to achieve campaign objectives in support of the war effort.

One of the more interesting points of divergence between Douhet and Mecozzi is over the role of civilians in war. In his book, Douhet asserted that 'the battlefield will be limited only by the boundaries of the nations at war', meaning that civilians would be combatants and consequently there would be 'no distinction any longer between soldiers and civilians'.[35]

While there is evidence that Mecozzi did not diverge significantly from Douhet's views on civilians such as munitions workers as components of an enemy's war effort, as early as 1922 he argued that 'unarmed' civilians were not legitimate targets because it placed airmen in the invidious position of committing the 'crime of aerial terrorism'. For practical purposes, also, terror bombing was not acceptable with so much of Italy's more densely populated areas being in the north, close to the border and vulnerable to revenge attack. Italy could ill-afford a massive bomber attack force and certainly could not create an effective defensive aerial screen on top of that. Douhet died of a heart attack on 15 February 1930, while tending his garden at Ceschina, near Rome.

In 1931, the most abundant fighter in use in the Italian Air Force was the excellent all-metal Fiat CR.20 biplane armed with four machine guns. Development of a monoplane fighter, believed to be less manoeuvrable, was resisted – until the advent of the Bf109 changed the whole picture. Bombers were still the Fiat BR.2 and BR.3, which had performed well but were now ten years in service. The Caproni Ca.73 and Ca.74 made up the bulk of the night bomber fleet. Given its extensive coastline, seaplanes, including the twin-hulled Savoia-Marchetti SM.55, were also a major component of the air service. When orders were placed for new aircraft, Balbo, given his penchant for travel and spectacle, invested rather more than his predecessor in civil and general aviation at the expense of the military. Engine design too was biased towards long-haul reliability rather than combat performance, resulting in a shortage of domestic production that had to be filled by foreign imports. Industry blamed 'weak and uncertain directives' for their failure to meet demand. The plain fact was that Italy was not a major industrial power and did not have the infrastructure to match French or German production and also, to get foreign currency, many of the aircraft that did come out of the factories were sold abroad, including to the Soviet Union which bought sixty-two Isotta Fraschini Asso in 1931.

It is said that Balbo was initially unable to make much of a mark on the aviation industry because of his lack of technical background, but he was able to collect around him a band of experts who quickly brought him up to speed. Confrontations with major manufacturers began with them complaining about government inefficiency but ended by Balbo demanding 'without discussion' a competitive bidding process and an end to companies 'overlooking flaws in the prototypes'.[36]

One aspect that troubled Balbo from the start was the shortage of pilots; young military-minded men were drawn more to the traditions of the army and navy. He set about changing this by elevating the status of his officers within society. He fitted them out with smart blue uniforms and promised that promotion would be open to all. He then presented his young flyers to the country through a series of air shows and competitions. The Aeronautica quickly started to project a professional image and by 1930 had a full quota of pilots. The strongly fascist doctrines with which the service was imbued was also a draw for young men whose national pride saw in it a means of projecting Italian values and prestige. Balbo actually directed his officers to 'speak out in favour of fascism', and demanded of them the highest standards of morality.[37] His stated ambition was to create an esprit de corps and a 'military spirit which would take into account the wholesome individualism of every flyer'. In an attempt to show off this spirit to the world, Balbo organised two exhibitions in 1930 and 1932 designed to rival the RAF displays at Hendon, with spectacular aerobatics and formation flying and as many as 200 aircraft in the air at one time, which vividly illustrated Douhetian principles. In recognition of Balbo's commitment to mass-formation flying, any large formation of aircraft flying in the 1930s was commonly referred to as a 'Balbo'. It is worth noting that in 1931, the Chief of the Italian General Staff was still denying the value of air power and Balbo was careful to devote much time and energy to cooperation in army manoeuvres.

Balbo became famous for his many 'cruises', or long-distance flights around the Mediterranean, across the Atlantic to South America and Odessa in the Soviet Union. In July 1933, he took an armada of twenty-five Savoia S-55, twin-hull seaplanes each powered by two Isotta Fraschini 18-cylinder Asso 500-hp engines and manned by nearly 100 officers from Orbetello in Italy on what was to be the greatest mass flight in aviation history. Their objective was Chicago, returning to Rome via New York. On 7 November 1933, he was appointed Governor General of Libya and died there on 28 June 1940 when his Savoia-Marchetti SM.79 was shot down by 'friendly fire' over Tobruk.

In 1932 several large Italian banks and investment concerns faced bankruptcy as a result of having invested so much in struggling industries during the years of the Great Depression. In response, Mussolini's government founded the Istituto per la Ricostruzione Industriale (Institute for Industrial

Reconstruction) to buy up and take control of many of the country's failing industries as a means of maintaining a high level of employment. This, unfortunately, led to poor oversight of budgets which, together with labour unrest, resulted in an economic climate of inefficiency and complacency. Many smaller manufacturers were kept going only through government contracts which were spread widely across the industrial base. In the case of the air force this meant that too many small contracts were agreed for too large a range of aircraft types, which required parts from too many disparate manufacturers. In terms of efficiency it was not a model anyone would want to follow. Lacking any capacity for mass production, costs remained high and end-product remained low. Much raw material had to be imported at considerable cost as other countries, also in the throes of rearmament, competed for the same supplies. Lacking competition for orders, the state-owned companies lacked incentive to invest in research and development and cronyism between industrialist and government ministers, sometimes one and the same, encouraged corruption and waste.

During the 1920s and early 1930s Italian aircraft engine manufacturers continued to produce modular in-line engines whose design resulted in heavier engines as well as longer, costlier production compared with other types. Engine manufacturers had no incentive to re-equip their production lines given Mussolini's insistence on subsidising domestic industry without regard to quality control. By 1933, however, the technical limits of modular in-line design had been reached and Balbo ordered that all subsequent Italian military aircraft designs be powered by the more reliable radial engines. Italian manufacturers had little prior experience with radial engine design and construction, and neither were they willing to invest in a lengthy research and design process so, instead, they purchased cheap licences from foreign manufacturers such as Bristol, Pratt & Whitney and Gnome-Rhône, which were not necessarily of the latest designs. This meant that they had to be modified in an attempt to obtain more power without having to design new engine parts. The extra stress this imposed on other parts of the engine made them susceptible to overheating and failure.

The problems with the modified engines were exacerbated by the inferior-quality materials going into the steel alloys from which the engines were cast, and the lack of high-octane aviation fuel resulted in lower power output. Many of the locally produced lubricants used for aero engines were vegetable-based and proved to be unstable at high temperatures, resulting in excessive engine wear. Many of these problems were self-inflicted resulting from Mussolini's insistence on strategic material self-sufficiency. Other issues were the shortage of well-educated and well-trained engineers both to design and build the engines.

Italy was quick to send military aid to support General Franco's troops in Spain when the Civil War broke out. Mussolini had bold ambitions of empire building in the Mediterranean and within that, he hoped to use Spain to weaken British control of Gibraltar, or at least acquire transit rights through Spanish territory to the Atlantic. Several Italian warships, two militia divisions and a great deal of materiel was supplied. The level of participation by Italian forces was initially much higher than that of Germany, whose interest was more of an exploratory nature, but Hitler had no interest in letting Italy increase its power in the region and soon authorised the setting up of the Condor Legion to counter Mussolini's influence with Franco. Although smaller in quantity, the level of German aid was to prove itself much superior in quality. There was a measure of cooperation between the two initially when German aircraft flying to Spain via Rome were aided in their flight across the Mediterranean by Italian warships stationed at intervals to act as navigation points, but once their forces were established in Spain they tended to fight separate wars. Naturally with both countries having ambitions that were, to some extent, conflicting, there was an urgent requirement for liaison if they were to work together. Fortunately, Germany had the perfect answer in the form of Reichswehr intelligence officer, Capitan Wolfram von Richthofen, who had served with the Regia Aeronautica for six months in 1929 to familiarise himself with its technology, training and doctrinal theories. He had stayed on for a further two years as Air Attaché, with specific instructions to study the theories of Douhet, by then 'well-known and followed carefully in the magazines'.[38]

The First Fiat CR.32 biplane fighters arrived in Spain in mid-August 1936 and went straight into action on the 20th at Córdoba, having set up their base at Cácares.[39] More arrived soon after and by October there were three squadrons operational along with twenty-one Romeo Ro37s (Lynx) reconnaissance biplanes. The Fiats were much superior as fighters to any other aircraft operating in Spain at this time and were successful in shooting down the antiquated Republican aircraft in combats, but even so, nine had been lost by the end of September. Savoia-Marchetti SM.81 tri-engine bombers had joined by the time of Franco's first attack on Madrid. These were fast and well armed aircraft and undertook night-time bombing of Cartagena, along with German Ju 52s, in an effort to disrupt supplies of Soviet military aid coming into the country through that port, but on the Madrid front they were 'forbidden ... to bomb the city' by the Spanish air force General Kindelán.[40]

The first big aerial battle of the war came on 5 November when nine Fiats took on fifteen Soviet Chatos, which had made their first appearance over Madrid the previous day, resulting in losses on both sides. The Fiat squadrons were back up to strength by this time and were heavily involved against the Chatos, along with the SM 81s, all through the Madrid offensive operating, at times, alongside the German Junker Ju 52s and Heinkel He 51s. The formidable Soviet Rata monoplane fighters had now arrived and were set to challenge the Fiats for dominance of the sky. Government forces had resisted the attack on Madrid and went onto the counter-offensive by bombing Gamonal and Prada del Arca airfields, forcing the Italian aircraft to pull back. The Soviet Katiuska bombers continued their assault with fighter escort and during the fierce air battles, the Fiats lost all three of their squadron leaders, which had a deleterious effect on morale. To forestall further losses and stabilise what was becoming a worrying scenario, the Fiats were now forbidden to engage enemy aircraft unless they were at least fifteen-strong and able to operate at three different heights for mutual protection, which resulted in better performance against the Ratas.[41] Neither were the German He 51 squadrons much help, as they also were ordered not to tackle the Ratas unless they had a significant numerical advantage.

With the conflict 'hotting up', Mussolini met Hitler in Rome to compare notes and try to ensure that their involvement in Spain would not lead to a wider European conflagration. Publicly, they agreed to a British and French initiative to send no further arms and it is likely that the Italians at least had got as far into the war as they wanted, but Hitler was anxious to use the war as a testing ground for his new weapons and a 'gentlemen's agreement' was of no consequence to him. On the ground, the German officers initially welcomed fighting alongside the Italians whose fascist system they admired so much, but it soon became apparent that Mussolini had his own agenda and would pursue it without regard to overall Nationalist ambitions. He had sent a huge contingent of men and materiel, far exceeding that of the German Condor Legion, but it was clear that they would operate almost as an independent force, which they soon did at Málaga. In the middle of January 1937, the four Fiat squadrons, named Nobili, Lodi, Viola and Francois, had moved south to support Italian Corpo Truppo Voluntarie (CTV) ground forces in the attack against Málaga, which had begun without consultation with the Spanish. The Republican force was defeated within days, which Mussolini lauded as a 'spectacular success'. Although the attack was successful, during the build up Chatos had wreaked havoc against the Nationalist bombers, who simply had no answer to them.

When the winter weather closed in the Fiats were relocated to the Madrid sector to support Nationalist forces at El Jamara. Government aircraft continued to dominate over Madrid and so, with losses mounting, the Fiats were ordered to stay over their own lines and not stray into enemy air space which meant that bombing missions, unescorted by a protective fighter screen, had to operate by night with minimal effect. The Spanish leaders were becoming agitated over their aerial casualties and urgently called on Italy to expedite delivery of the two dozen Fiats that had been promised. They were somewhat relieved to see the German Condor Legion now boosted by a squadron of Messerschmitt Bf109-Bs, but these were still underpowered compared to the later versions and were, as yet, no match for the Soviet Ratas.

At Guadalajara during March, the Nationalist air contingent was almost exclusively Italian and operating from airfields in Soria, but the Italian ground forces suffered a major setback which caused much embarrassment in Rome, and one they struggled to live down. The victory at Málaga would be little more than a mirage to be abruptly shattered by the nightmare of Guadalajara. Fiats and Romeos were severely hampered by having to operate from flooded airfields and often failed to get airborne, which gave Republican aircraft free rein to attack the Italian columns on the Madrid road almost at will. This debacle threatened to terminate Italian involvement but Mussolini, unwilling to lose face, chose instead to reinforce his air force in the peninsula. Another ten Fiats were sent in April to create a further squadron piloted by Spanish flyers and carrying Spanish insignia. There were now ten Fiat squadrons each having between six and nine aircraft. Together with the squadron of Bf109Bs they were up against, at this time, twelve squadrons of Soviet Ratas and Chatos, each with twelve aircraft. The government fighter force had a clear superiority of numbers, but the number of bombers on each side was roughly equal.

In 1938, the Italians again launched an independent operation in defiance of Spanish Nationalist opposition. General Kindelán had insisted that there should be no indiscriminate bombing of civilian targets and the Germans had understood that it was 'politically unacceptable' to do so, but Mussolini took the unilateral decision to launch his bombers against the city of Barcelona. This was not an unprecedented act, since the Italian Air Force had repeatedly targeted urban centres such as Lleida on 2 November 1937, Barbastro on 4 November and other towns in Aragon. Attacks on Barcelona started on New Year's Day 1938 and were led by General Valle who would 'give the Reds in Barcelona a New Year's welcome that will cause them to meditate on the Teruel defeat.' On 20 January the level of bombing increased, but it was the three-day blitz, a 'violent action on Barcelona' as Mussolini called it, between 16 and 18 March that brought widespread condemnation, even from German allies who called the 'destructive bombardment without clear military targets ... senseless'.[42] This did little to repair the rift that had clearly opened up between the Italians and their Nationalist allies. The CTV continued to be active in support of Nationalist forces during the Catalonia Offensive at the end of 1938, but were withdrawn from the country in February 1939. By this time all the Italian aircraft operating in the war were flown by Spanish pilots and the Italian airmen had left.

The Spanish Civil War more or less won the argument for Mecozzi. The Italian Air Force had performed admirably, carrying out interdiction bombing, close air support, and anti-shipping strikes in support of Italian and Nationalist ground troops. The argument was not all one-sided, however, with Mussolini leaning towards Douhet – as evinced by his ordering the mass-bombing of Barcelona in March 1938 to try to break the will of the civilian population to resist, but the response of the population under attack was a clear refutation of Douhet's doctrine. They had refused to be cowed and emerged from their shelters with renewed determination to resist. The Republican army stood firm and held Catalonia for another year before surrendering.[20]

At the end of 1939, an internal investigation in Italy's Air Force, the Regia Aeronautica, revealed that of the total 2,802 combat aircraft in service, there were only 536 bombers and 191 fighters that could be considered modern front-line aircraft, and of these only 396 bombers and 129 fighters were serviceable. This was in marked contrast to the frequent mass aerial displays and public demonstrations that had taken place all through the 1930s which had been designed not only to impress Italy's population, but also to intimidate its neighbours and international rivals. The reasons for the dire state of Italy's Air Force were the failure of its manufacturing industry to produce modern aircraft in numbers, the failure of the Italian aeronautical industry to design and produce powerful engines, and the fact that so many of the aircraft produced were exported to get foreign currency. Despite this, Mussolini set out to expand his Fascist empire at the expense of the other Mediterranean powers and prepared for war. In 1940, even the most advanced Italian fighters were underpowered and under-armed compared to those of France and Germany, but its bomber force was roughly comparable despite the tri-motor configuration of most of their aircraft. Air doctrine, however, was under-developed and lacked intellectual rigour within an overall military ambition that was simple and wide-ranging but unfocused.

By 1939, the Italian Air Force boasted a well-balanced force of bombers and fighters as well as assault and reconnaissance aircraft. Mecozzi's doctrine, tested and found reliable in Spain, was extensively applied. What would be the undoing of the Italian Air Force thereafter was more to do with trying to employ the doctrine with aircraft that were inadequate both technically and numerically as a result of years of underfunding the armed services. They had simply been left behind and lacked the resources to match their ambitions.

Notes

Chapter 1: Air Doctrine

1. **Biddle,** Tami Davis, *Air Power And Warfare: A Century Of Theory And History* p.1
2. **Cain**, Anthony Christopher, *The forgotten Air Force; French Air Doctrine in the 1930s* p.34
3. **Corum,** James S., *The Luftwaffe, Creating the Operational Air War 1918–1940* p.93
4. **Kennett**, Lee, *The First Air War 1914–1918* p.4
5. **Ibid** p.2
6. **Ibid** p.8
7. **Hippler,** Thomas, *Governing from the Skies* p.32
8. **Hallion,** Richard P. *Rise of the Fighter Aircraft 1914–1918* p.9
9. **Kennett** p.21
10. **Murray**, Williamson, *War in the Air 1914–1945* p.36
11. **Lawson,** Eric and Jane, *The First Air Campaign August 1914 – November 1918* p.205
12. **Hippler** p.37
13. **Kennett** p.69
14. **Stephens**, Alan, *The Development Of Air Power Doctrine 1911–1945* p.5
15. **Lawson** p.45
16. **Hippler** p.46
17. **Lawson** p.51
18. **Molketin,** Michael, *Policy, Prophecy and Practice: Air Power between the Wars* p.25

19. **Hippler** p.55
20. **Higham**, Robin, *Air Power A concise History* p.29
21. **Ibid** p.20
22. **Ibid** p.31
23. **Hallion** p.14
24. **Barros**, Andrew, *Strategic Bombing and Restraint in Total War, 1915–1918* p.421
25. **Ibid** p.422
26. **Ibid** p.424
27. **Kennet** p.94
28. **Lawson** p.218
29. **Molketin** p.25
30. **Hallion** p.37
31. **Hippler** p.79
32. **Hallion** p.46
33. **Higham** p.9
34. **Hippler** p.xviii
35. **Molketin** p.26
36. **Corum,** James S., *The Luftwaffe, Creating the Operational Air War 1918–1940* p.92
37. **Ibid** p.95
38. **Hallion** p.60
39. **Ibid** p.63
40. **Ibid** p.64
41. **Ibid** p.66
42. **Molketin** p.26
43. **Hallion** p.83
44. **Ibid** p.87
45. **Hippler** p.86
46. **Ibid** p.111
47. **Molketin** p.27
48. **Corum** p.236
49. **Higham** p.13
50. **Stephens** p.22
51. **Drum,** Karl, *The German Air Force in the Spanish Civil War* p.27
52. **Larrazábal,** Jesus Salas, *Air War over Spain* p.142

Chapter 2: The Evolution of Fighter Aircraft during the First World War

1. **Lawson,** Eric and Jane, *The First Air Campaign August 1914 – November 1918* p.31
2. **Ibid** p.11
3. **Hallion,** Richard P., *Rise of the Fighter Aircraft 1914–1918* p.iv
4. **Hallion,** Richard P., *Strike from the Sky The History of Battlefield Air Attack, 1911–1945* p.121
5. **Hallion,** Richard P., *Rise of the Fighter Aircraft 1914–1918* p.7
6. **Ibid** p.16
7. **Ibid** p.21
8. **Ibid** p.13
9. **Ibid** p.23
10. **Ibid** p.28
11. **Ibid** p.30
12. **Ibid** p.58
13. **Ibid** p.59
14. **Ibid** p.60
15. **Ibid** p.67
16. **Ibid** p74
17. **Ibid** p.34
18. **Ibid** p.73
19. **Hallion,** Richard P., *Strike from the Sky The History of Battlefield Air Attack, 1911–1945* p.122

Chapter 3: German Air Power before 1939

1. **Hooton,** E.R., *Phoenix Triumphant, The Rise and Rise of the Luftwaffe* p.17
2. **Corum,** James S., *From Biplanes to Blitzkrieg: The Development of German Air Doctrine Between the Wars* p.99
3. **Corum,** James S., *The Luftwaffe, Creating the Operational Air War 1918–1940* p.51
4. **Corum,** James S., and **Muller,** Richard R., *The Luftwaffe's Way of War; German Air Force Doctrine 1911–1945* p.113

5. **Smith** Arthur L. Jnr, *General von Seeckt and the Weimar Republic* p.348
6. **Ibid** p.351
7. **Ibid** p.354
8. **Ibid** p.257
9. **Corum,** James S., and **Muller,** Richard R., p.113
10. **Ibid** p.114
11. **Corum**, James S., *Airpower Thought in Continental Europe between the Wars* p.168
12. **Corum**, James S., *The Old Eagle as Phoenix: The Luftstreitkräfte Creates the Operational Air war Doctrine 1919–1920* p.13
13. **Corum,** James S., and **Muller,** Richard R., p.48
14. **Corum,** James S., *The Luftwaffe, Creating the Operational Air War 1918–1940* p.51
15. **Corum,** James S., and **Muller,** Richard R., p.72
16. **Corum**, James S., *Airpower Thought in Continental Europe between the Wars* p.170
17. **Muscha,** William R., *Strategic Airpower Elements In Interwar German Air Force Doctrine* p.32
18. **Corum,** James S., *From Biplanes to Blitzkrieg: The Development of German Air Doctrine Between the Wars* p.89
19. **Corum**, James S., *The Old Eagle as Phoenix: The Luftstreitkräfte Creates the Operational Air war Doctrine 1919–1920* p.16
20. **Ibid** p.15
21. **Corum,** James S., *From Biplanes to Blitzkrieg: The Development of German Air Doctrine Between the Wars* p.90
22. **Ibid** p.88
23. **Mitcham,** Samuel W., *Eagles of the Third Reich* p.21
24. **Wood,** Derek, with **Dempster**, Derek, *The Narrow Margin* p.16
25. **Hooton,** E.R., p.96
26. **Ibid** p.97
27. **Wood,** Derek with **Dempster**, Derek, p.17
28. **Korbel**, Josef, *Poland Between East and West* p.11
29. **Ibid** p.75
30. **Ibid** p.114
31. **Ibid** p.112

32. **Hooton,** E.R., p.37

33. **Gatzke,** Hans W., *Russo-German Military Collaboration During the Weimar Republic* p.51

34. **Ibid** p.55

35. **Hooton,** E.R., p.40

36. **Ibid** p.50

37. **Johnson**, Ian, *The Faustian Pact: Secret Soviet-German Military cooperation in the Interwar Period*

38. **Suchenwirth**, Dr Richard, *The Development of the German Air Force 1919–1939* p.8-11

39. **Corum,** James S., *The Luftwaffe, Creating the Operational Air War 1918–1940* p.52

40. **Ibid** p.90-91

41. **Ibid** p.104

42. **Ibid** p.83

43. **Corum,** James S., *From Biplanes to Blitzkrieg: The Development of German Air Doctrine Between the Wars* p.93

44. **Wood,** Derek, with **Dempster**, Derek, p.17

45. **Hooton,** E.R., p.58

46. **Ibid** p.51

47. **Corum,** James S., *The Luftwaffe, Creating the Operational Air War 1918–1940* p.86

48. **Ibid** p.120

49. **Suchenwirth**, Dr Richard, p.20

50. **Hooton,** E.R., p.79

51. **Suchenwirth**, Dr Richard, p.37

52. **Murray**, Williamson, *Strategy for Defeat; The Luftwaffe 1933–1945* p.15

53. **Suchenwirth**, Dr Richard, p.20-21

54. **Hooton,** E.R., p.78

55. **Korbel**, Josef, p.255

56. **Corum,** James S., *The Luftwaffe, Creating the Operational Air War 1918–1940* p.117

57. **Hooton,** E.R., p.85

58. **Murray**, Williamson, *Strategy for Defeat; The Luftwaffe 1933–1945* p.10

59. **Suchenwirth**, Dr Richard, p.34-36
60. **Mitcham,** Samuel W., p.14
61. **Suchenwirth**, Dr Richard, p.46-50
62. **Corum,** James S., *The Luftwaffe, Creating the Operational Air War 1918–1940* p.125
63. **Hooton,** E.R., p.51
64. **Ibid** p.95
65. **Overy** R.J., *Goering: The Iron Man* p.17
66. **Muscha,** William R., *Strategic Airpower Elements In Interwar German Air Force Doctrine* p.41
67. **Overy** R.J., *Goering: The Iron Man* p.42
68. **Ibid** p.47
69. **Corum,** James S., *The Luftwaffe, Creating the Operational Air War 1918–1940* p.125
70. **Muscha,** William R., p.32
71. **Murray**, Williamson, *Strategy for Defeat; The Luftwaffe 1933–1945* p.16
72. **Wood,** Derek with **Dempster**, Derek, p.19
73. **Hooton,** E.R., p.104
74. **Gordon,** Brian J., *Long-Term Deception: The Rearmament of the German Air Force, 1919–39* p.1
75. **Ibid** p.2
76. **Ibid** p.3
77. **Johnson**, Ian, *The Faustian Pact: Secret Soviet-German Military cooperation in the Interwar Period*
78. **Gordon,** Brian J,. p.4
79. **Korbel,** Josef, p.286
80. **Corum,** James S., *The Luftwaffe, Creating the Operational Air War 1918–1940* p.165
81. **Murray**, Williamson, *Strategy for Defeat; The Luftwaffe 1933–1945* p.15
82. **Suchenwirth**, Dr Richard, p.51
83. **Corum,** James S., *The Luftwaffe, Creating the Operational Air War 1918–1940* p.128
84. **Ibid** p.141
85. **Ibid** p.143
86. **Ibid** p.211

87. **Hooton,** E.R., p.99
88. **Corum,** James S., *The Luftwaffe, Creating the Operational Air War 1918–1940* p.154
89. **Overy** R.J., *Goering: The Iron Man* p.106
90. **Corum,** James S., *From Biplanes to Blitzkrieg: The Development of German Air Doctrine Between the Wars* p.97
91. **Mitcham,** Samuel W., p.16
92. **Wood,** Derek with **Dempster**, Derek, p.23
93. **Hooton,** E.R., p.146
94. **Corum,** James S., *The Luftwaffe, Creating the Operational Air War 1918–1940* p.181
95. **Mitcham,** Samuel W., p.23
96. **Murray**, Williamson, *Strategy for Defeat; The Luftwaffe 1933–1945* p.16
97. **Corum,** James S., *The Luftwaffe, Creating the Operational Air War 1918–1940* p.172
98. **Hooton,** E.R., p.107
99. **Mitcham,** Samuel W., p.24
100. **Suchenwirth**, Dr Richard, p.59
101. **Mitcham,** Samuel W., p.17
102. **Corum,** James S., *The Luftwaffe, Creating the Operational Air War 1918–1940* p.230
103. **Mitcham,** Samuel W., p.19
104. **Corum,** James S., and **Muller,** Richard R., p.91
105. **Suchenwirth**, Dr Richard, p.65
106. **Ibid** p.68
107. **Corum,** James S., *The Luftwaffe, Creating the Operational Air War 1918–1940* p.185
108. **Hooton,** E.R., p.122
109. **Ibid** p.128
110. **Mitcham,** Samuel W., p.26
111. **Ibid** p.27
112. **Ibid** p.31
113. **Hooton,** E.R., p.143
114. **Larrazábal,** Jesus Salas, *Air War over Spain* p.101
115. **Drum,** Karl, *The German Air Force in the Spanish Civil War* p.181
116. **Ibid** p.198

117. **Mitcham,** Samuel W., p.32
118. **Ibid** p.17
119. **Ibid** p.18
120. **Corum,** James S., *The Luftwaffe, Creating the Operational Air War 1918–1940* p.230
121. **Mitcham,** Samuel W., p.20
122. **Ibid** p.33
123. **Ibid** p.34
124. **Suchenwirth**, Dr Richard, p.80
125. **Hooton,** E.R., p.168
126. **Suchenwirth**, Dr Richard, p.83
127. **Murray**, Williamson, *Strategy for Defeat; The Luftwaffe 1933–1945* p.21
128. **Young**, Robert J., *The Strategic Dream: French Air Doctrine in the Inter-War Period 1919–1939* p.72
129. **Corum,** James S., *The Luftwaffe, Creating the Operational Air War 1918–1940* p.271

Chapter 4: British Air Power before 1939

1. **Lawson,** Eric and Jane, *The First Air Campaign August 1914 – November 1918* p.21
2. **Meilinger,** Philip S., *Trenchard, Slessor and Royal Air Force Doctrine before World War II* p.40
3. **Wood,** Derek, with **Dempster**, Derek, *The Narrow Margin* p.38
4. **Harvey,** A.D., *The Royal Air Force and Close Support 1918–1940* p.463
5. **Lawson** p.48
6. **Ibid** p.212
7. **Kennett**, Lee, *The First Air War 1914–1918* p.6
8. **Lawson** p.213
9. **Robertson**, Scot, *Development of Royal Air Force Strategic Bombing Doctrine between the Wars* p.42
10. **Fahey,** John, *Airmindedness And The Development Of A British Theory Of Strategic Bombing* p.8
11. **Meilinger** p.42

12. **Hippler,** Thomas, *Governing from the Skies, A Global History of Aerial Bombing* p.103
13. **Ibid** p.109
14. **Hastings**, Max, *Bomber Command* p.32
15. **Meilinger,** p.43
16. **Overy**, Richard, *RAF: The Birth of the World's First Air Force* p.44
17. **Wood and Dempster** p.38
18. **Overy** p.48
19. **Harvey** p.470
20. **Murray**, Williamson, *War in the Air 1914–1945* p.69
21. **Meilinger** p.41
22. **Barros**, Andrew, *Strategic Bombing and Restraint in 'Total War', 1915–1918* p.3
23. **Hall,** David Ian, *Strategy for Victory, The Development of British Tactical Air Power 1919 – 1943* p.13
24. **Hastings**, Max, p.47
25. **Overy** p.87
26. **Ibid** p.88
27. **Meilinger** p.47
28. **Overy** p.93
29. **Robertson** p.43
30. **Hippler** p.66
31. **Ibid** p.58
32. **Hall** p.20
33. **Robertson** p.43
34. **Hippler** p.62
35. **Robertson** p.44
36. **Hall** p.19
37. **Ibid** p.21
38. **Higham**, Robin, *Two Roads to War, The French and British Air Arms from Versailles to Dunkirk* p.76
39. **Fahey** p.8
40. **Robertson** p.45
41. **Overy** p.95
42. **Hall** p.18
43. **Overy** p.91
44. **Gray,** Peter, *Air Warfare; History, Theory and Practice* p.18

45. **Meilinger** p.58
46. **Ibid** p.55
47. **Hippler** p.xvi
48. **Meilinger** p.55
49. **Ibid** p.50
50. **Ibid** p.51
51. **Robertson** p.46
52. **Higham** p.99
53. **Wood and Dempster** p.42
54. **Higham** p.78
55. **Robertson** p.46
56. **Hastings** p.37
57. **Fahey** p.11
58. **Robertson** p.48
59. **Ibid** p.48
60. **Fahey** p.9
61. **Ibid** p.10
62. **Hastings** p.43
63. **Murray** p.85
64. **LaSaine**, John T. Jnr., *Air Officer Commanding Hugh Dowding Architect of the Battle of Britain* p.42
65. **Ibid** p.49
66. **Smith**, Malcolm, *The Royal Air Force, Air Power and British Foreign Policy, 1932-37* p.154
67. **LaSaine** p.57
68. **Ibid** p.56
69. **Meilinger** p.58
70. **Macmillan,** Norman, *The Royal Air Force in the World War, Vol 1* p.21
71. **Ibid** p.22
72. **Baughen,** Greg, *The RAF in the Battle of France and the Battle of Britain* p.15
73. **Corum,** James S., *Legion Condor 1936–1939* p.55
74. **LaSaine** p.73
75. **Smith** p.168
76. **Ibid** p.172

77. **Robertson** p.50
78. **Gray** p.98
79. **Baughen** p.13

Chapter 5: French Air Power before 1939

1. **Murray**, Williamson, *War in the Air 1914–1945* p.82
2. **Corum**, James S., *Airpower Thought in Continental Europe between the Wars* p.151
3. **Baughen**, Greg, *The Rise and Fall of the French Air Force* p.13
4. **Lawson,** Eric and Jane, *The First Air Campaign August 1914 – November 1918* p.40
5. **Ibid** p.49
6. **Baughen** p.27
7. **Ibid** p.29
8. **Higham**, Robin, *Two Roads to War, The French and British Air Arms from Versailles to Dunkirk* p.29
9. **Ibid** p.29
10. **Ibid** p.34
11. **Corum,** James S., *The Luftwaffe, Creating the Operational Air War 1918–1940* p.4
12. **Cain**, Anthony Christopher, *The Forgotten Air Force; French Air Doctrine in the 1930s* p.10
13. **Ibid** p.10
14. **Corum**, James S., *Airpower Thought in Continental Europe between the Wars* p.151
15. **Higham**, Robin, *Two Roads to War, The French and British Air Arms from Versailles to Dunkirk* p.89
16. **Ibid** p.91
17. **Hippler,** Thomas, *Governing from the Skies, A Global History of Aerial Bombing* p.70
18. **Cain** p.25
19. **Ibid** p.25
20. **Ibid** p.17
21. **Baughen** p.88

22. **Higham**, Robin, *Two Roads to War, The French and British Air Arms from Versailles to Dunkirk* p.71
23. **Corum**, James S., *Airpower Thought in Continental Europe between the Wars* p.152
24. **Higham**, Robin, *Two Roads to War, The French and British Air Arms from Versailles to Dunkirk* p.119
25. **Cain** p.27
26. **Corum**, James S., *Airpower Thought in Continental Europe between the Wars* p.155
27. **Baughen** p.111
28. **Ibid** p.78
29. **Corum**, James S., *Airpower Thought in Continental Europe between the Wars* p.157
30. **Young**, Robert J., *The Strategic Dream: French Air Doctrine in the Inter-War Period 1919–1939* p.66
31. **Cain** p.28
32. **Baughen** p.95
33. **Thomas,** Martin, *French Economic Affairs and Rearmament: The First Crucial Months, June-September 1936* p.661
34. **Higham**, Robin, *Two Roads to War, The French and British Air Arms from Versailles to Dunkirk* p.129
35. **Ibid** p.120
36. **Baughen** p.108
37. **Ibid** p.119
38. **Higham**, Robin, *Unflinching Zeal* p.39
39. **Baughen** p.120
40. **Higham**, Robin, *Unflinching Zeal* p.12
41. **Baughen** p.124
42. **Young** p.72
43. **Baughen** p.135
44. **Ibid** p.138
45. **Young** p.76
46. **Baughen** p.126
47. **Ibid** p.129
48. **Cot**, Pierre, *The Defeat of the French Air Force* p.797
49. **Higham**, Robin, *Two Roads to War, The French and British Air Arms from Versailles to Dunkirk* p.279

50. **Ibid** p.281
51. **Cot** p.802
52. **Young** p.68
53. **Cot** p.803
54. **Ibid** p.804
55. **Higham**, Robin, *Unflinching Zeal* p.7

Chapter 6: Polish Air Power before 1939

1. **Cynk,** Jerzy B., *History of the Polish Air Force 1918–1968* p.101
2. **Ibid** p.10
3. **Ibid** p.12
4. **Schwonek,** Matthew R., *Improvising and Air Service; The Rise of Military Aviation in Poland 1918–1920* p.518
5. **Ibid** p.523
6. **Cynk,** Jerzy B. *History of the Polish Air Force 1918–1968* p.17
7. **Ibid** p.17
8. **Korbel**, Josef, *Poland Between East and West* p.20
9. **Ibid** p.22
10. **Schwonek,** Matthew R., *Improvising and Air Service; The Rise of Military Aviation in Poland 1918–1920* p.522
11. **Ibid** p.526
12. **Cynk,** Jerzy B. *History of the Polish Air Force 1918–1968* p.31
13. **Schwonek** p.534
14. **Ibid** p.527
15. **Ibid** p.531
16. **Ibid** p.532
17. **Ibid** p.533
18. **Cynk,** Jerzy B., *The Truth about The Operational Doctrine of the Polish Air Force in World War II – A rebuttal* p.176
19. **Cynk,** Jerzy B., *History of the Polish Air Force 1918–1968* p.46
20. **Hallion,** Richard P., *Strike from the Sky: The History of Battlefield Air Attack, 1911–1945* p.55
21. **Schwonek** p.535
22. **Hallion** p.58
23. **Cynk,** Jerzy B. *History of the Polish Air Force 1918–1968* p.50

24. **Peszke**, Michael Alfred, *The Operational Doctrine of the Polish Air Force in World War II, A Thirty-Year Perspective* p.142
25. **Cynk,** Jerzy B,. *History of the Polish Air Force 1918–1968* p.60
26. **Ibid** p.66
27. **Schwonek** p.528
28. **Belcarz,** Bartłomiej **& Pęczkowski**, Robert, *White Eagles: The Aircraft, Men and Operations of the Polish Air Force* p.88
29. **Cynk,** Jerzy B., *History of the Polish Air Force 1918–1968* p.72
30. **Belcarz & Pęczkowski** p.88
31. **Cynk,** Jerzy B., *History of the Polish Air Force 1918–1968* p.76
32. **Belcarz & Pęczkowski** p.95
33. **Cynk,** Jerzy B., *History of the Polish Air Force 1918–1968* p.79
34. **Ibid** p.80
35. **Cynk,** Jerzy B., *The Truth about The Operational Doctrine of the Polish Air Force in World War II – A rebuttal* p.177
36. **Belcarz & Pęczkowski** p.95
37. **Cynk,** Jerzy B., *History of the Polish Air Force 1918–1968* p.87
38. **Cynk,** Jerzy B., *The Truth about The Operational Doctrine of the Polish Air Force in World War II – A rebuttal* p.177
39. **Ibid** p.188
40. **Cynk,** Jerzy B., *History of the Polish Air Force 1918–1968* p.101
41. **Ibid** p.95
42. **Peszke,** Michael Alfred, *Pre-War Polish Air Force Budget, Personnel, Policies and Doctrine* p.186
43. **Cynk,** Jerzy B., *History of the Polish Air Force 1918–1968* p.99
44. **Peszke**, Michael Alfred, *The Operational Doctrine of the Polish Air Force in World War II, A Thirty-Year Perspective* p.143
45. **Cynk,** Jerzy B., *History of the Polish Air Force 1918–1968* p.101
46. **Ibid** p.104
47. **Ibid** p.111
48. **Cynk,** Jerzy B., *The Truth about The Operational Doctrine of the Polish Air Force in World War II – A rebuttal* p.179
49. **Peszke**, Michael Alfred, *Pre-War Polish Air Force Budget, Personnel, Policies and Doctrine* p.188
50. **Peszke**, Michael Alfred, *The Operational Doctrine of the Polish Air Force in World War II, A Thirty-Year Perspective* p.145
51. **Cynk,** Jerzy B., *History of the Polish Air Force 1918–1968* p.110

52. **Belcarz & Pęczkowski** p.107
53. **Ibid** p.107
54. **Peszke,** Michael Alfred, *Pre-War Polish Air Force Budget, Personnel, Policies and Doctrine* p.189
55. **Cynk,** Jerzy B., *The Truth about The Operational Doctrine of the Polish Air Force in World War II – A rebuttal* p.181

Chapter 7: Soviet Air Power before 1939

1. **Jones**, David R., *The Beginnings of Russian Air Power* p.18
2. **Kainikara**, Premchand Sanu, *Russian Concept Of Air Warfare: The Impact Of Ideology On The Development Of Airpower* p.18
3. **Jones** p.16
4. **Kainikara** p.31
5. **Jones** p.19
6. **Kainikara** p.34
7. **Lawson,** Eric and Jane, *The First Air Campaign August 1914 – November 1918* p.21
8. **Jones** p.23
9. **Ibid** p.19
10. **Kainikara** p.68
11. **Jones** p.24
12. **Kainikara** p.73
13. **Jones** p.22
14. **Ibid** p.21
15. **Ibid** p.23
16. **Lawson** p.56
17. **Kilmarx,** Robert A., *A History of Soviet Air Power p.29*
18. **Jones** p.27
19. **Kilmarx** p.42
20. **Whiting** , Kenneth R., *Soviet Aviation and Air Power under Stalin* p.65
21. **Schwabedissen,** G. Walter, *The Russian Air Force in the Eyes of German Commanders* p.4
22. **Kilmarx** p.63
23. **Ibid** p.34
24. **Ibid** p.58

25. **Ibid** p.47
26. **Ibid** p.72
27. **Ibid** p.73
28. **Whiting** p.50
29. **Johnson**, Ian, *The Faustian Pact: Secret Soviet-German Military cooperation in the Interwar Period*
30. **Kilmarx** p.73
31. **Higham**, Robin and **Kipp,** Jacob W., *Soviet Aviation and Air Power* p.42
32. **Corum**, James S., *Airpower Thought in Continental Europe between the Wars* p.164
33. **Corum,** James S., *The Luftwaffe, Creating the Operational Air War 1918–1940* p. 96
34. **Kilmarx** p.75
35. **Schwabedissen** p.2
36. **Ibid** p.3
37. **Ibid** p.4
38. **Higham** and **Kipp** p.270
39. **Whiting** p.47
40. **Ibid** p.51
41. **Schwabedissen** p.7
42. **Kilmarx** p.87
43. **Whiting** p.52
44. **Kilmarx** p.144
45. **Larrazábal**, Jesus Salas, *Air War over Spain* p.79
46. **Schwabedissen** p.45
47. **Payne**, Stanley G, *The Spanish Civil War* p.156
48. **Schwabedissen** p.56
49. **Richardson,** R. Dan, *The Development of Airpower Concepts and Air Combat Techniques in the Spanish Civil War* p.14
50. **Schwabedissen** p.48
51. **Bailes,**K. E., *Technology and Legitimacy: Soviet Aviation and Stalinism in the 1930s* p.59
52. **Ibid** p.73
53. **Larrazábal** p.155
54. **Ibid** p.159
55. **Bailes** p.71

Chapter 8: Italian Air Power before 1939

1. **Hallion,** Richard P., *Rise of the Fighter Aircraft 1914–1918* p.2
2. **Ungari**, Andrea, *The Italian Air Force from the Eve of the Libyan Conflict to the First World War* p.406
3. **Hallion** p.2
4. **Ibid** p.2
5. **Ungari** p.411
6. **Higham**, Robin, *Air Power A Concise History* p.23
7. **Ungari** p.420
8. **Martino,** Basilio di, *The Development of the Italian Air Force* p.9
9. **Ibid** p.9
10. **Ibid** p.10
11. **Ibid** p.18
12. **Ibid** p.34
13. **Hippler,** Thomas, *Governing from the Skies, A Global History of Aerial Bombing* p.119
14. **Meilinger,** Philip S., *Giulio Douhet and the Origins of Airpower Theory* p.1
15. **Holley,** I.B., *Reflections on the Search for Airpower Theory* p.579
16. **Gray,** Peter, *Air Warfare: History, Theory and Practice* p.53
17. **Meilinger** p.2
18. **Hippler** p.122
19. **Meilinger** p.5
20. **Ibid** p.5
21. **Ibid** p.5
22. **Hippler** p.120
23. **Meilinger** p.5
24. **Martino** p.44
25. **Meilinger** p.17
26. **Corum,** James S., *The Luftwaffe, Creating the Operational Air War 1918–1940* p.90
27. **Meilinger** p.13
28. **Douhet,** Guilio, *The Command of the Air, Translated by Dion Ferrari* p.xiii
29. **Corum,** James S., *Airpower Thought in Continental Europe between the Wars* p.159

30. **Taylor**, Blaine, *Fascist Eagle: Italy's Air Marshal Italo Balbo* p.11
31. **Ibid** p.15
32. **Ibid** p.25
33. **Corum**, James S., *Airpower Thought in Continental Europe between the Wars* p.160
34. **Sganga**, Rodolfo, **Paulo** G. Tripodi and **Wray** R., *Douhet's Antagonist: Amedeo Mecozzi's Alternative Vision of Air Power* p.3
35. **Ibid** p.9
36. **Taylor** p.31
37. **Ibid** p.36
38. **Corum**, James S., *The Luftwaffe, Creating the Operational Air War 1918–1940* p.101
39. **Larrazábal**, Jesus Salas, *Air War over Spain* p.76,
40. **Ibid** p.97
41. **Ibid** p.108
42. **Corum**, James S., *The Luftwaffe, Creating the Operational Air War 1918–1940* p.211
43. **Corum**, James S., *Airpower Thought in Continental Europe between the Wars* p.161

Sources

Aigner, Frank, *Stopping the Unstoppable: Douhet, Mitchell, and Arnold vs. Chennault and 'Defensive Pursuit'* (Airpower & Modern Conflict, 2011)

Alegi, Gregory, *War in the Air: Visions of a Weapon Foretold* (Academia. edu, 2016)

Bailes, K E. *Technology and Legitimacy: Soviet Aviation and Stalinism in the 1930s* (Johns Hopkins University Press, 1976)

Barros, Andrew, 'Strategic Bombing and Restraint in "Total War"', *1915–1918. (The Historical Journal*, vol. 52, no. 2, 2009)

Baughen, Greg, *The Rise and Fall of the French Air Force* (Fonthill, 2018)

Baughen, Greg, *The RAF in the Battle of France and the Battle of Britain* (Fonthill, 2016)

Beevor, Antony, *The Spanish Civil War (Cassel, 1982)*

Belcarz, Bartłomiej & **Pęczkowski**, Robert, *White Eagles: The Aircraft, Men and Operations of the Polish Air Force* 1918–1939 (Hikoki Publications, 2001)

Biddle, Tami Davis, *Air Power And Warfare: A Century Of Theory And History* (Strategic Studies Institute, US Army War College, 2019)

Bloch, Charles, *Great Britain, German Rearmament, and the Naval Agreement of 1935* (Quadrangle Books, 1972)

Budiansky, Stephen, *Air Power: From Kitty Hawk to Gulf War* (Viking, 2003)

Cain, Anthony Christopher, *The Forgotten Air Force: French Air Doctrine in the 1930s* (Smithsonian Institute Press, 2002)

Cerdá, Néstor, 'The Road to Dunkirk: British Intelligence and the Spanish Civil War' (*War in History* Vol 13, 2006)

Corum, James S., *The Luftwaffe, Creating the Operational Air War 1918–1940* (University of Kansas Press, 1997)

Corum, James S., 'From Biplanes to Blitzkrieg: The Development of German Air Doctrine Between the Wars' (*War in History*, 1996)

Corum, James S., *Airpower Thought in Continental Europe between the Wars* (The School of Advanced Airpower Studies Air University Press, 1997)

Corum, James S., *The Old Eagle as Phoenix: The Luftstreitkräfte Creates the Operational Air War Doctrine 1919–1920* (Air Power History, 1992)

Corum, James S., *Legion Condor 1936–1939* (Osprey Publishing, 2020)

Corum, James S., and **Muller,** Richard R., *The Luftwaffe's Way of War: German Air Force Doctrine 1911–1945* (Nautical and Aviation Publishing, 1998)

Cot, Pierre, 'The Defeat of the French Air Force' (*Foreign Affairs* Vol 19, 1941)

Cynk, Jerzy B., *History of the Polish Air Force 1918–1968* (Osprey, 1972)

Cynk, Jerzy B., 'The Truth about The Operational Doctrine of the Polish Air Force in World War II – A rebuttal' (*Aerospace Historians*, Vol 25, 1978)

Dildy, Douglas D., *The Air Battle for England* (Air Force Historical Foundation, 2016)

Douhet, Guilio, *The Command of the Air, Translated by Dion Ferrari* (Air University Press, 2019)

Drum, Karl, 'The German Air Force in the Spanish Civil War' (New York, *USAF Historical Studies* No 150, 1957)

Fahey, John, *Airmindedness And The Development Of A British Theory Of Strategic Bombing* (University of Sydney)

Fahey, John, *The British Aircraft Industry* (University of Sydney)

Gatzke, Hans W., *Russo-German Military Collaboration During the Weimar Republic* (Quadrangle Books, 1972)

Gordon, Brian J., 'Long-Term Deception: The Rearmament of the German Air Force, 1919–39' (*Studies in Intelligence* Vol. 62, No. 1, 2018)

Gray, Peter, *Air Warfare; History, Theory and Practice* (Bloomsbury, 2016)

Guilmartin, John F., 'Aspects of Airpower in the Spanish Civil War' (*The Air Power Historian*, Vol. 9 1962)

Hall, David Ian, *Strategy for Victory, The Development of British Tactical Air Power 1919–1943* (Praeger, 2008)

Hallion, Richard P., *Strike from the Sky: The History of Battlefield Air Attack, 1911–1945* (Airlife, 1989)

Hallion, Richard P. *Rise of the Fighter Aircraft 1914–1918* (Nautical & Aviation Publishing, 1984)

Harvey, A.D., 'The Royal Air Force and Close Support 1918–1940' (*War in History,* 2008)

Harvey, A.D., 'Bombing and the Air War on the Italian Front, 1915–1918' (*Air Power History* vol. 47, 2000)

Hastings, Max, *Bomber Command,* Pan Books, 2010

Higham, Robin, *Air Power A Concise History* (Military Book Society, 1972)

Higham, Robin, *Two Roads to War, The French and British Air Arms from Versailles to Dunkirk* (Naval Insititute Press, 2012)

Higham, Robin, *Unflinching Zeal* ((Naval Insititute Press, 2012)

Higham, Robin and **Kipp,** Jacob W., *Soviet Aviation and Air Power* (Westview Press, 1977)

Hippler, Thomas, *Governing from the Skies, A Global History of Aerial Bombing* (Verso, 2017)

Holley, I.B., *Reflections on the Search for Airpower Theory* (The School of Advanced Airpower Studies Air University Press, 1997)

Holman, Brett, 'British Press Opinion between Disarmament and Rearmament' (*Journal of Contemporary History,* 2011)

Hooton, E.R., *Phoenix Triumphant, The Rise and Rise of the Luftwaffe* (Brockhampton Press, 1994)

House, Jonathan M., *Toward Combined Arms Warfare: – A Survey of 20th Century Tactics, Doctrine, and Organization* (US Army Combat Studies Institute 1984)

Johnson, Ian, *The Faustian Pact: Secret Soviet-German Military cooperation in the Interwar Period* (Ohio State University, 2016)

Jones, David R., *The Beginnings of Russian Air Power 1907–1922,* Soviet Aviation pp 15–34 edited by Robin Higham & Jacob W. Kipp (Westview Press, 1977)

Kainikara, Premchand Sanu, *Russian Concept Of Air Warfare – The Impact Of Ideology On The Development Of Airpower* (University of Adelaide, 2005)

Kasprzak, Janusz, *Przegląd Historyczno-Wojskowy* (Vol 1, 1981)

Kennett, Lee, *The First Air War 1914–1918* (Simon & Schuster, 1991)

Kilmarx, Robert A., *A History of Soviet Air Power* (Faber and Faber, 1962)

Kirby, M. and **Capey** R., 'The Air Defence of Great Britain1920–1940' (*The journal of the Operational Research Society*, 1997)

Korbel, Josef, *Poland Between East and West* (Princeton University Press, 1963)

Larrazabal, Jesus Salas, *Air War over Spain* (Ian Allan, 1974)

LaSaine, John T. Jnr., *Air Officer Commanding Hugh Dowding Architect of the Battle of Britain* (Fore Edge, 2018)

Lawson, Eric and Jane, *The First Air Campaign August 1914 – November 1918* (Combined Books, 1996)

Macmillan, Norman, *The Royal Air Force in the World War, Vol 1* (George G. Harrap & Co, 1942)

Martino, Basilio di, *The Development of the Italian Air Force* (Nacelles [En ligne], La Grande Guerre. Regards croisés franco-italiens, Dossier thématique / Thematic Section, mis à jour le, 2017)

McCannon, John, 'Soviet Intervention in the Spanish Civil War 1936-39' (*Russian History*, Vol 22, 1995)

Meilinger, Philip S., *Trenchard, Slessor and Royal Air Force Doctrine before World War II* (The School of Advanced Airpower Studies Air University Press, 1997)

Meilinger, Philip S., *Giulio Douhet and the Origins of Airpower Theory* (The School of Advanced Airpower Studies Air University Press, 1997)

Mitcham, Samuel W., *Eagles of the Third Reich* (Stackpole Books, 2007)

Molketin, Michael, *Policy, Prophecy and Practice: Air Power between the Wars* (United Service 69, 2018)

Murray, Williamson, *War in the Air 1914–1945* (Collins, 1999)

Murray, Williamson, *Strategy for Defeat: The Luftwaffe 1933–1945* (Air University Press, 1983)

Muscha, William R., *Strategic Airpower Elements In Interwar German Air Force Doctrine* (Faculty of the US Army Command and General Staff College, 2001)

Musciano, Walter A., *Spanish Civil War: German Condor Legion's Tactical Air Power (*Aviation History, 2004)

Niestrawski, Mariusz, *The Greater Poland Air Force 1919–1920* (greaterpolanduprising.eu)

Olsen, John Andreas, *A History of Air Warfare* (Potomac Books, 2010)

Overy R.J., *Goering: The Iron Man* (Routledge and Keegan, 1984)

Overy, Richard, *RAF; The Birth of the World's First Air Force* (Norton, 2018)

SOURCES

Payne, Stanley G., *The Spanish Civil War* (Cambridge University Press, 2004)

Peszke, Michael Alfred, 'Pre-War Polish Air Force Budget, Personnel, Policies and Doctrine' (*Aerospace Historian*, Vol 28, 1981)

Peszke, Michael Alfred, 'The Operational Doctrine of the Polish Air Force in World War II, A Thirty-Year Perspective' (*Aerospace Historian*, Vol 23,1976)

Peszke, Michael Alfred, 'The Forgotten Campaign; Poland's Military Aviation in September 1939' (*The Polish Review*, Vol 39, 1994)

Richards, Clive, 'The Royal Air Force in the Army cooperation Role 1919–1940' (*Royal Air Force Historical Society*, Journal 54)

Richardson R. Dan, 'The Development of Airpower Concepts and Air Combat Techniques in the Spanish Civil War' (*Air Power History* Vol. 40, No. 1, 1993)

Rodrigo, Javier, 'Italian fascism and war experience in the Spanish Civil War 1936–39' (*Sage Journals*, 2017)

Robertson, Scot, 'Development of Royal Air Force Strategic Bombing Doctrine between the Wars' (*Air and Space Power Journal*, 155 1998)

Sakwa, George, 'The renewal of the Franco-Polish Alliance in 1936' (*The Polish Review* 16, no. 2 , 1971)

Sakwa, George, 'The Franco-Polish Alliance and the Remilitarization of the Rhineland' (*The Historical Journal* 16, no. 1, 1973)

Schwabedissen, G. Walter, 'The Russian Air Force in the Eyes of German Commanders' (New York, *USAF Historical Studies* No 175, 1960)

Schwonek, Matthew R., 'Improvising and Air Service; The Rise of Military Aviation in Poland 1918–1920' (*War in History*, Vol 21, 2014)

Sganga, Rodolfo, **Paulo** G. Tripodi and **Wray** R., 'Douhet's Antagonist: Amedeo Mecozzi's Alternative Vision of Air Power' (*Air Power History*, Vol. 58, No. 2, 2011)

Silva, Marco Aurélio Vasques **and Migon,** Eduardo Xavier Ferreira Glaser, *On employing Air Power for the benefit of the Ground Force* (Collection Meira Mattos, Rio de Janeiro, v. 13, no. 48, p. 283-299, 2019)

Smith Arthur L. Jnr, 'General von Seeckt and the Weimar Republic' (*The Review of Politics* Vol 20 No 3, 1958)

Smith, Malcolm, 'Planning and Building the British Bomber Force 1934–1939' (*The Business History Review,* 1980)

Smith, Malcolm, 'British Strategic Air Doctrine before 1939' (*Journal of Contemporary History*, 1980)

Smith, Malcolm.The Royal Air Force, Air Power and British Foreign Policy, 1932-37' (*Journal of Contemporary History*, 1977)

Steinman, Victor A., 'Soviet Air Power In Perspective: Development And Impact, 1925–1942' (*United States Navy Conference Group*, 1995)

Stephens, Alan, 'The Development Of Air Power Doctrine 1911–1945' (Air Power Studies Centre, Paper 61, 1998)

Suchenwirth, Dr Richard, 'The Development of the German Air Force 1919–1939' (*New York, USAF Historical Studies* No 160, 1968)

Sumner, Ian, *The French Air Force in the First World War* (Pen and Sword, 2018)

Taylor, Blaine, *Fascist Eagle: Italy's Air Marshal Italo Balbo* (Pictorial Histories Publishing Company, 1996)

Thimme, Annelise, *Stresemann and Locarno* (Quadrangle Books, 1972)

Thomas, Martin, 'French Economic Affairs and Rearmament: The First Crucial Months, June-September 1936' (*Journal of Contemporary History* Vol 27, 1992)

Ungari, Andrea, 'The Italian Air Force from the Eve of the Libyan Conflict to the First World War' (*War in History* Vol 17, 2010)

Vourkoutiotis, Vasilis, *Making Common Cause, German-Soviet Secret Relations 1919–1922* (Palgrave Macmillan, 2007)

Wakelam, Randall, **Varey**, David, **Sica**, Emanuele, *Giulio Douhet And The Influence of Airpower Education in Interwar Italy (*Wilfrid Laurier University Press, 2018)

Wandycz Piotr S. 'France and the Polish-Soviet War, 1919–1920' (*The Polish Review* 62, no. 3, 2017)

Wark, Wesley K., 'British Intelligence on the German Air Force and Aircraft Industry, 1933–1939' (*The Historical Journal*, 1982)

Whiting, Kenneth R., 'Soviet Aviation and Air Power under Stalin 1928–1941' *Soviet Aviation* pp 47-68 edited by Robin Higham & Jacob W. Kipp (Westview Press, 1977)

Whitmarsh, Andrew, 'British Strategic Bombing 1917–1918: The Independent Force' (*Journal of the League of WWI Aviation Historians*, 2003)

Wood, Derek with **Dempster**, Derek, *The Narrow Margin* (Hutchison & Co, 1969)

Young, Robert J. 'The Strategic Dream: French Air Doctrine in the Inter-War Period 1919–1939' (*Journal of Contemporary History*, Vol 9 1974)

Index

Aircraft Index